Sabre Rattling in Space

Ahmad Khan · Eligar Sadeh

Sabre Rattling in Space

A South Asian Perspective

Springer

Ahmad Khan
Department of Strategic Studies
National Defence University
Islamabad, Pakistan

Eligar Sadeh
Astropolitics Institute
Boulder, CO, USA

ISBN 978-981-97-6049-7 ISBN 978-981-97-6050-3 (eBook)
https://doi.org/10.1007/978-981-97-6050-3

This Springer imprint is published by the registered company Springer Nature Singapore Pte Ltd.
The registered company address is: 152 Beach Road, #21-01/04 Gateway East, Singapore 189721, Singapore

Foreword

The exploration and utilisation of outer space have transitioned from being the prerogative of a few developed nations to a global concern. Space is recognized as the common heritage of humankind, a domain with boundless potential to benefit all nations. This book, with its focus on space-related issues in South Asia offers a comprehensive understanding of the challenges and opportunities in this evolving landscape. It presents a nuanced perspective on the implications of the space race for the region, advocating for policies that align technological advancements with peaceful, equitable use.

From Discovery to Widespread Application

Outer space, once a symbol of human curiosity and scientific ambition, has become an indispensable aspect of modern life. The services it provides—global navigation, climate monitoring, telecommunications, and financial security—touch almost every aspect of contemporary society. Satellites enable precise weather forecasts, enhance agricultural productivity, and provide vital data for disaster management. Space-based technology underpins global supply chains, financial networks, and communication systems.

These advancements underline the indispensable role of space in civil, economic, and military domains. South Asia, with its diverse challenges and aspirations, is increasingly utilizing space-based technology for development. In this context, advancement in space technology is not only a matter of prestige but also a vital tool for achieving sustainable development goals.

Historical Foundations: From the Space Race to International Frameworks

The early history of space exploration was dominated by the rivalry between the United States and the Soviet Union during the Cold War. This period, often termed the "space race," saw ground breaking achievements like the Apollo moon landings and the development of satellite technology. However, it also amplified geopolitical tensions, raising concerns about the potential militarization of outer space.

Recognizing these risks, the international community established legal frameworks to promote peaceful uses of space. The 1967 Outer Space Treaty (OST) remains a cornerstone of international space law. It prohibits the placement of weapons of mass destruction in outer space and emphasizes that outer space should be explored for the benefit of all nations. However, the OST has limitations, particularly in regulating conventional weapons and emerging technologies.

The United Nations Committee on the Peaceful Uses of Outer Space (COPUOS), established in 1959, has played a critical role in fostering international cooperation. Wide-ranging multilateral initiatives such as the Prevention of an Arms Race in Outer Space (PAROS) and the Long-Term Sustainability (LTS) guidelines seek to address evolving challenges, including space debris, resource exploitation, and the militarization of space.

Emerging Actors and New Realities

The exclusive monopoly of the two Cold War superpowers has diminished over time. Emerging powers like China and India have made remarkable strides in space technology. China's lunar missions, its Mars rover, and the establishment of its space station underscore its leadership in this domain. India's achievements, including its Mars Orbiter Mission and Chandrayaan lunar program, highlight its growing capabilities.

South Asia's entry into space has introduced both opportunities and challenges. The region's aspirations reflect its need for space-based solutions to address pressing issues like disaster management, climate change, and sustainable development. However, the competition for resources and prestige can exacerbate regional tensions, necessitating a balanced approach that emphasizes collaboration over rivalry.

Space Security: Challenges and Risks

As space technology advances, so do the risks to its security and sustainability. The growing militarization of space is evident in the establishment of space forces by major powers and the proliferation of anti-satellite (ASAT) tests. The use of nonkinetic methods, such as cyberattacks, to disrupt space assets further complicates the security landscape. These developments increase the likelihood of conflict in outer space and exacerbate the problem of space debris, which threatens the safety of satellites and human missions.

The 1967 Outer Space Treaty's prohibition on weapons of mass destruction provides some safeguards, but it does not adequately address the deployment of conventional or emerging weapons in space. The lack of a comprehensive legal framework has led to calls for binding measures under initiatives like PAROS. This is essential to prevent an arms race in space and to ensure the domain remains accessible for peaceful purposes.

The Role of the Private Sector

At this junction, it is also important to acknowledge the role played by the private sector, which has emerged as a key player in space activities, driving innovation and reducing the cost of access to space. Companies like SpaceX, OneWeb, and Blue Origin are pioneering advancements in satellite deployment, reusable launch vehicles, and space tourism. Their contributions have expanded the possibilities of space exploration, enabling services that were once the domain of national space agencies.

However, the increasing involvement of private entities raises critical regulatory questions. Private companies have played significant roles in geopolitical contexts, such as the use of SpaceX's Starlink in Ukraine. Starlink's satellite internet system has supported military communications during the ongoing conflict, demonstrating the potential for private sector tools to influence international security dynamics. Such instances underscore the urgent need for regulatory frameworks that ensure accountability and align private sector activities with global norms. While addressing the challenges and opportunities associated with the growing role of private companies in space is important, there is also need for deliberations on mechanisms to regulate private sector contributions, ensuring they complement international efforts to maintain space as a peaceful, sustainable domain.

Pakistan's Space Program: A Steady Ascent

Pakistan has made steady progress in its space program, emphasising peaceful applications and sustainable development. The Pakistan Space and Upper Atmosphere Research Commission (SUPARCO), established in 1961, has been at the forefront of the country's efforts. While its resources are limited compared to global leaders, SUPARCO has achieved significant milestones, including satellite launches and the development of space-based solutions for national challenges.

Pakistan's space policy reflects its commitment to leveraging space technology for socio-economic development. Remote sensing satellites, such as PRSS-1, support agriculture, urban planning, and disaster management. Communication satellites, like PAKSAT-1R, enhance connectivity across the country, contributing to digital inclusion.

Pakistan is also an active participant in international space governance. It has played an active part in and continued to support initiatives like the Prevention of an Arms Race in Outer Space (PAROS), Long Term Sustainability of Outer Space (LTS). It has also contributed to the work of establishing new platforms that will address coordination and cooperation on the moon, such as the Action Team on Lunar Activities Consultations (ATLAC). These efforts demonstrate Pakistan's recognition of the need for collaborative approaches to address the challenges of space security and sustainability.

Pakistan, despite its resource constraints, has the potential to play a leading role in fostering regional cooperation. By leveraging its expertise and engaging with international partners, Pakistan can contribute to building a framework that emphasizes mutual benefits and shared goals.

Towards Comprehensive Space Governance

The rapid evolution of space technology and the increasing number of actors necessitate a comprehensive approach to governance. Existing frameworks, while valuable, are insufficient to address the complexities of modern space activities. Issues like space debris, resource exploitation, and the militarization of space require urgent attention.

This book advocates for cohesive policies that integrate space law, security, and development. It emphasizes the need for coordinated efforts across international platforms, especially those in New York, with a focus on space security issues at the First Committee; Geneva, which hosts the Conference on Disarmament (CD); and, Vienna, where the Committee on the Peaceful Uses of Outer Space (COPUOS) conducts its session. In this regard, the establishment of binding agreements to regulate emerging challenges, such as private sector involvement and the weaponization of space, is critical to ensuring long-term sustainability.

Space sustainability, a recurring theme in this book, highlights the importance of protecting the orbital environment from threats like debris and overcrowding. The preservation of space as a peaceful and accessible domain for all nations is a shared responsibility.

The Value of This Book

This book is a timely and important contribution to the discourse on space issues in South Asia. By focusing on Pakistan's space program and its regional and global implications, it fills a critical gap in the literature. The book's emphasis on public awareness is commendable, encouraging broader engagement with spacerelated issues.

For students and researchers, this work serves as a comprehensive resource that bridges theory and practice. It provides insights into the complexities of space law, policy, and security, while also exploring the specific challenges and opportunities in South Asia. By engaging with this book, readers can develop expertise and contribute to the ongoing dialogue on space governance.

Conclusion

As outer space becomes an integral part of human civilization, the need for equitable access, sustainable practices, and robust governance frameworks cannot be overstated. This book provides a nuanced understanding of the interplay between technology, policy, and security in South Asia. It highlights Pakistan's role in the global space community, emphasizing the importance of collaboration and innovation.

By addressing these critical issues, the book inspires a vision of outer space as a domain that benefits all of humanity. It serves as both a call to action and a guide for ensuring that space remains a shared heritage for future generations.

Vienna, Austria

Muhammad Kamran Akhtar
Pakistan Permanent Representative
(PAREP)

Acknowledgments

The realization of this dissertation as a completed research project has only been made possible through support, guidance, encouragement, and perseverance of so many people primarily under supervision of Dr. Eligar Sadeh, who is also co-author of this book. Thanks to Almighty Allah for His blessings. First and foremost, my greatest thanks to my family, my wife Ayesha, my three sons Arham, Areeb and Turab. Thanks to my father Mohammad Ishaq (late) who has been there in heaven sending his prayers since his departure in August 2015. Likewise, my mother was instrumental, especially after her brave recovery from breast cancer in bringing me to this stage. Her undying love, words of encouragement, and care were a blessing for me. In the same breath, I must thank to my wonderful brother Adeel Khan and sisters Sara Khan and Rabia Khan for their understanding and support.

My eternal thanks and appreciation also go out to the faculty of the Department of Strategic Studies. To begin, my utmost thanks to Prof. Dr. Zulfqar Khan, my Ph.D. supervisor in NDU, whose sage advice and patience have been instrumental to my success in this monumental endeavour.

Many thanks also go to Arms Control and Disarmament Affairs (ACDA), Strategic Plans Division (SPD).

I am certainly thankful to my dearest friends, Ali and Asim of the U.S.

I would like convey my regards to Maj Gen Syed Shahab Shahid, (Retd) Present DG ACDA for his encouragement to complete the project. I am grateful to Former DG ACDA Brig Zahir Kazmi, Retd. for his support and guidance throughout this project. I would be amiss if I did not thank Brig Hamid Farooq, Retd., for extending support. I am also thankful to former DG ACDA Mr Khalid Banuri for suggesting title of the book. Once again, I want to thank Dr. Eligar Sadeh for his support, encouragement, and willingness to always have my "six" from day one.

Contents

1 Introduction 1
Space Security Trilemma in South Asia 4
Structure of the Book 7
Xxx 11
Notes 12
References 13

2 Schools of Thought: Doctrines and Policy Perspectives 15
War and Anarchy 15
Nature and Character of War 17
Mediums of War 18
Space Schools-of-Thought 20
Space Doctrines 22
Space Sanctuary Perspectives 23
Space Weaponization Perspectives 24
Space Weaponization Camps 25
Conclusion 26
Notes 27
References 29

3 Conceptualizing Space Security at Three Levels of Security 31
Introduction 31
Understanding Security 32
Theoretical Aspects of the Arms Race 40
Evolution of RMA 41
Conceptualizing Space Security 43
Conclusion 48
Notes 50
References 54

4 **Space Policy, Strategy, and Doctrine: The U.S, China, India, and Pakistan** 59
Introduction 59
Theory of Space Power 60
Elements of Space Power 62
What is Space Policy? 65
U.S' Space Policy 66
United States Space Strategy and Doctrine 69
China's Space Policy 70
India's Space Policy 73
Pakistan's Space Policy 76
Conclusion 78
Notes 79
References 82

5 **Space Militarization and Weaponization Capabilities** 87
Introduction 87
Military Uses of Space 89
The U.S 100
China 108
India 114
Pakistan 121
Conclusion 127
Notes 129
References 136

6 **Global and Regional Space Order** 145
Introduction 145
The Concept of International Order 145
Examples of International "Orders" 146
Cold War Space Order 149
Second Space Age and Present Space Order 158
Asian Space Race 165
Conclusion 168
Notes 169
References 173

7 **U.S.—China Bilateral Relations in Space** 179
Introduction 179
U.S.—China Dynamics 180
Political Relation 182
Economic Relations 183
Deterrent Relations 184
Complex Interdependence 186
U.S and China in Space 188

Conclusion 194
Notes 195
References 197

8 Space Security Trilemma and Strategic Implications for South Asia 203
Introduction 203
China-India 204
China-Pakistan 206
India-Pakistan 207
Strategic Implications 209
Conclusion 212
Notes 213
References 214

9 Contemporary Challenges to International Space Governance 215
Introduction 215
Contemporary Challenges to Space Governance 216
Renewed Interest in Lunar Resource Exploration 218
Legality of Space Exploration 220
Conclusion 225
Notes 226
References 226

Conclusions 229

Index 237

About the Authors

Dr. Ahmad Khan has completed his Ph.D. degree in Strategic and Nuclear Studies at the Department of Strategic Studies, National Defence University, Islamabad, Pakistan. He has co-authored seven international publications in impact factor journals on space and nuclear studies including two book chapters in the *Handbook of Space Security*, published by Springer. He is a visiting faculty member in the same department. Previously, he was visiting fellow at South Asia Center, Atlantic Council, USA.

Dr. Eligar Sadeh is an Aerospace professional and founder and President of Astroconsulting International. Sadeh is Editor of the academic journal Astropolitics and an adjunct professor, teaching courses in astrophysics, aerospace engineering, technology development, project management, and astropolitics. Sadeh has held professorships in the Center for Space Studies at the University of Colorado; College of Aerospace Sciences at the University of North Dakota; and in the Eisenhower Center for Space and Defense Studies U.S. Air Force Academy. Sadeh was a Systems Engineer for Lockheed Martin Space Systems working on NASA spacecraft and served as a Research Associate at George Washington University. Sadeh holds a Ph.D. from Colorado State University. Sadeh founded the Astropolitics Institute in 2019 to promote the discipline.

Acronyms

A2/AD	Anti-access/Area-denial
ABM	Anti-ballistic Missile
ACDA	Arms Control and Disarmament Affairs
AFP	Agence France-Presse
AP-MCSTA	Asia-Pacific Multilateral Cooperation in Space Technology and Applications
APRSAF	Asia-Pacific Regional Space Agency Forum
APSCO	Asia-Pacific Space Cooperation Organization
ARPA	Advanced Research Projects Agency
ASAT	Anti-satellite
ASLV	Augmented Satellite Launch Vehicle
ASPI	Australian Strategic Policy Institute
BDS	BeiDou Navigation Satellite System
BMD	Ballistic Missile Defence
BMEW	Ballistic Missile Early Warning
BoP	Balance of Power
C^2	Command and Control
C^4I^2SR	Command, Control, Communication, Computers, Intelligence, Information, Surveillance, and Reconnaissance
CARs	Central Asian Republics
CartoSAT	Cartographic Satellite
CAST	China Academy of Space Technology
CBMs	Confidence-Building Measures
CD	Conference on Disarmament
CEIP	Carnegie Endowment for International Peace
CEP	Circular Error Probability
CFR	Council on Foreign Relations
CGWIC	China Great Wall Industry Cooperation
CHM	Common Heritage of Mankind
CIA	Central Intelligence Agency
CISS	Center for International Studies

CMD	Credible Minimum Deterrence
CNSS	Compass Navigation Satellite System
COMINT	Communication Intelligence
CPEC	China-Pakistan Economic Corridor
CSIS	Center for Strategic and International Studies
DARPA	Defence Advanced Research Projects Agency
DEWs	Direct Energy Weapons
DF	Dongfeng (missile)
DIA	Defence Intelligence Agency
DIPAC	Defense Imagery Processing and Analysis Center
DoD	Department of Defence
DRDO	Defence Research and Development Organization
DSA	Defence Space Agency
DSC	Defensive Space Control
DSMAC	Digital Scene Matching Area Correlation
DSP	Defence Support Program
ELINT	Electronic Intelligence
EMP	Electromagnetic Pulse
ESA	European Space Agency
ESPI	European Space Policy Institute
EW	Electronic Warfare
FAB	Frequency Allocation Board
FMCT	Fissile Material Control Treaty
GAGAN	GPS-aided GEO augmented navigation
GDP	Global Domestic Product
GMD	Ground-based Midcourse Defence
GPALS	Global Protection against Limited Strike
GPS	Global Positioning System
GSAT	Geostationary Satellite
GSLV	Geosynchronous Satellite Launch Vehicle
GSLV	Satellite Launch Vehicles
GWOT	Global War on Terror
HEO	Highly Elliptical Orbits
HMD	Homeland Missile Defence
IAF	Indian Air Force
ICBM	International Continental Ballistic Missile
ICoC	International Code of Conduct
ICTP	International Centre for Theoretical Physics
IDS	Integrated Defence Services
IDSA	Institute for Defence Studies and Analyses
IISS	International Institute of Strategic Studies
INCOSPAR	Indian Committee for Space Research
INSAT	Indian National Satellite
INW	Isotropic Nuclear Weapons
IO	Information Operation

IPCS	Institute of Peace and Conflict Studies
IPFM	International Panel on Fissile Materials
IR	International Relations
IRNNS	Indian Regional Navigation Satellite System
IRS	Indian Remote Sensing
ISC	Integrated Space Cell
ISR	Intelligence, Surveillance, Reconnaissance
ISRO	Indian Space Research Organization
ISS	International Space Station
ISSI	Institute of Strategic Studies Islamabad
ITAR	International Traffic in Arms Regulations
JAXA	Japan Aerospace Exploration Agency
JP	Joint Publication
KKVs	Kinetic Kill Vehicles
LEO	Low Earth Orbit
LPAR	Large Phased-Array Radar
LRBM	Long-Range Ballistic Missile
LSE	London School of Economics
LTBT	Limited Test Ban Treaty
MAD	Mutual Assured Destruction
MAS	Mutual Assured Survival
MCs	Multinational Companies
MHV	Miniature Homing Vehicles
MIRV	Multiple Independent Re-entry Vehicle
MIT	Massachusetts Institute of Technology
MRB	MsMedium Range Ballistic Missiles
MTCR	Missile Technology Control Regime
NASA	National Aeronautics and Space Administration
NATO	North Atlantic Treaty Organization
NavIC	Navigation with Indian Constellation
NAVWAR	Navigation Warfare
NC^2	Nuclear Command and Control
NCA	National Command Authority
ND	Nuclear Disarmament
NESCOM	National Engineering and Scientific Commission
NMD	National Missile Defence
NOAA	National Oceanic and Atmospheric Administration
NPR	Nuclear Posture Review
NPS	Naval Postgraduate School
NPT	Nuclear Non-proliferation Treaty
NSA	Negative Security Assurances
NSA	Non-state Actors
NSS	Nuclear Security Summit
NSSP	Next Steps in Strategic Partnership
NSSS	National Security Space Strategy

NTC	National Telecommunication Corporation
NTM	National Technical Means
OBOR	One-Belt-One-Road
OCS	Offensive Counterspace Strategy
ORF	Observer Research Foundation
ORS	Operationally Responsive Space
OST	Outer Space Treaty
OTV	Orbital Test Vehicle
PAA	Phase-Adaptive Approach
PAD	Prithvi Air Defence
PAEC	Pakistan Atomic Energy Commission
PAROS	Prevention of Arms Race in Outer Space
PLA	People's Liberation Army
PNT	Positioning, Navigation, Timing
PPP	Public-Private Partnership
PPWT	Prevention of Placement of Weapon
PRC	People's Republic of China
PSLV	Polar Satellite Launch Vehicle
PTA	Pakistan Telecommunication Authority
PTBT	Partial Test Ban Treaty
PTV	Pakistan Television
QZSS	Quasi-Zenith Satellite System
R&D	Research and Development
RCO	Rapid Capabilities Office
RISAT	Radar Imaging Satellite
RLV	Reusable Launch Vehicle
RMA	Revolution in Military Affairs
RS	Restricted Service
RSC	Regional Security Complex
RSDP	Remote Sensing Data Policy
SAARC	South Asian Association for Regional Cooperation
SAR	Synthetic Aperture Radar
SatCom	Satellite Communications
SBSP	Space-Based Solar Power
SDI	Strategic Defence Initiative
SDIO	Strategic Defence Initiative Organization
SIGINT	Signal Intelligence
SLBM	Submarine-Launched Ballistic Missiles
SM	Standard Missile
SPD	Strategic Plans Division
SSA	Space Situational Awareness
SSF	Strategic Support Force
STAS	Program in Science, Technology, and Society
STB	Space Test Bed
SUPARCO	Space and Upper Atmosphere Research Commission

TCBMs	Transparency Confidence-Building Measures
TERCOM	Terrain Contour Matching
THAAD	Terminal High Altitude Area Defence
TMD	Theatre Missile Defence
TSTO	Two-Stages-To-Orbit
UAE	United Arab Emirates
UCS	Union of Concerned Scientists
UK	United Kingdom
UN	United Nations
UNEP	United Nations Environment Program
UNGA	United Nations General Assembly
USAAF	U.S Army Air Force
USAF	United States Air Force
USSPACECOM	U.S. Space Command
VSSC	Vikram Sarabhai Space Center
WMDs	Weapons of Mass Destruction
WWW	World Wide Web

Chapter 1
Introduction

Space is now a congested, contested, and competitive domain. Space technologies and programs have become vital to major spacefaring nations' national power. In the past three decades, space has gained importance for spacefaring nations' security and socioeconomic development. However, most of the activities in this domain are unchecked primarily due to the lack of an internationally agreed treaty. In addition, the challenges to international space governance in ensuring space is a safer and more secure environment are enormous. These include the increasing pool of actors, growing commercialization, expanding military space programs, the proliferation of anti-satellite weapons, and a lack of consensus among states on a conclusive and universally negotiated treaty prohibiting an arms race in space. The expanding number of spacefaring actors and dual-use technologies have made the skies and space more competitive. The competing states followed a path from space militarization to weaponization, which aggravated the threat of space war.

The Sputnik-I launch by the former Soviet Union in 1957 demarked the beginning of an intense space race between the U.S. and the former Soviet Union.

[1]The animosity of the strategic rivalry prompted the two states to exploit the final frontier. Space as the "fourth medium of warfare"[2] compelled both countries to expedite their research and development (R&D) to surpass each other. During the Cold War, both remained engaged in a space race.

Space-based satellite systems are of vital importance for building military power. Military satellites provide intelligence, surveillance, reconnaissance (ISR) of the opponent's force development in peacetime and crises. Primarily, military satellites were sent into outer space to get the ISR of the adversaries' denied territories. In general, such early warning systems help reduce the "fog of war" and help the

This chapter draws from the PhD research work of the author titled "Arms Race in Outer Space: A Paradigm Shift in International Security and Implications for South Asia," which was completed in 2019 and successfully defended in 2020 at Department of Strategic Studies, National Defence University, Islamabad.

A. Khan and E. Sadeh, *Sabre Rattling in Space*,
https://doi.org/10.1007/978-981-97-6050-3_1

state prepare a quick response before the adversary launches an attack. Sun Tzu famously said, "If you know your enemies and know yourself, you will not be imperiled in a hundred battles."[3] Knowing the enemy's ground and sea force formation before any crisis would increase survival chances by responding to the adversary proportionately. This will increase a state's survival and help win the war, depending upon the understanding and knowledge of the adversary's capabilities. Likewise, deploying ISR capabilities would reduce the chances of inadvertent, miscalculated, and unauthorized war between the two adversaries.

After the Soviet Union's demise, there was a pause in the space arms race, which ended after the Chinese anti-satellite (ASAT) test in 2007, which proved to be a significant development towards space weaponization. Space weaponization is a "transformation" in international security, and the Chinese ASAT test is one of the constructs that have brought this transformation.[4] As proliferation is one of the constructs of global security, fears are associated with the horizontal proliferation of ASAT weapons.

Indian Ballistic Missile Defence (BMD) system resulted in the ASAT test in 2019, posing implications for security in South Asia. India tested Prithvi Defence Vehicle (PDV) - MK II as a ASAT missile by destroying its military satellite, the global arms race in outer space, the Cold War product, has strongly impinged upon South Asian security calculus. Indo-Pak strategic relationship is viewed through an action-reaction prism. Pakistan's space program, in principle, focuses on peaceful space exploration. However, the space security trilemma between China, India, and Pakistan may prompt these nations to revisit their space program.

Theoretically, "Space Controllers" or "Space Hegemons" view new actors in outer space as a threat to space security.[5] Likewise, the absence of an International Code of Conduct (ICoC) or "norms of responsible stewardship for this global commons" to monitor states' activities in space threatens international security.[6] This has implications for South Asia's security environment. Since, the arms race in space is a threat to the international security environment, it is also a significant security challenge for South Asia's security.

Space militarization is "using space assets to enhance state's war-waging capability."[7] Space was militarized when Sputnik-I was launched. Space weaponization is a subset of militarization.[8] However, there is less consensus among experts on the definition of space weaponization. Satellites for intelligence gathering, photographic reconnaissance, ocean and terrestrial surveillance, navigation, communication, early warning, nuclear explosion detection, weather, meteorological and geodetic features are used for passive defence purposes, enhancing the state's war-fighting capabilities and represent space militarization. The actual deployment of weapons in space and space weapons is generally viewed as space weaponization. However, orbital mechanics and laws of physics indeed defy such deployment. However, Chinese Fractional Orbital Bombardment System (FOBS) test in 2021 as a space weapon has defied laws of Physics. In 2010, the U.S. launched a highly secretive Space Test Bed (STB) X-37B, carrying a whole constellation of kinetic kill vehicles (KKVs) in low Earth orbit (LEO).[9] The X-37B launch was a crucial step in space weaponization.

Michael D. Intriligator and Dagobert L. Brito, in their joint work "Arms Races," theoretically analysed the dynamics of arms races.[10] After the Cold War, the number of significant arms races dramatically decreased. Nevertheless, the Cold War's legacy continued, strongly impacting international security. The recent strategic developments reflect the changing nature of arms races, as "the scale in production and sophisticated projections of weapons systems" has risen in the twenty-first century. The arms race in outer space is not a new phenomenon.[11] Historically, the U.S. and the former Soviet Union militarized space by sending military-featured satellites to secure "high ground." The space significance for both strategic competitors was high, and the Sputnik-I launch marked the beginning of space militarization. Space became another medium of intense rivalry between two rivals.[12]

The definition of an arms race is "the competitive, resource-constrained, dynamics process of interaction between two states or coalitions of states in their acquisition of weapons."[13] The "arms races, as exemplified by the accumulation of weapons stocks, represent an exceptional case of weapons as an instrument of power."[14]

War fears existed between the U.S. and the former Soviet Union during the Cold War. Both superpowers continued to shift the balance of power in their favour to prepare for a surprise attack. Building military capabilities was the primary tool to shift the balance of power. Space paved the way for both competitors to develop and deploy military satellites. Concomitantly, this led to the beginning of the "First Space Age."

The space arms race substantially impacts international peace and stability, bringing a paradigm shift in international security. Space arms race is a danger posed by advances in the anti-ballistic missile defence system and ASAT development.[15]

Revolution in Military Affairs (RMA) and revolution in "Art of War" compelled the U.S. to think beyond its conventional and nuclear forces and contemplate a comprehensive military force that may reside on Earth and integrate with space to fight a future war.[16] A practical manifestation is an announcement from the President Donald Trump Administration to establish a Space Force in December 20, 2019.

Understanding outer space's international arms control measures is essential to address contemporary space security issues. The United Nations General Assembly (UNGA) adopted an initiative in 1981 to prohibit the weaponization of outer space. Later on, it was added to the Conference on Disarmament (CD) agenda. Subsequently, in March 1985, an ad-hoc committee on the Prevention of Arms Race in Outer Space (PAROS) was established after an agreement in the CD. Since then, a stalemate has been observed in the CD on PAROS, stalling any possible international mitigation of space weaponization. PAROS is the fourth core issue in CD's permanent agenda. Russia and China are making efforts to initiate negotiations on a PAROS. However, the U.S. has opposed these efforts in CD. In this context, the U.S. argued that the existing multilateral and bilateral agreements are adequate since there is no overt arms race in outer space. Russia proposed the "No First Placement of Weapons in Outer Space" and the Prevention of Placement of Weapons Treaty (PPWT) in 2008. Furthermore, the PPWT still lacks clarity on prohibiting an arms race; it would require an international consensus in the CD.[17] There is member of resolutions tabled in the UN First committee on PAROS. These are Prevention of an Arms Race in Outer

Space, Further Practical Measures on PAROS, No First Placement of Weapons in Outer Space, Transparening Confidence Building Measures, reducing threats in space through responsible behaviour through norms, rules and behaviour, etc., A group of Govermental Experts on PAROS was established in 2018 under resolution titled Further Practical Measures on PAROS. But it failed to adopt a consensus report. However, GGE on PAROS was reconvened in 2023-24 and adopted a consensus report as on possible elements of a Legally Binding Instrument on PAROS.

Space Security Trilemma in South Asia

A prominent feature of the Cold War is the action-reaction model of an arms race between the former Soviet Union and the U.S. at multiple levels and in other mediums. It generated insecurities due to each other's military build-ups in conventional and strategic domains. One state's action made the other vulnerable and insecure, resulting in a massive conventional and strategic arms build-up. This whole phenomenon was tagged as security dilemma during the Cold War.

States' security in the post-Cold War world became complex, garnering a critical understanding of states' behaviour in the anarchic system. In the pre-Cold War period, the two states—the U.S. and the former Soviet Union—competed with each other on land, sea, air, and space for hegemony, prestige, and to preserve their security. However, the post-1991 period presented a different picture altogether in which security of states required a deeper understanding of their allies and adversaries.

Robert Einhorn and W.P.S. Sidhu described that rival and friendly states' actions and reactions are linked in the shape of a "Strategic Chain." Gregory Koblentz better explains this strategic chain dynamic as a security trilemma. Koblentz describes the chain reaction as extension of the security dilemma. In the security dilemma, two states respond to each other's actions. In security trilemma, "actions taken by one state to protect itself from a second make a third feel insecure." The principal assertion about the security trilemma is that states respond to each other's political, economic, and military provocations to create a ripple effect on their relations.

Consequently, the ripple effect could lead to strained relations. Then, states would adjust their political, economic, and military responses to create a delicate balance of power in a lawless world. The theme of security trilemma is based on India and Pakistan's bilateral relations, China and India, China and Pakistan, and China and the U.S.[18] Einhorn and Sidhu's observation highlights that security trilemma is a prominent feature of contemporary South Asia's security calculus. All three countries are significant military and nuclear-weapon states. However, the U.S.' role and political, economic, and strategic interests in South Asia persisted since 1945.[19]

The continuous strategic orientation in South Asia has engendered changes in India's threat perceptions. The Chinese ASAT test in 2007 changed India's preferences towards space militarization and weaponization. Indian space assertiveness is primarily a reaction to the Chinese ASAT test. India's space program is a top political priority, and focus of the program encompasses commercial, social, economic, and military purposes. India's ASAT test marked its space program, supporting the very notion of space weaponization.[20] Pakistan remains the primary threat level to India.[21] Pakistan's overt nuclearization has impelled India to modify its military strategy to neutralize any threat emanating from Pakistani territory. India's Army Doctrine (2004) laid a foundation stone for building its space program to augment its command, control, communication, computers, intelligence, information, surveillance, and reconnaissance (C^4I^2SR) system. These developments facilitate dominant battle-space awareness and constitute a significant thrust area.[22]

At the same time, India has demonstrated space power capabilities by sending a space mission to Mars.[23] Likewise, India has sent spacecraft to the Moon—Chandrayaan-1, 2, and 3. This reflects sophisticated technological and scientific advancements in India's space program, projecting India as a global space power. Further, in 2005, India and the U.S. agreed to the Next Steps in Strategic Partnership (NSSP), which primarily focused on civil nuclear and space cooperation. As a follow-on, the U.S. Obama Administration in 2011 removed the Indian Space Research Organization (ISRO) and Defence Research and Development Organisation (DRDO) from its export control "Entity List."[24] Technological developments in India's space program illustrate a path from space militarization to weaponization. This is clear with India's BMD system, and in this area, India seeks space-based sensors to bolster and solidify its system's effectiveness.

India's BMD has ramifications on South Asian security. The conventional asymmetry between India and Pakistan is growing, accounting for the asymmetry in space-based military assets. The conventional and space asymmetries have further increased Pakistan's dependence/reliance on its nuclear weapons to survive against India. India's BMD developments "necessitate Islamabad to improve its missile inventories quantitatively."[25] This implies that India's BMD system impinges upon Pakistan's security. Also, Indian BMD developments and its military space endeavours have fostered a security dilemma for Pakistan, intentionally indulging it in an expensive conventional arms race.

The ongoing space competition between the U.S. and China has created a space security trilemma for Pakistan and India. Multiple interconnected factors, including global and regional geostrategic transformations, have played a critical role in bringing this security trilemma. The Indo-US space and strategic partnership continue to impact South Asia's security dynamics, particularly for Pakistan. In space, in technological and military terms, Pakistan is at a clear disadvantage compared to India. Using space power for states' national defence has become integral to the national security strategy, especially for India and Pakistan. In addition to geoeconomic, military, and geopolitical advantages, India is also enthusiastically focusing on expanding its space program for national defence and power projection goals. This is likely to prompt Pakistan to follow suit. India's growing space progress is due to its perceived fear of China's expanding space program and emphasis on militarization and weaponization capabilities.

China's primary concern is the U.S.' burgeoning space weaponization capabilities. The circumstances, vulnerabilities, and challenges in space have further triggered. It has magnified the security trilemma for the South Asian rivals. It visibly interconnects all three states—China, India, and Pakistan—linking it to international security and causes geopolitical dynamics/predicaments like China versus the U.S., India versus China, and Pakistan versus India. India has accelerated international space cooperation to complement its BMD system. The Indo-U.S. space cooperation has aggravated Pakistani perception as a potent security threat, and a highly destabilizing development would undermine South Asia's future strategic stability. This would put Pakistan under the sway of India's increasing dominance in military and space capabilities. The U.S., China, and India's ambitious space and technical programs would magnify the security trilemma between the regional states, chiefly for Pakistan.

Pakistan's space program is not a high political priority. Credible Minimum Deterrence (CMD) is "the survivable, sufficient number of nuclear forces with effective early warning system, reconnaissance, and surveillance system."[26] From this perspective, a space-based component of nuclear command and control (NC^2) would raise the effectiveness and survivability of NC^2 in adversary strikes. However, Pakistan's C^4I^2SR system lacks a space-based component, depending heavily on its terrestrial infrastructure, whose survivability is questionable if a pre-emptive nuclear strike launched by India. Hence, the question arises: what would be the efficacy of Pakistan's C^4I^2SR without an effective space-based ISR and early warning systems? The lack of space-based assets is a challenge for Pakistan's C^4I^2SR.

Pakistan's civil space program was established in the 1960s. Since then, Pakistan's progress in exploring space has developed slowly. The slow speed was primarily because of technological denials from high-end technology states and the changing geostrategic landscape of South Asia.

At the 68th UNGA First Committee (Disarmament and International Security) meeting, the Pakistani representative criticized the significant powers for developing "anti-ballistic missile systems and their integration into space assets."

> These systems have worrying dimensions, and the resultant arms race in space would aggravate the intensity of conflicts on Earth, with potentially disastrous consequences.[27]

The monopoly of central spacefaring states could not last long. All those who want to achieve full spectrum dominance have caused destabilizing effects on international and regional security. The international space arms control agreements are inherently destabilizing and of dubious effectiveness.[28]

India has yet to determine the cost-effectiveness of its BMD system since the system's life cycle costs need to be considered by decision-makers. Moreover, India's BMD system faces problems of immature technology coupled with a lack of clearly defined goals. These capital costs of building a BMD system and technological challenges allow Pakistan to expedite its R&D towards countermeasures. The countermeasures to an Indian BMD system are the development of its land and space-based assets. Pakistan's Ababeel a MIRVed Medium Range Ballistic Missile (MRBM), is a countermeasure to India's BMD Shield. Fateh-II and SMASH P282 with state-of-the-art navigation and maneuverability are ballistic missiles tested as countermeasures to India's S-400 air defence system.

One significant achievement in the history of the Pakistan space program is the deployment of the ground capability to use the Chinese-based Positioning, Navigating, Timing (PNT) system (Beidou). The initial phase of the ground installation in Pakistan provides a geographic positioning network, mainly covering Karachi, and the second stage will provide coverage for the whole area of Pakistan. The network would help Pakistan in urban planning, surveying and mapping environmental supervision, disaster relief efforts, and traffic monitoring.

Pakistan's space cooperation with China is noteworthy, as it helped launch its first communication satellite (PakSAT-1R). Likewise, PRSS-1, PakTES-IA, and PakSAT-MMI were also launched with China's help. Space cooperation with China would also allow Pakistan to build its space launch facility (SLF) and develop a Space Launch Vehicle (SLV) in future. Pakistan could expedite its space cooperation with China as a founding member of the Asia–Pacific Space Cooperation Organization (APSCO), where it can also cooperate with other countries, like Bangladesh, Indonesia, Iran, Mongolia, Peru, Thailand, and Turkiye, in space R&D.

Pakistan's 19th National Command Authority (NCA) announced *Space Vision 2047* in 2011. *Space Vision 2047* intends to bring the full spectrum benefits of space technology to the people of Pakistan.[29] Pakistan plans to build its Earth observation satellites (remote sensing) constellation and communication satellites to benefit from space technologies. Pakistan could also increase its space cooperation with Russia and the European Space Agency (ESA). Even though the National Aeronautics and Space Administration (NASA) helped Pakistan establish its space agency, Space Upper Atmosphere Research Commission (SUPARCO), in the 1960s, space cooperation with the U.S. has stalled due to strategic issues. Therefore, Pakistan's efforts in international space cooperation with China, Russia, and ESA are linked to the *Space Vision 2047*.

Structure of the Book

The design of the study is based on deductive reasoning. The qualitative method is employed to understand the research problem. First, qualitative methods are used to understand the phenomenon of an arms race in outer space and study the implications for South Asia. The paradigm shift in international security was analysed in the preview of scientific and technological revolutions, encompassing RMA and the modern art of war. The methodology combines theoretical analysis with historical illustration by examining official documents and statements. The book offers an analytical approach to the arms race's regional and international dimensions in outer space, a paradigm shift in international security, and the implications (positive and negative) of the arms race in outer space for South Asia. The study would rely on available primary and secondary sources. The primary sources include the official documents of government departments of the central spacefaring states and statements and interviews of policymakers and experts; secondary sources are books, academic journals, and internet-based documents. Additional sources reviewed include newspaper articles, blogs, and other website opinions focusing on expert views. Document analysis involves examining and interpreting available data to elicit meaning and understand the topic of the research and problem statement. The available documents on the issue were produced without the researcher's intervention. These documents, including primary data, will be analysed and assessed to support the arguments and deduce conclusions.

The global trends in space militarization and weaponization threaten global security. The non-existence of Legally binding Instrument or international code of conduct prohibiting space weaponization is a challenge for the international community to maintain space as a global commons based on all states' free use and access. Concerning South Asia, the Indian approach towards space militarization and weaponization is a challenge to the security of South Asia. The Indo-Pak relationship magnifies this challenge; i.e. it is predominantly viewed through an action-reaction prism.

The introductory chapter briefly highlights space militarization and weaponization. It further explains the rationale behind choosing the topic of the book.

The second chapter establishes a broader understanding of the theoretical debate on space doctrines and policies narrated in literature. This chapter explores different schools-of-thought on space security, encompassing various theoretical perspectives by space security experts. The chapter focuses on the strategic importance of space as the fourth medium of warfare and the difference between schools-of-thought of thought on the policy-oriented outcome, further identifying a framework to understand the behaviour of states in space. The chapter concludes that the discourse on space security, particularly space militarization, and weaponization, is multifaceted, multidimensional, multilayered, and complex. The advocates, proponents, supporters, and major camps emphasize the development and placement of space weapons and weapons in space. On the contrary, space doves oppose space weaponization, stressing the major spacefaring states to negotiate arms control agreements and treaties to seek cooperation.

The third chapter provides a theoretical understanding of international security to develop a framework to conceptualize space security at three levels of analysis. Chapter three provides a context for how space security will be understood. The categorization of security studies took place after the Cold War. In that period, most research on security studies focused on understanding the behaviour of the state as a referent object. After the end of the Cold War, academics widened the scope of security studies to include societal security. In this way, individuals or citizens of a state became another referent object besides the state's national and global security. Scholars of space security demarked the successful launch of Sputnik-I as the first step towards militarizing space. The chapter offers theoretical aspects of an arms race among states with this development in mind. It primarily aims to collect different academic accounts of an arms race in space. The chapter also discusses the evolution of the RMA during the space age. The effort is to understand the shift in international security due to space militarization. Evidently, "space has become increasingly crowded, contested, and competitive since the Cold War, with new countries, companies, and even private citizens operating satellites." As a result, the fear of a potential military conflict may arise among developed, emerging, and aspiring spacefaring states because of the development of space weapons and possible deployment. The chapter concludes that there has been a paradigm shift in international security since the launch of Sputnik-I, and states are moving towards space weaponization. Likewise, the chapter offers a comprehensive analysis of major spacefaring states' space policies, doctrines, and capabilities in the twenty-first century, promulgating military and peaceful exploration of space. The history of the Cold War highlights a timeline of the space arms race between the U.S. and the former Soviet Union. With the growth of Chinese space capabilities, India is also trying to become a space power. As a result, the probability and possibility of an arms race in outer space between the U.S. and China would have possible implications for the Regional Security Complex (RSC) in South Asia.

The fourth chapter investigates the nature of space policies, strategies, and doctrines of the U.S., China, India, and Pakistan. This chapter studies space power theory and analyses the relevant states' space doctrine and policy. This chapter highlights the fundamental contours of space doctrines and policies of the U.S., China, India, and Pakistan. The analysis provides a core aspect of space doctrines and policies in the context of space militarization and weaponization. Additionally, this chapter addresses several concerns regarding officially declared space policies and the White Papers. Only a few states have officially declared space doctrines and policies. The document analysis tells little about the states' actual space operations and development of capabilities.

The fifth chapter is an analytical study of the space capabilities of the abovementioned states. The U.S., China, and India have shown their intent and demonstrated space weaponization capabilities. India has global space intentions but is still on the path of acquiring capabilities. Its space capabilities are advancing and increasing, following a path from a regional space power to becoming a global space power. Likewise, at the lower level of the continuum, there are state aspirants of space technologies for their national development and meeting their national security challenges. These states are emerging space powers. Understanding the strategic triangular relations between China, India, and Pakistan from a space security lens is essential. Many believe that there is no arms race in outer space at present. However, the analysis of the current space weaponization capabilities tells the opposite. The study of space capability developments of the major, emerging space powers envisages the dynamic of a space arms race. The discord over whether or not a space race exists is because it is difficult to understand the exact nature of payloads sent on space rockets. It is easier to determine rival military power developments in other dimensions of power, like nuclear and conventional arms. Mapping space militarization and weaponization capabilities of these global, regional, and emerging powers will provide a holistic picture of the states' intent, whether they want to weaponize space.

The sixth chapter focuses on the dimensions of global and regional space order. This chapter answers the following questions: What was the Cold War space order, its main actors, and what is the present space order and its dynamics? Studying the past and present global space orders provides a closer look at the nature of relations between the U.S. and China at the global level and between China, India, and Pakistan at the regional level. This effort will highlight the nature of relations and their subsequent effects or implications for global and regional security. This chapter has explored the answers to the questions to prove that states follow a path from space militarization to weaponization due to geostrategic and geopolitical compulsions.

The next chapter examines the U.S.-China spillover effects of power dynamics in space and the effects on South Asian security calculus. The chapter explains the nature of Sino-U.S. political, military, and economic relations. It will further explain the nature of Sino-U.S. relations in the medium of space.

Without examining the U.S. space program, it would be impossible to understand the dynamics of global and regional space orders and astropolitics. A prominent part of Sino-U.S. relations is the implications for South Asia. China, India, and Pakistan's military, political, and economic relations will be highlighted to understand their relations in space. Space capabilities work as a force enabler, and space power military, political, and economic benefits, creating security challenges for adversaries. Hence, the chapter will focus on the space security trilemma and its military, political, diplomatic, economic, and environmental implications for South Asia. Chapter eight focuses on a key important feature of South Asia's geopolitical and geostrategic environment: security trilemma. The chapter will be incomplete if the implications of space power and the security trilemma for South Asia are not adequately studied. A more comprehensive review will investigate the role of the U.S. as a core state, which has political, economic, and military power, resources, and influence to shape global, regional, and sub-regional space order. The U.S. possesses enough power in space to influence other states to change their behaviour in space. However, the U.S. faces specific challenges from additional global space powers, China and Russia. China has ascertained the second position in the international space order, built sufficient space capabilities, and showed its Astro-intentions to Asia. China has also become a global space power, creating challenges and vulnerabilities for U.S. space supremacy. Chapter nine explores the contemporary challenges to intenational space governance and renewed interests of states in lunar exploration. Pakistan joined International Lunar Research Station (ILRS) in 2021. Whereas, India signed Artemis Accords in 2023 with the U.S. The chapter explores the challenges to the international space governance and highlights that preventing an arms space in outer space in a still a tough job to ask for the international negotiators to negotiate a legally binding instrument on PAROS.

Despite political, technological, and economic constraints, Pakistan is considered an emerging space power with a relatively modest space program compared to China and India's more significant, successful ones. Innovative leadership, smart allocation of national resources, and political will are necessary for any country to progress in such a high-technology field. Since its inception, space activities have remained slow; however, Pakistan achieved substantial milestones in space primarily for socioeconomic benefits. Pakistan can utilize available resources to improve its space infrastructure through collaborative efforts to gain eventual self-sufficiency for socioeconomic and strategic purposes in the South Asian region. Likewise, Pakistan supports multilateral agreements to prevent space weaponization and has ratified all United Nations space treaties. Furthermore, multilateral collaboration, utilizing available resources and public–private partnerships empowering its space program, enhances its domestic scientific and technological base and builds an indigenous space industry that can reap dividends at home and abroad. This can also benefit Pakistan's need to mainstream its national space program for its overall growth and meet future requirements.

Xxx

1. For further detail on the history of space race, see Dickson [1].
2. "Vision for 2020," *Federation of American Scientists,* www.fas.org/spp/military/docops/usspac/visbook.pdf
3. "Sun Tzu: Quotes," Goodreads, www.goodreads.com/17976-if-you-know-the-enemy-and-know-yourself-you-need
4. "Concept of Security," *Department for Disarmament Affairs,* United Nations, 1986, May 30, 2014; ASAT test caused huge man-made space debris, which is indeed a construct of international security.
5. Mueller [2].
6. Krepon [3].
7. Lele [4].
8. Mueller, "Totem and Taboo," 10.
9. "Atlas V launches with X-37B orbital Test Vehicle," *NASA Spaceflight,* www.nasaspaceflight.com/20130/04/live-atlas-v-lunch-x-37b-otv/
10. Intriligator and Brito [5]
11. Intriligator and Brito, "Arms Races," 45–55.
12. Intriligator and Brito.
13. Intriligator and Brito.
14. Intriligator and Brito.
15. Intriligator and Brito.
16. For further reference see, Handberg [6].
17. For further detail, see Sharma [7].
18. Einhorn and Sidhu [8].
19. Einhorn and Sidhu, "Strategic Chain," 1–59.
20. Listner [9].
21. For further details, see Ahmed [10].
22. *Indian Army Doctrine (*New Delhi: Headquarters Army Training Command, India, October 2004).
23. "Indian GSLV successfully lofts GSAT-7 Satellites," *NASA Spaceflight,* January 4, 2014, www.nasaspaceflight.com/2014/01/indian-gslv-launch-gast-communications-satellite/
24. "US removes ISRO and DRDO from entities list," *Indian Express,* January 25, 2011. "The other entities trimmed from the entity list are: Bharat Dynamics Ltd, DRDO subsidiaries; Armament Research and Development Establishment, Defence Research and Development Lab, Missile Research and Development

Complex and Solid State Physics Laboratory Liquid Propulsion Systems Center, Solid Propellant Space Booster Plant, Sriharikota Space Center, and Vikram Sarabhai Space Center are the four ISRO subsidiaries."
25. Jaspal [11].
26. For further details, see Cheema [12]
27. United Nations, "Space-Based Ballistic Missile Defence 'Very Worrying Dimension', with Potentially Devastating Consequences on Earth, Speaker Tells First Committee," news press release no. GA/DIS/3488, October 28, 2013, http://www.un.org/press/en/2013/gadis3488.doc.htm
28. United Nations, "Ballistic Missile Defence."
29. "NCA Okays Nuclear Power Program 2050, Space Program 2040," *Defence.pk,* http://www.defence.pk/forums/pakistan-strategic-forces/120262-nca-okays-nuclear-power-prog-2050-space-prog-2040-a.html.

Notes

1. For further detail on the history of space race, see Dickson [xxx1].
2. "Vision for 2020," *Federation of American Scientists,* www.fas.org/spp/military/docops/usspac/visbook.pdf
3. "Sun Tzu: Quotes," Goodreads, www.goodreads.com/17976-if-you-know-the-enemy-and-know-yourself-you-need
4. "Concept of Security," *Department for Disarmament Affairs,* United Nations, 1986, May 30, 2014; ASAT test caused huge man-made space debris, which is indeed a construct of international security.
5. Mueller [xxx2].
6. Krepon [xxx3].
7. Lele [xxx4].
8. Mueller, "Totem and Taboo," 10.
9. "Atlas V launches with X-37B orbital Test Vehicle," *NASA Spaceflight,* www.nasaspaceflight.com/20130/04/live-atlas-v-lunch-x-37b-otv/
10. Intriligator and Brito [xxx5].
11. Intriligator and Brito, "Arms Races," 45-55.
12. Intriligator and Brito.
13. Intriligator and Brito.
14. Intriligator and Brito.
15. Intriligator and Brito.
16. For further reference see, Handberg [xxx6].
17. For further detail, see Sharma [xxx7].
18. Einhorn and Sidhu [xxx8].
19. Einhorn and Sidhu, "Strategic Chain," 1–59.
20. Listner [xxx9].
21. For further details, see Ahmed [xxx10].
22. *Indian Army Doctrine (*New Delhi: Headquarters Army Training Command, India, October 2004).
23. "Indian GSLV successfully lofts GSAT-7 Satellites," *NASA Spaceflight,* January 4, 2014, www.nasaspaceflight.com/2014/01/indian-gslv-launch-gast-communications-satellite/

24. "US removes ISRO and DRDO from entities list," *Indian Express,* January 25, 2011. "The other entities trimmed from the entity list are: Bharat Dynamics Ltd, DRDO subsidiaries; Armament Research and Development Establishment, Defence Research and Development Lab, Missile Research and Development Complex and Solid State Physics Laboratory Liquid Propulsion Systems Center, Solid Propellant Space Booster Plant, Sriharikota Space Center, and Vikram Sarabhai Space Center are the four ISRO subsidiaries.".
25. Jaspal [xxx11].
26. For further details, see Cheema [xxx12].
27. United Nations, "Space-Based Ballistic Missile Defence 'Very Worrying Dimension', with Potentially Devastating Consequences on Earth, Speaker Tells First Committee," news press release no. GA/DIS/3488, October 28, 2013, http://www.un.org/press/en/2013/gadis3488.doc.htm
28. United Nations, "Ballistic Missile Defence.".
29. "NCA Okays Nuclear Power Program 2050, Space Program 2040," *Defence.pk,* http://www.defence.pk/forums/pakistan-strategic-forces/120262-nca-okays-nuclear-power-prog-2050-space-prog-2040-a.html.

References

1. Paul Dickson, *Sputnik: The Launch of Space Race* (Toronto: Macfarlane Walter and Ross, 2001).
2. Karl P. Mueller, "Totem and Taboo: Depolarizing the Space Weaponization Debate," in *Space Weapons: Are They Needed?* eds. John M. Logsdon and Gordon Adams (Washington D.C: George Washington University, 2003), 10.
3. Michael Krepon, "Space Code of Conduct: Inadequate Mechanism," in *Decoding the International Code of Conduct for Outer Space Activities,* ed. Ajey Lele (New Delhi: Pentagon Security Press, 2012), 10.
4. Ajey Lele, "The US Space Priorities under the Obama Administration," *Strategic Analysis* 35, no.1 (2010): 31.
5. Michael D. Intriligator and D. L. Brito, "Arms Races," *Defence and Peace Economics* 11, no.1 (2000): 45–55.
6. Roger Handberg, *Seeking New World Vistas: The Militarization of Space* (London: Praeger, Publishers, 2000), 7–8.
7. Munish Sharma, "Space Treaty Mechanism," in *Decoding the International Code of Conduct for Outer Space Activities*, ed. Ajey Lele (New Delhi: Pentagon Security Press, 2012), 53–59; and also see "Outer space Multilateral Mechanism," in *Decoding the International Code of Conduct for Outer Space Activities,* ed. Ajey Lele (New Delhi: Pentagon Security Press, 2012), 62–71.
8. Robert Einhorn and W.P.S. Sidhu (eds.), "The Strategic Chain: Linking Pakistan, India, China and the United States," *The Bookings Arms Control and Non-Proliferation Series, No. 14,* March 2017, 1–59.
9. Michael Listner, "India's ABM test: A validated ASAT capability or a paper tiger?" *The Space Review,* March 28, 2011, http://www.thespacereview.com/article/1807/; and also see DRDO Chief V.K. Saraswat's statement on March 21, 2010, on the development and deployment of two-tier BMD system in South Asia. "India Ballistic Missile Defense news and discussions thread," *Indian Defence,* February 3, 2011, http://indiandefence.com/threads/india-ballistic-missile-defense-news-and-discussions-thread.4121/
10. Ali Ahmed, *India's limited war doctrine: The Structural factors* (New Delhi: Institute of Defence Studies and Analyses, December 2012).
11. Zafar Jaspal, "Ballistic Missile Defence: Implications for India-Pakistan Strategic Environment," *NDU Journal*, 2011.
12. Zafar Iqbal Cheema, "Pakistan's Posture of Credible Minimum Deterrence," *Margalla Papers,* 2008.

Chapter 2
Schools of Thought: Doctrines and Policy Perspectives

War and Anarchy

Understanding why states opt for military solutions (war) to achieve political goals is crucial. After the First World War (1914–1919), the subject of International Relations (IR) was introduced to understand behaviour of states in the international political system. Primarily, the subject was based on key assertion of existing political science. However, "Why war?" has become essential for scholars and experts in their respective fields.[1]

The term "anarchy" is one of the fundamental features of international political system. States act like organisms in international political system; hence, when they [states] interact, they tend to preserve their vital national interests. So, while preserving their national interests, states do not follow any internationally or universally accepted order, resulting in anarchy.[2]

Table 2.1 highlights the dimensions of anarchy using multiple theoretical approaches, including realism, institutionalism, liberalism, and constructivism.

What is the relationship between anarchy and war? Is this anarchical international system the cause of war? Such questions often arise after discussing the term anarchy.

This assertion from a preeminent realist suggests that war among states is a prominent feature of this anarchic global system. War becomes inevitable when political, ideological, geographical, and social differences between organisms of this anarchical system lead towards a point of no return, where states often exercise their military capabilities to preserve their supreme national interests.[7] Traditionally, preserving any state's national interest in this anarchic world is baseline of interstate conflict. The interest of any state may differ from another and is thus measured in

This chapter draws from the Ph.D. research work of the author titled "Arms Race in Outer Space: A Paradigm Shift in International Security and Implications for South Asia," which was completed in 2019 and successfully defended in 2020 at Department of Strategic Studies, National Defence University, Islamabad.

A. Khan and E. Sadeh, *Sabre Rattling in Space*,
https://doi.org/10.1007/978-981-97-6050-3_2

Table 2.1 Anarchy according to major theories of IR

Theory of IR	Key perspective on anarchy
Realism (Structural Realism and Neorealism)	1. Anarchy is an inherited feature of international system 2. Primarily referred to absence of a central authority in international system regulating states' behaviour 3. State's military and economic power permit it to defend itself in "hope to survive."[3]
Institutionalism	1. Like realist perspective, international political system is inheritably anarchic in its very nature, but cooperation among states is very much possible 2. Anarchy does not hold states back from cooperating; instead, states can act like rational actors "seeking to survive while increasing their material conditions." 3. Importantly, if institutions are built, they can provide information about behaviour of the state[4]
Liberalism	1. States essentially share the same goals and behaviour in the international political system, thus causing less anarchy. Liberalists believe in more cooperation between states in sharing objectives and common goals[5]
Constructivism	1. "Constructivism is not a theory"; instead, it is "a set of assumptions about human motivation." Alexander Wendt believes that interests are socially constructed[6] 1. Many argue that although international political system is very anarchic, this anarchy does not prevent states from acting upon their strategic cultures and belief systems

relative terms. Hence, anarchy prevails without a supreme body that could regulate or mould state behaviour in a conflict situation. Essentially, realist perspectives germinate this critical assumption that anarchy allows any two states or a group of states to wage war.

Why do states fight the war? Realists believe states try to maximize their strategic power, which may allow them to influence other states' behaviour according to their interests. In doing so, morality becomes a mere ethic to be followed by the state. Here, another issue arises the significance of morality in international relations. Realists regard morality of the state as a controversial issue.[8] Morality has no place in international political system because of its non-universally accepted definitions.

Realists thought that since states always pursue power (military and economic) to maximize their security and power, they tend to forego morality. States adopt aggressive behaviour in pursuit of power and security. But at what cost? It is generally believed that maximizing a state's power and security causes a security dilemma for its rival state(s).[9] The cost of gaining power in this anarchic political system is measured in economic terms and relative damage caused to security of rival state(s). If such power gains by one actor are viewed to cause significant damage to the rival(s)' security, they can go for countermeasures and increase their military capabilities. This would cause an arms race between the adversaries. Because of theory of balance of power (BoP), the action-reaction syndrome germinating security trilemma is one of many causes of war among states.

Nature and Character of War

The dynamics of the war have changed significantly over time. A documented history of 5000 years of warfare tells how the nature and character of war have changed. Humans have fought in the three mediums of land, sea, and air, but not in space yet.[10] However, the war in space is no longer an idea out of science fiction; instead, states aggressively pursue modern technologies to weaponize this fourth medium. The phenomenon of war has evolved over 5,000 years of recorded history in human civilization through five generations of warfare. History of warfare narrates that humans first adopted guerrilla tactics to fight as it required the least amount of training and skills. From the early recorded history of warfare, guerrilla skirmishes or battles were fought between small organized armies. The Roman army developed exceptional fighting skills with a well-organized, well-structured military with proper ranks that engaged adversaries in well-thought-out and executed war formations. This first generation of warfare arguably laid the foundation of the present-day army culture. This first generation of warfare was also documented between 1648 and 1860, keeping in mind improvements in weapons, equipment, and logistics.[11] Battles were formal, and the battlefield was orderly because of the column tactics.

War became mechanized due to the Industrial Revolution fuelling a growing assembly line of naval vessels and military fighting vehicles for land and air, as seen in the first half of the 20th century. The workforce was supplanted or consolidated with firepower in the second generation of warfare. Firepower was centrally controlled and carefully organized such that infantry and artillery allowed the war to be fought as a "conducted battle."[12] These first two generations of warfare were linear.

At the end of Second World War, character of war drastically changed, completely revolutionizing the art of war. As discussed earlier, the armies were organized in the first and second generations of warfare and on the battlefield.[13] While still raised in an organized manner, the armies now adapted to a war conducted beyond the battlefield. It is generally believed that this third generation of war was not based on firepower; instead, it was all about speed, surprise, and mental and physical dislocation. Moreover, the third generation has completely revolutionized war tactics. Now, the enemy chooses to attack from the rear.[14] The third generation of war was principally a contest of ideas rather than technology. The fourth generation of war became a mixture of ideas and technology, which is still emerging. The third and

Table 2.2 Changing nature and character of war

Generation	Time	Basis	Mode
First	1648 to present	Technology	Guerrilla Warfare
Second	1815 to present	Technology	Conventional Warfare
Third	1918 to present	Ideas	Conventional (kinetic means of warfare) and Nuclear Warfare
Fourth	Emerging	Technology + Ideas	Non-kinetic means of warfare; terrorism, presence of NSA

Source The group study highlights the theoretical understanding of war's changing nature and character. See Saeed et al.[28]

fourth generations of the war saw a nonlinear pattern on the battlefield throughout the nineteenth and twentieth centuries.

Clausewitz defined war as "an act of violence intended to compel an adversary to fulfil our will." Because of this definition, the further explanation of the phenomenon tells that war is a legitimate instrument of state violence. However, the state has lost its monopoly over war at this fourth-generation level. The rising phenomenon of Non-State Actors (NSA) has further complicated warfare. Any act of violence in the modern world first creates confusion about the attribution of the attack. The terrorist attacks on the Twin Towers in the United States (U.S.) are an example of state-level confusion. Primarily, Al-Qaeda was blamed for carrying out the 9/11 terrorist attacks. After the terrorist attacks, while the identity of the terrorists was mostly from Arab countries, the war against terror by the U.S. was itself fought in Afghanistan and elsewhere. Hence, the changing character of war resulted in loosening the state's monopoly over organized violence in the contemporary world. Table 2.2 briefly shows the changing character of all four generations of war over human civilization's documented history.

Mediums of War

After briefly explaining the character of five generations of war, it is essential to understand the different physical mediums of war: land, sea, air, and space. Many argue that space's strategic importance is connected to the other three mediums. General John Jay Raymond speaking at thirty-third Space and Missile Defence Symposium, stated that "space is a warfighting domain just like air, land, and sea."[15] The policy statement from a high-ranking military official of today's space superpower highlights importance of this emerging medium of warfare. Not surprisingly, the U.S. Department of Defence (DoD) and U.S. Congress have established a Space Force, the sixth branch of the U.S. military, to provide security and fight wars in space more effectively. U.S. policymakers view Russia and China as threats to U.S. space assets.[16] Accordingly, the Sino-Russia nexus in space is now considered a severe existential threat to American national security. Table 2.3 compares all different war mediums on the following parameters: the influence of history, geography, technology, and periods of evolution.

The first Gulf War in 1991 highlights the strategic importance of space power and space assets' military applications. In Operation Desert Storm, coalition forces utilized space and "introduced yet another Revolution in Military Apace-based intelligence, surveillance, reconnaissanceffairs (RMA)."[17] Desert Storm is sometimes called the "first Space War," in which the "U.S and allied forces excessively used Global Positioning System (GPS) and Satellite Communications (SatCom) for combat operations on Land," writes Kenneth Bergman.[18] He also quoted Michael Krause, who said that "space has been part of today's evolving RMA since the first satellite launch in 1957."[19] Krause states that the evolving RMA pivots around four areas: "space, information warfare, precision strike, and dominant manoeuvre."[20] This is shown in Fig. 2.1.

A.K. Tiwary opines that "the uncertainty of one's position and its relation with another's position, especially over the featureless desert terrain, was eliminated for the first time."[21] The coalition forces successfully used military satellites, proving a quantum leap in modern warfighting techniques.[22] The U.S. space-based intelligence, surveillance, reconnaissance (ISR) global enterprise has further revolutionized the old-age warfighting techniques on Earth.

Table 2.3 Comparative analysis of mediums of warfare

Medium	History	Geographic influence	Technology	Period of evolution
Land	Oldest medium of warfare	High	Few skills were required to fight on land	From the beginning of human civilization
Sea	Long history of warfare	High	Highly trained personnel are needed	Four to five centuries old
Air	A century-old	Less dependent on territory	High skills and technology are necessary	From aerial dogfights to strategic bombing
Space	Emerging	Common human heritage; no state has declared sovereignty	Hi-tech sophistication is required for combat forces in space	Sputnik 1957 began space militarization

Source Nair [29]

Fig. 2.1 Intersection of four areas with evolving RMA

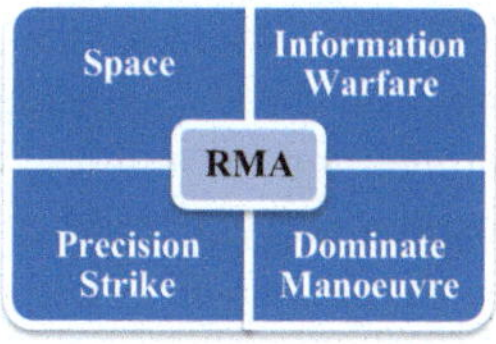

The former Soviet Union and the U.S. competed during the Cold War to exploit all spectrums of space, thus laying the Space Age foundation. It also demarked beginning of the militarization of outer space when both superpowers continued to send hundreds of military payloads into orbit, making it a new medium of warfare. After China emerged as a significant spacefaring state in the early 1990s and the rise of other states with space power capabilities,[23]space has become congested, crowded, and contested.[24]

The first school-of-thought advocates the weaponization of space. On the contrary, the second school-of-thought propagates that space should remain conflict-free since it is a global commons. The proponents of conflict-free space believe that fighting a war in space would have devastating effects worldwide. It also opposes prospects of space militarization and argues that any effort to weaponize space would impact global security. However, the opposing camp states that space militarization provides enormous military benefits to states and increases the chances of winning any terrestrial armed conflict. This school-of-thought also supports the idea of placing weapons in Earth's orbit. Hence, a debate between two prominent schools-of-thought generates multifaceted and complex policy directions for policymakers. The discourse encourages policymakers to explore space for peaceful purposes or to militarize and weaponize it to achieve national security objectives. A detailed survey of the existing literature highlights these different schools' diverging arguments on space used for various purposes. This chapter aims to gather all the converging and diverging ideas, arguments, and opinions in one place.

Space Schools-of-Thought

The subsequent sections highlight the schools-of-thought on space militarization and weaponization and possibility of space cooperation. James Moltz is known for his views and analyses of space security issues[25] analysed space security issues at theoretical and policymaking levels and presented a comprehensive breakdown of the existing schools-of-thought on space security. Space security primarily revolves around two main ideas: space defences and space sanctuary.[26] However, Moltz believes that space security discourse can be better understood if abovementioned schools are studied under space nationalism, global institutionalism, technological determinism, and social interactionism.[27]

The primary factor contributing to the formation of space nationalism was the study of space rivalry between the former Soviet Union and the U.S. during the Cold War. Moltz argues that the rivalry between two Cold War competitors was based on three sources/factors:(1) the political theory of realism, (2) the strategic competition on multiple frontiers (land, sea, air, and space), and (3) the Cold War hostility and belligerence between the arch-rivals. The limited cooperation between the former Soviet Union and the U.S. during the Cold War reveals how perspectives of space nationalism mentioned above came into being.[28] The advocates of space nationalism believe that this narrow cooperation in the era was essential because of the divergent space doctrines and approaches. Generally, both states only cooperated where they were assured that none of them would create hurdles for each other. Moltz gave the example of U.S.-Soviet cooperation prohibiting nuclear weapons deployment on celestial bodies in outer space.[29] However, both states cooperated reluctantly when deploying new technologies or weapons there and space·weapons international arms control agreements in space do not show an impressive record of cooperation.[30] This assertion clarifies that states predominantly behaved under the realist framework. This realist behaviour is the baseline for strong space nationalism space nationalists reject the notion of transnational cooperation and are more inclined towards competition in space. Furthermore, space nationalists argue in favour of a more "militaristic drive by the leading space powers to secure geostrategic advantages over their rivals, as during the age of sea power."[31]

Global institutionalism shares most of the values of idealism. Global institutionalism advocates see space as a medium in which state interactions benefit all humankind (absolute versus relative benefits/gains). They support building global institutions that would regulate activities in space, and they starkly oppose the approach of space nationalism. The focus is on cooperation rather than competition among states for the peaceful exploration use and of space. The advocates of this idealist approach oppose states' militaristic views that desire to wage war in space.[32] Moltz explains that although space nationalists do not promote utopian ideas regarding space cooperation between the states, the Partial Test Ban Treaty (PTBT) can be exemplified as a utopian thought that materialized into an actual cooperation mechanism.[33] The growing competition between significant spacefaring states and the continuous threat of future space weaponization may negate the core objectives of space idealism.

Technological determinism focuses on the states' technological advancements in space rather than merely paying attention to the politics regarding space security. Moltz argued that the foundations of this school were laid during the early 1950s in the U.S. It was thought that nuclear technology would give enormous benefits as it would be harnessed to produce energy. Likewise, space exploration would also benefit by yielding spin-off effects to improve human lives on Earth.[34] Nevertheless, state's national interests facilitated using nuclear and space technologies for military purposes. The superpowers indulged in an intense competition to exploit both technologies to serve their national security objectives.

At that critical junction of time, space technologists drew an analogy between nuclear and space technologies, primarily based on the Cold War experience. Even though both strategic competitors were in an arms race to gain nuclear superiority over each other, nuclear weapons' possession reduced nuclear war chances during the Cold War period. Further explanation of this school suggests that "technological determinists predicted the cooperation among the states in space, which would rise out of the objective of advanced scientific research and development."[35] This eventually prompted states to cooperate since the massive space exploration programs would force the states to share technology, eventually enforcing "international stability and creating new forms of social engagement by urging caution on their possessions."[36] In this school-of-thought, political conflict may not necessarily restrict states from cooperating during "technologically oriented tasks."[37] In conclusion, technological determinists believe in states' cooperation in space and do not consider it a rare possibility; however, this possibility "will rely on favourable structural conditions, communications, and political bargaining."[38]

The premise of social interactionism is based on rejecting the notion of the weaponization of space. The foundation of this school was established just before the end of the Cold War rivalry. Essentially, after the demise of the former Soviet Union and the subsequent U.S. failure to complete planned Strategic Defence Initiative (SDI) in the 1980s, advocates of social interactionism thought that cooperation in space could occur even among the fiercest enemies.

Primarily, social interactionism propagates prohibition of deployment and employment of space weapons. To promote social interactionism, arms control agreements in space are only measure to prevent militarization and weaponization. However, Moltz stressed that "social interactionism requires knowing what will work in existing political and military conditions."[39]

Space Doctrines

David Lupton, discussed four types of space doctrines in his book, *On Space Warfare,* published in 1998.[40] He discussed the contours of space doctrine, force, and weapons in his research. Lupton's research work provides a theoretical understanding of space weaponization. He compared and contrasted multiple perspectives to illustrate the foundation of space doctrine. However, "it is often defined using four different operative words—principles, rules, beliefs, and ideas."[41] Based on these four operative words used to define doctrine, Lupton understood space doctrine.

The first type of space doctrine is known as sanctuary.[42] Sanctuary doctrine emphasizes the development of space-based assets to allow a state to gather all the information about the unfriendly states' space capabilities, doctrines, policies, and strategies. This implies states should develop offensive and defensive military space forces and "capabilities to see within the sovereign states' boundaries."[43] This doctrine promulgates that the U.S. should develop a space-based system, strengthening and enhancing its nuclear deterrence from assured destruction to assured survival. Proponents of this school-of-thought view space systems as applicable for the treaty verification process with stabilizing effects on international peace and stability.

The second type of space doctrine, survivability, differs from the sanctuary doctrine. The proponents of this doctrine understand that the threats to military space assets and space forces (referred to as space weapons) are more vulnerable than weapons placed on land, sea, and air. They believe that space weapons are not cost-effective, sustainable, and survivable. Furthermore, forces in space can easily be countered mainly through terrestrial forces of rival states. Although they recognize reality of military space assets, their survivability remains constantly threatened. Therefore, survivability advocates view military space assets as more suitable for peacetime situations than during conflicts.[44]

The proponents of the high-ground doctrine view the space domain as ultimate high ground; domination of the ultimate high ground will "ensure domination of the lower-lying areas."[45] They support the development and subsequent deployment of Ballistic Missile Defence (BMD) systems to ensure the survival of strategic forces on the ground. For that, they argue in favour of development of Direct-Energy Weapons (DEWs) as well as Kinetic-Kill Vehicles (KKVs) to intercept rival states' Intercontinental Ballistic Missiles (ICBMs) in space during any conflict situation. "In their view, space-based defensive forces can reverse the current stalemate caused by the pre-eminence of the offence and create either an offensive-defensive balance or a preferred defensive stalemate," writes Lupton.

The premise of control doctrine is laid on argument that states should build such space assets to control all the spectrums of space. This strategy is very much analogous to sea and air power strategies. This school-of-thought advocates that terrestrial conflicts can be won if states conquer air and build indisputable airpower. For the control doctrine proponents, space assets provide complete dominance over all physical mediums of war, such as land, air, and water space-based ISR capabilities give military commanders a holistic picture of the various battlefields. The capability of real-time image generation and the GPS coordination may give military commanders a better ground position to conduct defensive and offensive operations more effectively.[46]

Karl P. Mueller, has divided the debate on space security into six intellectual perspectives.[47] James Moltz and David Lupton primarily covered the previous discussion on the various schools-of-thought. In this context, Moltz's intellectual construct was based on Mueller's division on space weaponization. Like Moltz, Mueller made his arguments based on two significant positions in space security: Space Hawks and Space Doves. Both scholarly approaches focus on Lupton's Space Sanctuary and Space Defence doctrines. The following discussion compares Mueller's intellectual and academic work on space security with that proposed and discussed earlier by Moltz.

Space Sanctuary Perspectives

Mueller states that space idealists oppose the idea of space weaponization, similar to social interactionism. Both schools share similar fundamentals and principles. Mueller labelled this school's advocates as sanctuary idealists; therefore, it is tagged as sanctuary idealism. The policymakers in the U.S. were more inclined towards technological determinism and were also motivated towards space nationalism during and after the Cold War. The advocates oppose deployment of weapons in space and development of new ones.

Are weapons the cause of the war or not? The debate on causes of war is centuries old; it has its roots deeply entrenched in history of human civilization. Idealism, an old school of thought in political science and international relations, shares most of its values with sanctuary idealism.

Mueller writes that sanctuary internationalists oppose developing and deploying new weapons in new domains because of their strategic implications for international security and stability; Mueller argues that "the nature of space weapons makes them far better suited to offensive than defensive warfare."[48] The development of orbital weapons places the weapons' possessor in an advantageous position, allowing for a first-strike capability. In this scenario, the development of orbital weapons is harmful to international security.

Mueller posits that "sanctuary internationalism warns potential coupling between space weaponization and nuclear instability, on several levels."[49] These include the development of BMD systems with destabilizing effects on global security. Likewise, the real-time testing of Anti-Satellite (ASAT) weapons contributes to nuclear instability. Lastly, orbital weapons allow their possessor to strike first, which links to nuclear weapons instability if the first-strike is directed at a nuclear weapon state. Practically, sanctuary internationalists "are inclined to oppose space weaponization in general, and although they would tend to embrace other stabilizing means of reducing vulnerability to attack in or from space."[50]

The sanctuary nationalists present their arguments based on realism. The development of space weapons does not necessarily damage or weaken global security, but it does cast dangerous military space assets. Their assertion is based on the argument that there are new spacefaring states. If they can develop space weapons, existing space powers, like the U.S., China, and Russia, would not make sense to stay out of the competition. This would make it dangerous not just for space powers but also for all spacefaring states. Currently, the U.S. is an indisputable space power and an existential threat to its civil and military space assets, which would break the present status quo in space. The advocates also imply that the U.S. led any alliance in space and sought deployment of space weapons would undoubtedly antagonize other space powers, namely Russia and China, to challenge such U.S. dominance in space. "Sanctuary nationalists do not think U.S. space weapons would be intrinsically bad. Instead, their eventual cost would greatly outweigh their benefits, particularly as U.S. space weaponization would lead to other states building their space weapons," writes Karl Mueller.[51]

Space Weaponization Perspectives

Even though space racers have some converging interests in space sanctuary, they emphasize the inevitability of space weaponization. They are not extremists in their views as far as space weaponization is concerned. Space racers are reluctant to recognize pro-weaponization because space also offers cooperation among rival space powers. At the same time, they argue that the U.S. should not allow other rival states to compete and surpass its military space capabilities. Interestingly, space racers believe that space weaponization depends on spacefaring states' intentions and capabilities. This implies that other states' measures to place arms should be closely monitored.

Space controllers assert that space weapons are inevitable, and the development of space weapons provides a space power with ultimate superiority over its rival states, not only on the land, air, and sea but also in space. "Space controllers may accept that weaponizing space will be politically costly." However, its strategic benefits for space power are enormous in terms of further shifting the BoP in space.[52] They advocate that a space power like the U.S. should continue building space weapons irrespective of the other states' time, intentions, and capabilities.

The most extremist point of view regarding space weaponization emanates from the space hegemonists. They propagate that space is the ultimate frontier and now the fourth medium of warfare. States have fought wars with each other on land, sea, and air throughout human history. However, space is becoming a new medium of conflict among the major powers. Hence, hegemonists argue differently from space controllers because deploying weapons in space should be a top priority.

Space hegemonists' actual argument informs that space powers should realize existing space capabilities and pursue control of space, and they should seize control of the final frontier and "deny its use by unfriendly States."[53] Space powers lack critical technologies to control all spectrums and spheres of space and cannot altogether deny unfriendly states from exploring it. Therefore, as the exemplar of space power, "needs to quash any challenges" posed by Russia and China that attempt to "launch vehicles attempting to enter space without U.S. authorization and any terrestrial ASAT weapons that unfriendly state might build."[54]

Space Weaponization Camps

Peter L. Hays authored *Space and Security: A Reference Handbook,* in which he discussed various camps on space weaponization. He raised some critical questions, which he also answered in his book. He asked whether space would be weaponized or not. Furthermore, when and how might that happen? Is the U.S. interested in placing space weapons, or would it be compelled to do so? The answers to these questions helped him divide the debate on space into four major space weaponization camps.[55]

The thought process of space hawks is similar to the prepositions of realists. Space hawks support the deployment of space weapons. Likewise, they see space as having all the characteristics and potential to be the next war medium. Hence, it would be necessary for space powers to develop space weapons and deploy them without delay. Of the strategic importance of space, the proponents of this school-of-thought support the development of space-based BMD systems "as a potentially decisive weapon capable of fundamentally reordering the strategic balance."[56] Space hawks do not support any arms control agreement in space and support space's complete control to deny rival states the ability to reach space.

A closer look at the views shared by space hawks and inevitable weaponizers suggests that the latter disagree with the former on space's strategic importance. The history of the war on land, sea, and air tells that space is the next medium of war, but inevitable weaponizers do not believe that space would be the ultimate combat zone for states. They view space weaponization as inevitable, but that would not necessarily be the "decisive theatre of combat operations."[57] Inevitably, weaponizers do not entirely support arms control agreements regarding the prevention of an arms race in space; however, they value transparency confidence-building measures (TCBMs) to ensure an environment for safe space operations. According to inevitable weaponizers, efforts to cease the arms race in outer space may go "futile," and states, due to inherited security challenges in the international system, continue to see space weaponization as a real possibility.[58]

Advocates of this school oppose space weaponization because it may lead to a space weapons arms race. If the U.S. deployed space weapons, it would face in-kind deployments by other states that work against the military and economic superiority over major powers in different mediums of war (land, sea, and air) that the U.S. currently possesses. Further, space has different physics, differentiating it from other war mediums. If a war is fought in space, it is likely to be dangerous as the collateral damage of space debris threatens critical military space assets for all space powers. Hays says, "fighting into space looks feasible, and the U.S. should plan for this eventuality."[59] However, "fighting in space currently has little utility, while fighting from space looks impractical for the foreseeable future, with or without arms control."[60] For militarization realists, states should emphasize negotiated arms control treaties and agreements for space security.

Space doves oppose the concept and deployment of space weapons and support arms control measures to regulate space utilization for non-military purposes. They further argue that any deployment other than "National Technical Means (NTM), early warning and hotline communications" would be highly provocative for international security and stability and make other states pursue space weaponization.[61] This is a "slippery slope" towards a space weaponization arms race. According to Space Dove, arms control agreements with effective measures are essential to prevent this scenario.[62]

Table 2.4 shows a compilation of all the schools-of-thought on the issues of space militarization and weaponization, including the development and placement of space weapons, multilateral arms control agreements and treaties, and TCBMs.

Conclusion

The discourse on space security, militarization, and weaponization is multifaceted, multidimensional, multilayered, and complex. Multiple perspectives germinate multiple arguments on whether space should be weaponized or not. Besides, can states cooperate in space or continue to deny the establishment of multilateral arms control treaties and agreements to make space competition-free? It is a fact that states have various conflicts resulting in wars on land, sea, and air. States have built military capabilities to fight each other in these mediums, but the world has yet to witness full-fledge all out war in space, although states have conflictual relations.

Table 2.4 Schools-of-thought on space militarization and weaponization

Space schools-of-thought: advocates, doctrines, and policy perspectives	Space weaponization: development and placement of space weapons	Multilateral arms control agreements and treaties	Confidence-Building Measures (CBMs)
Space nationalism	Support competition	Oppose	Oppose
Global institutionalism	Oppose	Support treaties	Support
Technological determinism	Support cooperation	Strongly support	Unclear
Social interactionism	Strongly Oppose	Strongly support	Strongly support
Sanctuary doctrine	Support	Limited support	Not clear
Survivability doctrine	Limited support	Support	Not clear
High-ground doctrine	Strongly support	Oppose	Oppose
Control doctrine	Strongly support	Strongly oppose	Strongly oppose
Sanctuary Idealist	Strongly oppose	Strongly support	Strongly support
Sanctuary Internationalists	Limited opposition	Limited support	Limited support
Sanctuary Nationalists	Reluctantly oppose	Limited support	Limited support
Space Racers	Weak opposition	Weak support	Weak support
Space Controllers	Strongly support	Oppose	Oppose
Space Hegemonists	Strongly support	Strongly oppose	Strongly oppose
Space hawks	Strongly support	Strongly oppose	Strongly oppose
Inevitable weaponizers	Weak opposition	Limited support	Limited support
Militarization realists	Weak opposition	Limited support	Limited support
Space doves	Strongly oppose	Strong support	Strong support

However, the advocates, proponents, supporters, and major camps related to space hawks emphasize space weapons development and placement.

Other schools-of-thought recognize states' security interests but also advocate space cooperation and TCBMs in space. On the other hand, space doves oppose space weaponization and ask major spacefaring states to negotiate arms control agreements and treaties to make space a weapon-free medium.

Notes

1. The realists' view is so far best explained by a prominent realists, like Waltz [1]; also see von Clausewitz [2]
2. On anarchy, see Kenneth [3].

3. Mearsheimer [4].
4. Burchill [5].
5. Burchill, "Liberalism," 55–83.
6. Reus-Smit [6]; Wendt [7].
7. Nye [8].
8. McGrath [9].
9. Baldwin [10]; and also see Buzan, *People, States and Fear,* 3–5.
10. Echevarria II [11].
11. Papaj [12].
12. Lind [13].
13. Polk [14].
14. von Clausewitz [15].
15. Fabey [16].
16. Davenport [17]..
17. Tiwary [18]
18. Bergman [19].
19. Bergman, "Space," 58.
20. Bergman, 58.
21. Bergman, 58.
22. Lord [20].
23. On Chinese emerging space power, see Khan and Khan [21].
24. Many space security experts state that space is now contested. Since the research highlight China as arising global space power, space has become contested. A detail research work was carried out to study the growing number of new actor in space, see Moltz [22].
25. Moltz [23].
26. Moltz, *The Politics of Space Security*, 24.
27. Moltz, 24.
28. Moltz, 24 & 25.
29. Moltz, 25.
30. Moltz, 25.
31. Moltz, 27.
32. Moltz, 28.
33. Moltz, 29.
34. Moltz, 31.
35. Moltz, 32.
36. Moltz. 32.
37. Moltz, 32.
38. Moltz, 36.
39. Moltz, 38 and 59.
40. Lupton [24].
41. Lupton, *On Space Warfare,* 2. A brief definition of doctrine is given as "a doctrine is a formal political-military consensus of the external threats facing the state, the ways by which these threats are countered, and the resources and organization needed by the arms forces to eliminate them." In addition, the doctrine in more particular terms is viewed as a contract between the government and the military which "defines a state-approved system of views on the essence, goals, and character of a future war; on the preparation of the armed forces and the country of war; and on the means of conducting war. Ultimately, it reflects the political goals of the state, as well as, the military, economic, social and legal means of achieving these goals during a future war." For details see, Wolkov and Balatsky [25].
42. Eligar Sadeh refers to the term sanctuary as "free use and access to space without the interference of other states."
43. Lupton, *On Space Warfare,* 20.
44. Lupton, 38–49.
45. Lupton, 21.

46. Lupton, 60–69.
47. Mueller [26].
48. Mueller, "Totem and Taboo," 14.
49. Mueller, 15.
50. Mueller, 15.
51. Mueller, 18.
52. Mueller, 22.
53. Mueller, 25.
54. Mueller, 25.
55. Hays [27].
56. Hays, *Space and Security*. 86, 87 and 88.
57. Hays, 86, 87 and 88.
58. Hays, 86, 87 and 88.
59. Hays, 86, 87 and 88.
60. Hays, 86, 87 and 88.
61. Hays, 86, 87 and 88.
62. Hays, 86, 87 and 88.

References

1. Kenneth Waltz, *Man, the State and War: A Theoretical Analysis* (New York: Columbia University Press, 2001), 6, 29 and 64
2. Carl von Clausewitz, *On War,* trans, J.J. Graham(London: N. Trubner, 1873), XV.
3. Kenneth Waltz, *Theory of International Politics* (London: Addison-Wesley Publishing Company, 1979), 102–129.
4. John J. Mearsheimer, "Structural Realism," *University of Chicago,* accessed September 10, 2016, http://mearsheimer.uchicago.edu/pdfs/StructuralRealism.pdf, 1–18.
5. Scott Burchill, "Liberalism," in *Theories of International Relations,* ed. Scott Burchill et al., (London: Palgrave Macmillan, 2001), 66
6. Christian Reus-Smit, "Constructivism," in *Theories of International Relations,* ed. Scott Burchill et al., (London: Palgrave Macmillan, 2001), 188-200
7. Alexander Wendt, "Anarchy is what States Make of It: the Social Construction of Power Politics," *International Organization* 46, no. 2 (Spring 1992): 391–425; *Social Theory of International Politics* (Cambridge: Cambridge University Press, 1885); and also see "On the Via Media: A Response to the Critics," *Review of International Studies* 26, no.1(2000): 165–180.
8. Joseph Nye, *Understanding International Conflicts: An Introduction to Theory and History* (New York: Pearson Longman, 2007).
9. Sarah McGrath, "Moral Realism with Convergence," *Philosophical Topics* 38, no, 2 (Fall 2010): 65; and also see, "Moral Realism," *Stanford Encyclopaedia of Philosophy,* revised February 3, 2015, http://plato.stanford.edu65. entries/moral-realism/.
10. David A Baldwin, "The Concept of Security," *Review of International Studies* 23, no.1 (1997): 5–26
11. Antulio J. Echevarria II, *Globalization and the Nature of War* (Carlisle, PA: Strategic Studies Institute, 2003); and *Fourth-Generation War and Other Myths* (Carlisle, PA: Strategic Studies Institute, 2005).
12. Christopher J. Papaj, *Clausewitz and 21st Century Warfare* (Carlisle, PA: Strategic Studies Institute, 2008), 2.
13. Willian S. Lind, "Understanding Fourth Generation War," *Antiwar,* January 15, 2004, http://www.antiwar.com/lind/?articleid=1702
14. Robert. B Polk, *Fourth Generation Warfare and Its Impact on the Army* (Kansas: School of Advanced Military Studies, U.S Army Command and General Staff College, 2000).

15. Carl von Clausewitz, *Principles of War,* trans, Hans W. Gatzke (New York: Dover Publication, 1942).
16. Mike Fabey, "U.S. Space Command develops operational concepts for waging war in orbit," *Space News,* August 8, 2017.
17. Christian Davenport, "Some in Congress are pushing for a 'Space Corps,' dedicated to fighting wars in the cosmos," *The Washington Post,* September 15, 2017.
18. AK Tiwary, "Aerospace Power: The Need for Unity of Command and Control," *Indian Defence Review* 18, no. 2 (April-June 2003): 63.
19. Kenneth R. Bergman, "Space and Revolution in Military Affairs," *Marine Corps Gazette* 79, no.5 (May 1995): 58.
20. Lance W. Lord, "Commanding the Future: The Transformation of Air Force Space Command," *Air and Space Power Journal* 18, no.2 (Summer 2004).
21. Zulfqar Khan and Ahmad Khan, "Chinese Capabilities as a Global Space Power," *Astropolitics* 13, no. 2-3 (2015): 185–204.
22. James Moltz, *Crowded Orbits: Conflicts and Cooperation in Space* (New York: Columbia University Press, 2014).
23. James Moltz, *The Politics of Space Security: Strategic Restraint and the Pursuit of National Interests* (Stanford, CA: Stanford University Press, 2008), 23.
24. David E. Lupton, *On Space Warfare* (Alabama: Air University Press, 1998).
25. Benjamin Wolkov and GalyaBalatsky, "Changes in Russia's Military and Nuclear Doctrine," *Los Alamos National Laboratory*, July 25, 2012, http://permalink.lanl.gov/object/tr?what=info:lanl-repo/lareport/LA-UR-12-23486, 1.
26. Karl P. Mueller, "Totem and Taboo: Depolarizing the Space Weaponization Debate," in *Space Weapons: Are They Needed?* ed. John M. Logdon and Gordon Adams (Washington DC: Space Policy Institute, The George Washington University, 2003), 1–51.
27. Peter L. Hays, *Space and Security: A Reference Handbook* (Santa Barbara: ABC-CLIO, 2011), 86, 87 and 88.
28. Javed Saeed et al., *National Strategy Paper: Non-Kinetic Challenges to the States of Pakistan* (Islamabad: National Defence University, February 2012).
29. Kiran Krishan Nair, *Space: The Frontiers of Modern Defence* (New Delhi: Center for Air Power Studies and Knowledge World, 2006), 63.

Chapter 3
Conceptualizing Space Security at Three Levels of Security

Introduction

After the end of the Cold War, academics debated widening the scope of security studies to include societal security. Societal security consists of the individuals or citizens of a state as referent objects. Besides, security levels also have the state's national and international security.[1]

Evidently, "space has become increasingly crowded, contested, and competitive since the Cold War, with new countries, companies, and even private citizens operating satellites."[2] Because of the development and deployment of space weapons, the fear of a potential military conflict may arise among developed, emerging, and aspiring spacefaring states. There has been a paradigm shift in international security since the launch of *Sputnik*-I, and states are following a path from space militarization to weaponization in the twenty-first century.

Major spacefaring states' space policies, doctrines, and capabilities promulgate military and peaceful uses in the twenty-first century. With Chinese space capabilities growing, India is also trying to become a global space power as it has already achieved a regional space power status. The probability and possibility of an arms race in outer space between the U.S. and China would have possible Regional Security Complex (RSC) implications for South Asia.

This chapter draws from the Ph.D. research work of the author titled "Arms Race in Outer Space: A Paradigm Shift in International Security and Implications for South Asia," which was completed in 2019 and successfully defended in 2020 at Department of Strategic Studies, National Defence University, Islamabad.

A. Khan and E. Sadeh, *Sabre Rattling in Space*,
https://doi.org/10.1007/978-981-97-6050-3_3

Understanding Security

There is no universally accepted definition of "security." Practitioners and academics continually debate this concept.[3] Instead of defining security, there is a need to lay down a framework that can be understood and studied in different scenarios, conflicts, and contexts.[4] The rationale is that security is affected by multiple factors in different scenarios, conflicts, and contexts, including socioeconomic, military, political, cultural, and ecological factors. Nevertheless, several definitions are widely accepted in noteworthy security studies.

During the Cold War, security was traditionally attributed to the state's military power, with the practitioners and academics understanding security as the "derivative of power."[5] States' security was gauged by their ability to develop their militaries for defence. The modern theoretical aspects were studied during the Cold War when the U.S. and Soviet Union locked in a deadly conventional and nuclear arms race to shift the balance of power (BoP) in their favour. The competition led to building arms to fight a land, sea, and air war. Both superpowers tried to offset the threat emanating from each other. Consequently, they competed in space by sending hundreds of military nature satellites to augment their military power.

States' security during the Cold War was succinctly analysed by studying the BoP theory. The theory assumes that states in the anarchical international system tend to accumulate military power "as a means to security"[6] and struggle to maximize it.[7] In classical realism, the core assumption is that there is little difference between human nature and state behaviour in the international political system. A state's behaviour pivots around its self-interest, and theory suggests that states pursue their narrow self-interests within the hierarchy of states.

BoP succinctly defines states' behaviour. This means the "creation or aggregation of military power through either internal mobilization or forging of alliances to prevent or deter the occupation and domination of the state by a foreign power or a coalition."[8] A state's balancing behaviour is "to prevent the loss of territory, either one's homeland or vital interests abroad (e.g. sea lanes, colonies, or other territory considered of vital strategic interest)." BoP maps the behaviour of the state, which aims to preserve the integrity of its international political system. BoP argues that states always try to maximize their political, economic, and military goals at the cost of other states' interests, and states cannot be trusted with "inordinate power." The real antidote to power is power.[9]

BoP primarily argues for building military capabilities for maximum security against an adversary's military capabilities. A state builds its military capability as the countervailing power. State(s) tend to stimulate internal and external balancing. Internal balancing is in the form of arms build-up, and BoP further suggests that external balancing encourages the state to go into a military alliance. BoP is a means to fight a war and an end in itself. In the case of an armed conflict between two significant military powers, the capability to fight a war is the actual military power to be gauged.[10]

However, understanding the context of conflict is necessary to gauge the state's power. This means that in *realpolitik*, power of the state is measured through;

a. Its military capabilities;
b. Political stability and will to fight the war (internal balancing);
c. Reliability of commitments of the allies; and
d. The geographical location of the state.

Furthermore, economic balancing has emerged as the most potent counterbalancing tool in this changing political and strategic landscape. The relationship between power, security, and economy was merely discussed during the Cold War. The states mobilized their internal resources to build maximum military power to neutralize the threat from rival states or alliances. In middle of the twentieth century, economic context profoundly impacted the balance of power politics. The Game Theory was explained in political science and business studies for over two decades to understand balancing policies between rival states or alliances. Currently, states cannot be successful unless they are not embedded in economic interdependency.[11] This shows the importance of the economy in the twenty-first century and informs proper contextualization of a comprehensive security strategy for any state.

The scholarly discourse on security studies during the Cold War era discusses the centrality of the state, which is main theme of classical and neorealism. Furthermore, modern concept of state suggests its two core characteristics: sovereignty and territory. Sovereignty and territory have primarily evolved in twentieth century. Scholars in political science and international relations have divided the central character—sovereignty—into two levels: internal sovereignty and external sovereignty. The internal level is the state's power to hold its authority within its territory. External sovereignty deals with maintaining a state's autonomy and independence while interacting with other actors (states) in international political system.[12]

Power is fundamental feature of realism and a prominent theme in international relations. One of the many fundamentals of security studies is studying state behaviour. Likewise, another core aspect is state's ambition to seek power to securitize its sovereignty and territory against threats, challenges, and vulnerability. Classical literature on security suggests that a state seeks military power. The proponents of realism linked preserving the state's sovereignty and territory with its lust for power.

The traditional school-of-thought on security studies argues that military capabilities are the only measure to repel attacks. Therefore, state should build military power to ensure security against its adversary's belligerence. Non-traditionalists believe that traditionalists do not fully comprehend other security contexts, namely societal, environmental, economic, and political security. During the Cold War, security was mainly linked with military power and invited classical and neorealist schools. The criticism of realism has germinated other perspectives; it contextualized security in a new dimension. By the end of the Cold War, the discipline of security studies was forced to widen its scope.[13]

The subject of security studies in the early 1990s took new forms, including threats to state's sovereignty and territory. The new forms of threats are challenging a single state's security and hierarchy of states. In the past, security discourse professed military competition among states. It encouraged states to build military capabilities to repel adversaries' attacks. States were focused on preserving their sovereignty and territory from other states, threatened by their adversary's military build-up, adding complexity of challenges when facing a changing global environment (climate change) and rising economic disparities. Besides climate change, economic disparity, and population growth, other threats impact the individual (human), state, and global security levels. These threats include transnational and global terrorism, global epidemics, food shortages, poverty, economic mismanagement, refugees, and ecology and natural destruction.

The Cold War ended a bipolar world.[14] The "Cold War world has germinated unipolarity, with the U.S. as only pole left."[15] The Soviet Union's retreat from Afghanistan and the first Gulf War were the two significant events that helped the U.S. emerge as the sole global power. Furthermore, Operation Desert Storm enabled the world to witness the U.S. military power, including the active use of space assets for warfighting. At that critical juncture, the world witnessed a new political order with a new security agenda. The experts and academics disseminated the discourse on three levels: human security (societal security), state's security, and international security or global security.[16]

The Copenhagen school-of-thought, a mix of neorealist and social constructivist concepts, offers a better understanding of human security.[17] Primarily, human security is referred to as societal security. "The individual represents the irreducible basic unit to which the concept of security can be applied."[18] The referent object in societal security is the human being. Societal security is "the ability of a society to persist in its essential character under changing conditions and possible or actual threats."[19] It is linked with "sustainability of traditional language patterns, culture, association, and religious and national identity and customs."[20]

Nevertheless, sustainability of earlier factors is linked to acceptable evolution conditions. The concept of social security is meant to study the threats, challenges, and vulnerabilities to humans' language, culture, association, religion, and identity and how to securitize society from these threats.[21] Several threats to individual security encompass physical, political, economic, and environmental factors.

The interplay between state and individual concludes that as "state power grows, it also becomes a source of threat against the individual."[22] This chemistry is paradoxical in nature. Society depends on the state as a "lynchpin for social and economic structures."[23] The "state is irreversible," and "security of the individuals is inseparably entangled with the state."[24] Without understanding the individual's needs, the state's security would be incomplete and remain weak against mounting strategic, socioeconomic, political, and environmental threats.

One of the threats to overall international security is the weak or failed/failing state. The strong states "control their territories and deliver a high order of political goods to their citizens."[25] On the other hand, weak or failing state does the opposite. A "state's failure threatens global stability because national governments have become the primary building block of international order."[26] The debate on the relationship between individual and state suggests that state's survival is inheritably linked to the individual's security. It is the promise made by state to its inhabitants to provide security against political, socioeconomic, and political threats.[27] International security relies enormously on this state's promise to "protect against chaos at home and limit the cancerous spread of anarchy beyond their borders and worldwide."[28] A state can be considered substantial if it can provide "political good of security" to its citizens.[29] In modern security studies, state survival is linked with its promise to provide societal security to its components (government and citizens). A state's survival is primarily based on fulfilling its promise to its inhabitants.[30]

State security is referred to as national security. There are several thought-provoking definitions of national security. Defining the national security of any state in its general form is challenging. However, it is still possible to define national security in this changing contemporary world, where threats, challenges, and risks are multidimensional and multifaceted. Kim Homles, describes national security as "safekeeping and protection of the nation and its society from attacks and other external dangers by maintaining armed forces and guarding state secrets."[31] Toby Mendel, defines national security as "it is referred especially to the maintenance of foreign relations, to the extent that this is linked to the protection of national security, per se."[32] Mortan Berkowitz and P.G. Bock described it as "the ability of the nation to protect its internal values from external threats."[33] Albeit all these scholars give different definitions of national security, their definitions suggest a commonality between them rooted in the external threats from the other state(s).

Security is a contested concept. There are varying answers to questions, including security for whom, how much security, what it means, at what cost, and in what period.[34] These questions need answers to understand the security of the state, society, civilization, and the individual. Understanding a state's national security in the hierarchy of states is necessary for the referent object's survival.[35] To augment national security, state rationalizes, organizes, and develops a framework to structure its national objectives in the form of a national security policy to deal with the emerging threats, vulnerabilities, challenges, and risks to its survival, especially to its sovereignty and territory, from its adversary state(s).[36] States usually try to identify their core interests and develop a security policy to achieve national security objectives. The core interests of any state could be as follows[37]:

a. State's survival and its society [population][38].
b. Protecting its territorial integrity and maintaining physical, economic, and political sovereignty, which are its fundamental rights.
c. Fulfilling the promise of providing security to its citizens from societal threats.

After defining core national objectives, the referent objects measure relative threats, challenges, vulnerabilities, and risks to its security. To deal with subjective form of dangers and concerns, state formulates and develops its foreign, defence, economic, social, environmental, health, food, energy, educational and cultural policies to ensure that it can meet national security objectives. Furthermore, state develops a structure of organizations and institutions to formulate its national security policy. This policy's baseline is developed by chalking out defence and internal policy options to deal with internal and external threats. In the modern world, external threats, challenges, vulnerabilities, and risks may be regional and global rivalries between states, territorial disputes, severe economic disparities, ethnic and religious conflicts, the proliferation of Weapons of Mass Destruction (WMD), and transnational organized crime and terrorism. Likewise, internal risks, challenges, threats, and vulnerabilities impinge upon the security of a state, such as organized crime, political instability, poverty, poor governance, corruption, terrorism, and lack of education.[39] To deal with external threats, in defence elements of national security, regular army, police, and specialized military-police or paramilitary forces are raised to solidify the state's defence against threats, challenges, vulnerabilities, and risks posed to its territorial sovereignty and integrity. To augment the policy further, state identifies internal threats, vulnerabilities, challenges, and risks posed to its society. These dangers and concerns to societal security are dealt with by establishing a police force and a justice system to give citizens the right to benefit from the states' promises to provide societal security.[40]

There is a shift in international security patterns, commonly known as global security. Before that, "international security was dominated by ideological confrontation between the superpowers during the Cold War."[41] The Cold War world was polarized, and the threat of war and political and military confrontation between the two superpowers was imminent. The rivalry intensified when both supplied arms to their allies, the periphery states. The supplying of arms to their periphery states raised their existing hostilities.[42] However, the fall of the Berlin Wall completely changed the pattern of global security.[43] This also shifted international security patterns as the debate tilted towards studying new threats to society, states, and the international system. The states still focus on their national defence against military threats to their sovereignty and territory. However, non-kinetic threats, such as economic, societal, and environmental threats, "are pushing their way into the top ranks of the international security agenda."[44] The shift in the international security agenda is primarily linked with the emergence of non-military/kinetic threats to the individual, the state, and the "international community".[45] The threats are increasingly important in the twenty-first century security agenda, including international terrorism, criminality, dangers and risks to economy, global environment, information systems (cybersecurity), natural and manufactured disasters, and poverty.[46]

States are still facing military threats from other states as they are inevitable.[47] The states are still involved in arms race and military build-up to counter the military threats emanating from their adversaries. Several academic efforts thoroughly discussed new challenges to international security and their relative implications for the security of the individual, the state, and the international system.

It is a fact that modern concept of security is incomplete without traditional concept of security. However, the traditionalist view on security has not displaced its original presumptions about predicting the states' behaviour in an anarchical international system. In the twenty-first century, the core dangers to international security are the evolving nature of the nuclear doctrines and postures, state's grand strategies, arms and disarmament affairs, asymmetrical nature of conventional weapons, "the determinants of the defence policies of states," civil-military relations, strategic stability, and military history.[48]

Traditional and non-traditional thinking on security is significant in studying the security calculus at the regional and global levels. Besides, a relatively new concept has emerged in international security studies: the Global Commons. It is "referred to resource domains or areas that lie outside of the political reach of any one nation-state."[49] These common areas are the high seas, air (atmosphere), Antarctica, and outer space.[50] Interestingly, some experts also argue that cyberspace is another global commons.[51] Identifying these areas can lead to extracting vital resources, which could be used for states' welfare. According to International Law, a broader understanding of the global commons highlights that it is governed by the Common Heritage of Humankind (CHM).[52] The extraction of resources in these areas is an uphill task. However, technological advancement has made these areas more accessible. Space is one of the essential areas of global commons, and its security is highly important for humans. Notably, the CHM establishes that all humanity can freely use the resources, and every state has free access to these areas. The changing nature of international security has forced the states to extend the securitization process to even the CHM. The national defence of any state in this contemporary world is not limited to securing its physical sovereignty and territory; it has extended its scope to deal with the emerging threats from global commons. Global commons enable "militaries to protect national territory and interests and facilitate the passage of goods, people, communication, and data upon which every member of the international community depend."

Regional economic and military alliances are particularly looking to access the global commons due to their growing national interests in these areas.[53] Space as a global commons is rich in resources, especially its ability to provide accessible communication on the Earth. It has been crowded with new countries, Non-State Actors, and even private citizens operating satellites to utilize the area's resources. However, it has some cost to pay, as the increasing activities have created threats, challenges, vulnerabilities, and risks to space use.[54] The actions of significant spacefarers resemble the concept of the tragedy of the commons. Their actions refer to a particular environment in outer space where the vast resources of this global commons have become a restricted area for others. The major spacefarers continue sending more satellites to fulfil their national needs and denying space to other states, which refers to the global commons' tragedy.

States in the international system always protect their interests and security. It is exciting that they interact within a global structure where nearly 200 states reside. Some have neither political will nor military strength to threaten most of the state's interests. However, neighbouring states and major political and military powers feel threatened by other states and their rising military and political powers in many parts of the world. Likewise, threats and dangers emanate from rising economic disparities, environmental changes, and transnational terrorism. These threats, challenges, risks, and vulnerabilities affect individual, state, and international security. Measures have been taken at three levels, and security has been structured to neutralize these threats.

More precisely, threats to international security have been securitized by structuring an international system of institutions, organizations, and alliances.[55] The

United Nations (U.N.) was established after the Second World War in 1945 to maintain international security and promote fundamental human rights. The U.N. has authority to use force; however, it has failed to prevent major wars and armed conflicts since its inception. Likewise, the North Atlantic Treaty Organization (NATO) is another multilateral military alliance headed by the U.S. States that has developed norms, best practices, treaties, and principles under international law to guard people and states against international security threats. Although these are mere ethics, states have agreed to regulate their behaviour under international law. At the same time, they continue to violate International Law. Besides, forums, bodies, and committees work under the U.N. to examine arms control and disarmament matters. Institutions' role in maintaining international peace and stability can be assessed by applying two different theoretical frameworks: liberal institutionalism and realism. Realism contradicts institutionalism so that global institutions do not "markedly affect the prospects for international stability" and symbolize global power distribution.[56] Liberal institutionalists argue in ways different from international institutions' work to alter state behaviour. In this tug of argument, institutions have minimal influence on the state's behaviour and thus hold little promise for promoting stability in the post-Cold War world.[57]

The realist perspective can analyse international institutions' role in studying the framework of space security. This study presumes that international institutions regulate the states' behaviour and that states' national security policies represent their actual positions. The reason is that space is now attributed mainly as one of the global commons and is also the fourth medium of warfare. Now, the question arises: what are the prospects of maintaining peace and stability in space without a global authority regulating the states' behaviour in space? Is it possible for states to have a universally accepted framework to establish peace and stability in space? How does it affect security at three levels?

Security is a relational phenomenon between three levels. A state's national security cannot be seen in isolation; its citizens and national security are seemingly interconnected with international security in the form of a "seamless web."[58] The debate on this relational aspect of security yields sublevels of security as regional RSC, where states' security primarily interacts. Regional security is "a level between national and international security with a certain degree of interaction."[59] The argument is based on Stephen Walt's assumption of states' relations with their neighbours. He believes that "simple physical adjacency generates more security interaction among neighbours than states located in different areas."[60] In this middle level, "one finds only the hazy notions of regional balances of power and subsystems," where an interplay of national security and the international system suggests a location that "contains a new worthy level of political turbulence."[61] This interaction level adds more complexity to the state's security as it cannot be viewed in isolation; instead, it needs a comprehensive understanding of the prevailing regional and international environment.[62]

National and international security interactions propagate at the regional level, theorized as RSC. In the research, they are identified as regional structures/complexes. For example, Latin (South) America, the Middle East, Southern Africa,

South Asia, and Southeast Asia. Every region has its security distinction. There are some buffer states between the security complexes. However, every region has its power and political and economic problems, and a single regional security framework cannot be adopted to study the states' behaviour.[63]

The primary feature of RSC is that it "hinges on patterns of amity [friendship] and enmity among the units [actors] in the system." The impact of "geographical proximity on security interactions is strongest and most obvious in the military, political, societal and environmental sectors."[64] Superpowers have a wide range of interests interconnected within and outside the region. RSC has several categorizations: the standard, centred, and great power levels.[65] The standard RSC suggests that regional power defines a pattern of rivalry, BoP, and alliance patterns among the leading powers within the region and polarity.[66] In the centred RCS, the role of a centred power is essential as it defines the standard complex. For details, see Table 3.1[67]

The rationale behind this study on regional security complexes is to understand the security dynamics in South Asia. Space developments could significantly influence regional power structures. India and China are rigorously pursuing space power to augment their national power. Likewise, Pakistan cannot be separated from its relations as a regional actor. The U.S.' role as a superpower has continued to influence the region. This makes the South Asian RSC super complex, creating a space security trilemma.

The framework of three levels of security and their relational aspect resulting in a relatively new concept of RSCs is applied in this study to assess the security relationship between India, Pakistan, China, and the U.S.

Table 3.1 Regional security complexes

Levels	Characteristics	Security Issue (s)	Example (s)
Standard	Dominated by regional power	Security Interdependence Amity/enmity Polarity Civilization area Domestic spillover	Middle East, South America, Southeast Asia, Southern Africa
Centred	Superpower as central state Great power as central state Regional power as central state The region requires actors' quality through institutions	Security Interdependence Amity/enmity Polarity Civilization area Domestic spillover	• North America • South Asia? • None • E.U
Super complexes	Strong interregional level of security dynamics arising from great power spillover into adjacent regions	Security Interdependence Amity/enmity Polarity	East/South Asia

Source: Barry Buzan and Ole Wæver, *Regions and Power,* 62; also see Buzan, *People, State and Fear,* 226.

It is also important to understand that the adversarial relationship between China and the U.S.[68] South Asia is categorized as an RSC where the two regional powers, India and Pakistan, compete in an arms race.[69] This suggests an enmity between the two states and an adversarial relationship between India and China. So, in the super RSC of interest here, great power in the region dominates the sublevel of security. More complexity is generated in the security of this part of the world. The U.S. has a strategic partnership with India and a declared policy (The Pivot to Asia) of containment of China.[70] Pakistan is a close strategic ally of China. But has unstable relations with the U.S.[71]

Theoretical Aspects of the Arms Race

> An arms race is defined as a progressive, competitive peacetime increase in armament by two states or coalition of states resulting from conflictual purposes or mutual fears.[72]

—Huntington, a Famous American Political Scientist.

The above-stated definition of an arms race between any two states or coalitions of states is still relevant today. Michael Intriligator and Dagobert Brito give a more standard definition to Huntington's definition of an arms race, which is "the competitive, resource-constrained, dynamic process of interaction between two states or coalitions of states in their acquisition of weapons."[73] Colin S. Gray, defined an arms race as "two or more parties [states] perceiving themselves to be in an adversary relationship, who are increasing or improving their armament at a rapid rate and structuring their respective military postures with a general attention to the past, present, and anticipated military and political behaviour of the other parties."[74] The definition suggests several aspects of adversarial relations between two states or a coalition of states. The theoretical understanding of the definition is how states perceive each other. This factor is still crucial in defining the rules of engagement between the adversarial states in the modern world. Robert Jervis argues that security-related perception between states A and B is that "the effect of initiatives and threats depends largely on the other's intentions and its perceptions of the first state."[75] Likewise, the adversarial relations between states pivot around each other's perception, especially when they are significant military powers. When states could not gauge their aggression, it caused a security dilemma. The security dilemma lets states acquire as many weapons as they can "afford."[76]

A survey of Sino-U.S. security-related perceptions conducted by Carnegie Endowment for International Peace suggests that "international cooperation and conflict in the twenty-first century hinge upon whether Chinese and Americans view of each other, and foreign countries more generally, as trustworthy or not."[77] Besides, Sino-U.S. competition is not limited to land, sea, and air; it has also gone into space. As far as misperception is concerned, China and the U.S.' challenges to their national security are because of the misunderstanding and lack of clarity on the threats and dangers to each other's security.

Fig. 3.1 Causal link between arms race and war[79]

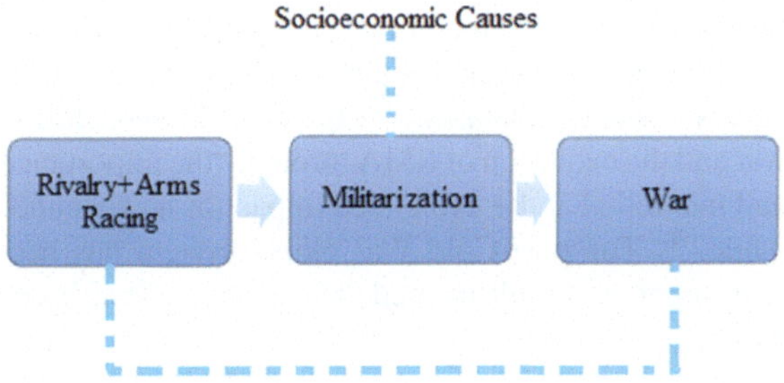

The arms race does not necessarily create sufficient war conditions.[78] However, there is a causal link between arms races and war. War is possible if two rival states are engaged in a build-up of arms. Adding more complexity to the equation, the possibility of war cannot be excluded if relations between the two rival states have misunderstanding-misperception dynamics. See Fig. 3.1.

Indo-Pakistan case study suggests that the arms race between the arch-rivals applies to an action-reaction model. It is "an intense and continuous interaction between two states"[80] that could still be the mechanism by which states compete militarily in purely quantitative terms."[81] Further to this, "arms racing has only become a distinctive international phenomenon since the industrial revolution unleashed the force of mass production and institutionalized innovation into international system."[82] The phenomenon of arms racing becomes a distinctive part of relations between arch-rivals (India and Pakistan) or between two coalitions (only during the Cold War) when the states realize that war is the likely outcome of their aggressive accumulation of weapons.[83] In Indo-Pak case, a declassified U.S. document written in 1959 suggests that the arms race was a visible part of the relations between the two countries.[84] The arms race between the two states can be exemplified as an action-reaction syndrome.[85]

A space arms race is also a distinctive phenomenon in the international political system. However, the present arms race trends in outer space can be studied by applying the above-mentioned arms race models; for example, the action-reaction model can be applied to study the pattern of Sino-U.S. relations in space. Similarly, Indo-Pak relations could be another relevant case study for the space domain's action-reaction syndrome. The impacts of the arms race, no matter which domain, are devastating at the regional and global levels.[86]

Evolution of RMA

Operation Desert Storm "was the first time we integrated strategic space information into a theatre of operations."[87] However, how has space evolved as RMA? There are many factors involved in the evolution of warfare. However, one cannot exclude that RMA would be the primary factor in this evolution.[88] RMA primarily "emphasized the greater use and better communication of information among commanders, analysts, and combatants."[89] Operation Desert Storm showed the modern nature of war and the evolution of RMA through "the importance of firepower over manoeuvre and marvelled at the associated impact of new technologies in changing the face of battle."[90] The post-Cold War global system has become more complex, multidimensional, and multilayered. The global system's complexity is because the "four tributaries feed into this river of turbulent change," one of the streams is the RMA.[91] It has made the global system's complexity more effortless for the great powers to "extend deterrence without relying on WMDs." The great powers are trying to make their capabilities "stealthier, smarter, faster, smaller, and therefore, much harder to target by conventional or nuclear weapons."[92] Hence, the effects of these efforts are visible and profound. The most profound is the development of medium and long-range missiles by smaller nuclear weapons states in the global nuclear order, e.g. India, Pakistan, and North Korea. Furthermore, the U.S., China, and Russia invest in their nuclear force structure and rapid innovation in their defence-dominant strategy and technologies.[93]

Space has become part of the evolving RMA since the first satellite launch in 1957."[94] Space technologies are integral to the present RMA.[95] The present RMA intersects four areas: space, information warfare, precision strike, and dominant manoeuvre (see Fig. 2.1).[96] Space technologies are integral to the RMA. They are smarter, not cheap, but stealthier, more precise, accurate, and enhance target acquisition and striking. Desert Storm is exemplified for this reason.[97] Because of fighting a war, Operation Desert Storm gave "the U.S. force to dominate manoeuvre" during the first Gulf War. It established that space technologies could play a decisive role in warfighting. Deibert stresses that "outer space technologies provide high ground essential to communicating information worldwide, coordinating force movements, rehearsing simulated interventions, and targeting attacks.[98]

Other critical issues may be essential in shaping the major spacefarers' space power, especially the U.S. These issues are similar to Information Operation (I.O.), transformation, and the space power's organizational structures, which help bring the evolution of RMA. Operation Desert Storm enabled U.S. forces to craft a "space-enabled operational integrated reconnaissance complex capable of tailoring military strikes for unprecedented effects in unprecedented ways."[99] Experts within the U.S. space policymaking sphere have argued for establishing a "system of systems."[100] Some analysts also believe that net-centric warfare capabilities are also required. The U.S. should build a global enterprise of "I.O. and technologies" to radically improve U.S. combat and warfighting effectiveness in this system of systems.[101] Nevertheless, the space-based global enterprise of intelligence, surveillance, reconnaissance (ISR) enables space power to establish that system of systems.

Concomitantly, if space power becomes analogous to land, sea, and air power, "it will show that space power is on the threshold of something much more prominent."[102] "This emergence of space power will mark it out as an RMA."[103]

As far as space power characteristics are concerned, there is a need to understand to what extent the characteristics of space power are similar to other power domains, i.e. air, land, and sea. Geography will be an essential factor in making any medium part of the evolution of RMA. Geography influences the "policymakers, planners and experts to prepare strategies, tactics, logistics and force postures."[104] Therefore, it is important to understand space's characteristics and their familiarity with the land, air, and sea power. It is undeniable that space is a vast area, and it has no limit to its exploration. Instead, space is a unique medium, unlike land, sea, and air, having no north, south, east, or west.

A comparison of space and other mediums of warfare shows military forces' characteristics as "strategic agility, ability to demonstrate commitment and credibility, economic consideration, military consideration, and political consideration."[105] The political flexibility, which pivots around *realpolitik*, carries the day regardless of the force structure and doctrines. Ultimately, "it is the political applicability of a force, not operational dissimilarities from another, which is most meaningful."[106] This suggests that the political applicability of force on land, sea, and air is similar to space.

In conclusion, space is considered the fourth medium of warfare, and since Desert Storm, space power has been realized as RMA.[107] For example, the U.S. military has a global ISR enterprise, early warning system, navigation, and communication, providing strategic agility, commitment, and credibility to its military forces on land (terrestrial) and sea and sea air from its space power. Moreover, "it seems space power can be more politically useful in most situations"; however, the sea, land, and air powers still have unique advantages and applications.[108]

Giving a "real basis for the vision of current RMA," the impact of space on RMA and vice versa is enormous. In today's world, the Research and Development (R&D) in space technologies, e.g. the development of Anti-Satellite (ASAT) weapons and ballistic missile defence (BMD) systems, are some of the manifestations of space technologies.[109] Space has become a strategic domain, and states compete to maximize their power. Major spacefaring states are developing new space technologies for dual-use purposes, and in addition to this, the digital revolution is a new manifestation of RMA. States, especially the U.S., are looking to develop further and exploit communication and navigation satellites. The space power revolution linked to RMA serves to militarize space further.[110]

Conceptualizing Space Security

As one of the global commons and a strategic asset, the security of space for humans, the state, and the international system is fundamental. Humans have been thinking of exploiting the skies and outer space for centuries. Since the rise of the First Space Age, exploring and using space began an unending process. Space has also gained political, economic, and military importance in the last seven decades (the 1950s to the present) as a strategic asset and global commons.

The importance of space power cannot be ruled out in twenty-first century. Great Britain became a superpower in the nineteenth century due to its super navy. The

British Empire controlled the seas through its naval power. It extended its grip beyond the European continent to rule the Indian subcontinent eventually, the Middle East, many parts of Africa, and Oceania. In *The Influence of Sea Power Upon History*, Alfred T. Mahan reviewed the British Empire's emergence due to its super navy.[111] Sea power resulted in the establishment of the British Empire in nineteenth century.

Similarly, Operation Desert Storm showed the U.S.' emergence as a superpower in the last decade of the twentieth century thanks to its space power. This, combined with its already conventional and nuclear superiority, allowed it to become the only truly global power in the history of humankind. Likewise, Israel is an example of a super-regional power in the 1990s when it realized the importance of space power; Israel understood that it could not influence its neighbours' behaviour without space.[112]

Space security is usually defined as: "the secure and sustainable access to, and use of, space and the freedom from space-based threats." To draw a holistic picture of space security, there is a need to understand the major and emerging spacefaring states' space policies, doctrines, and capabilities. Further, the picture will be incomplete if there is no analysis of the states' international and regional space programs because of their multilateral and bilateral space relations. This constitutes a global space environment that can better understand space security.

Major spacefaring states' military space programs are important to understanding space security. Military space capabilities have profound implications for international security. Space systems protection and negation and space-based strike weapons are important areas of space security. A complete picture of global space security is drawn by assessing states' capabilities to build space systems protection and negation.[113]

Of note are the threats to space assets that can cause physical damage and hamper the standard abilities of satellite systems. These threats are of kinetic and non-kinetic means, which states are developing. The kinetic measures include developing Kinetic-Kill Vehicles (KKVs) tagged as ASAT missiles. The non-kinetic measures include means of Electronic Warfare (E.W.). These are jamming capabilities against dedicated military satellite communications, imaging satellites, and Global Positioning Systems. Further, operational hacking software, dazzling sensors, spoofing, and cyber-attacks exist. Furthermore, artificial debris is another threat to operational satellite systems.[114]

Hundreds of reports of jamming, spoofing, and dazzling by states exist.[115] China, Russia, India, and the U.S. have recently tested ASAT capability. It cannot be predicted that there will not be any further ASAT tests by other space powers in the future. India in 2019 tested ASAT missile in Low Earth Orbit, destroying a live military satellite. The threat of ASAT proliferation has increased due to the Chinese, Indian, and American tests in the recent past.

Additionally, "Russia and China are conducting sophisticated on-orbit satellite activities, such as rendezvous and proximity functions, at least some of which are likely intended to test dual-use technologies with inherent counterspace functionality."[116] States seek space access due to the proliferation of new technologies. The reliance on satellites and the absence of a universally accepted code of conduct in space and regulation have made space weaponization inevitable. Space militarization began with *Sputnik*-I, and while states have yet to place space weapons, they are building capabilities on the ground to be weaponized there. The U.S., China and Russia can place space weapons. These states are just waiting for each other to place weapons first. Simultaneously, states are more inclined towards space sanctuary than controlling space and denying free access to other states. U.S. space doctrine predominantly pivots around the high-ground and space control doctrines and has yet to operationalize its capabilities.[117]

The global trends in space industry expansion suggest that states briefly extend space-enabled capabilities and space situational awareness to public and private actors. This would provide necessary imagery, communications, weather, Positioning, Navigation, Timing (PNT) capabilities for intelligence gathering, early warning, and scientific and commercial uses of outer space.

As indicated earlier, the three space powers of note are the U.S., China, and Russia. Their relationship may be better understood through the lens of a BoP in space. Space security can be analysed internationally in political, military, and economic environments. All three states have given tremendous importance to their space power, with the U.S. being the three's undisputable space power.[118] Russia is a significant space power.[119] It aims to improve its ISR satellite system to solidify its Space Situational Awareness (SSA) and tactical weapons targeting satellites.[120] China is an emerging global space power, and in recent decades, it has surpassed Russia in terms of the number of operational space assets.[121] It is increasing its space power by developing space capabilities for dual-use purposes.

India has emerged as a regional space power with global ambitions, and Japan also has an adequate space program.[122] Pakistan is a regional power and can further augment its aspiring regional space power status.[123] Emerging space users in the Middle East, e.g. United Arab Emirates (UAE) and Saudi Arabia. Private entities are also in space, making space crowded and congested, which may eventually lead to conflict.

Overall, space security is comprehensively understood if the relations of major and emerging spacefaring states are analysed in previewing their space policies, reflecting upon the intentions and visions of their space programs and capabilities. Space assets, i.e. satellites, are the fastest, most reliable, and most sustainable communication source. In this globalized world, the reliance on satellites for communication, navigation, and broadcasting makes space indispensable. They prove that any military space conflict would harm human and economic security (Fig. 3.2).

The BoP theory helps predict major spacefaring states' behaviour in global space activities. Major space powers have advanced technologies, capabilities, and significant operational satellite systems for military and peaceful purposes. However, "the political applicability of a force, not operational dissimilarities from another, is most meaningful."[124] They all compete to shift the balance of power by building space weapons and advancing assertive space policies and doctrines. U.S. policymakers assessed that Russia and China perceive "a need to offset any U.S. military advantage derived from military, civil or commercial space systems and are increasingly considering attacks against satellite systems as part of their future warfare doctrine."[125] Both

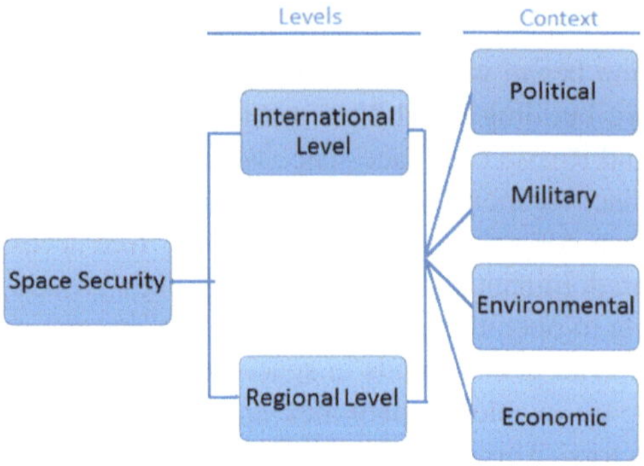

Fig. 3.2 Framework of space security at international and regional level

states, Russia and China, are actively pursuing ASAT weapons systems to reduce U.S. military effectiveness.

"U.S. is currently the preeminent global space power"[126] because of its military and civilian space capabilities. It plays a dominant hegemonic role. China is second in the global space order, and Russia comes third.[127] China is more inclined to ally with Russia to counter U.S. space hegemony, build its space capabilities, and increase international cooperation with other space actors. The high-ground and space control schools of thought dominate U.S. space policy and doctrine.

The operational parts of the U.S. space control doctrine are offensive to Chinese and Russian space programs. U.S. space intends to control the high ground and only let friendly countries operate in outer space. This is likely to shape the global space order in the U.S.'s favour. It develops space capabilities to negate the adversary through deception, disruption, denial, degradation, or destruction. U.S. "assets designed for offensive counterspace mission may be used to conduct or support counterair, countersea, counterland, counterinformation, or strategic attack missions by performing offensive counterspace actions where the adversary's vulnerable node is a space system."[128] This scenario makes it easy to assess that the U.S. is still vulnerable to China and Russia because of their counterspace capability development.[129] However, the "Five Ds: deception, disruption, denial, degradation, or destruction actions," which represent the continuum of options, are not only meant for China and Russia but also meant to persuade other states[130] as well as the non-state actors from committing any course of action against the U.S. space assets.[131] The activities of private actors and states are increasing, and space is now crowded and congested. It is important to follow how the U.S. will manage to control it. Will the balance of power work when other states with fewer space assets reach the final frontier? The answers are difficult to find, but the impacts of the Sino-U.S. space rivalry will likely affect international security. Russia is making significant international cooperation with China and others in space, which concerns U.S. control doctrine and capabilities. India in 2019, self proclaimed the status of global space power. It military space capabilities are aimed to counter China with the help of the U.S..

From a traditionalist lens, BoP is about developing military capabilities to prepare for a possible war. Furthermore, military capabilities are meant to create or aggregate "military power through either internal mobilization or the forging of alliances to prevent or deter the occupation and domination of the state by a foreign power or a coalition."[132] The theory suggests that the states target the adversary's military hardware in preparation for a possible war. Hence, the core assumption is that states always try to maximize their political, economic, and military goals at the cost of other states' interests, and states cannot be trusted with "inordinate power." Simply put, the natural antidote to power is power.[133] By applying these core assumptions to power relations in space, new actors are "capable of challenging the hierarchical situation in space."[134] The newcomers are developing space capabilities intending to acquire any status there.

A crowded, congested, and contested space threatens U.S. space supremacy. Likewise, newcomers and two other major space powers, Russia and China, have challenges and vulnerabilities to their space assets from U.S. space power's offensive space control components. In this case, states make alliances in space and indigenously develop military space assets. The Indo-U.S. co-operation in space under the umberalla of COMCASA, BECA, LEMOA and STA-I status is an example of new alliance in space against China in Asia. Sino-U.S. rivalry in space has its dimension. China often views U.S. space power and capabilities as offensive to its space power. The U.S. sees Chinese space development, especially after the Chinese ASAT test in 2007, as an emerging challenge to its space supremacy.[135] Sino-U.S. space relations are involved in a security dilemma. However, China-U.S. competition is unlike the U.S.-Soviet space race.

Nevertheless, significant developments from each side are detrimental to international security. The asymmetrical space power structure between spacefaring states (the U.S. and China) destabilizes global strategic stability effects. At the same time, both countries are economically interdependent.

There are three significant military powers in the South Asian region: China, India, and Pakistan. Although there are good relations between Pakistan and China, India has strained relations. This suggests that the type of relations is a mix of amity and enmity. RSC theory is most suitable for analysing relations regionally. The U.S. also has a strong presence and influence in South Asia. China, India, and Pakistan have a strategic triangular relationship.[136] The Sino-U.S. relationship has impacted this triangle, making it a quadrilateral relation. The study's scope is limited to their relationship in outer space as it may affect regional strategic stability. Space power, doctrines, policies and capabilities will be analysed in strategic triangular relations in South Asia. However, the U.S. is a preeminent space power with a dominant role in shaping the global space order, but it can also influence the regional space regime in South Asia. The U.S. plays a prominent role in space because of its adversarial relations with China. It once collaborated with India and Pakistan. India continues to enjoy friendly relations with the U.S. However, Pakistan is not. The U.S. does not consider Pakistan its foe in space. Therefore, its relations with China are the triggering point of space security trilemma in South Asia, whereas its status in the trilemma is just the tip of the iceberg.

India is a regional space power whose space program is a top political priority. However, in South Asia, Sino-India relations are adversarial. Both countries fought a war with each other in 1962. India perceives China as a strategic adversary. "China is a more fraught subject in Indian national debates," and "India displays tremendous insecurities in the face of Chinese economic and military expansion." "The security relationship can act as a spoiler in the larger relationship, ultimately determining whether the two Asian giants will clash or cooperate." For mutual gains,[137] both countries have had minimal contact and understanding in the past. However, it is a profound bilateral relationship in twenty-first century.[138] Sino-India relations have been strained overall in past decades due to territorial disputes. China is a significant military and economic power. It has the potential to grow globally. India is also a leading power with significant military and economic strength. It has the resources to change the regional balance of power.[139] There is an asymmetrical space power structure between India and China. Both countries also see each other as potential adversaries in space, just like in different realms of power.[140] "Both countries are expanding their strategic reach from the open seas to outer space."

Indo-Pak relations suffered from historical legacy of the 1947 subcontinent Partition. A brief history of both countries' relations highlights three major wars, the nuclearization of the subcontinent, and unresolved territorial regional disputes. Both countries possess conventional and nuclear power to change regional power polarity. From space security point of view, India is a significant space power, expanding. However, Pakistan is regarded as an aspiring space power with an expanding missile capability. India's space program trajectory has had a pacifist orientation, but it has developed space military capabilities in navigation, remote sensing, communication, and reconnaissance. This presents implications for Pakistan's and China's national security.

Any armed conflict in space would have devastating impacts on regional and international security. Securing space for free access and use necessitates avoiding space war. A war in space would be devastating to all, and preventing it, rather than finding ways to fight it, will likely remain the goal of the study.[141] The current trajectory of newcomers and major spacefaring states' activities affects strategic stability and deconstructs the present status quo in space. This can lead to the weaponization of space. An "increased competition in space revives fears of a war there, one with devastating consequences."[142] To avoid conflict in space, international and regional cooperation is required. Also, the misperception-misunderstanding dynamic should not be part of any multilateral or bilateral engagement to secure free access and use space.

Conclusion

Understanding space security internationally and regionally is complex as space is now more crowded, congested, and competitive. Understandably, the U.S. is the sole space superpower, and China is following in its footsteps. The BoP theory is applicable to assess the bilateral space relations between the two major powers. Even though China is still lagging behind the U.S. regarding operational satellite systems, its current path of space activities will be challenging to U.S. space supremacy. Russia is a significant space power and experienced competing with the U.S. during the Cold War space race. It is also developing space capabilities (kinetic and non-kinetic) to offset threats from the U.S. The U.S. has highlighted and assessed all necessary measures to remain dominant in space at policy and doctrine. China and Russia are also developing counterspace capabilities. Hence, it is essential to know why states are pursuing these capabilities. What will be the likely outcome of space militarization and potentially space weaponization?

The power of state is always attributed to its military power. In the past, states developed conventional and nuclear power to bolster their military muscles. States always gauged their military strength to offset risks, challenges, and vulnerabilities to their national security, with military defence forces repelling any physical attack on their territory. The introduction of RMA in the early 1950s, its evolution during the Cold War, and its applicability during the first Gulf War completely revolutionized warfare. Space is the product of the evolution of RMA. It has enhanced the agility, communication, and credibility of the battlefield's terrestrial, air, and sea forces. Space is now considered a strategic asset with enormous resources for peaceful and military uses. However, its security is as important as the security of states on land, sea, and air. States' self-centric approach to maximize their security and power can lead to armed conflict in space. They are expanding space capability for dual-use purposes, which may damage other states' security and the domain of space itself. This likely leads to interstate conflict with implications for international security and regional peace and stability.

Sino-U.S. relations are an important aspect of the global strategic environment. The U.S. has enormous military, political, and economic strength and influence to shape the global strategic environment. All components of its national power make it an undisputed global power. Its enormous strength has allowed the U.S. to influence the global political and strategic landscape. Concomitantly, U.S. power faces risks, vulnerabilities, and challenges on land, sea, air, and space. China is also solidifying its national power through military and economic means. There are chances of Sino-U.S. conflict in all mediums of warfare. However, both have economic interdependence and strategic competition with each other. This complex interdependence suggests that they will continue to compete without struggling to shift the balance of power. Their fortunes are inextricably tied together. It is analysed whether the complex interdependence will prevent weaponizing space or a rigorous competition involving an arms race.

In conclusion, Sino-U.S. relations posit implications for South Asia. India and China both have adversarial relations. Similarly, India and Pakistan relations suffer from the action-reaction syndrome and are involved in a conventional nuclear arms race. Hence, in South Asia, a complicated regional security complex exists in which all three states (China, India, and Pakistan) can change the polarity of power balances through their military power. The U.S. also influences China, India, and Pakistan; this can be viewed as strategic triangular relations with a core state (the U.S.).

Notes

1. Buzan [1]
2. For further details, see Moltz [2].
3. Heurlin and Kristensen [3].
4. For further details, see Buzan [4].
5. Buzan, 8.
6. Wohlforth et al. [5].
7. One of the main proponents of structural realism was Hans Morgenthau. See, Morgenthau [6]. Likewise, John Mearsheimer's scholarly work is primarily based on criticizing the traditional concept of security and giving alternative concepts of security in the twenty-first century. For details, see Mearsheimer [8]
8. Schweller [9].
9. Schweller, "The Balance of Power."
10. Schweller, 2016.
11. Papayoanou [10].
12. The scholar has developed a general framework of security, which may be applied to study space security as well. The initial thoughts on the overall structure of security were studied by the scholar in a chapter focusing on the three levels of security, particularly focusing on the systemic level of security in international relations. The systemic level of security is mostly discussed by Bary Buzan and the scholar has aptly discussed and laid a framework for security to study the interplay of relations between international security and regional security. For further details, see Mirarab [11].
13. Tarry [12].
14. Heurlin and Kristensen, "International Security."
15. Spielman [13].
16. Brooks [14]; and also see Stone [15].
17. McSweeney [16]; and also see Diskaya [17].
18. Buzan, *People, States and Fear,* 35.
19. Wæver [18].
20. Wæver, 23.
21. See, van Munster [19]; and also see Chifu [20] (site discontinued).
22. Buzan, "New Patterns of Global-Security," 431–451.
23. Buzan, 431–451.
24. Buzan, 39.
25. Rotberg [21].
26. Rotberg, 130.
27. Buzan and Hansen [22], 35; Brooks, "What is Security." 225–239; Stone, "Security Approach to Buzan," 2–11; and also see, Buzan, "New Patterns of Global-Security," 431–451.
28. Rotberg, "Failed States," 130. And also see, "The New Nature of Nation-State Failure," *The Washington Quarterly* 25, no.3 (summer 2002): 85–96.
29. Rotberg [23].
30. Harris [24]; Buzan, "New Patterns of Global-Security," 431–451.
31. Holmes [25].
32. Mendel [26].
33. Berkowitz and Bock [27].
34. Baldwin [28].
35. Brauch [29].
36. Grizold [30].
37. Quoted in Vojin Dimitrijevic, professor of international relations. Grizold, "The Concept of National," 37–53.
38. Realists believe that the state develops its national security policy on three centerpieces of the theory of realism, which are statism, survival and self-help. For details, see Dunne and Schmidt [31].

39. "Threat to National Security," *De La Salle University,* Philippines, accessed October 23, 2021, http://www.dlsu.edu.ph/offices/sps/rotc/pdf/ms1/threat-NatlSecurity.pdf, 1–3, (site discontinued).
40. Grizold, "Concept of National Security," 46.
41. Buzan, "New Patterns of Global Security," 433.
42. Buzan, 433.
43. In this research, he pointed out several factors which have made impacts on the new security agenda after the end of Cold War. He commented on the rise of multipolar power structure in the place of the Cold War's bipolar one; a much lower degree of ideological division of rivalry; the global dominance of security community; and the strengthening of international society. See Buzan, "New Patterns in Global Security," 431–451.
44. Buzan, 433.
45. The definition of international community is important to highlight as it will give a necessary understanding of the role of the international community in contextualizing space security. While defining the International community, Michel Rocard, former Prime Minister of France, believes that the international community can be defined as "any country whose identity and sovereignty is recognized, and that chooses to participate in global discussions and decision-making." See, Records [32]; Barry Buzan quoted Hedley Bull and Adam Watson that the international community can be defined as "a group of states (or, more generally, a group of independent political communities) which not merely form a system, in the sense that the behaviour of each is a necessary factor in the calculations of the others, but also have established by dialogue and consent common rules and institutions for the conduct of their relations, and recognize their common interest in maintaining these arrangements." Buzan, "New Patterns in Global Security," 438.
46. "Contemporary Threats to National and International Security, and Appropriate Security Measures," *Ministry of Foreign Affairs, and Defence, Slovenia and NATO*, Government of Slovenia, accessed October 24, 2021, http://nato.gov.si/eng/topic/threats-to-security/.
47. The Westphalian school of thought is considered international security as the mixture of alliance politics, collective security, multilateralism and national security policies. See for details, Bastien Irondelle, "The New Parameters of International Security: Conceptual Introduction," in *New and Evolving Trends in International Security,* ed. Anne-Marie Le Gloannec (Rome, Italy: Transworld, April 2013), 13.
48. The reason behind Lynn-Jones assertion is that war is not obsolete as many believe that after the Cold War, war will be a relatively less discussed issue in the future. But, war is not yet obsolete; in fact, it has taken new forms and dimensions, e.g. space War, and cyberspace war. States are building both physical capabilities to fight war at all mediums of warfare; air, sea, land and space. In cyberspace or at the information front, many believe that a war is ongoing, which has its implications for national security and individual security. In this case, the traditional concept still remains largely valid.
49. "IEG of the Global Commons," *The United Nations Environment Program, United Nations,* accessed October 24, 2021, http://staging.unep.org/delc/GlobalCommons/tabid/54404/Default.aspx.
50. "Global Commons."
51. Murphy [33].
52. CHM is a very specific legal construct. A global commons can exist without a CHM designation. This is the case for space. For details, see "Global Governance and Governance of the Global Commons in the Global Partnership for Development beyond 2015," United Nations, January 2013, http://www.un.org/en/development/desa/policy/untaskteam_undf/thinkpieces/24_thinkpiece_global_governance.pdf, 5–7.
53. "Governance of the Global Commons," 7.
54. For details on the subject, see Moltz, *Crowded Orbits.*
55. Many experts of international politics believe that international institutes are established to promote international peace. Some of these institutes are, e.g. European Community, the NATO, Conference on Security and Cooperation in Europe (CSCE), and the European

Union. The aim to establish these international institutions is to achieve durable peace and international security.

56. Mearsheimer [34].
57. Mearsheimer, "False Promise," 7.
58. Mirarab, "Power Relations in the Persian Gulf Region," 85.
59. Mirarab, 85.
60. Quoted in Buzan and Walt [34]; and also see Waltz [35].
61. Buzan, *People, State and Fear,* 187.
62. Buzan and Wæver [36].
63. For complete details on the RSC, Buzan and Wæver, *Regions and Powers*, 37–67; and also see Buzan, *People, State and Fear,* 226.
64. Buzan and Wæver, *Regions and Powers,* 45.
65. Buzan and Wæver, 65.
66. Buzan and Wæver, 47.
67. Buzan and Wæver, 62.
68. For over Sino-U.S. security relations see, Lieberthal and Jisi [37]; Eric Heginbotham et al. [38]; and also see Saunders [39].
69. Spain [40]; and also see Shah [41].
70. For details on the Pivot to Asia Policy, see Burgess [42]; Zhao [43]; and also see Friedberg [44].
71. The strategic chain project report published by Brookings Institute can be viewed as a summarized understanding of all four actors' relational security, the U.S., China, India and Pakistan. See Einhorn and Sidhu [45].
72. Huntington [46].
73. Intriljgator and Brito [47].
74. Gray [48].
75. Jervis [49].
76. Jervis, 112.
77. Johnston and Shen [50].
78. Schofield [51]; and also see, George and Bennett [52].
79. Schofield, 11.
80. Quoted in Schofied [53].
81. Buzan has extensively worked on the issue of arms racing between rival states. He argues that there are three different models of arms racing, which are: - (1) the action-reaction model; (2) the domestic model; and (3) the technological imperatives. The central point in rationalizing the arms racing debate according to three different models is force build-up against the rival state. The force build-up or arms production may be because of the anarchic international system or the internal pressure exerted by the Defence and security institutions or by the rapid technological innovations or developments in the world. See for further details, Khan [54]. Buzan and Herring [55].
82. Buzan and Herring, *Arms Dynamic in World Politics,* 84.
83. Buzan and Herring, 84.
84. Spain, "Indo-Pakistani tensions."
85. Khan, *Pakistan's Nuclear Policy,* 73 & 74.
86. Intriljgator and Brito, "Arms Race," 45–54.
87. Bennett [56].
88. Chapman [57].
89. See for further details, Lewis [58]; and also see Alwardt [59].
90. Quoted in Sloan [60]; and also see Lambeth [61].
91. Lambeth, 69.
92. Lambeth, 69.
93. Lambeth, 69.
94. Bergman [62].
95. Deibert [63].

96. Deibert, 108.
97. Billman [64].
98. Billman, 510.
99. Hays [65].
100. Hays, 366.
101. Hays, 366.
102. Hays, 366.
103. Hays, 366.
104. Billman, "Inherent Limitations of Space Power," 516.
105. Billman, 522.
106. Billman, 523.
107. Eligar Sadeh (Editor-in-chief Astropolitics) in discussion with the author, 3 November 2017.
108. Billman, "Limitations of Space Power," 546 & 547.
109. Fučík [66].
110. Mansoor [67].
111. Mahan [68]; Sempa [69]; Carpenter [70].
112. Eligar, discussion.
113. Space Security Index is the first and only annual, comprehensive and integrated assessment of space security. Some of the world's renowned space experts assessed the security in space by using the aforementioned variables. For further details visit the website of Space Security Index to access their annual reports since 2003.
114. From the Kessler syndrome, if the current trajectory of testing ASAT missile is continued, then it will create "a self-sustained cascading collision of space debris in low earth orbit (LEO)." For details, see "The Kessler Syndrome: 10 Interesting and Disturbing Facts," *Space Safety Magazine,* accessed November 8, 2017, http://www.spacesafetymagazine.com/space-debris/kessler-syndrome/.
115. For further details, see Weeden and Samson [71].
116. *Worldwide Threat Assessment of the U.S. Intelligence Community, Before Select Comm. on Intelligence* (May 11, 2017) (statement of Daniel R. Coats, Director of National Intelligence), 8.
117. Eligar, discussion.
118. Johnson-Freese [72].
119. Luzin [73]
120. In Ukraine war, Russia quickly degraded Ukrainian internet access, showing resilience in its space assets being used for denial of services.
121. Khan and Khan [74]
122. Howell [75].
123. Prof Dr Ram Jakhu (Associate Professor Institute of Air and Space Law, McGill University) in discussion with the author, 6 November 2017. Prof Ram believes that Pakistan is not an aspiring space power rather it is a regional space power. Pakistan has space capabilities and its building its space launch station and it's a matter of political well and intention that Pakistan will have its own space launch vehicles and space launch stations. However, Clay Moltz argues that Pakistan is an emerging regional space power. For details see Moltz [76]. Likewise, Correll [77].
124. Billman, "Inherent Limitations of Space Power," 523.
125. Statement of Coats, Director of National Intelligence, 8.
126. Johnson-Freese, *Space as a Strategic Asset*, VII.
127. Khan and Khan, "Chinese Capabilities."
128. Hays [78].
129. Bateman [79].
130. "There are more than 130 countries possessing sophisticated space programs or developing them, using information from space assets for their own Defence, the representative of Kazakhstan." See for further details, United Nations, "Full-Spectrum Dominance of Outer Space Can Turn Frontier into 'Military Theatre', Build Walls of Suspicion, Breach Global Security, First Committee Told," press release no. GA/DIS/3464, October 23, 2012, https://www.un.org/press/en/2012/gadis3464.doc.htm.

131. *Counterspace Operations* (Maxwell AFB, AL: Headquarters Air Force Doctrine Center, 2004)
132. Schweller, "Balance of Power."
133. Schweller, 2016.
134. Burzykowska [80].
135. Weeden and He [81]; Weeden [82]
136. Kapur [83].
137. Kanwal [84].
138. Banerjee [85].
139. Tellis [86].
140. The authors believe that the nuclear gap between India and China has been narrowed over the past decades and India has done significant developments in its missile and space program. India's long-range ballistic missile can now can reach the heartland of China. Likewise, India is develop Multiple independently targetable re-entry vehicle, submarine launch ballistic missiles, ballistic missile defence (BMD), and much advance outer space, which is causing concerns in China. Einhorn and Sidhu (eds.), "Strategic Chain," 22.
141. Lamrani [87].
142. Lamrani, 2016.

References

1. Barry Buzan, "New Patterns of Global-Security in the Twenty-First Century," *International Affairs* 67, no.3 (July 1991): 431–451.
2. James Moltz, *Crowded Orbits: Conflicts and Cooperation in Space* (Columbia University Press; New York, 2014).
3. Bertel Heurlin and Kristensen, "International Security," in *International Relations,* ed. Jarrod Weiner and Robert A Schrire (Oxford, UK: EOLSS Publishers, 2009), 172.
4. Barry Buzan, *People, States and Fear: An Agenda for International Security Studies in the Post-Cold War Era* (Boulder, Colorado: Lynne Rienner Publishers, 1991), 8.
5. William C. Wohlforth, Stuart Kaufman and Richard Little, "Introduction: Balance and Hierarchy in International Systems," in *the Balance of Power in World History*, eds. Stuart J. Kaufman, Richard Little and William Wohlforth (London: Palgrave Macmillan, 2007), 19.
6. Hans J. Morgenthau, *Politics Among Nations: The Struggle for Power and Peace* (New York: Alfred A. Knopf, 1978).
7. John J. Mearsheimer, *The Tragedy of Great Power Politics* (New York: W.W. Norton, 2001).
8. Randall L. Schweller, "The Balance of Power in World Politics," *Oxford Research Encyclopaedia of Politics,* May 2016, http://politics.oxfordre.com/view/https://doi.org/10.1093/acrefore/9780190228637.001.0001/acrefore-9780190228637-e-119.
9. Paul A. Papayoanou, "Economic Interdependence and the Balance of Power," *International Studies Quarterly* 41, no. 1 (March 1997): 113–140.
10. Mehrdad Hadji Mirarab, "The Role of the United States in the New System of Power Relations in the Persian Gulf Region, with Particular Reference to the Security and Stability," (PhD. Diss., Newcastle University, 1996), 85–130
11. Sarah Tarry, "Deepening and Widening: An Analysis of Security Definitions in 1990s," *Journal of Military and Strategic Studies* 2, no.1 (1999): 15–27.
12. Richard Spielman, "The emerging Unipolar World," *The New York Times,* August 21, 1990.
13. David J. Brooks, "What is Security: Defining through knowledge categorization," *Security Journal* 23, no.3 (2010): 225–239.
14. Marianne Stone, "Security Approach to Buzan: A Comprehensive Security Analysis," *School of International and Public Affairs,* Columbia University, 2009, 2–11.
15. Bill McSweeney, "Identity and security: Buzan and the Copenhagen school," *Review of International Studies* 22, no.1 (1996): 81–93.

16. Ali Diskaya, "Towards a Critical Securitization Theory: The Copenhagen and Aberystwyth Schools of Security Studies," (MSc. Diss., Aberystwyth University, 2012).
17. Ole Wæver, "Societal Security: the Concept," in *Identity, Migration and the New Security Agenda in Europe*, ed. Ole Wæver et al., (London: Pinter, 1993), 23.
18. Rens van Munster, "Logics of Security: The Copenhagen School, Risk Management and the War on Terror," *University of Southern Denmark,* October 2005, http://citeseerx.ist.psu.edu/viewdoc/download?doi=10.1.1.472.8628&rep=rep1&type=pdf, 2–4
19. Lulian Chifu, "Societal security: An agenda for the Eastern Europe," *Center for Conflict Prevention and Early Warning,* accessed October 22, 2017, http://www.cpc-ew.ro/pdfs/societal_security.pdf, 1–18
20. Robert I. Rotberg, "Failed States in a World of Terror," *Foreign Affairs* 81, no.4 (July-August 2002): 132.
21. Barry Buzan and Lene Hansen, *The Evolution of International Security Studies* (Cambridge: Cambridge University Press, 2009).
22. 23. Robert I. Rotberg, "Failed States, Collapsed States, Weak States: Causes and Indicators," in *State Failure and State Weakness in a Time of Terror,* ed. Robert I. Rotberg (Washington DC: Brookings, 2003), 1–3.
23. Harris, "Thinking About Security," (MSc. Diss., The University of Manitoba, 2008), 25
24. Kim R. Holmes, "What is National Security?" in *2015 Index of U.S. Military Strength: Assessing America's Ability to Provide for the Common Defence,* ed. Dakota L. Wood (Washington DC: The Heritage Foundation, 2015), 23–24.
25. Toby Mendel, "Defining the Scope of National Security: Issues Paper for the National Security Principles Project," *Center for Law and Democracy,* March 2013, http://www.right2info.org/resources/publications/mendel-on-defining-national-security, 4
26. Mortan Berkowitz and P.G. Bock, eds., *American National Security* (New York: Free Press, 1965), X.
27. 28. David A. Baldwin, "The Concept of Security," *Review of International Studies* 23, no.1 (Jan 1997): 5–26.
28. Hans Günter Brauch, "Concepts of Security threats, Challenges, Vulnerabilities and Risks," in *Coping with Global Environmental Change, Disasters and Security,* eds. Hans Günter Brauch et al., (Verlag, Berlin: Springer, 2001), 62.
29. 30. Anton Grizold, "The Concept of National Security in the Contemporary World," *International Journal of World Peace* 11, no.3 (September 1994): 37–53.
30. Tim Dunne and Brian C. Schmidt, "Realism," in *The Globalization of World Politics,* eds. John Baylis, Steven Smith and Patrica Owens (Oxford, UK: Oxford University Press, Seventh Edition 2017), 101–116.
31. Michel Records, "What is the International Community," *Project Syndicate,* May 30, 2013, https://www.project-syndicate.org/commentary/defining-the-international-community-s-role-and-responsibility-by-michel-rocard
32. 33. Tara Murphy, "Security Challenges in the 21st Century Global Commons," *Yale Journal of International Affairs* 5, no. 2 (2010): 29–43.
33. John J Mearsheimer, "The False Promise of International Institutions," *International Security* 19, no.3 (Winter 1994–95): 7.
34. 35. Barry Buzan and Stephen M. Walt, *The Origins of Alliances* (Ithaca: Cornell University Press, 1987)
35. Stephen Waltz, "International Relations: One World, Many Theories," *Foreign Policy,* no.110 (1987): 29–46.
36. Barry Buzan and Ole Wæver, *Regions and Powers: The Structure of International Security* (Cambridge: Cambridge University Press, 2003), 40.
37. Kenneth Lieberthal and Wang Jisi, "Addressing U.S.-China Strategic Distrust," *The Brookings,* John L. Thornton China Center Monograph Series, Number 4, March 2012, 1–49
38. Eric Heginbotham et al., "Introduction." In *The U.S.-China Military Scorecard: Forces, Geography, and the Evolving Balance of Power* (Santa Monica, CA: RAND Corporation, 2015), 1–22

39. 38. Philip C. Saunders, "U.S.-China Military Relations: Competition and Cooperation," *Journal of Strategic Studies* 39, no. 5–6 (2016): 662–684.
40. J W Spain, "Analysis of the Indo-Pakistani tensions: Canal waters, Kashmir, Arms Race, Boundary Disputes," (official memorandum, Washington DC: The Department of State, March 23, 1959), tinyurl.galegroup.com/tinyurl/5PJKp3
41. Saeed Shah, "India and Pakistan Escalate Nuclear Arms Race," *The Wall Street Journal,* 31 March 2017.
42. 41. Stephen Burgess, "The U.S. Pivot to Asia and Renewal of the U.S.–India Strategic Partnership," *Comparative Strategy* 34, no.4 (2015): 367–379
43. 42. Suisheng Zhao, "A New Model of Big Power Relations? China–US strategic rivalry and balance of power in the Asia–Pacific," *Journal of Contemporary China* 24, no. 93 (2015): 377–397
44. 43. Aaron L. Friedberg, "The Debate Over U.S. China Policy," *Survival* 57, no.3 (2013): 89–110.
45. Robert Einhorn and W.P.S. Sidhu (eds.), "The Strategic Chain: Linking Pakistan, India, China and the United States," *The Bookings,* Arms Control and Non-Proliferation Series, No. 14, March 2017, 1–59.
46. 45. Samuel Huntington. "Arm s Races: Prerequisites and Results," *Public Policy* 8, no.1 (1958): 41–86.
47. 46. Michael Intriljgator and Dagobert Brito, "Arms Race," *Defence and Peace Economics* 11, no.1 (2000): 45–54
48. Colin Gray, "The Arms Race Phenomenon," *World Politics* 24, no. 1 (1971): 39–79.
49. 48. Robert Jervis, *Perception and Misperception in International Politics* (Princeton: Princeton University Press, 1976), 112.
50. Alastair Iain Johnston and Mingming Shen (eds.), "Perception and Misperception in American and Chinese Views of the other," *Carnegie Endowment for International Peace,* 2015, http://carnegieendowment.org/email/SecurityPerceptions_final.pdf, 43.
51. 50. Julian Schofield, "Arms Races: Militarization and War," (PhD. Diss., Graduate School of Arts and Sciences, University of Columbia, 2002), 21
52. 51. Alexander L. George and Andrew Bennett, *Case Study and Theory of Development in Social Sciences* (Massachusetts: MIT Press, 2004), 281.
53. Schofied, Colin Gray. "The Arms Race Phenomenon," *World Politics* 24, no. 1 (1971): 39–79; "The Urge to Compete," *World Politics* 36, no.2 (1974): 207–233; and also see "Social Science and the Arms Race," *The Bulletin of the Atomic Scientist* 29, no.6 (1973): 25.
54. 53. Zafar Khan, *Pakistan's Nuclear Policy: A Minimum Credible Deterrence* (London: Routledge, 2015), 73–75
55. Barry Buzan and Eric Herring, *The Arms Dynamic in World Politics* (Boulder & London: Lynne Rienner Publishers, 1998), 84.
56. Jay Bennett, "Space War: How the Air Force Plans to Defend the Final Frontier," *Popular Mechanics,* 6 November 2017, http://www.popularmechanics.com/military/news/a28851/us-air-force-gears-up-for-expanded-role-in-space/
57. Gary Chapman, "An Introduction to Revolution in Military Affairs," *XV Amaldi Conference on Problems in Global Security*, Helsinki, Finland, September 2003, http://www.lincei.it/rapporti/amaldi/papers/XV-Chapman.pdf, 1–21.
58. James Andrew Lewis, "Neither Mahan nor Mitchell: National Security Space and Space power, 1945–2000," in *Space Power*, ed. Charles Lutes et al., (Washington DC: National Defence University Press, 2004), http://ndupress.ndu.edu/Portals/68/Documents/Books/spacepower.pdf
59. Götz Neuneck Christian Alwardt, "The Revolution in Military Affairs, its driving forces, elements and complexity," *Institute for Peace Research and Security Policy*, University of Hamburg, Working Paper no. 13, May 2008.
60. Steven E. Sloan, "The Revolution in Military Affairs and the Politics of Innovation in the U.S. Navy," (MSc. Diss., Naval Postgraduate School, Monetary, 1994).

61. 60. Benjamin S. Lambeth, *Desert Storm and Its Meaning: The View from Moscow* (Santa Monica: RAND Corporation, 1992), 69.
62. 61. Kenneth Bergman, "Space and Revolution in Military Affairs," *Marine Corps Gazette* 79, no.5 (May 1995): 58.
63. Ronald Deibert, "Unfettered Observation," in *Space Policy in the 21st Century*, ed. W. Henry Lambright(Baltimore & London: The Johns Hopkins University Press, 2003), 108.
64. Gregory Billman, "The Inherent Limitations of Space Power: Fact or Fiction?" in *Beyond the Paths of Heaven: The Emergence of Space Power Thought,* ed. Bruce DeBlois (Maxwell Air Force Base, Alabama: Air University Press, 1999), 510.
65. Peter Hays, "Space and the Military," in *Space Politics and Policy: An Evolutionary Perspective*, ed. Eligar Sadeh (Boston: Kluwer Academic Publishers, 2002), 366.
66. 65. Jakub Fučík, "Revolution in Military Affairs and Outer Space," *International Conference Knowledge-Based Organization* 23, no.1 (2017): 106–111.
67. Peter R. Mansoor, "The Next Revolution in Military Affairs," *Hoover Institute*, March 15, 2017, https://www.hoover.org/research/next-revolution-military-affairs.
68. Alfred T Mahan, *The Influence of Sea power Upon History: 1660–1783* (Cambridge: Cambridge University Press, 2010)
69. Francis P. Sempa, "The Geopolitics Vision of Alfer Thayar Mahan," *The Diplomat,* December 30, 2014, https://thediplomat.com/2014/12/the-geopolitical-vision-of-alfred-thayer-mahan/; "Mahan's The Influence of Sea Power upon History: Securing International Markets in the 1890s," Office of the Historian, *The Department of State*, United States, accessed November 6, 2021, https://history.state.gov/milestones/1866-1898/mahan
70. 69. Ronald Carpenter, "Alfred Thayer Mahan's style on sea power: A Para message conducing to ethos," *Speech Monographs* 42, no.3 (1975): 190–202;
71. Brian Weeden and Victoria Samson, *Global Counterspace Capabilities: An Open Source Assessment* (Washington, DC.: Secure World Foundation, April 2018).
72. Joan Johnson-Freese, *Space as a Strategic Asset* (New York: Columbia University Press, 2007), VII.
73. Pavel Luzin, "Space Power: What is Russia's Military Strategy in Outer Space?" *Intersection,* October 25, 2017, http://intersectionproject.eu/article/security/space-power-what-russias-military-strategy-outer-space (site discontinued)
74. 73. Zulfqar Khan and Ahmad Khan, "Chinese Capabilities as a Global Space Power," *Astropolitics* 13, no. 2–3 (2015): 185–204.
75. Elizabeth Howell, "JAXA: Japan's Aerospace Exploration Agency," *Space.com,* May 19, 2016, https://www.space.com/22672-japan-aerospace-exploration-agency.html.
76. Moltz, *Asia's Space Race: National Motivations, Regional Rivalries and International Risks* (New York: Columbia University Press, 2012), 158–190.
77. Randall R. Correll also highlights Pakistan as an emerging space power, for details see, "Emerging Actors," in *Space Power*, ed. Charles Lutes et al., (Washington DC: National Defence University Press, 2004), http://ndupress.ndu.edu/Portals/68/Documents/Books/spacepower.pdf.
78. 77. Peter Hays, "United States Military Space: Into the Twenty-First Century," *USAF Institute for National Security Studies,* INSS Occasional Paper No. 42, 2002, 36.
79. Aaron Bateman, "In outer space, the US is vulnerable to China and Russia," *The Hill,* July 20, 2017, http://thehill.com/blogs/pundits-blog/defense/342992-in-outer-space-the-us-is-vulnerable-to-china-and-russia.
80. 79. Anna Burzykowska, "Smaller states and the new balance of power in space," *Space Policy* 25, no.2 (2009): 188.
81. Brian Weeden and Xiao He, "Use Outer Space to Strengthen U.S.-China Ties," *War on the Rocks,* April 26, 2016, https://warontherocks.com/2016/04/use-outer-space-to-strengthen-u-s-china-ties/
82. Brian Weeden, "Insight - Building Stronger U.S.-China Relations in Space," *Secure World Foundation,* February 1, 2017, https://swfound.org/news/all-news/2017/02/insight-building-stronger-us-china-relations-in-space

83. 82. Ashok Kapur, *India and South Asian Strategic Triangle* (London: Routledge, 2011).
84. Gurmeet Kanwal, "India-China Strategic Relations Further Improvement is Contingent on Resolution of the Territorial Dispute," *CLAWS Journal* 5, no.1 (Summer 2010).
85. Dipankar Banerjee, "India-China Relations: Negotiating a Balance," *Institute of Peace and Conflict Studies,* IPCS Issue Brief No. 160, December 2016, http://www.ipcs.org/pdf_file/issue/IB160-Banerjee-India-China.pdf.
86. Ashelly Tellis, "India as a Leading Power," *Carnegie Endowment for International Peace*, April 4, 2016, http://carnegieendowment.org/2016/04/04/india-as-leading-power-pub-63185
87. Omar Lamrani, "Avoiding a War in Space," *Startfor,* May 17, 2016, https://worldview.stratfor.com/article/avoiding-war-space

Chapter 4
Space Policy, Strategy, and Doctrine: The U.S, China, India, and Pakistan

Introduction

The previous two chapters' research was focused on explaining and understanding the framework for space security at international and regional levels. This is useful to analyse actual space policies of global and emerging space powers. This chapter studies space power theory and researches the relevant states' space doctrines and policies. Many prominent space experts have defined what space power is. Moreover, they have included space power as one of the elements of a state's national power. Besides, they have discussed the requirements for a state to build it. It is undeniable that space power has significance for modern military; however, it has also grown in private and commercial sectors. To substantiate academic arguments on space power, definitional and conceptual frameworks are discussed in existing literature.

This chapter also highlights fundamental contours of space doctrines and policies of the U.S., China, India, and Pakistan. The research provides an understanding of space doctrines and policies concerning space militarization and weaponization. Additionally, this chapter addresses several questions of concern regarding officially declared space policies and white papers. What is nature of space policies? Do space policies and doctrines support space militarization and weaponization?

Furthermore, what are space policies of emerging space powers? Of note is that this research has some limitations. Only a few states have officially declared space doctrines and policies so far, and the documents tell little about the states' actual space operations and development of capabilities. On the other hand, while some countries do not have officially declared documents, they have space policies. After

This chapter draws from the PhD research work of the author titled "Arms Race in Outer Space: A Paradigm Shift in International Security and Implications for South Asia," which was completed in 2019 and successfully defended in 2020 at Department of Strategic Studies, National Defence University, Islamabad.

A. Khan and E. Sadeh, *Sabre Rattling in Space*,
https://doi.org/10.1007/978-981-97-6050-3_4

analysing global and emerging space power doctrines and policies, the next chapter will focus on the states' space capabilities.

Why must the global and emerging space powers' intentions, doctrines, and policies be assessed? This book's title suggests that space arms race brings a shift in international and regional security. The U.S. remains dominant in global space order, while China is an emerging global space power. Russia is still a significant global space power and will likely improve its space capabilities. India has self pro-claimed global space power, status after testing ASAT missile in 2019. Pakistan has a modest space program with emerging behaviour at regional level. These three space powers significantly shape the global and regional space orders. It is generally understood that there is global competition between these space actors. Also, emerging actors in space with growing space capabilities will likely create conflict due to congestion and competition. In this regard, the chapter assesses doctrines and policies of global and emerging space powers to study their thinking and perceptions about exploration and use of space.

Theory of Space Power

This section probes theory of space power. What are its elements and applications in modern world? What are advantages and disadvantages of space power? The answers are essential for better understanding the relevant state actors' doctrines, policies, and capabilities.

In political science, especially in strategic studies subfield, a state's intentions and capabilities are rigorously assessed by scholars. Both intentions and capabilities of states are interwoven in an equation which predicts state's behaviour. The state's intentions impact its overall behaviour when interacting with other states in international political system. Capabilities are actual manifestation of power of a state to take action on its intentions.

A British International Relations theorist, Ken Booth, makes an interesting argument that pivots around state's intentions and capabilities. He argues that assessing capabilities of a state is an imperfect art. It entails capabilities (military) and intentions (aggressive or offensive) as two major causes of war, per the understanding of idealist school of thought.

[1]Booth also stresses that intentions are important in predicting state's behaviour during peacetime and conflict. He concludes his thoughts by stating, "capabilities do represent a standing threat by providing options, but it is important to make as rigorous an examination of intentions as possible if an effective and efficient policy emerges."[2] From Booth's perspective on state's capabilities and intentions, it is evident that military planners and policymakers should assess an adversary's doctrine, policy, and capabilities. Assessing regional and global environment and landscape in political, strategic, and economic contexts is essential. In this way, a comprehensive policy can be formulated.

Sun Tzu gives a more comprehensive framework to understand enemy's capabilities and intentions. He said, "if you know the enemy and know yourself, you need not fear the result of a hundred battles."[3] Tzu's saying tells about why it is vital to assess capabilities and intentions of adversary. This also highlights how this factor impinges upon national security policy of state. Furthermore, policymaking process will be imperfect without a holistic review of global and regional security environments. Sun Tzu signalled this factor in his writings and how it impacts policymaking.

Currently, there is no comprehensive or universally accepted definition of space power. However, when combined, certain elements frame a definition of space power. From a historical point of view, space power was primarily attributed to sea and air power. Peter Hays states,

> It is a cosmic concept that is complex, indeterminate, and intangible...Confusion swirls on the semantic level because no commonly accepted definition or wording exists for this concept.[4]

Space experts agree with Peter Hays in this regard. They think space power is a confusing term. In an alternative argument, Samuel McNeil thinks using the term "space power" is accurate, appropriate, and precise with no ambiguity.[5] Martin France argues that space power lacks definitive work. However, early writings on space power suggest that "the U.S. has centred on space as a logical extension of airpower theory."[6] As space power lacks a comprehensive, agreed-upon definition, it is evident that it will be compared to the other powers, like sea and air. In this regard, Colin S. Gray argues that space power is akin to land, sea, and air power in all strategic essentials.[7] This gives a more logical way to define space power. However, it is also worth mentioning that space is a unique medium and has significance for military and peaceful purposes other than land, sea, and air.

There are similarities between characteristics of sea and space power. Alfred T. Mahan, an American naval officer and historian exponent of sea power in late nineteenth and early twentieth centuries, said six elements constitute state's sea power. These elements include geographical position, physical conformation, territory extent, population, people's character, and state's government.[8]

Likewise, there are characteristics of airpower, which also resemble space power. Characteristics of airpower include flexibility, responsiveness, survivability, and surveillance.[9] The fundamental characteristic of airpower is operating its essential item, aircraft, in the medium of air.[10]Similarly, fundamental characteristic of space is operation of satellites, spacecraft and missiles. Due to these similarities, air and space forces have the potential to dominate the conduct of enemy operations in all mediums.[11] Both air and naval power characteristics facilitate the development of a definition of space power.

Elements of Space Power

Scholars have advanced studies to understand various elements of space power. James E. Oberg conducted one critical scholarly study on space power in *Space Power Theory*.[12] He penned down basic elements of the space power of state, including hardware and human resources. The hardware includes launching sites, Space Launch Vehicles (SLVs), and satellite-building capabilities.

On the other hand, human resources are primarily about "people whose intelligence and dedication drive innovation, and a parent society which understands and values space activities, and considers the payoff worth major effort."[13] Based on these core elements and their synergy, Oberg defines space power. Moreover, based on hardware and human resources, states can be categorized as global, regional, and emerging space powers.

According to Oberg, essential elements of space power are stated below.[14]

a. *Facilities*. This is fundamental to space power, including state's manufacturing, launch, telemetry tracking, and command and control facilities. Other facilities include SLV manufacturing and payload manufacturing.
b. *Technology*. Technology plays a vital role in building space power, and governmental and non-governmental institutions are technology's main drivers to building capabilities.
c. *Industry*. Private actors can be instrumental in "designing, manufacturing, deploying and operating space systems." Non-governmental organizations/ non-profitable organizations are the central tenets of the industry.[15]
d. *Economy*. It is backbone of any power. Space power is associated with achieving economic, strategic, and political goals. These goals are meant to generate economic and social advantages. Space power is an expensive adventure, requiring investments in state's economy.
e. *Populace*. There should be adequate numbers of engineers and scientists who can significantly contribute to building a state's space power. Likewise, the masses should also be awarded the expenditure of states on their space activities. In this way, human resources and an awarded society are crucial in building space power.
f. *Research and Development (R&D)*. The state should have adequate R&D capabilities, including universities with space-related departments, institutions, and centres; government-run organizations that preserve national security and intelligence purposes; and public and private laboratories. These are tentacles of a space-based education system that generates knowledge and produces a pool of engineers and scientists to "support and grow a vibrant and vigorous space industry."[16]
g. *Geography*. It is a common understanding of political science that their geography works when states fail in politics. Robert Rotberg stresses that "the extent of a state's failure can be measured by how much of its geographical expense is genuinely controlled by the government."[17] For a state to become a space power, its location is essential, as it provides a "launch site with ample downrange safety

zones." Likewise, geographical location helps states establish good diplomatic relations with host nations to launch their satellites. For example, Pakistan has friendly relations with China and received Chinese help to launch PakSat-IR, PRSS-1, PakTES-IA, iCube-Qamar, and Pak-SAT-MMI satellites in the orbit.

h. *Tradition and Intellectual Climate.* To bolster space power, the state should spread as much information as possible to its population to gain public support to achieve its short-term and long-term space exploration objectives.
i. *Leadership.* Leadership is instrumental in building space power. Visionary leadership always looks beyond the horizons. Space is a vast horizon, allowing leadership to link its political goals with developing state's space power.

Within the context of above elements, Michael Moran defines a state's space power as combining several factors, including demography, economy, industry, military, technology, national will, and diplomacy. Likewise, state's coercive and persuasive power and diplomatic ability to politically influence other states to achieve national goals through space activitiess reflect its space power.[18]

The Defence Technical Information Center's document on Space Operations gives a more concise definition of space power as "the total strength of a nation's capabilities to conduct and influence activities to, in, through, and from space to achieve its objectives."[19] This refers to space capabilities to conduct space activities to influence activities in space.[20] USAF gives a military-oriented but straightforward definition as "the capability to employ space forces to achieve national security objectives."[21] From a general understanding of security studies, national security objectives are security, economic, and political. Nicolas Peter further elaborates that these national security objectives are meant "to affect desired outcomes in the presence of other actors on world stage and, if necessary, to change the behaviour of others by exploiting space systems and associated ground-infrastructure as well as political leverage it has garnered."[22] Peter adequately summarized definition of space power. All definitions provide multiple perspectives on space power and how states can build it. Building capabilities are not only meant to construct space power. Visionary leadership and political will are what are required to orchestrate space power. The state's political will develops national security strategy and policy to exploit elements of space power.[23] Moreover, based on elements, it can be understood what states' space doctrines and policies are and what kind of strategic, political, and security objectives are highlighted in their officially and unofficially declared statements.

In changing geopolitical environment, space power is a vital instrument of a state's national power to exert its strategic, political, and economic influence at regional and international levels. Space power solidifies national power and improves its international standing.[24] It conveys various benefits to space actors, including prestige, internal and external security, military power, economic growth, and scientific prowess. Likewise, space programs source hard military and economic power and project state's soft power. Gray describes the military advantages of space. He argues that space systems provide necessary advantages over the adversary's force on battlefield. Likewise, space power has infinite military depth and provides a constant overhead presence in peacetime and on battlefield.[25] The U.S. exemplifies its space program contributing to its military power, economic growth, and soft power projection.

There are also other advantages of space power. Space power provides global perspectives, exploration, a free-fall environment for microgravity applications, and vast natural resources.[26] Space power helps a state ascertain its global position to exert its influence at international and regional levels. It helps state build a technical and innovative workforce of engineers and scientists. Space power is vital for shortening the communication gaps between citizens and "can promote awareness of a common identity among citizens and demonstrate increased confidence in future."[27]

At the same time, there are disadvantages and limitations associated with space power. It is indeed an expensive venture. The capital cost of building hardware part of space power is beyond most states' economies; the building cost of launching capabilities, especially transportation, is very high. Gray argues that the cost almost "limits the pace of advancing military, scientific and commercial space systems."[28] Hence, emerging spacefaring states tend to launch their satellites from other states. Besides financial cost, Gray further argues that "it is like space power to be distant from terrestrial events. Although militarily beneficial distance overhead, a distance from Earth is still an important limitation."[29]

Based on space power theory, the strength of space power encompasses global, expanding, emerging (regional) space power, and emerging users.

Global. A global space power can be defined as a state that:

a. Officially declared military, economic, and political objectives in the form of doctrine, policy, and domestic laws to explore space.
b. Have necessary indigenous manufacturing and building capabilities to construct mission architecture.
c. Adhere to international space treaties, principles, and declarations.
d. Have strong international cooperation in sharing space technologies with other states.
e. Have mission architecture with a state-of-the-art command, control, and communication structure.
f. Have the capability to build spacecraft and abundant launching facilities to send military and civilian payloads in the orbits to build a global constellation of satellites.
g. Have ground stations to receive data to process and analyse it for ISR, early warning, communication, and navigation purposes.
h. Have a robust R&D infrastructure with global education focusing on space technologies.
i. And enjoys complete freedom of access and use in space.[30]

Expanding. Expanding space power is the subset of global space power with enough capabilities to achieve its space exploration objectives, but its capabilities are expanding to become a global power.

Emerging Regional. An emerging regional space power lacks sufficient manufacturing and building capabilities, though it has ambitions to develop them. Following attributes characterize an emerging regional type:

a. Clear space objectives, both officially declared and/or undeclared policies.
b. Developing educational and R&D infrastructure.
c. Signatory of space treaties and adherence to international norms, principles and declarations.
d. Furthermore, political, economic, and military objectives use their space power to wield regional influence.

Emerging Users. Emerging users are defined as those states using other states' space capabilities or subscribing to services provided under a multinational or bilateral agreement for their domestic purposes for political, economic, and military uses. These states do not have indigenous capabilities to manufacture and launch spacecraft in outer space.

What is Space Policy?

Policy for a state is a framework in which decisions are made to achieve goals and objectives of national governments. The policymaking process has three levels at which it is conceived, shaped, and implemented. The process involves a) setting national goals and objectives because of the state's national security, b) finding means and ways for government to achieve goals, and c) implementing policy by allocating resources.[31] Besides, the primary focus of space policy is to develop a framework to conduct an in-depth analysis of a) space activities for the citizens' needs, b) industrial space development for technical and scientific purposes, and c) dual-use applications.[32] Figure 4.1 is a general model that studies any state's overall policymaking process.

Fig. 4.1 Policymaking process

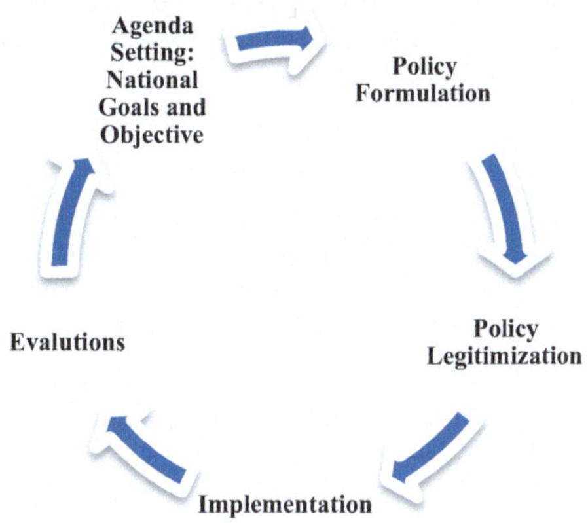

U.S' Space Policy

Space policy has always been on priority list of any U.S. administration. During the Cold War, space policy was included as one of the top priorities because of an intense space race with the former Soviet Union. After end of the Cold War, space gained tremendous significance, and it was termed a strategic asset in the U.S. Space policymaking in the U.S. has been institutionalized because of its military uses and, more importantly, due to advanced commercial space industry.

Dwight D. Eisenhower's administration drafted and passed the National Aeronautics and Space Act of 1958.[33] Eisenhower's space policy focused on building space capabilities to achieve political and economic goals. The policy's main emphasis was establishing the U.S. space program for citizens' welfare in science, technology, education, and industry, as well as tracking and preventing space assets from near-Earth objects.[34]

On May 25, 1961, President John F. Kennedy delivered his famous speech on "Urgent National Needs" at a joint session of U.S. Congress. Kennedy highlighted U.S' space exploration achievements, emphasizing "time for this nation to take a leading role in space."[35] Three main parts of the speech cum policy statement were; a) human landing on Moon, b) development of the Rover nuclear rocket, and d) accelerating the use of satellites for global communications.[36]

Jimmy Carter's space policy highlighted the U.S. goals to explore space for military and intelligence functions to pursue national security. The policy did not depart from the previously announced policy and emphasized maintaining the U.S. leadership role in space."[37]

Ronald Regan announced his administration's space policy through National Security Decision Directive 42 on July 4, 1982.[38]The policy significantly focused on private sector's role in space activities and arms control measures. Nevertheless, Reagan's policy re-emphasized "the U.S. preeminence in critical major space activities."[39] The policy also discussed measures to negate hostile space systems and establish deterrence in space.[40]

President Bill Clinton announced his national space policy through National Science and Technology Council Directive-8 on September 19, 1996.[41] The policy's main emphasis was enhancing scientific knowledge, strengthening national security, increasing economic competitiveness and technical capabilities, and promoting international cooperation to solidify the U.S. internal, national and foreign policies.[42]

George W. Bush announced his space policy on August 31, 2006, when the U.S. and its allies were fighting wars in Afghanistan and Iraq. The wars were initiated after the 9/11 terrorist attacks on U.S. soil in 2001. Hence, there was a spillover effect over U.S. space policy. As a result, it shifted its gear from civil and cooperative activities to strengthening national security. The policy focused on deploying U.S. space assets for intelligence, interagency cooperations, photo-reconnaissance, overhead measurements, and signature intelligence collection.[43] The 2001 Rumsfeld Commission report was drawn, discussing a "Space Pearl Harbour" threat.[44]

On June 28, 2010, Obama's administration released its space policy, which departed from his predecessor's space policy. The 2010 policy discussed adopting responsible behaviour in space "to help prevent mishaps, misperceptions, and mistrust."[45] The policy pivots around three Cs: congestion, crowdedness, and competition. The Obama administration was more focused on maintaining a strategic restraint in space through its space policy.[46] The 2010 policy is more about boosting domestic industry, enhancing international cooperation, and strengthening strategic stability in space in terms of goals. Moreover, the policy was focused on preserving the space environment and responsible use of space, fostering effective export policies, and establishing commercial, civil, and national space security guidelines for the U.S.

According to James Moltz, there is a strong belief in the U.S. that it is the only space power that regularly releases its space policy document.[47] From Moltz's point of view, Eisenhower's policy did not mention the Soviet Union, and the policy was not a "true strategy."[48] Kennedy's policy "failed to provide a broader place for space and a clear reason for seeking to stay on the Moon," and also the rationale for planetary exploration.[49] He criticized Carter's policy of not declaring specific goals and making any "clear statement of why the U.S. was there and how it should organize its priorities over the long term."[50] From his point of view, Clinton's policy fell short of a space strategy. Likewise, Bush's policy lacked long-term national goals as it failed to give a clear vision for space. On Obama's policy, he writes that it was a more comprehensive space policy than previous ones and gives a better sense of a space strategy.[51]

Moltz termed previous U.S. space policies full of "laundry-list" qualities and contained bureaucratic languages. The previous policies were a more diminutive form of a valid national space strategy. The policies focused more on achieving near-term objectives and falling short of seeing beyond the horizons. [52] There were flaws in civil space policy, including export control, which ramified competitiveness in space commerce and industry. Likewise, the ongoing export controls are negatively impacting scientific space research.

Moreover, the U.S. civil space program is declining. From Eligar Sadeh's point of view, the U.S. should not abandon its space shuttle program.[53] He believes it was a severe setback to the U.S. civil space program, whereas Russia and China run their space shuttle programs and can reach space. On the other hand, the U.S. scrapped its space shuttle program in 2011, and this is a severe policy lag in U.S. space policy.

The U.S.' space policies have all the characteristics necessary to make it a global power. However, the U.S. civil space program suffers from severe bureaucratic and administrative issues. At the moment, NASA is a weeping boil.[54] President Trump's administration was in serious disarray of running space issues by taking ad-hoc measures. "The U.S. is no more like the U.S. as it was in the 1980s. The U.S. power is declining, and it is not in a great position to change the global power structure," according to Michael Simpson.[55] The U.S. was a dominant power in the 1980s. However, its space and global prominence are in danger now.

In the past, U.S. space policies were mainly devised under the umbrella of space nationalism. It was because the U.S. was competing with the former Soviet Union in an intense space race. All the space policies made during the Cold War followed the principles of realism and were predisposed to space nationalism. However, a few guiding principles were focused on global institutionalism. U.S. space policies were never meant to follow the guidelines provided by global institutionalism. On the other hand, a comprehensive study of U.S. space policies, strategy, and doctrine suggests that its predominant theme of freedom of action is against social interactionism. However, it is quite understandable that social interactionism is inevitable.

2017 President Donald J. Trump came into power after winning the 2016 election. The Trump administration went for a space policy based on recollection of principles, goals, and guidelines of previous administrations' space policies or devised some new steps to achieve above policy goals. The policy combined old rhetoric and new directions. James Vedda recommended that "the President promulgated a revised rhetoric and, more importantly, sought budget request."[56] He argued that above policy encompassed a comprehensive review of changes that happened over the past seven years.

President Trump announced the Space Corps' establishment with a directive to create a sixth military branch. Space has become more contested and congested, leading to more competition between major spacefaring nations. It is argued that the competition has jeopardized security of thousands of satellites, enabling the Pentagon to enhance force. Trump believed that space is a strategic domain in which the U.S. must try to maintain its dominance. President Trump established the sixth military branch, comprising 8,000 military personnel. President Trump's establishment of the Space Force suggests that the U.S. wants complete freedom of action in space, intending to deny the space to others. Likewise, the U.S. does not consider China and Russia to be its adversaries with superior space technologies. This has triggered a misperception-misconception-misunderstanding dynamics between U.S-China and U.S-Russia in space. The dynamics has accelerated arms race between the U.S. and China and the U.S. and Russia.

President Trump's policy was based on "to do more than just catch up today—it should look ahead to tomorrow."[57] Besides, Trump's policy focused on maintaining the U.S. leadership role in space. U.S. policymakers consider other states' increasing space capabilities a looming threat to U.S. leadership.[58] The following policy was also consider a policy based on strengthening its commercial space industry and expanding its space capabilities at a gradual pace, In 2021, the Biden administration accounced "Space Priorities Framework". The Framework highlights that the U.S will defend its national security interests from growing threats in space. The U.S will work with its partners and allies to deter aggression against the U.S, allies and partners. While establishing a more resilient national security space posture, DoD released its space policy review and strategy of protection of satellites in september 2023. The documents are more focused on China and Russia and policy to defend against space-enabled threats.

United States Space Strategy and Doctrine

The Obama administration paid considerable attention to developing national space policy and successfully crafted the National Security Space Strategy (NSSS) for release in 2011. The NSSS primarily discussed the strategic environment in space, highlighting U.S'. Strategic objectives and approaches are addressing challenges to its space supremacy. The NSSS mentions emerging opportunities for the U.S. to strengthen its "national security space posture while maintaining and enhancing the advantages gained from space."[59] The NSSS highlights that "space is becoming increasingly congested, contested and competitive." Because of these three Cs, it states that there may be an armed conflict in space in future. Dealing with these challenges highlights strategic objectives of the U.S. in space. It wants to strengthen its space assets' safety and security to maintain stability in space. Likewise, the U.S. wants to maintain its leadership role in space. For this purpose, it will promote the responsible, peaceful and safe use of space under a defined set of rules and strategic approaches.

The U.S. also wants to address lingering challenges to space security globally. In this regard, the U.S. wants to enhance collaboration with its allies to "establish norms and Transparency Confidence-Building Measures (TCBMs); enhance space situational awareness (SSA); and foster greater transparency, and sharing space-derived information."[60] However, Moltz has criticized U.S. policies for not including U.S. civil space policy, and the strategy remained "vague on the kinds of diplomatic efforts that it will pursue in space."[61]

The U.S. has a joint space doctrine titled Joint Publication (JP) 3–14, Space Operations, linked to Air Force and Army Service space doctrines.[62]Christopher King and Edward Byrne discuss fundamentals of military space operations, including a) military space contributions to joint operations, b) operational consideration for space, c) space mission areas, d) command and control of space forces, role and responsibilities of military leadership, and e) planning.[63]

The Space Operations document identifies U.S. military space operations, including SSA, space force enhancement, space support, space control, and space force applications.[64] The mission areas talk about counterspace operations, offensive and defensive. The space control doctrine suggests these operations as offensive space control (OSC) and defensive space control (DSC). The OSC entails 5Ds: deception, disruption, denial, degradation or destruction of adversary's capabilities. DSC means "preserving U.S. access to space and space capabilities using active and passive means while protecting friendly space capabilities from attacks, interference, or unintentional hazards."[65] Many space experts believe that X-37B space plane is a practical manifestation of U.S. space control doctrine.[66] Likewise, this doctrine may employ many more missiles.[67] Importantly, space control doctrine stresses and supports freedom of action in space.

Interestingly, Gen Ralph Eberhart, former Commander of the old U.S. Space Command (USSPACECOM), highlighted that "the importance of space control and space superiority will continue to grow as our [U.S.] economy becomes more reliant on space." He also argued that the U.S. must pay more attention to critical issues of space control and superiority as space is linked with critical military land, sea, and air operations.[68] Bruce DeBlo is summarized the debate on space control and argues that it supports space weaponization at moderate and high levels.[69] A retired USAF Colonel, Wesley Hallman, argues that "weaponization of space by some state in foreseeable future is a foregone conclusion."[70] Hallman states that the U.S. cannot afford to be second to the weaponization of space.

Furthermore, the U.S. already has advanced capabilities to weaponize space before any states like China or Russia can. The U.S. would not wait for it to happen. That is because of the operational part of its doctrine, primarily based on space control. The U.S. can employ anti-satellite missiles quickly; however, it has only remained in the testing phase. Another important aspect of space control doctrine is SSA. "SSA involves characterizing the space capabilities operating within the terrestrial environment and space domain." OSC and DSC are heavily dependent on robust SSA.[71]

John Klein identifies discrepancies between U.S. space doctrine and space power theory. Klein argues that these discrepancies are due to the operational focus of the joint publication document. These discrepancies are linked with freedom of action, SSA, and space superiority, "which the derived space strategy does not include."[72] However, these discrepancies are minor compared to the strategic space environment and the context of these terms. In 2020, the United States Strategic Command released two documents: Joint publication 3-14 and Joint Space Operations. Joint Publication 3-14 was recently updated. The document shed right on space superiority and suppression of enemy space capabilities. In 2023, the USSF released Space Doctrine Publication 3.0 Operations. The document notes that "the most effective operation to deny, distrupt, damage, or destroy anadrersavy's space capability, and preserve freedom of action in space, may originate from a domain other than space".

China's Space Policy

China has officially declared space policy documents and the White Papers covering its space activities, defining goals, principles, and aims for future space endeavours. These space policy cum White Papers were published in 2000, 2006, 2011, 2016, and 2021 respectively, for release by the State Council. The White Papers have mapped Chinese activities in space in the past five years and aim to spread awareness of Chinese progress and plans for the next five years. The papers also talk about China's development in the space industry and underline its cooperation in space.

China considers space power as a vital element of its national power. It has built "impressive" indigenous space capabilities with the development of remote sensing, telecommunication and broadcasting, and regional navigation satellite systems with the ambition to expand for global use.[73] China has surpassed Russia regarding several operational satellites in space by 2015. All these space achievements are made under the guiding principles declared in the White Papers.

The purposes of Chinese space activities are[74]:

a. To explore space and enhance understanding of Earth and cosmos;
b. To utilize space for the benefit of human civilization and social progress;
c. To strengthen economy, scientific, and technological development given achieving national security objectives; and
d. To foster scientific and cultural knowledge, protect national rights, and build up overall national power.

Likewise, China's space activities pivot around four guiding principles: (a) innovative development, (b) coordinated development, (c) peaceful development, and (d) open development. These four guiding steps are "subject to and serve the national overall development strategy."[75]

The primary purpose of these White Papers is to show transparency in China's space activities. China's space strides were focused mainly on space transportation, launching Earth observation, communication and broadcasting, navigation and positioning satellites, development of human-crewed spaceflight, deep space exploration, launch sites, space telemetry, tracking, command and communication, and space science and applications.[76]

The 2016 White Paper suggests that China will "launch non-toxic and pollution-free medium-lift launch vehicles with low cost" to expand its existing space infrastructure and industry, start building assembly and operation of the space station, conduct deep space exploration, and perform experiments on new space technologies.[77]

The 2016 White Paper focuses on increasing international exchanges and cooperation. It suggests the Chinese government is eager to increase cooperation with developing countries based on mutual commercial benefits through peaceful space exploration. The Chinese space program is playing a significant role in constructing the Belt and Road Initiative. A key element of Chinese space activities for the next five years is to build a Space Silk Route. Malcolm Davis writes that China is looking "to add a Space Silk Road to its proposed land-based Silk Road Economic Belt."[78] In this regard, China is expanding its Asia–Pacific navigation satellite system to a global navigation system. China will likely add more satellites to its Beidou satellite constellation by 2020 to enhance its positioning, navigation, timing (PNT) capability. The 2016 White Paper suggests that China form a global navigation satellite system consisting of 35 satellites and provide its clients with more accurate and reliable services.[79]

The 2016 White Paper highlights that China adheres to peaceful uses of space and does not want weapons in space. Significantly, China has criticized the weaponization of space. Ajay Lele writes that China's ASAT tests negate its policy of adherence to peaceful uses of space. China's ASAT tests had generated a significant amount of artificial space debris, a potential threat to the orbiting satellites of other states.[80] In 2021, China released another white paper highlighting its goal, objectives, principles and achievements in space. The White Paper 2021 highlights that "China will integrate space science, technology and applications to meet high-quality development in space domain in next five years." The White Paper 2021 highlights that there are number of new countries in space which may create new investment avenues. China wants to accelerate work on its space industry to meet rising demand of space applications, services and development to boost its national growth.

China has not released any space strategy document. However, Gregory Kulacki has published a paper highlighting some key aspects of China's military space strategy.[81] Chinese language is a barrier to understanding the essence of Chinese space activities and intentions due to "non-authoritative, poorly chosen or poorly translated Chinese-language sources into its space program."[82] This barrier has dramatically influenced the debate on China's military space endeavours in the U.S. China is building space capabilities that the U.S. had already developed decades ago. These include intelligence, surveillance, reconnaissance (ISR), navigation, communication, and weather satellites. Kulacki's assessment is based on a Chinese military textbook published in 2003 by the General Command of China's People's Liberation Army (PLA) titled *The Science of Second Artillery Operation.* The documents highlight that Chinese ASAT capability is not meant to attack U.S. satellites.[83] China is also concerned about its satellite systems, which is an effort to increase the effectiveness of China's missile forces. A major emphasis in Chinese military space strategy is to protect its "missile forces from surveillance"; however, it is through camouflage, concealment, and deception rather than attacking satellites.

Moreover, Chinese military space strategy "emphasized the importance of its space systems and missile forces and operating in ways that protect its missile forces by fooling foreign satellites, rather than attacking them."[84]Many space experts from the U.S. disagree with this notion and argue that China could target U.S. satellites. Geoffery Forden disagrees with Kulachi's assessment.[85] He thinks that in case of an armed conflict between China and the U.S., China can attack U.S. navigation, communication, early warning, and low-altitude satellites. However, "China could destroy a large fraction of strategic intelligence-gathering capabilities but not all of it." In this worst-case scenario, the U.S. would retain enough deep space capabilities to monitor "Chinese troop movements, harbours, and strategic forces, although at a reduced level."[86]

China would not like to have space weapons without a strategy. The Chinese ASAT system may not be a symbolic weapon, and its military strategy may consider it a weapon of use in a worst-case scenario. However, it would be interesting to know how far the complex interdependence between China and the U.S. will play a role in establishing a strategic deterrence in space.

Likewise, Chinese space policy and strategy are close to survivability doctrine and slightly similar to space control doctrine. An overall assessment of China's past and present space policy, strategy and doctrine suggests a global space power significantly influencing global space order. Although Chinese space program is not as advanced as its competitor, the U.S., its space policy provides all necessary principles, guidelines and objectives to establish it a global space power.

China's space policy predominantly focuses on technological determinism to broaden Chinese space vision from scientific exploration to technological development.[87] Chinese space policy was motivated to bring technological innovations and economic development in the past. However, after the 1991 Gulf War, China realized this as it needed to invest in such space assets and capabilities to create a multiplier effect in other warfare domains.[88] This suggests a shift in Chinese policy from technological determinism to space nationalism. China invests in its research and development (R & D) facilities to build its space assets for dual-use purposes. It tested its ASAT capability in 2007 to showcase its building space weapons expertise.[89] Space experts believe China is competing with the U.S. globally and sees India's space capability as a threat to its regional space supremacy.[90]

India's Space Policy

Prime Minister Jawaharlal Nehru first visualized Indian space policy during the Sputnik era when the Cold War competition between two superpowers was at its peak. Nehru's vision was to use space for India's economic and social development. In 1962 the Indian Committee for Space Research (INCOSPAR) and the Department of Space were established. Indian Space Research Organization (ISRO) was initially part of India's nuclear program. Later, Vikram Sarabhai, the Indian space program's father, convinced Indian political and military leadership to separate Indian space agency from its nuclear program. He played a leading role in this regard. Right from the beginning, the entire focus was on achieving socioeconomic objectives.

India does not have any officially declared national space policy till 2023.[91] India's motivations, objectives, and goals can be understood through its space development and activities. India's space program has strong political motivation and is integral to its foreign and defence policies.[92]At the moment, it is among the top political priorities in India. The regional rivalries with Pakistan and China have influenced Indian space policy. India has realized that its space program can contribute towards its economic, political, and strategic power build-up.[93] Moreover, India's space program includes gaining international prestige and soft power. India's space program's political ambition is to achieve self-reliance to build and manufacture its launching vehicles without any foreign technical assistance.[94]

Indian space policy objectives emphasize "space for national development." ISRO and the Department of Space are essential in highlighting some of India's space policy's specific features.[95]

India aims to develop a space program as a "core national capability." It 2023 space policy talks about achieving a) high-end technology capability, b) autonomous access to space, c) fostering the commercial space industry in India, and d) bolstering international cooperation in space.[96] India's goal in space is to harness a capability to manage its resources on Earth. Likewise, its policy is about monitoring natural disasters, expanding and strengthening the broadcasting and telecommunication services nationwide, promoting Earth sciences, positioning and navigation, technological development, and, most importantly, building a space capability for its national security and defence.[97]

India has officially released several policy documents in the past. India's Satcom policy provides a framework for satellite communication approved by the government in 1997.[98] Likewise, the Indian government formulated the norms, guidelines, and procedures for implementing the Satcom Policy.[99] In addition to Satcom, India has also released a document for registering Indian satellites, and there is an official policy guideline for INSAT/GSAT capability. [100] India also released its Remote Sensing Data Policy (RSDP) in 2011. The RSDP-2011 document suggests two primary guidelines to recognize remote sensing data and national interests.[101]

ISRO, India's premier space agency, coordinates and collaborates with the Prime Minister's office and the Department of Space for India's space policy formulation. The Prime Minister's office oversees the Department of Space, under which ISRO comes.[102] ISRO's vision is to "harness space technology for national development while pursuing space science research and planetary exploration."[103] Current Prime Minister Narendra Modi stated, "No space should be left between the common man and space technology."[104] He addressed a conference held in 2015 to project Indian space activities for harnessing space technologies for communication, navigation, preserving the ecosystem, and better managing and conversing India's natural resources.

In 2023, Prime Minister's Office officially approved India's space policy. The policy vision is "to augment space capabilities; enable, encourage, and develop a flourishing commercial presence in space". The policy also highlights that space applications and technology will also cater for security. However, it does not explicity highlights the countours of security and emphasis remained in general form. It does not provide exclusive insight of its national security space programs. India's space policy is also focusing on planetary exploration. Its space program focuses beyond the Earth's orbits, sending spacecraft to explore celestial bodies, including the Moon and Mars. Planetary exploration in India has become a symbol of excellence and the quest for prestige.[105]

Another dimension of the Indian space program is its military component. India's present space policy is a clear shift from Nehru's vision of socioeconomic development and has become increasingly militarized in the past two decades.[106] The Indian space program has significantly grown and has become a vital element of its national security strategy. Joint Doctrine Indian Armed Forces-2017 document recognizes the importance of space for military purposes, highlighting the relevance of space power for national security as:

> Civil and commercial requirements mostly drive India's space capabilities. Steps for the exploitation of space for military applications are being undertaken. Leveraging space power would include protecting our National space assets and exploiting space to enable defence capabilities across the conflict spectrum.[107]

Indian space policymakers pay significant attention to developing space-based command, control, and communication assets with advanced C^4I^2SR capability. India has been developing a Ballistic Missile Defence (BMD) system and paid considerable attention in developing an ASAT capability.[108] IDSA's Ajay Lele assumes that India's space security policy is to establish a tri-service space command. India's space program may build capabilities to enhance SSA and develop strategic technologies to increase its reliance on space assets "for intelligence gathering, communications, navigation and operating various weapon systems."[109]

India has advanced Long-Range Ballistic Missiles (LRBM) and has tested MIRVed Intercontinental Ballistic Missile (ICBM) Agni-V, with an undeclared range of 8000 km. India continued to expand the ranges of Agni-series ballistic missiles e.g. Agni-VI has a range of 10000-12000 km (under development). Likewise, it developed Agni-Prime (1000-2000 km) and Surya ICBM with 12000-16000 km range (under development). DRDO officials denied the existence of Surya program. However, Zafar Nawaz Jaspal reasoned that there could be indirect U.S. pressure on India on such development. Jaspal argues that both countries have enjoyed close cooperation in space. In view of this assertion, Indian space program has indirectly assisted its ICBM project. India is not disclosing longer ranges as most the ranges will bring the Western Capitals in its targeting range. After the Chinese ASAT test in 2007, India has shown a keen interest in building its ASAT capability. Many space techies believe that ASATs are a spin-off effect of ABMs . Considering this technological reality, India has built an ASAT system. India takes Chinese ASAT capability as a threat to its space assets. Rajeswari Rajagopalan, argues that "even if the Chinese ASAT test has not yet changed Indian policy on space militarization, it is safe to assume that it has increased Indian concerns with ensuring space security."[110] Former Indian Defence Research and Development Organization (DRDO) chief V.K. Saraswat had announced that India would make an ASAT system in future.[111] Gene Milowicki and Joan Johnson-Freese of U.S Naval War College argue that India's intentions to build ASAT in response to Chinese tests as:

> All countries essentially protested the test... However, at least one country justified its intent to assess the need for and pursue its ASAT capabilities. Notably, India declared its intent to explore such development, thereby raising the risks of an eventual space arms race with Pakistan, Indonesia and other Asian nations.[112]

Bhupendra Jasani argued similarly and wrote that the state would attempt to acquire considerable ASAT capabilities before any National Missile Defence (NMD) was developed.[113] Considering these arguments, it can be assumed that India's space doctrine resembles the survivability doctrine. India has built an ASAT as planned, this shows that its space doctrine is similar to space control doctrine.

An assessment of India's space policy, strategy and doctrine suggests that India is expanding its space program to become a global space power. However, it is currently a regional space power due to its location or geography, and India can be termed a regional space power with global ambitions.

India's space policy focused on country's scientific and socioeconomic development. It has been a top political priority to consider its space program as a prestige symbol and improve its international standing. India has successfully achieved its policy of technological determinism and continues to gain more from it. However, Joint Doctrine Indian Armed Forces-2017 and Land Warfare Doctrine-2018 clarify India's position on space weaponization. India is taking steps to utilize space to achieve its national security objectives. In an email correspondence, Clay Moltz argued that "India realized after the 1999 Kargil conflict that it too could not draw effectively on space assets for reconnaissance and targeting information. It has recently made significant investments to overcome these gaps."[114] Likewise, India has made significant capacity building. It has built its ASAT capability nevertheless, its policy had suffered a significant transformation from technological determinism to space nationalism at the regional level. It sees Chinese development as a threat to its space and national objectives.

Pakistan's Space Policy

Pakistan is an aspiring space power in Asia. The history of the Pakistani space program goes back to the 1960s when Pakistan collaborated with NASA to launch its first sounding rocket, Rahber-1, in outer space to become the third country in Asia to launch a rocket in outer space. Pakistan's national space agency, the Space and Upper Atmosphere Research Commission (SUPARCO) was established in 1961. Initially, SUPARCO was part of the Pakistan Atomic Energy Commission (PAEC). Prof Dr Abdus Salam, Pakistan's only Nobel Laureate in Physics, founded the International Centre for Theoretical Physics (ICTP) in Italy and was the first director of SUPARCO. Later on, it became an independent space commission in 1981.

Prof Salam showed a keen interest in taking space science in Pakistan to the highest level. However, he left SUPARCO in 1974, and the commission lost a visionary leader. SUPARCO did not make any progress and suffered from the government's neglect. Zafar Nawaz Jaspal argues that Pakistan's space program has not been a severe priority to its military top brass.[115] Jaspal's critical observation suggests that the security situation in the 1970s and 80 s compelled Pakistan's civil and military leadership to pay all attention and divert resources to build Pakistan's nuclear program to make a deterrence capability against arch-rival India.

Pakistan has no declared space policy, regulatory regime, or space law until 2023. Before the release of National Space Policy (NSPy) in 2023, in the absence of legislation related to space activities in Pakistan, laws and acts belonging to different areas provided temporary legal coverage to space activities. Likewise, SUPARCO also "lacked the constitutional and legal mandate to regulate and control national space activities and to implement space policies." As a result, Pakistan's space program made slow progress.[116]

In 2011, the National Command Authority (NCA), under the chairmanship of former Prime Minister Yusuf Raza Gillani, approved Pakistan's Space Vision 2047. In 2012, Chairman SUPARCO, at the National Space Conference 2012 held in Islamabad, highlighted some of critical characteristics of Space Vision 2047. In his speech, SUPARCO Chairman highlighted the mission statement: "Space as a strategic sector, exploit all aspects of space science, technology and its application for national well-being and security." SUPARCO mission states that Pakistan aims to build, launch, and operate its satellite to perform various functions in outer space, including communication, remote sensing, navigation, and meteorology, to achieve socioeconomic and national security goals.[117]

Before 2023 NSPy, in the absence of space law and policy and the undeclared constitutional status of SUPARCO, it was challenging to run Pakistan's space program. However, these hindrances did not restrict Pakistan from continuing its space activities. SUPARCO has published a space policy after government approval granting SUPARCO a status of national space agency. Some of salient of space policy are[118]: -

a. Space technology applications for socio-economic development and national security.
b. Development of facilities, infrastructure, and space professionals.
c. Research and development in science, technology, and innovation.
d. Development of local industry and commercialization of space products and services.
e. Space education and awarness.
f. International cooperation and collaboration.
g. Sustainable, safe, and secure space environment,
h. Space laws, regulations and governance mechanisms.
i. Creation of Pakistan space Activities Regulatory Board (Established in 2024).

Pakistan's space program is still underdeveloped and primarily dependent on the goodwill of China. China launched Pakistan's first communication satellite, PAKSAT-IR, in 2011. China also launched PRSS-1, PakTES-1A, iCube-Qamar and PakSAT-MMI for Pakistan. However, Pakistan's international space cooperation is also increasing, which will bolster its space program. Pakistan has specific opportunities and challenges to explore its space program despite little international cooperation and expanding Chinese support.[119]

Pakistan has not publicaly declared space strategy or doctrine, and it recognizes space as a strategic domain vital for its national security, just like its nuclear and conventional military power. Pakistan will eventually aim to develop its Satellite Launch Vehicles (SLVs) and manufacture satellites. It has formulated space laws and legislation to conduct space activities in Pakistan. This suggests that Pakistan is an aspiring space power as its space policy characteristics resemble emerging space power characteristics.

Pakistan's space policy 2023 and Space Vision 2047 suggest that its policy is predominantly devised on technological determinism. Pakistan sees its space program for peaceful purposes and its country's socioeconomic development through its power. Space Vision 2047 highlights that Pakistan will build, manufacture, build, and launch satellites; however, Clay Moltz believes that Pakistan's economic condition is a significant obstacle in achieving its Space Vision 2047 objectives of indigenously manufacturing, building, and launching satellites.[120]

Conclusion

In this changing world, human reliance on space is inevitable. It is difficult for humanity to communicate and navigate on Earth without satellites. Satellites have revolutionized these fields, making communication, navigation, and other satellite applications more reliable, accurate, and precise. Although there is no single theoretical framework to study space power in existing literature except for some academic endeavours nearest to developing a space power framework, states continue to bring more advancements in their space programs. Some states have brought advancements in their space program to a level where they can be recognized as a global space power. Likewise, some are in the process of entering into the club of global space powers.

Importantly, understanding the intent of a state and its national security objectives gives a taste of their thinking about how they will behave in this international political system. One of the steps to understanding the state is to study declared policies, strategies, and doctrine. However, states do not need to release their policies, strategies, and doctrines in a document form because states do not want to be transparent about their strategic programs. Understandably, space activities of most states are for peaceful purposes. However, importance of space has increased manifold with time. Hence, some states consider their space programs a critical element of their national power. A general overview of space policies of India, Pakistan, China, and the U.S. suggests that space is now an essential part of their national security policy and strategy. Space is considered a strategic domain, and space technologies are for dual-use purposes; military purposes achieve national security objectives.

Space policies of global space powers have paid considerable attention towards achieving national security objectives. It is undeniable that states are building such capabilities, which will lead to weaponization of space. It is a general understanding that a state's intention can change overnight; however, it will be a matter of choice and political will of the states to weaponize space.

The space strategy of the U.S. pivots around the notion of freedom of action. It talks about counterspace measures under its space control strategy. China's military space strategy argues in favour of building ASAT and electronic measures for counterspace operations. However, no state has explicitly declared building such capabilities in official documents. Nevertheless, all global space powers are building capabilities to weaponize space. So far, very little has been discussed in their declared policies about arms control and disarmament measures in space. Although their space policies explicitly discuss the peaceful exploration of space, it is hardly mentioned in their policies regarding the prohibition of space weaponization. China's white papers talked about diplomatically, which contradicts its capability development process. Likewise, the U.S. endeavours to get freedom of action in space but is not supportive of preventing the weaponization of space. All the capability development suggests that there is a space arms race.

India's declared space policy in 2023 is about peaceful as well as security uses. The Joint Doctrine Indian Armed Forces-2017 and Land Warfare Doctrine-2018 stress that steps are being taken to use space technologies for national security purposes. This suggests shifting India's space policy from Nehru's space vision to achieving national security objectives. This policy change can lead to an intense space rivalry in South Asia. China's ASAT test gained considerable attention in India. India has tested its ASATs in 2019 and its military space intentions are apparent. Pakistan's space policy has been published, and it talks about peaceful uses of space. Space Vision 2047's statement emphasized using space for national security.

In conclusion, while many states do not publish their official space policy, that does not mean states do not have a space policy. However, as a global space power, the U.S. has always released its space policy, strategy, and doctrine to remain transparent about its global leadership.

Notes

1. See for details, Booth [1]
2. Booth, 1979.
3. Tzu [2].
4. Hays [3].
5. McNiel [3]
6. France [5]
7. Gray [6]
8. Mahan [7] and also see Speller [8].
9. Mazarr et al. [9].
10. Heflin [10].
11. Kent and Ochmanek [11].
12. For further details, see Oberg [12].
13. Oberg, 44.
14. Oberg, 44–47.
15. Oberg, 45.
16. Oberg, 46.
17. Rotberg [13].
18. Moran [14].
19. *Space Operations,* Joint Publication 3–14 (Washington DC: Joint Chief of Staff, May 29, 2013), GL-8, http://www.dtic.mil/doctrine/new_pubs/jp3_14.pdf.
20. Evans [15].
21. *Space Operations,* Air Force Doctrine Document 2–2 (Maxwell AFB, AL: Chief of Staff of the United States Air Force, August 23, 1998), 1, http://webapp1.dlib.indiana.edu/virtual_disk_library/index.cgi/4240529/FID2862/pdfdocs/jel/service/afdd2_2.pdf.
22. Peter [16].
23. Peter, "Space Power and Europe," & "Space Power and Europe in the 21st Century.".
24. Correll [17].
25. Gray [18].
26. France and Sellers [19].
27. Peter, "Space Power and Europe," 3.
28. Gray, *Modern Strategy,* 263 & 264.
29. Gray, 263 & 264.
30. In the U.S. space doctrine, the phrase "freedom of action" has profound understanding. The phrase suggests that the U.S. wants to have complete freedom of action to exploit to achieve its national security objectives and commercial activities without any kind of international overhead.

31. Sadeh [20].
32. Gibbs [21].
33. "National Aeronautics and Space Act (Unamended)," *NASA*, accessed November 16, 2017, https://history.nasa.gov/spaceact.html.
34. Hand et al. [22].
35. Kennedy [23].
36. Gibson [24].
37. "Presidential Directive/NSC-37: National Space Policy," (official memorandum, Washington DC: Director of Central Intelligence, June 13, 1978), https://www.cia.gov/library/readingroom/document/cia-rdp80m00772a000300010027-8.
38. "Unclassified Version of NSDD-42: National Space Policy," (official memorandum, Washington DC: The White House, July 12, 1982), https://www.cia.gov/library/readingroom/docs/CIA-RDP84B00148R000100320009-2.pdf.
39. "Unclassified Version of NSDD-42.".
40. Gibson, "Current Space Law," 49.
41. "Fact Sheet: National Space Policy," *George C. Marshall Institute*, September 19, 1996, http://marshall.wpengine.com/wp-content/uploads/2013/09/PDD-NSC-49-PDD-NSTC-8-National-Space-Policy-19-Sep-1996.pdf.
42. "Fact Sheet.".
43. "U.S. National Space Policy (Unclassified)," *Federation of American Scientists*, NSPD-49, August 31, 2006, https://fas.org/irp/offdocs/nspd/.
44. Stoullig [25], Burke [26] and also see Kheel [27].
45. "National Space Policy of the United States of America," *The White House*, June 28, 2010, = https://obamawhitehouse.archives.gov/sites/default/files/national_space_policy_6-28-10.pdf.
46. Malcolm Davis (Senior Fellow, Australian Strategic Policy Institute) in discussion with the author, November 20, 2017.
47. Moltz [28].
48. Moltz, 23.
49. Moltz, 23.
50. Moltz, 24.
51. Moltz, 25 & 26.
52. Moltz, 27.
53. Eligar Sadeh (Editor-in-Chief, Astropolitics) in discussion with the author, November 18, 2017.
54. Dr Michael Simpson (Executive Director, Secure World Foundation) in discussion with the author, November 27, 2017.
55. Simpson, discussion.
56. Vedda [29]
57. Vedda, 6.
58. Hendrix and Routh [30].
59. *National security space strategy: unclassified summary* (Washington, DC: Dept. of Defence, 2011).
60. "Fact Sheet: National Security Space Strategy," *Department of Defence*, January 19, 2011, http://archive.defense.gov/home/features/2011/0111_nsss/docs/2011_01_19_NSSS_Fact_Sheet_FINAL.pdf.
61. Moltz, "Space and Strategy," 27.
62. King and Byrne [31].
63. King and Byrne, 61–68.
64. *Space Operations*, Joint Publication 3–14 (Washington DC: Joint Chief of Staff, May 29, 2013), GL-8, http://www.dtic.mil/doctrine/new_pubs/jp3_14.pdf.
65. Hays [32].

66. Joanne Irene Gabrynowicz, editor-in-Chief of the Journal of Space Law and currently teaching at the Beijing Institute of Technology School of Law, believes that X-37B is not a space weapon. She argues that X-37B is not a weapon as perceived by many space experts. Irene Gabrynowicz (Editor-in-Chief of the Journal of Space Law) in discussion with the author, November 17, 2017. On the other hand, Malcolm Davis, (Senior Fellow ASPI) argues that Russia and China fears that X-37B can use a space weapon; in discussion with the author, November 22, 2017. Also see, "Why Russia and China Should Fear the X-37B Space Plane," *The National Interest*, October 19, 2016, http://nationalinterest.org/blog/the-buzz/why-russia-china-should-fear-the-x-37b-space-plane-18099?page=2; Jameson [33].
67. Waller [34].
68. Waller, 2001. Quoted in Jameson, "X-37 Space Vehicle," 12; and Hays, "Space and the Military," 352.
69. DeBlois [35]; Also quoted by Hays [36].
70. Hallman [37].
71. King and Byrne, "Space Doctrine," 63.
72. Klein [38].
73. Gibbs, "Space Policies of the Major Space Faring Nations," 310.
74. China National Space Administration [39].
75. "China's Space Activities in 2016.".
76. "Full Text of White Paper on China's Space Activities in 2016," *The State Council*, updated December 28, 2016, http://english.gov.cn/archive/white_paper/2016/12/28/content_281475527159496.htm; "China's Space Activities in 2011," December 2011, http://english.gov.cn/archive/white_paper/2014/08/23/content_281474983043142.htm; "White Paper on China's Space Activities Published," *China.org.cn*, 2006, http://www.china.org.cn/english/2006/Oct/183588.htm; and also see "China's Space Activities in 2006," 2006, http://www.china.org.cn/english/features/book/183672.htm.
77. "China's Space Activities in 2016.".
78. Davis [40].
79. "China's Space Activities in 2016.".
80. Lele [41].
81. Kulacki [42].
82. Kulacki, 1.
83. Kulacki, 1.
84. Kulacki, 11.
85. Forden [43].
86. Forden, 151.
87. Khan and Khan [44].
88. Ames Moltz (Professor at Naval Postgraduate School, U.S. and writer of *Asia's Space Race* (2012)) email message to author, November 28, 2017.
89. Khan and Khan, "Chinese capabilities," 188.
90. Khan and Khan, 188.
91. Lele [45].
92. Paikowsky and Ben-Israel [46].
93. von Welck [47].
94. Mistry [48].
95. Rao [49].
96. Rao, "Indian Space Policy.".
97. Rao, 2014.
98. "A Policy Framework for Satellite Communication in India," *ISRO*, 1997, https://www.isro.gov.in/sites/default/files/article-files/indias-space-policy-0/satcom-policy.pdf.
99. "The norms, guidelines and procedures for implementation of the policy frame-work for satellite communications in India," *ISRO*, 2000, https://www.isro.gov.in/sites/default/files/article-files/indias-space-policy-0/satcom-ngp.pdf.

100. "Guidelines for Registration of INSAT/GSAT Capacity Requirement," *Department of Space,* Government of India, SCNP/F.ICRF, accessed November 21, 2017, https://www.isro.gov.in/sites/default/files/dos_guidelines_for_insat-gsat_capacity_reservation_-_release_2.pdf.
101. "Remote Sensing Data Policy (RSDp-2011)," *ISRO*, accessed November 21, 2017, https://www.isro.gov.in/indias-space-policy-0.
102. Rao, "Indian Space Policy.".
103. "Vision and Mission Statements," *ISRO*, accessed November 21, 2017, https://www.isro.gov.in/about-isro/vision-and-mission-statements.
104. "No space should be left between the common man and space technology, says Modi," *India Info News Service,* September 8, 2015, https://www.indiainfoline.com/article/news-top-story/no-space-should-be-left-between-the-common-man-and-space-technology-says-modi-115090800008_1.html.
105. Bhola [50].
106. Paracha [51]
107. *Joint Indian Armed Force 2017* (New Delhi: Ministry of Defence, India, April 2017), 25–26, http://ids.nic.in/dot/JointDoctrineIndianArmedForces2017.pdf.
108. For details on Indian BMD development, see Khan [52], Jaspal [53], Yusuf and Banuri [54] and also see, Jalil [55].
109. Lele [56].
110. Rajagopalan [57].
111. "India Readying Weapon to Destroy Enemy Satellites: Saraswat," *Indian Express*, January 3, 2010, quoted in Lele [58].
112. Milowicki and Johnson-Freese [59]; and also see Paikowsky and Ben-Israel [60].
113. Jasani [60].
114. Moltz, email message.
115. See details, Jaspal [61].
116. Jaspal, 2008.
117. Bilal [62].
118. Khan [63] and also see, Bilal, "National Space Program.".
119. Siraj [64].
120. Motz, email message.

References

1. Ken Booth, *Strategy and Ethnocentrism* (London: Routledge, 1979)
2. Sun Tzu, *The Art of War,* trans., Lionel Giles (El Paso: El Paso Norte Press, 2005).
3. Peter Hays, *United States Military Space: Into the Twenty-First Century* (Maxwell AFB, AL: Air University Press, 2002), 5.
4. Samuel McNiel, "Proposed Tenets of Space power: Six Enduring Truths," (MSc. Diss., Air Command and Staff College, Air University, 2003–04), 3.
5. Martin France, "Mahan's Elements of Sea Power Applied to the Development of Space Power," (MSc. Diss., National Defence University National War College Washington DC, 2000), 1.
6. Colin Gray, *Modern Strategy* (Oxford: Oxford University Press, 1999), 258.
7. Alfred T Mahan, *The Influence of Sea power Upon History: 1660–1783* (Cambridge: Cambridge University Press, 2010)
8. Ian Speller, *Understanding Naval Warfare* (London: Routledge, 2014), 42.
9. Michael Mazarr et al., *Strategic Planning and U.S. Air Force: Characteristics of Success* (Santa Monica, CA: RAND Corporation, 2017).
10. Woodford Agee Heflin ed., *The United States Air Force Dictionary* (Washington, D.C.: Air University Press, 1956), 74.
11. Glenn Kent and David Ochmanek, *Defining the Role of Airpower in Joint Missions* (Santa Monica, CA: RAND Cooperation, 1998), 11.

12. James Oberg, *Space Power Theory* (Colorado Springs, CO: United States Air Force Academy, 1999).
13. Robert I. Rotberg, "Failed States, Collapsed States, Weak States: Causes and Indicators," in *State Failure and State Weakness in a Time of Terror,* ed. Robert I. Rotberg (Washington DC: Brookings, 2003), 5-6.
14. Michael Moran, "An Evolving Doctrine: Force Application from Space," (MSc. diss., Air Command and Staff College, Air University, 2000–04), 2.
15. Tyler Evans, "Space Coordinating Authority: Information Service from Space," in *Space Power Integration: Perspectives from Space Weapons Officers*, ed. Kendall Brown (Maxwell AFB, AL: Air University Press, 2006), 4.
16. Nicolas Peter, "Space Power and Europe, in the Need for a Conceptual Framework," (paper, 59th International Astronautical Congress, Glasgow, United Kingdom, 2008); and also "Space Power and Europe in the 21st Century," *European Space Policy Institute,* ESPI Perspective No. 21, April 2009, https://www.espi.or.at/images/stories/dokumente/Perspectives/espi%20perspectives%2021%20.pdf.
17. Randall R. Correll, "Emerging Actors," in *Space Power*, ed. Charles Lutes et al., (Washington DC: National Defence University Press, 2004), http://ndupress.ndu.edu/Portals/68/Documents/Books/spacepower.pdf.
18. Colin Gray, *Modern Strategy* (New York: Oxford University Press, 1999), 260.
19. Martin France and Jerry Jon Sellers, "Real Constraints on Space Power," in *Space Power*, ed. Charles Lutes et al., (Washington DC: National Defence University Press, 2004), http://ndupress.ndu.edu/Portals/68/Documents/Books/spacepower.pdf.
20. Eligar Sadeh, "Politics of Space," in *the Politics of Space: A Survey*, ed. Eligar Sadeh (London: Routledge, 2011), 3.
21. Graham Gibbs, "An Analysis of the Space Policies of the Major Space Faring Nations and Selected Emerging Space Faring Nations," *Annals of Air and Space Law* 37, no.1 (2012): 282-331.
22. Richard Hand et al., *Space Handbook: A War Fighter's Guide to Space* (Maxwell AFB, AL: Air University Press, 1993), Chap 1.
23. John Kennedy, "Urgent National Needs," (speech, Washington DC, May 1, 1961), *NASA*, https://history.nasa.gov/Apollomon/apollo5.pdf.
24. Jane Gibson, "Current Space Law and Policy," in *AU-18: Space Primer* (Maxwell AFB, AL: Air University Press, 2009), 47, http://www.au.af.mil/au/awc/space/au-18-2009/au-18_cover.pdf.
25. Jean-Michel Stoullig, "Rumsfeld Commission Warns Against Space Pearl Harbour," *Space Daily,* January 11, 2001, http://www.spacedaily.com/news/bmdo-01b.html
26. Alan Burke, "Space Threat Warning: Foundation for Space Superiority, Avoiding A Space Pearl Harbour," (MSc. Diss., Air War College, Air University, 2005)
27. Rebecca Kheel, "Backers of Space-based Military Branch: We Will not allow a Space Pearl Harbour," *The Hill,* August 11, 2017, http://thehill.com/policy/defense/359438-space-corps-backers-we-will-not-allow-a-space-pearl-harbor
28. James Moltz, "Space and Strategy," in *Space Strategy in the 21st Century,* ed. Eligar Sadeh (London: Routledge, 2013), 16.
29. James Vedda, "Consideration for the Next National Space Policy," *Center for Space Policy and Strategy,* Aerospace Cooperation, Policy Paper, March 2017, 3.
30. Jerry Hendrix and Adam Routh, "U.S. Space Policy Should Aim to Preserve Advantage on the New Frontier," *Defence One*, November 9, 2017, http://www.defenseone.com/ideas/2017/10/us-should-act-preserve-americas-advantages-space/142028/.
31. Christopher King and Edward Byrne, "Space Doctrine," in *AU-18: Space Primer* (Maxwell AFB, AL: Air University Press, 2009), 61, http://www.au.af.mil/au/awc/space/au-18-2009/au-18_cover.pdf.
32. Peter Hays, "United States Military Uses of Space: Issues and Challenges," (paper, International Symposium on Security Affairs 2015, Tokyo), 1–20, http://www.nids.mod.go.jp/english/event/symposium/pdf/2015/E-01.pdf

33. Austin Jameson, "X-37 Space Vehicle: Starting A New Age in Space Control?" (MSc. diss., Air Command and Staff College, Air University, 2001–04), IX.
34. Michael Waller, "Militarizing Space," *Insight,* March 19, 2001.
35. Bruce DeBlois, "The Advent of Space Weapons," *Astropolitics* 1, no.1 (2003): 29–53
36. Peter Hays, "Space and the Military," in *Space Politics and Policy: An Evolutionary Perspective*, ed. Eligar Sadeh (Boston: Kluwer Academic Publishers, 2002), 343.
37. Wesley Hallman, "A Fast-following Space Control Strategy," *Astropolitics* 3, no.1 (2005): 35-42.
38. John Klein, "Space Warfare: A Maritime-Inspired Space Strategy," *Astropolitics* 2, no.1, (2004): 53.
39. China National Space Administration, "China's Space Activities in 2016," (presentation, United Nations Office for Outer Space Affairs, Vienna, Austria, February 2017)
40. Malcolm Davis, "The Coming of China's Space Silk Road," *Australian Strategic Policy Institute*, August 11, 2017, https://www.aspistrategist.org.au/coming-chinas-space-silk-road/.
41. Ajay Lele, "China's 2016 Space White Paper: An Appraisal," *Institute of Defence Studies and Analyses,* issue brief, January 6, 2017, https://idsa.in/system/files/issuebrief/ib_china-2016-space-white-paper_060117.pdf.
42. Gregory Kulacki, "An Authoritative Source on China's Military Space Strategy," *Union of Concerned Scientists,* March 2014, https://www.ucsusa.org/sites/default/files/legacy/assets/documents/nwgs/China-s-Military-Space-Strategy.pdf.
43. Geoffrey Forden, "Viewpoint: China and Space War," *Astropolitics* 6, no. 2 (2008): 139.
44. Zulfqar Khan and Ahmad Khan, "Chinese Capabilities as a Global Space Power," *Astropolitics* 13, no.2-3 (2015): 185-204.
45. Ajay Lele, "India's Policy for Outer Space," *Space Policy* 39-40, no.1 (2017): 26-32.
46. Deganit Paikowsky and Isaac Ben-Israel, "India's Space Program: An Israeli Perspective on Regional Security," *India Review* 10, no.4 (2011): 394-405.
47. Stephen F. von Welck, "India's Space Policy: A Developing Country in Space," *Space Policy* 4, no.1 (1987): 326-334.
48. Dinshaw Mistry, "India's Emerging Space Program," *Pacific Affairs* 71, no.2 (1998): 151-174.
49. Mukund Rao, "Indian Space Policy for Technological and Social Development," (presentation, Space Policy and Law for Social Development in Asia, Tokyo, Japan, December 3, 2014)
50. Gaurav Bhola, "India and China Space Programs: Form Genesis of Space Technologies to Major Space Program and What That Means for the International Community," (MSc. Diss., Department of Political Science, University of Central Florida, 2009), 62-66.
51. Soobia Paracha, "Military Dimensions of the Indian Space Program," *Astropolitics* 11, no. 3 (2013): 156-186.
52. Zafar Khan, "India's Ballistic Missile Defence: Implications for South Asian Deterrence Stability," *The Washington Quarterly* 40, no.3 (2017): 187-202
53. Zafar Nawaz Jaspal, "India's Missile Capabilities: Regional Implications," *Pakistan Horizon* 54, no.1 (January 2001): 33–64; "Ballistic Missile Defence: Implications for India-Pakistan Strategic Environment," *NDU Journal* (2011): 1–26; http://www.ndu.edu.pk/publications/NDU_Journal_2011.php
54. Moeed Yusuf and Khalid Banuri, "India's Quest for Ballistic Missile Defence: A Slippery Slope," in *South Asia at Crossroads: Conflict or Cooperation in the Age of Nuclear Weapons, Missile Defence, and Space Rivalries*, eds. Subrata Ghoshroy and Gøtiz Neuneck (Hamburg: Nomos, 2010), 106–7
55. Ghazala Yasmin Jalil, "Indian Missile Defence Development: Implications for Deterrence Stability in South Asia," *Strategic Studies* 35, no.2 (2015): 29-46.
56. Ajay Lele, "India's Space Security Policy: A Proposal," *IDSA*, policy brief, April 28, 2016, https://idsa.in/policybrief/indias-space-security-policy_alele_280416.
57. Rajeswari Pillai Rajagopalan, "India's Changing Policy on Space Militarization: The Impact of China's ASAT Test," *India Review* 10, no.4 (2011): 354-378.
58. Ajay Lele, "Indian Armed Forces and Space Technology," *India Review* 10, no.4 (2011): 379-393.

59. Gene Milowicki and Joan Johnson-Freese, "Strategic Choices: Examining the United States Military Response to the Chinese Anti-Satellite Test," *Astropolitics* 6, no.1 (2008): 1-21
60. Bhupendra Jasani, "New Approaches to Achieving Space Security," in *Collective Security in Space: European Perspectives,* eds. Johan Logsdon, James Moltz and Emma Hinds (Washington DC: Space Policy Institute, Elliott School of International Affairs, The George Washington University, January 2007), 34.
61. Zafar Jaspal, *Militarization and Weaponization: A critical Analysis*, (Islamabad: South Asian Strategic Stability Institute, 2008).
62. Ahmed Bilal, "National Space Program: Past, Present and Future," (presentation, National Space Conference 2012, September 17–19, 2012, Islamabad).
63. Abdullah Khan, "National Regulatory Framework for Outer Space Activities in Pakistan," (presentation, United Nations/China/APSCO Workshop on Space Law The Role of National Space Legislation in Strengthening the Rule of Law, November 17–21, 2017, Beijing); and also see, Bilal, "National Space Program."
64. Arshad Siraj, "Pakistan's Space Program," (presentation, Conference on Security and Cooperation in South Asia, October 8–10, 2007, Berlin).

Chapter 5
Space Militarization and Weaponization Capabilities

Introduction

The previous chapters highlight policies, doctrines, and strategies of major, regional, and aspiring space powers. Likewise, these primarily focused on the general security framework at three levels of analysis: individual security, state security, and international security. A "seamless web" of sublevels exists between these three levels. The interplay of state and international security yields a sublevel known as regional security.

It is known that there are three global space powers: the U.S., China, and Russia. These states have shown intent and demonstrated space militarization and weaponization capabilities to be recognized as global space powers. India has global space intentions but is still on the path of acquiring capabilities. India's space capabilities are advancing and increasing, following a path from regional to global space power. There are aspirants of space technologies for their national development at the lower level of the continuum and to meet their national security challenges. These states are emerging space powers. The study's scope has been limited to major spacefaring states, the U.S., China, India, and Pakistan. This chapter studied the space militarization and weaponization capabilities of the U.S., China, India, and Pakistan.

Understanding China, India, and Pakistan's strategic triangular relations from a space power lens is essential. Many believe that there is no arms race in outer space at present. However, analysis of the current development of space weapon capabilities and experts' views and writing tells that the opposite. The study of space capability developments of primary, regional, and emerging space powers envisages the dynamic of a space arms race. The discord over whether or not a space race exists

This chapter draws from the Ph.D. research work of the author titled "Arms Race in Outer Space: A Paradigm Shift in International Security and Implications for South Asia," which was completed in 2019 and successfully defended in 2020 at Department of Strategic Studies, National Defence University, Islamabad.

A. Khan and E. Sadeh, *Sabre Rattling in Space*,
https://doi.org/10.1007/978-981-97-6050-3_5

makes it difficult to understand the exact nature of payloads sent on space rockets. It is easier to determine rival military power developments in other dimensions of power, like nuclear and conventional arms. For example, missile developments can be understood by observing their launching and testing. Another vital factor in gauging nuclear arms race between two competitors by analysing development and production of delivery vehicles: ballistic missiles (short-range to intercontinental), cruise missiles, Submarine-Launched Ballistic Missiles (SLBM), and the air leg of a nuclear triad. Likewise, in nuclear realm, developments are measured in terms of number of nuclear weapons. Actions in building nuclear weapon facilities, testing nuclear devices, and launching nuclear-capable missiles reflect a country's military power. If these developments respond to an adversary's developments, this constitutes a nuclear arms race between two competitors.

The Cold War history suggests an intense nuclear arms race between the former Soviet Union and the U.S. Both powers were trying to achieve nuclear superiority. Both were also involved in an intense space race as their intentions and capabilities responded to each other's space capability developments. Another example of nuclear arms race is Indo-Pakistani competition. India unveiled its "Smiling Buddha" in its first nuclear detonation in 1974, prompting Pakistan to initiate its nuclear program. Likewise, India detonated five nuclear weapons at Pokhran in May 1999, and in response, Pakistan detonated six devices at Chagai just two weeks later. Afterwards, both countries continued to test their missiles and changed their doctrines and postures in response to their capability development. Hence, South Asia's power dynamics suggest a continuous and intense nuclear arms race between India and Pakistan.

The aim of highlighting nuclear arms race is to make an analogy for space arms race. In an arms race, numbers do matter. In a nuclear arms race, an essential part of the equation is each state's number of nuclear weapons.[1]

The central, regional, and emerging space powers have a variety of space assets. Space assets can also be used for dual-use purposes, making it challenging to understand whether a space asset is specially designed for military purposes or peaceful uses only. At present, 1957 operational satellites orbit the Earth, performing various functions. The U.S. has maintained pre-eminence in space by possessing the world's largest fleet of space assets. China has surpassed Russia in recent years in terms of several active space assets. India's space program is progressing and is far from changing its regional status into a global space power. Other actors in space, e.g. the European Space Agency (ESA), France, Israel, and international companies, are consistently making progress in space sciences and technologies.

The competition between China and the U.S. is progressing at global level. At regional level, India is on the path to becoming a global space power. However, what states are developing in space technologies is an essential factor.

The militarization of space began with the launch of Sputnik-I in 1957. It is evident from RAND's feasibility report titled Preliminary Design of An Experimental World-Circling Spaceship on developing spacecraft for military purposes.RAND's report was about building a spacecraft for space exploration, but satellites' dual-use nature was also highlighted. Satellites are developed primarily for communications, navigation, remote sensing, and meteorology and have dual-use purposes.

The number of active space satellites is significant, but it is not decisive to change space conflict. Numbers are important in defining nature and context of the competition between two adversaries or two blocs (the Cold War term) or in a multipolar world (post-Cold War term). A general assessment of any adversarial relations starts with comparing number of military weapons, vehicles, and personnel (active and reserve) possessed by each side. On the other hand, space is a unique medium where number of satellites can change fundamental nature of the conflict or relations and context. Nevertheless, becoming a global space power involves other crucial variables. Besides each country's number of space assets, their quality and designated functions and operations directly affect competition among major spacefaring states.

It is evident that "nobody knows what the nature of the payload is" when a rocket is sent to space.[2] This assertion shows that space race phenomenon is difficult to understand in post-Cold War era. Adding more complexity to it, assessing military space capabilities would be the world's most imperfect art. However, this imperfect art needs attention to clear the dust from a space arms race phenomenon. From Eligar Sadeh's point of view, present space arms race phenomenon is complex to understand as he thinks there is none. However, he suggests that states from space militarization follow a path to space weaponization.[3]States are rigorously following this path, and the time is near when major spacefaring states will reach a defining moment to place their weapons in space.

This chapter aims to answer following questions: what are the military uses of outer space, and what are the different space capabilities of major, regional, and aspiring space powers? This chapter aims to find the answers to abovementioned questions to compare global, regional, and emerging space powers. Mapping space militarization and weaponization capabilities would provide a holistic picture of major, regional, and aspiring states' intent, whether they have weaponized, space or not.

Military Uses of Space

Michio Kaku, a renowned theoretical physicist and author of *Physics of the Impossible,* criticized U.S. policies to weaponize space.[4] In his view, the probability of fighting a nuclear war between the former Soviet Union and the U.S. has receded after the Cold War. However, he stressed that if "one danger is fading, another rises ominously."[5] Kaku refers to another danger that emerged drastically in post-Cold War world. This is a path followed by states from space militarization to weaponization. Clay Moltz thinks that space weaponization has already happened.[6] Likewise, Kaku argues that "space weaponization is a reality to the security of everyone on Earth."[7] The pursuit of building weapons to weaponize outer space will accelerate a new arms race.[8] The U.S., China, and Russia are building space weapons on the ground and are waiting for the other to weaponize space first so they can flex their military muscles in space in response.[9] Kaku believes that if this "madness is not stopped, then a whole new round of the arms race in outer space could begin."[10]

A comprehensive study on space security is incomplete without highlighting difference between militarization and weaponization. From a definitional point of view, both have different frameworks and characteristics. Militarization and weaponization of space are fundamentally different in their physical manifestation and from a legal perspective. The militarization of space began after the first communication satellite, *Sputnik-I,* was launched by the former Soviet Union in 1957. Space militarization is the first step in the continuum, with space weaponization at its end. Between space militarization and weaponization, there is an intervening factor of an arms race between central spacefaring states (see Table 5.1).

The use of space for passive defence (non-destructive) is called the militarization of space.[11] This passive defence means creating a network of satellites to support terrestrial military operations and increase their effectiveness. Space militarization is the launch and orbital placement of passive space systems. Likewise, using these passive space military systems to enhance military effectiveness is also part of space militarization. Passive systems include reconnaissance, communications, weather,

Table 5.1 Space militarization and weaponization

Space Doctrine and Posture	Perceived level of threat to foreign countries due to space posture	Threat Level	Type of Activity/Weapons
High Ground	High	10	Permanently Orbiting Space-to-Terrestrial Weapons (Unilateral)
		9	Temporary, or "pop-up" Space-to-Terrestrial Weapons (Unilateral)
		8	Space-to-Terrestrial Weapons (Multilateral)
		7	Permanently Orbiting Space-to-Space (Unilateral)
		6	Temporary, or "pop-up" Space-to-Space Weapons (Unilateral)
Space Control	Moderate	5	Space-to-Space Weapons (Multilateral)
		4	Terrestrial-to-Space Weapons (Unilateral)
Space Survivability	Low	3	Terrestrial-to-Space Weapons (Multilateral)
		2	Space-to-Terrestrial ISR, MCS, Communications
		1	Space-to-Space ISR, MCG, Communications,
Space Sanctuary	None	0	Terrestrial-to-Space ISR, MCG Communications

(Brackets beside the table: A spans threat levels 10–3; C spans 10–0; B spans 2–0.)

A = Weaponization of Space, B = Militarization of Space, C = Arms Race in Outer Space
Source Deblois [137]

navigation, geodesy, and early warning satellites. Importantly, passive space systems do not function as weapons themselves.

In 2001, the United Nations General Assembly (UNGA) adopted a resolution calling for the Prevention of Arms Race in Outer Space (PAROS) Treaty. The resolution called for "recognizing the common interest of all mankind in the exploration and use of outer space for peaceful purposes."[12] Likewise, the Outer Space Treaty (OST) text, adopted by UNGA in its 1963 resolution and a binding international treaty supported by all space powers, tells about the peaceful exploration of space, the Moon, and other celestial bodies.[13] The word "peaceful" does not restrict passive military space systems' deployment from a legal perspective.[14]

Peace is interpreted differently by different countries; for example, the U.S. considers peaceful purposes inclusive of non-destructive means of defence, which endorses the militarization of space. Many Western analysts also view "peaceful purposes," including non-aggressive military uses of space. On the other hand, Japan interpreted peace as non-military use of space. "Peaceful purposes" carried a different interpretation for the former Soviet Union. Its jurists considered "peaceful purposes" as non-military uses of space. This interpretation is still a part of Russia's space policy. However, the former Soviet Union and the U.S. rigorously competed to militarize outer space. This inherited contradictory interpretations, and ambiguous language of the OST has let other states militarize space. Another interpretation of Article IV of the treaty suggests that it does not prohibit all military activities. The passive military defence systems are used for "direct bombing raids or to orchestrate a prompt global strike, which is the ability to control any situation or defeat any adversary across the range of military operations."[15] Identifying space's "peaceful purposes" is challenging as space objects (satellites) have dual-use purposes. There are two prominent military uses of satellites: communications and remote sensing.[16] Bruce Hurwitz argues that "communication satellites do not provide any unique legal problems."[17] On the other hand, remote sensing is an issue among nations because of their right to "disseminate the data and information derived from satellites."[18]

Karl Mueller defines weaponization of space as a subset of the militarization of space.[19] Space weaponization is about employment of space weapons. Moreover, in simple terms, it means placing military space systems that can be used for active defence to destroy adversaries' space and terrestrial assets.[20] No legal regime or universally accepted treaty prohibits a space arms race and space weaponization. States are developing and testing space weapons, and in recent years, some systems have been temporarily employed in space, which has opened a backdoor in space weaponization.[21]

Satellites for reconnaissance, communications, weather, navigation, geodesy, early warning, and Global Positioning System (GPS) purposes act as "force multipliers,"[22] "force enablers,"[23] and "force enhancement capabilities."[24] These force multiplier, enabler, and enhancement capabilities represent space militarization capabilities. They are unnecessary for hard killing of adversary's space and terrestrial capabilities. However, space militarization capabilities can kill adversary satellites, like orbital jamming and interference with radio-frequency signals. However, they are also categorized as anti-satellite weapon systems.

In past decades, satellites have significantly improved the "performance, lethality, and effectiveness of ground, air, and naval forces and weapons during peace and war."[25] Paul Stars highlights the importance of passive military space systems enhancing precision, accuracy, lethality, survivability, and agility of all terrestrial, sea, and air military operations.[26] The space assets contribute to overall aerospace superiority and support the "full spectrum of military actions in theatres of operations."[27] Table 5.2 shows details of non-aggressive/non-destructive military space systems. Primarily, space force enhancement includes intelligence, surveillance, reconnaissance (ISR), missile tracking/detection, monitoring, communications, positioning, navigation, timing (PNT), and Navigation Warfare (NAVWAR) satellite capabilities.

First, there is a need to define space weapons comprehensively. A space weapon is defined as "any device or system designed to cause damage within outer space or targeted from space to cause damage; or any device or system which, when fully developed, would eventually thoroughly accomplish either of those objectives."[28] The definition of space weapon also identifies different types of weapons and their characteristics, especially their damage level. Bhupendra Jasani defines space weapons as "which can damage, destroy, permanently disrupt the functioning of, or change the flight trajectory of space objects of other states."[29] Another definition suggests:

> Space weapons and offensive space warfare initiatives as terrestrially based devices specifically designed and flight-tested to physically attack, impair, or destroy objects in space, or space-based devices designed and flight-tested to attack, impair, or destroy objects in space or on earth.[30]

Michael Krepon and Michael Katz-Hyman argue that this definition is not comprehensively written. This definition and previous ones do not talk about soft killing of satellites through non-kinetic means.[31] The definitions of space weapons do not include those systems and methods through which someone can interfere with uplinks and downlinks of satellites and hamper their function.[32] This can seriously damage functioning of satellite, though not necessarily destroy it. These systems disrupt or permanently damage satellites' command, control, and communications necessary for their smooth and efficient function. Jasani defines these systems as non-dedicated space weapons.[33] States are rigorously developing hard-kill capabilities like ASATs. However, soft-kill capabilities are simpler to develop and require a bit of an industrial base. In this case, states want to build hard simultaneously and soft-kill capabilities. Primarily, soft-kill capabilities are included in modern Electronic Warfare (EW).

Defining space weapons is difficult as "what constitutes a space weapon means we cannot know with confidence whether a satellite launched by a potential enemy is on a peaceful mission."[34] More importantly, there is a linkage between capability and intention. Former Commander U.S. Strategic Command General James Cartwright argues about Earth-based space weapons, stating that if a state intends to launch an interceptor in space and has created desired after-effects, an interceptor will be considered a space weapon. He believes that every state has its perspective on space weapons.[35] Some experts believe that if a missile intercepts an incoming missile (mostly ICBM) in its mid-course flight (in space), its interception capability will likely be considered an Earth-based space weapon.[36] Brian Weeden divides space weapons into two general categories. First, Earth-based weapons, and second, space-based weapons. From his point of view, medium- to long-range ballistic missiles, ASATs, LASERs, and direct energy weapons are Earth-to-space weapons.[37] Medium to long-range ballistic missiles can be used for the Ground-based Mid-course Defence (GMD).[38] The GMD system detects a missile in its mid-course flight stage to intercept and destroy it before it re-enters the Earth's atmosphere and hits its target on the ground.[39] However, George Lewis and Theodore Postol while analysing the efficacy of GMD and Standard Missile (SM)-3 interceptors, state that "GMD and SM-3 systems are highly susceptible to the massive confusion that leads to complete performance breakdowns when they encounter objects that have characteristics that are unexpected."[40] Krepon and Katz-Hayman argue that medium or long-range ballistic missiles are adaptable as space weapons.[41] However, they criticize those who think that space is weaponized by employing these capabilities. They think these residual or latent space warfare capabilities serve more as "an insurance policy and deterrent against the initiation of dedicated space warfare programs by potential adversaries."[42]

Malcolm Davis supports the need to redefine space weapons.[43] In this regard, Xavier Pasco argues that a comprehensive definition of space weapons requires including "orbital and ground-based equipment intended to affect targeted space systems."[44] Other non-kinetic means exist to damage the adversary's space assets, such as the soft killing of satellites. The damage to space and terrestrial assets from space is not limited to physical means; instead, new means and methods exist to damage space and terrestrial assets. There are kinetic and non-kinetic space weapons in this discussion of defining space weapons.

Generally, space weapons are divided into three major categories. First, Earth-to-space weapons are used to attack targets in space, which move through space to get targets on the ground. Second, space-to-Earth weapons acquire targets in the air, sea, or ground. Third, space-to-space weapons that move through space to attack targets in space.[45] The second and third categories can be combined into a single category of space-based weapons, which achieve their targets in space, air, land, and sea. Importantly, all three types of space weapons exhibit different physical characteristics, work differently, and achieve various targets for attack with different scales of destruction. Bruce Deblois describes space weapons based on development and employment in space. Deblois categorizes space weapons on their unilateral or multilateral deployment and temporary or permanent employment in space (see Table 5.1). For weapons that fall under the category of space weapons, see Table 5.2.

States are developing space weapons and will continue to develop more if they remain vulnerable to each other and feel less secure.[46] The dangers of employment of space weapons are frightening.[47] War is inevitable, but is there any possibility that war will be fought in space?[48] This possibility cannot be ruled out in contemporary world. States have fought wars on land, sea, and air.

Consequently, space is now the fourth medium of warfare. Space policies, doctrines, and strategies in the past and present of major spacefaring nations have recognized space warfare as a possible reality. It is no longer a novelistic idea, given that states are building space weapons. The development of space weapons has now

Table 5.2 Passive military space systems: space force enhancement

Orbits	Distance from Earth (Km)	Passive Defence Use
Low-Earth Orbit	180-2,000	Telecommunications
		Imaging
		Navigation
		Radio Intelligence
		Meteorology
Medium Earth Orbit	19,000-20,000	Navigation
		Imaging
		Telecommunications
Geostationary Orbit/	35,780	Missile Warning Systems
		Radio Intelligence
		Telecommunications
High-Earth Orbit	35,780-384,000	Navigation
		Missile Warning Systems
		Radio Intelligence
		Telecommunications

A = Communication Satellites B = Remote-Sensing Satellites, C = Navigation/Positioning Satellites
Source [9]; Watts [138]; Jasani and Lee [139]; and Topychkanov [140]

moved towards the tail of continuum, which ends with space weaponization. This trend has implications not only for global security but also for regional and state security. In previous decades, states have tested and demonstrated space weapon capabilities.[49]

Many argue that in a potential conflict over Taiwan, China can attack U.S. satellites in space and vice versa. This could initiate a space war between two states.[50] It is also quite understandable that further development of space weapons and their subsequent deployment in outer space will prompt other countries with advanced missile capabilities to "resort to some low-cost and relatively low-technology anti-satellite devices to counter critical and vulnerable" space assets of global and regional space powers.[51] James Oberg argues that space powers were investing their time and skills to develop technical means for countermeasures in space. He thinks states, emerging space powers and still at entry-level, have "rudimentary space weaponry within grasp."[52] Krepon and Katz-Hayman believe that if space weapons are deployed, this placement could have adverse effects on nuclear non-proliferation regime as it may further degrade. States are then incentivized to build more nuclear weapons.[53]

Bhupendra Jasani also stresses the possible vertical proliferation of nuclear weapons after the deployment of space weapons. He believes that space weaponization can prompt vertical proliferation in South Asia. Jasani thinks that the National

Missile Defence (NMD) system is employed with sufficient space assets and that states are more vulnerable and insecure about NMD deployment. Jasani opines that if the U.S. deployed its NMD and Theatre Missile Defence (TMD), China would be vulnerable and likely to enhance its nuclear arsenal with more lethality and yield.[54] To illustrate, the U.S. deployed Terminal High Altitude Area Defence (THAAD) in South Korea in the wake of North Korea's nuclear tests, which China criticized.

There is disagreement on the definition of space weapons, their types, and the weaponization of space. The disagreement is mostly on the technical and political understanding of space weapons. The deployment germinates a difference of opinion on space weaponization and militarization. For example, the difference is mostly in Earth-based space weapons. Brian Weeden considers long-range and ICBMs part of any missile defence system, which can intercept missiles in their mid-course as space weapon. From this perspective, the U.S. has tested SM-3 and SM-6 as part of its GMD system as space weapon. So far, the GMD system has more than "25 successful space interceptions, and more than 240 interceptors have been delivered to U.S. and Japanese navies," according to its manufacturer Raytheon.[55] Lewis and Postol have challenged the effective target acquisition of SM-3 and 6 and raised serious questions regarding the GMD's effectiveness. Therefore, the discourse on space weaponization is challenging to understand as there are many technical and politically divergent points on which a convergence of opinion is difficult to achieve. As far as space weaponization and development in GMD are concerned, Krepon and Katz-Hyman emphasized that:

> Although some assert that space is already weaponized because ocean-spanning missiles pass through this domain during testing, this argument is akin to claiming that world subways have been weaponized because the AumShinrikyo cult used sarin gas in the Tokyo subway system in 1995.[56]

This is a strong argument by the authors about space weaponization. Other experts also think there is no current deployment of space weapons, and space is not weaponized, in contrast to the above argument on space weaponization. Eligar Sadeh thinks that space is already militarized but not yet weaponized. He thinks that space weapons are not deployed for operational purposes.

Krepon and Katz-Hyman argue that those who think the GMD system has weaponized space mix "residual or latent" capabilities with dedicated space weapon capabilities. Both view that ground-based medium and long-range missile interceptors may be considered space weapons, but these residual capabilities are not dedicated space weapon capabilities. In response to those who think space is not weaponized, Clay Moltz argues that space is weaponized. The reason behind his comprehension of space weapons and weaponization is state's intent. If states test ground-based missile interceptors intending to hit incoming target in its mid-course, then it is considered a space weapon, and it will eventually lead towards weaponization of space. The intent to intercept missile in its mid-course is related to the aftereffects of the test or launch. The states' intentions and motivation to weaponize outer space are the paths to inevitable space weaponization.

Krepon argues that verifying payload aboard a rocket launched into space is challenging. This makes it difficult for independent experts and researchers, especially the adversary, to know the launch's actual intent, what is inside it, and for what purpose it will be launched. Space powers quietly unveil their space capabilities, especially with significant spacefaring states of the U.S., China, and Russia deploying "new and more sophisticated weaponry in space."[57] Axe's argument is understandable because it is difficult to monitor and verify nature of the payload. It is a fact that space technologies are essential for dual use and dual purposes. Given the militarization of space, do states think about space weaponization and developing such capabilities? Although space weaponization is expensive, a state's reliance on space assets is directly proportional to the increasing risks, vulnerabilities, and challenges to its operational space assets. The more space assets are operationalized, the more vulnerable they are to attacks in space from the state adversary, including non-state actors. Axe opines that "many inspection satellites lurk in orbit, possibly awaiting commands to sneak up on disabling or destroying other satellites."[58] Advancements in ground-based missile systems are also likely to change the debate on space weaponization as with the increasing level of accuracy and guidance, ground-based missiles "could reach into orbit to destroy enemy spacecraft."[59]

Space weaponization is essentially pivoted around conventional thought on weapon deployment in which a weapon is developed and deployed in response to enemy's weapon development and deployment. From a non-traditional perspective, which is mainly about employment of non-kinetic means, weaponization of space has offered a different understanding. Sun Tzu argued, "to win one hundred victories in one hundred battles is not the acme of skill. "To subdue the enemy without fighting is the acme of skill."[60] Sun Tzu also believed that supreme method of fighting a war is without fighting a war. His argument for winning and fighting the war points towards non-kinetic means, including jamming, spoofing, dazzling, blinding, and hijacking. From a non-traditionalist perspective, these EW means do fall within scope of space weapons. It means capabilities on the ground or in space if they can damage, impair, hamper, disrupt (permanently), or change satellites' trajectory. They will be considered space weapons. The reason behind acceptance of these Earth and space-based capabilities as space weapons is that satellites are dedicated systems with almost no self-correct or self-repairing mechanisms; however, the U.S is developing Operationally Responsive Space (ORS) capabilities to quickly repair and replace damaged satellites that enable the delivery of timely warfighting effects.[61]

Today, non-kinetic means are more lethal, dangerous, and effective weapons of warfare than kinetic means. The major spacefaring states like the U.S., China, and Russia have demonstrated their kinetic kill space weapons capabilities in ASATs. The states with non-kinetic space weapons have outnumbered those with kinetic space weapons. There are incidents of jamming, spoofing, and hacking of terrestrial and space assets by those states that are emerging space powers. These capabilities are primarily possessed by Non-State Actors (NSAs), i.e. commercial actors. This suggests that in case of an eventuality, i.e. a state's space asset is hacked, blinded, or jammed by a commercial actor. There is a need to widen the scope of definition of space weapons. Likewise, there is a need to understand that non-kinetic means are as lethal and dangerous as kinetic means of warfare.

Furthermore, if there is a need to widen definition of space weapons, it will spill over into space weaponization discourse. The political, economic, strategic, and environmental effects of space weaponization through kinetic means are enormous. Perhaps this is why traditional thought on deploying dedicated space weapons system is not ready to accept that space has been weaponized. However, if non-kinetic means are accepted as dangerous and lethal as kinetic means, space is weaponized from this perspective as states effectively employ these capabilities against each other's assets (Table 5.3). [62]

A BMD system technology is developed, tested, and deployed to intercept or counter incoming ballistic missiles of all ranges: short, medium, intermediate, and long. The U.S. has developed, tested, and deployed world's most sophisticated BMD technology.[63] India is also developing a two-layered BMD shield in South Asia to intercept ballistic missiles launched from Pakistan; however, India also considers its BMD shield to intercept Chinese missiles.[64] China has been critical of U.S. BMD development, but it has demonstrated its BMD capability with a successful test of the high-altitude anti-ballistic missile in 2010. Many defence experts outside China consider it a BMD test, but China provided few details.[65] On February 5, 2018, China demonstrated an anti-missile test. The Chinese Ministry of Defence demonstrated

Table 5.3 Kinds of space weapons

Types		Kinetic	Non-kinetic (electronic interference)
		Weapon systems	
Earth-to-space (Earth-based weapons)		Medium to long-range ballistic missiles	Hijacking, spoofing
		Direct-ascent ASATs	
		Lasers and directed energy weapons (DEWs)	Scanning, dazzling, blinding
Space-to-Earth	Space-based weapons	Hypervelocity rods (kinetic bombardment "Rods from God"	Terrestrial and orbital jamming
Space-to-space		Space-based lasers	
		Co-orbital ASATs, dual-use satellites (microsatellites)	

Source For Electronic interference methods, see Space Security Index, *2017Space Security Index*, September 2017, http://spacesecurityindex.org/2017/10/space-security-2017/;For details on categories of space weapons, see Weeden, "Space Weapons from a Technical Perspective," and "China's BX-1 Microsatellites: A Litmus Test for Space Weaponization," *The Space Review*, October 20, 2008, http://www.thespacereview.com/article/1235/1;For details on targets, characteristics, physics and types of space weapons, see, Preston et al. [141]. For details on microsatellites as dual-use satellites as a threat to space, security see Archinard[142] "ground-based mid-course anti-missile intercept technology" without aiming at any country.[66] The latest anti-missile test reflects that China has been conducting BMD tests for the last decade. It is to counter Southeast Asia's U.S. missile defence shield, especially the latest U.S. THAAD deployment system in South Korea.

A ballistic missile's flight from the starting point to its target on the ground is typically divided into three phases. The first phase is called the boost phase, the second is known as mid-course, in which a missile travels in space, and the last phase is known as the terminal phase or the re-entry phase, in which a missile re-enters the Earth's atmosphere and falls with tremendous speed under the influence of gravity to reach its target. The U.S. has proposed a BMD system that follows a four-phased trajectory: boost, ascent, mid-course, and terminal. However, the current developments are limited to intercepting an incoming missile in its mid-course and terminal phases. However, the U.S. is developing a BMD with space-based components to hit a ballistic missile in its boost phase. The thinking is not new; instead, it dates back to President Reagan's concept of Strategic Defence Initiative (SDI), conceived to build an "iron shield" to intercept the incoming Soviet ballistic missiles and simultaneously launch American missiles to hit targets on enemy territory. Ground-based and space-based systems were initially proposed to build SDI with various interceptors and sensor systems. However, due to high cost of space-based sensors and interception,[67] SDI ideas were never fully hatched, and only a few components were developed.[68] Another reason behind SDI failure is easy countermeasures, which prompted the subsequent administrations after Reagan to discard it with plans to build other programs, like Brilliant Pebbles (BP), Global Protection Against Limited Strikes (GPALS), National Missile Defence (NMD) and BMD.[69]

An important aspect of space weaponization is Earth and space-based BMD. As discussed in detail about Earth-based BMD systems components, which are medium and long-range interceptors, they are generally considered Earth-based space weapons. Experts give one particular reason for these interceptors: they are dual-use. Laura Grego analysed the U.S. hitting its defunct satellite USA-193 in 2008 with its modified missile interceptor SM-3. Before this event, former USSTRATCOM commander General Cartwright announced that the U.S. would destroy Low Earth Orbit (LEO) satellites using Aegis' sea-based BMD system.[70] It was the first time an Earth-based missile interceptor was modified into an anti-satellite missile and successfully achieved its target. The test showed that SM-3 missile interceptor was modified through a Phase-Adaptive Approach (PAA) with a divert capability.[71] Grego assessed the characteristics of missile interceptors of the GMD system and suggests that missile defences have embedded capabilities to target a missile in its mid-course and a satellite moving in orbit around the Earth. If equipped with sensors, locate a target other than a moving missile.[72] Codenamed Operation Burnt, the test of SM-3 to hit a defunct satellite in 2008 saw Aegis BMD and THAAD considered the first point.[73] THAAD consideration is that it can effectively hit a target in LEO. Grego further explained BMD interceptors as ASATs. They can achieve their LEO targets, where most reconnaissance, Earth-observing, Signal Intelligence (SIGINT), and meteorological satellites are stationed. Hence, it is easy to infer that these interceptors can be considered space weapons, thus creating vulnerability to the survival of the adversary satellites in LEO. Likewise, Russia's S-500 missile system is equipped with the same capability as the SM-3.[74]

A space-based BMD system is mainly conceived to intercept an adversary's ballistic missiles in its boost phase. Likewise, a ground-based launch is located inside adversary's territory in case of a land-based ICBM; however, significant powers, the U.S, Russia, China, France, India, and the United Kingdom (UK), have Submarine-Launched Ballistic Missiles (SLBMs). Recently, Pakistan also fired a cruise missile, Babur-2, from a submerged platform, opening its entry into the elite group of nations having such capabilities. So, from this aspect, two factors largely account for developing a space-based BMD system: the launching site and the time required to complete the boost phase of the ballistic missile. A space-based BMD deployment aims to hit a ballistic missile in its boost phase, deny it from entering its mid-course, and intercept it before escaping the Earth's gravitational field. Therefore, a space-based BMD system is like hitting a ballistic missile just after it takes off. However, for a space-based BMD system, a full range of space- and Earth-based early warning and detection satellites are required for deployment during peacetime and in a potential crisis. For an effective space-based BMD, a network of satellites with advanced multipurpose sensors and detection is required to achieve the primary objectives of directing a missile interceptor launched from space to hit its target as it launches from the ground. Likewise, if a missile escapes from Earth's gravitational field, early warning satellites do not detect it, or a missile interceptor fails to intercept in its boost phase. The second layer of the space-based BMD system will hit the target in its mid-course. These are the two-layered space-based BMD systems. In this system, direct energy weapons (DEWs) in high-energy lasers and kinetic kill vehicles (KKVs) will intercept the missile in its boost phase and mid-course.[75] However, a space-based BMD system has not emerged and will be realized in its proper operational form or deployment. If states build a space-based BMD system, there will be no disagreement on land that space has not been weaponized.[76]

A space-based BMD system has suffered from numerous constraints and has ramifications for international strategic stability. Likewise, analysts believe that it has some easy countermeasures. Instead of developing their own space-based BMD in response, they would develop cost-effective and technologically less advanced countermeasures. Alwyn Young writes about three significant factors blocking the path towards achieving a space-based BMD: "A space-based BMD must deal with: a) defending the target set and successfully coping with penetration aids and countermeasures; b) defending the BMD components themselves to prevent a total collapse of the system, and c) gaining favourable cost-exchange ratios concerning the offensive."[77] However, cost-effective countermeasures have not stopped the states from thinking about developing such systems.

The definition of an ASAT weapon is very similar to the broad definition of a space weapon. Primarily, ASAT weapons are developed to hamper or disrupt (temporary or permanent) or physically damage the activities or functions of the adversary's satellite in space. Moreover, the destruction or damage of the enemy's satellites is for "strategic military purposes and to protect home satellites."[78] Based on their ability to cause damage to a target, ASAT can be divided into different categories:

Isotropic Nuclear Weapons (INW), kinetic-energy weapons (KEWs), and DEWs. See Table 5.4 for details.

The debate on the definition and utility of space weapons suggests that significant space powers have developed them as a matter of political, strategic, and economic choice to deploy these weapons in space. A critical question regarding space weaponization is whether space weapons are needed or states should develop these lethal capabilities only for deterrence. Before answering the question, it is essential to understand major and emerging space powers' space militarization and weaponization capabilities. One limitation of the research is that there is very little information about exact number of capabilities the significant spacefaring states possess and nature of the assets, whether for military or peaceful purposes. As a result, it would be difficult to make a head-on count of military space assets of even selected states like the U.S., China, Russia, India, and Pakistan. The research has adopted simple qualitative and quantitative tools to measure these space powers' military space capabilities. For this purpose, space militarization and weaponization capabilities, and any future space weapons programs of the U.S., China, India, and Pakistan are discussed.

The U.S

The U.S. is undoubtedly leading global space order with world's largest space fleet, which has expanded since the dawn of the Space Age. It has 5,184 satellites including 30 civil, 4,741 commercial,167 Government owned and 246 military purpose satellites. U.S. reliance on space assets has increased since the Cold War. It effectively utilized its space power during the first Gulf War. It was a mini space war as it decimated the Iraqi military with its airpower in collaboration with space capabilities.

The Joint Publication 3–14, titled *Space Operations,* highlights that the U.S. military space program aims to develop most of its capabilities to build a Space Situational Awareness (SSA) network, space force enhancement, space support, space control, and space force application.[79] The U.S. has been creating these capabilities since the beginning of space age. It has sent thousands of satellites into space to build its current space militarization capabilities. Table 5.5 gives a bird's eye view of U.S. force enhancement, application, support, and enabling capabilities, including ISR early warning, metrological, communication, navigation PNT, geodesy, and oceanography satellite capabilities.

The U.S. National Oceanic and Atmospheric Administration (NOAA) is an important organ of its overall military space program. NOAA systems continuously monitor Earth's changing electromagnetic field, provide military readiness data, and are mostly used to monitor space weather. NOAA systems are mainly used for geodesy, a force multiplier enhancing military dominance.

The *Digital National Security Archive* has published a detailed document titled *Chronology: U.S. Military Uses of Space, 1945–1991,* to highlight the U.S.' efforts to militarize space in the past. The document highlights the U.S. military space

Table 5.4 Types of ASAT weapons

Types	Position	Weapon	Lethality/Function/ Damage	Target orbit
Isotropic nuclear weapons	Ground-based	Co-orbital interceptor	The explosion causes radiation and electromagnetic pulse (EMP), physical damage, and hampers, disrupts, and destroys the function of the satellite 1967 Outer Space Treaty prohibits the placement of nuclear weapons in the orbits	Low and high Earth orbit
		Direct-ascent interceptor		
	Space-based	Co-orbital interceptor (space mines)	Nuclear explosive direct energy weapons (NDEW) are not available	
Kinetic-energy weapons	Ground-based	Co-orbital interceptor	Direct impact with low and high speeds resulted in the physical destruction of the target	
		Direct-ascent interceptor		
	Space-based	Co-orbital interceptor (space mine)		
		Non-orbital interceptor		
Direct energy weapons	Ground-based	High-power radio-frequency (HPRF) and active electronic countermeasures (ECM)	**HPRF**: overload and damage satellite electronic equipment **Low-PRF**: merely to temporarily overload satellite electronic systems (i.e. for "jamming ")	All levels of conflict
		High-energy laser (HEL) and active electro-optical countermeasures (E-OCM)	**HPRF**: Permanently damaging the satellite **Low-PRF**: • Jamming, • spoofing (deceive), • dazzling (temporarily blinding)	
	Space-based	High-power radio-frequency (HPRF) and active electronic countermeasures (ECM)	Same as ground-based HPRF and HEL	All levels of conflict

(continued)

Table 5.4 (continued)

Types	Position	Weapon	Lethality/Function/ Damage	Target orbit
		High-energy laser (HEL) and active electro-optical countermeasures (E-OCM)		
		Neutral-particle beam (NPB)	Physical damage to electronic parts of the satellite	Low-Earth orbit

Source U.S. Congress, Office of Technology Assessment [143]; Grego [144]

used to identify past U.S. military space activities.[80] Likewise, Jeffery Richelson has done more elaborate work in books on U.S. space satellites for spying purposes. In *America's Space Sentinels: A History of the DSP and SBIRS Satellite Systems*, Richelson briefly explained U.S. military space activities, especially focusing on creating and evolving the MIDAS/Defence Support Program (DSP). These programs were developed to analyse data collected through sensors and surveillance.[81]

The increasing U.S. reliance on space assets has increased its operational space assets. However, it has also increased perceived security challenges for U.S. space assets. With the advancement of space technology, the pool of emerging space powers and aspiring nations is increasing. However, the U.S.' worrisome development is Russia's and China's increasing space capabilities, especially their military space developments. Under President Donald Trump's Administration, National Security Strategy emphasized that the U.S. wants "unfettered access to and freedom to operate in space to a vital interest."[82] The document suggests that U.S. closely monitors all those states pursuing a range of ASAT weapons. In case any activity interferes or affects its interest in space, it "will be met with a deliberate response at a time, place, manner, and domain of our choosing."[83] In this scenario, two major challenges face the U.S.' space assets. First, emerging and aspiring space powers are developing their capabilities to achieve national security and economic goals. Second, states are developing capabilities that "can defeat or destroy American space assets."[84] According to Gene McCall and John Darrah, Russia and China are developing ASAT missiles, high-power laser, and microwave technology to counter U.S' space assets. From the U.S. point of view, these devices and technology developments are its mission-defeat assets.[85]

There is a need to secure space assets while maintaining a database of comprehensive awareness about activities of other nations and space weather and environment, especially the movement of asteroids and meteoroids in space. The U.S has created a modern and technologically advanced SSA structure to address the above. SSA is designed to track position of space objects, monitor communications, monitor activities in geostationary orbits, determine passive threats to U.S. space assets, and

Table 5.5 U.S. Space militarization capabilities: force multiplier/enhancement capabilities

Space militarization capabilities	Current systems
Intelligence, surveillance, reconnaissance (ISR)	• Space-Based Infrared System (SBIRS)-high and low • Defence Support Program (DSP) • For reconnaissance, major satellite series (Onyx and Topaz)
	• IMINT (Key Hole (KH) and Lacrosse Series) • ELINT (Orion, Mentor Series, Mercury, Nemesis, Sharp, Trumpet and Improved Trumpet, NROL-85) • MASINT (Nuclear Detonation System)
Missile launch (early warning) and tracking (14)	• Space Situational Network (SSN): Defence Support Program, GPS, space-based infrared system, space tracking, and surveillance system
Environmental monitoring (space weather) (4)	• Defence Meteorological Satellite Program (DMSP)
Satellite communications (66)	• Defence Satellite Communications System (DSCS) III • Military Strategic and Tactical Relay (MILSTAR) • AEHF • SDS III & IV • TacSat-4,6 • WGS SV 2 • Ultrahigh Frequency Follow-on (UFO) Satellites,
Positioning, navigation and timing (PNT) (30)	• Global Positioning System (GPS) IIR, IIR-M, IIF, III
Navigation and NAVWAR	• Global Positioning System (GPS-1, 2 and 3) • Major satellite series (Transit and Navstar)
Nuclear detonation detection	• Integrated Operational Nuclear Detection System (Vela Satellite Series)
Geodesy and oceanography	• GEOSAT, GFO, SECOR, TOPO, LIDOS, SALT

Source Union of Concerned Scientists [145]; Evans [146]; Sadeh [147]

provide facilities to control space assets and sensors.[86] Also, "it is a broad and fundamental set of activities that provide essential knowledge to improve the effectiveness of activities in the other space mission areas." (Figs. 5.1 and 5.2)[87]

To augment SSA capabilities and foster surveillance network, the U.S. government planned to spend US$ 6 billion. The figure is not "comprehensive, nonetheless represents one of the most detailed accounting of SSA programs and funding released to date." Significantly, the lion's share of the funding went to the Pentagon and NASA, "accounting for 10 per cent of the total."[90]

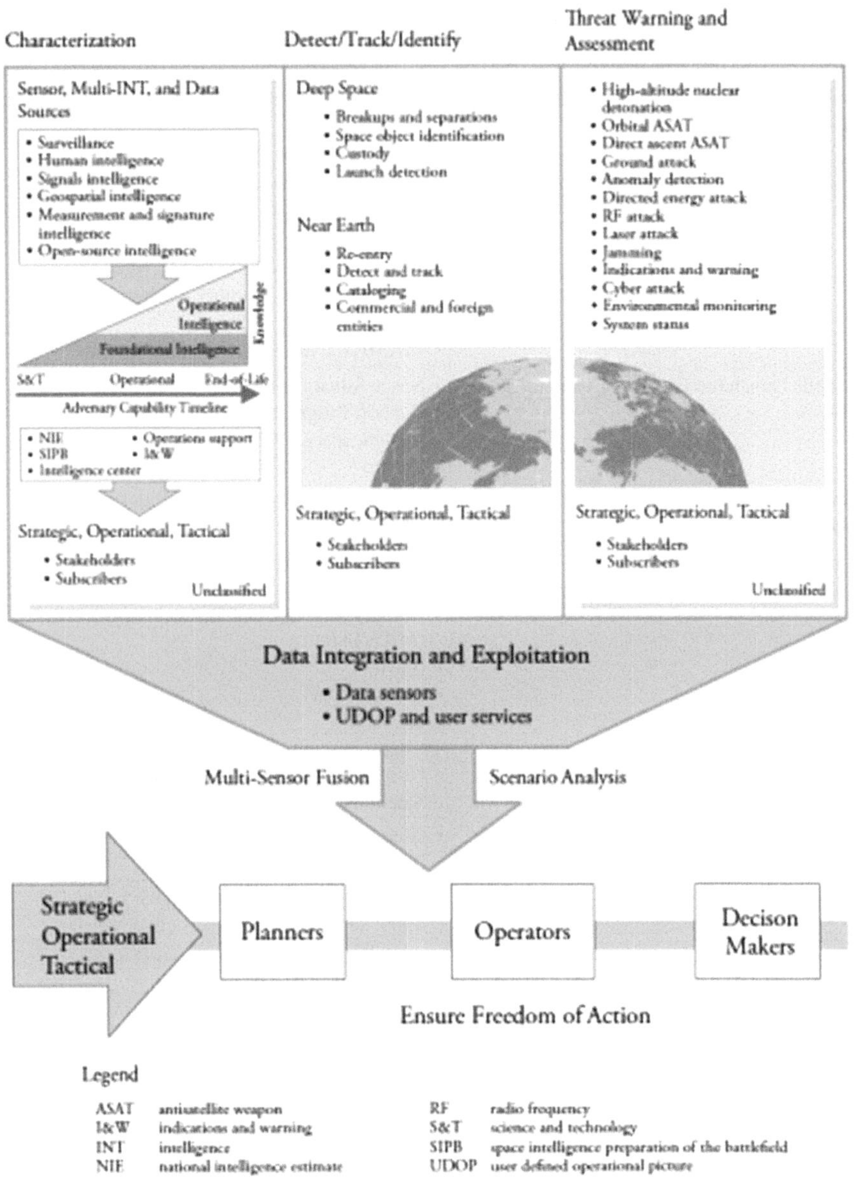

Fig. 5.1 SSA capabilities[88]

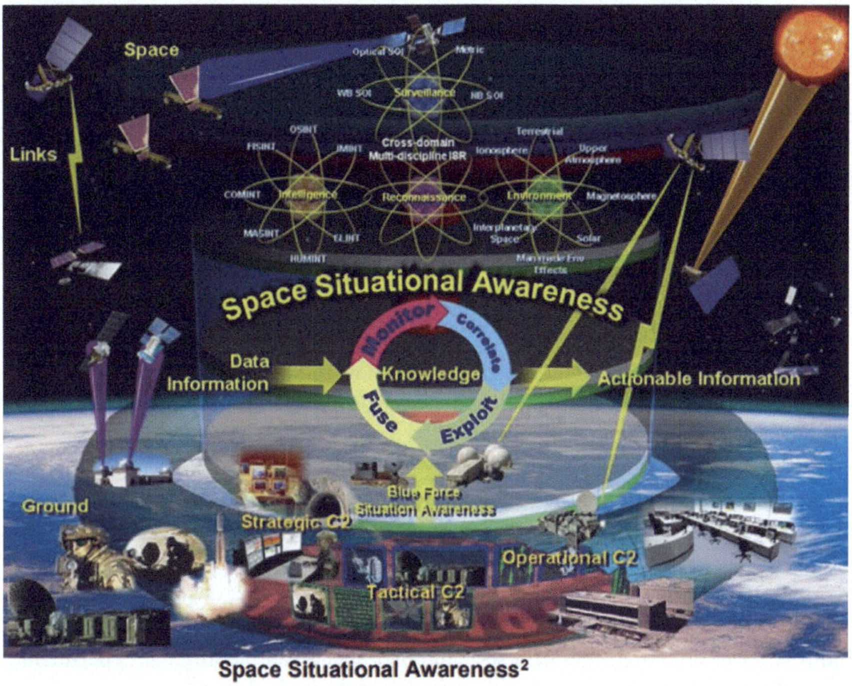

Fig. 5.2 SSA network[89]

In the future, the U.S. is looking to park its dual-use assets in Lagrange Points (see Fig. 5.3).[91] Lagrange points are between the earth and the moon. The Space Force and U.S commercial companies are looking to orbit cislunar monitoring satellites and /or space. DARPA recently launched its 10-year Lunar Architecture (Luna-10) capability study to tap technologies for a sustainable and profitable space ecosystem linking the earth and the moon, especially the cislunar space.

The U.S. is exploring these points in space for deep space exploration and building an advanced SSA network to monitor the activities of hostile forces in space. These

Fig. 5.3 Five Lagrange points associated with the Sun-Earth system

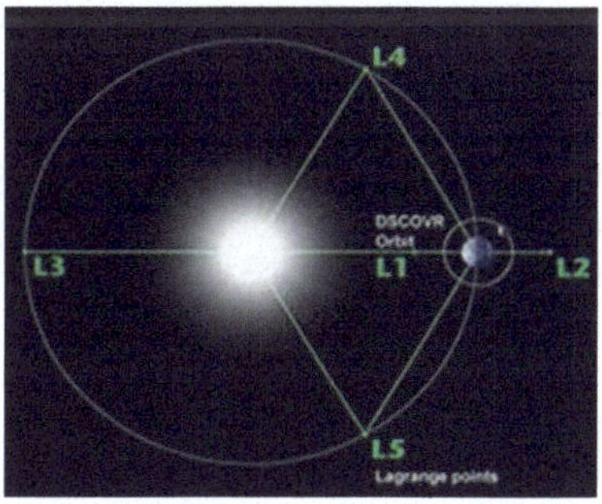

dual-use parking lots in space will allow the U.S. to build a platform to launch future deep space exploration missions and carry out military space activities.

The important point is that since these points or parking places will be explored under NASA, most of the payload will be carried under the supervision of U.S. defence forces. Hence, it can be inferred that if the U.S. Army or Air Force carries the payload, it will be an effort to militarise outer space further.[92]

The development, testing, demonstration, and launching of X-37B have been shrouded in secrecy. The X-37B program was initially conceived, developed, and demonstrated by the U.S. Air Force. According to the official USAF description, X-37B is an Orbital Test Vehicle (OTV) designed to test as a "technology demonstrator and experimental vehicle" to develop new technologies to build a reusable Space Launch Vehicle (SLV).[93] The program's official understanding is about building reusable SLVs; however, the vehicle can also be used for "orbital inspection, repair, and retrieval."[94]

The program has some specific military space uses directly proportional to space weaponization. Experts see the development and successful stay of X-37B as giving the U.S. a backdoor channel to space weaponization. Its secrecy has created fears and doubts in states like China and Russia about the actual beginning of space weaponization. It is widely believed that X-37B can carry a constellation of KKVs in the LEO, station there, and hit or intercept an incoming missile in its mid-course flight. After completing its four tests[95] in outer space and passing the experimental phase, the USAF has inducted and operationalized two X-37Bs.[96]

Subrata Ghoshory argues that the U.S is the principal driver of space weaponization, and its Space Test Bed (STB). "X-37B is indeed being used to help develop critical technologies that lead down the path to the eventual weaponization of space."[97] The development and subsequent induction of X-37B are integral to U.S. efforts to follow a path from space militarization to space weaponization.[98] Like many others, he has assessed the technologies used in building X-37B and finds that the plane can carry missiles and launch these missiles from space or re-enter into the Earth's atmosphere to hit targets in an anti-access/area-denial (A2/AD) environment.[99] The operationalization of X-37B is another step towards space weaponization, a significant space weaponization capability. Although many experts do not think in the same manner as explained by Ghoshory. Here a question germinates over why the USAF has still not shared details of the mission and its flight parameters. X-37B is believed to be a countermeasure to Russia and China's increasing ASAT capabilities. General John Hyten, Former Commander of USSTRATCOM, told CBS about present-day competition between the U.S., China, and Russia. "It is a competition that I wish was not occurring, but it is."[100] Likewise, Former Air Force Secretary Heather Wilson and General Hyten told CBS correspondent David Martin that "The U.S is prepared to fight a war in space today, but not in the future."[101] An analysis of their argument suggests that the U.S. possesses ample space weaponization capability to fight a war in space, and the operationalization and induction of X-37B are significant steps towards fostering its capabilities. Another key question on the X-37B is why the USAF has never shared technologies used in building these reusable spacecraft and why it has over-stayed in space. These questions still need answers to these questions related to the secrecy of X-37B, which can be used as a space weapon.

ORS is built and modelled on the USAF's old Rapid Capabilities Office (RCO) foundations. ORS's primary purpose is to build redundant capabilities and replace them promptly in case of physical damage or permanent blindness of a satellite. The idea is to build such capabilities to replace defunct or physically destroyed satellites in case an enemy's ASAT hits U.S. satellites in any orbit. Since its establishment in 2007, the ORS has shown progress, and according to the 2017 Space Security Index, the U.S. has remained focused on space mission assurance, emphasizing space resilience.[102]

It is difficult to determine a state's exact course of action in space for future. For the U.S., future is congested, crowded, and contested in space. There will be more actors in space and further expansion of space capabilities of its adversaries, Russia and China. Due to its immense reliance on its space assets for dual-uses purposes, any space conflict would eventually lead to further development and multilateral deployment of space weapons. U.S is looking towards developing a full-scale strategic review of space warfare. Four significant objectives are driving a strategic framework, which includes a) strengthening and safety of the U.S. space assets and activities, b) establishing assured space deterrence and building necessary and sufficient space capabilities to defeat adversaries, c) rapidly establishing Public–Private Partnership (PPP) within the U.S. commercial sector, and d) maintaining U.S pre-eminence in space science and defence.[103]

Heather Wilson notes that the U.S. needs offensive space weapons, and "we [U.S.] need the ability to create effects, defend ourselves, and deter actions."[104] The statement from Former U.S. Air Force Secretary is like putting new wine into old bottles. Likewise, new strategic framework objectives are similar to previous space posture reviews and policies. However, the U.S. is the principal follower of the path leading from space militarization to weaponization.

The U.S administrations are keen on augmenting U.S. militarization and weaponization capability. Future development will continue, and the U.S. may not look back until soon to shun its space weapon development capabilities. The current trajectory of U.S. space activities for dual-use purposes is strengthening its commercial industry and developing more space resilience capabilities. From the fundamental manifestation of deterrence, building capabilities are among the three elemental manifestations of any deterrence. For assured space deterrence, U.S. wants to build offensive counterspace capabilities in future to persuade its adversaries not to commit any course of action against it.[105] However, the U.S. is also committed to its primary objectives of freedom of action in space under its space control doctrine. For both objectives, the U.S. needs abundance and redundant space capabilities to maintain a status quo in global space order and its pre-eminence in future.

A report launch ceremony organized by CSIS, Former Commander of U.S. Army Space and Missile Defence Command, General James Dickinson, highlighted some critical threats to U.S. national security. One is the technological advancement of U.S. adversaries in EW, counterspace, hypersonic missiles, and cyberspace. He suggested that the U.S. expand its kinetic capabilities with a cost-effective approach. The

U.S. has demonstrated Ground-based Mid-course Defence (GMD) capability and expanded its capacity in recent years. In May 2017, the Homeland Missile Defence (HMD) System successfully intercepted a ballistic missile target during the FTG-15 flight test. It increased the number of ground-based interceptors from 14 in 2016 to 44 in 2017. HMD plans to conduct the GMD salvo flight test of FTG-19, and the U.S. Army anticipates long-range discrimination radar induction, added to the U.S. BMD architecture. In addition to these capabilities, the U.S. is also developing and testing new capabilities like high-energy lasers, EW capabilities, and high-powered microwaves, among other cost-effective solutions.

As an enterprise, the U.S. Army Space and Missile Defence Command invests in developing, acquiring, and integrating some of the emerging technologies that provide a technological edge against the emerging threats in all mediums of warfare, including space. Army Space and Missile Defence Command is investing in DEWs, and it has the potential to be a low-cost and effective complement to kinetic-energy options. The command is experimenting with a 50KW laser with a fire manoeuvre, a striker, and a mobile high-energy system with a fire manoeuvre. This has successfully achieved its broad targets, and the command is developing and operationalizing more high-power lasers up to 150 KW in the future. The U.S. Army actively pursues a "left-of-launch" strategy for many threat sets. The term refers to any capability that affects the enemy's ability to employ ballistic missiles, including cyber, space, and air capabilities, before they have missiles in flight. However, sustainable financial resources are required to build these capabilities, as a missile interceptor may cost millions of dollars to develop. Likewise, it would not be cost-effective if a single missile worth millions of dollars were launched to intercept a missile worth a few hundred thousand dollars. U.S. Army is also actively developing a concept of multidomain battles as a joint services concept for the twenty-first century. This includes developing warfighting capabilities for the physical domain and emphasizing space and information environments, including cyberspace and the electromagnetic spectrum.

The U.S. Army is also developing multidomain task force initiatives that may change it. The intent is to integrate organic and joint counterair, counterfire, cyberspace, and space capabilities to ensure joint force freedom of action, and earliest deterrence. The initial concept was approved in 2017, with a U.S. Pacific Command-led pilot program that will be conducted in the coming years. The U.S. Army is developing a new strategy to address emerging threats and develop capabilities to fight multidomain battles from land to space.[106]

China

The Chinese space launch rate remained low in first twenty years of China's space program. On the other hand, China continuously made progress in its space program, and in 2016, the Chinese space launch industry showed a "strong performance." China continued to increase them by developing its indigenous manufacturing of

SLVs and simultaneously showing significant progress in its satellite manufacturing industry through rigorous research and development (R&D). Due to its space program's linear but steady progress, China eventually surpassed Russia in 2015 to become the second global space power after the U.S. regarding active (operational) satellites in outer space. Although the combined number of space launches (successful and failed) of the former Soviet Union and modern-day Russia is more than the total number of space launches by the U.S., the number of dead Russian satellites has increased.[107]

China considers space as one of its national security organs and an essential factor in its overall national growth.[108] Likewise, its space program has significantly contributed to its national economy. China has increased its cooperation at the regional and global levels, providing comparatively lower space launch costs to developing countries than the U.S. and Russia. China has significantly increased its military space activities over the years, and in this regard, it has increased its space budget to meet the demand of its national security.[109] However, an essential aspect of Chinese space activities budget is that it does not mention how much has been spent on its civilian and military space programs.

A European space writer, Brian Harvey, argues that the twenty-first century has witnessed a significant emergence of space power after the U.S. and the former Soviet Union.[110] China has achieved a global space power status.[111] It has made tremendous development in its space program in the last decade.[112] China has sent hundreds of payloads into space and successfully placed them for dual-use purposes.

China has developed various space militarization and weaponization capabilities and has followed the path from space militarization to space weaponization. It has developed and intends to bolster its existing space technologies to expand space militarization and weaponization capabilities. It has invested in building a Large Phased Array Radar (LPAR) that supports offensive and defensive capabilities, supporting Chinese ASATs or Ballistic Missile Early Warning (BMEW). China has built SLVs that can carry communication, data relay, SSA, and airborne imaging systems and travel near space. China vigorously invests in imagery, navigation, communication, data relay, and ISR system satellites. Table 5.6 shows Chinese military space capabilities used as a force multiplier or enhancement. Its space program is expanding and has improved its space-based ISR, satellite communication, navigation, meteorology, human spaceflight, and robotic space exploration.

In 2016, China successfully launched the world's first quantum communication satellite, which shows a notable advancement in cryptography science in China and will further secure its existing communication network as Quantum satellites are hack-proof.[113] Likewise, China is heavily investing in building its (A2/AD) capabilities.[114] These capabilities manifest the Chinese A2/AD strategy "based around restricting enemy access to a certain strategic location."[115] A2/AD is primarily designed to "deter, dissuade, or defeat" a third party's involvement in an armed conflict over a territorial dispute.[116] Salients of Chinese A2/AD strategy include developing long-range precision strikes, BMD systems, offensive and defensive capabilities for surface and underwater operations, and space and counterspace capabilities. In implementing A2/AD, China is rapidly developing space and counterspace

Table 5.6 Chinese space militarization capabilities

Space militarization capabilities	Current systems
Communication (11)	Major satellite series (FH, ST) FH-1&2, ST-1&2
Early warning (5)	Huoyan-1
ISR (92)	Jianbing, Tianhui, LKW, Yaogan series satellites
Navigation (45)	Beidou-1, 2 and 3
Ocean surveillance (8)	Yunhai series
SIGINT, COMINT, ELINT (81)	Yoagan Series, Chuangxin, Jianbing, Qianshao, Shijian series satellites

FH = Feng Huo, TJS = Tongxin Jishu Shiyan, FSH = Fanhui Shi Weixing, JSSW = Ji Shu Shiyan Weixing, ST = Shen Tong
Source Heginbotham et al. [148]

capabilities, focusing on " ISR and advanced targeting, communications, naval, air, missile defence, and cyber capabilities."[117] China now has more satellites in space than Russia. However, it is still far behind the U.S. China's space program is expanding and is likely to complete its constellation of navigation satellites and launch more meteorological satellites used for amphibious military strikes.

China has released five White Papers since 2000 describing its space activities' principles, aims, objectives, goals, and plans. The 2016 White Paper says China plans to send more high-resolution land observation satellites into space for environmental and land surveying purposes. It is also planning to send marine and atmospheric observation satellites soon. Nonetheless, China has transformed its Asia–Pacific-oriented BeiDou navigation system into a dual-use global enterprise with an expansion of its PNT capabilities.[118] For this purpose, it has added remaining satellites into its BeiDou constellation, improving its positioning accuracy by about four times.[119] BeiDou has provided "low-rate data transmission for the People's Liberation Army (PLA) forces."[120] One of the main reasons behind Chinese investment in building its global navigation enterprise was the denial of GPS during the Taiwan Strait crisis. China decided to place its satellites in space in early 1980s to reduce its military reliance on the U.S. GPS. Initially, China had only developed a small navigation system named Compass. However, it building a larger constellation of navigation satellites in early 2004. From now on, China has stretched the scope of its BeiDou system and offered services to several of its regional partners, such as Pakistan and Iran. China extended its regional navigation system from a more extensive regional level to a global one, officially named Compass Navigation Satellite System (CNSS). A careful assessment suggests that China have 35 satellites in its global navigation system. These satellites have increased the PLA's reliance on the system, giving passive guidance for military applications and improving the precision and accuracy of its strategic strike weapons. As a result of CNSS, Chinese reliance on GPS has diminished.[121]

One of the global trends in space militarization is the improvement of SSA capabilities of the U.S., China, and Russia. The U.S. is the leading spacefaring state with expanding SSA capabilities. However, China is also following suit.[122] China is developing capabilities to monitor the space environment, focusing on risks of debris collision, mitigation, early warning, and protection of its space assets. China is assumed to have SSA sensors and a phased array radar network, "each likely to have 3,000 km range and 120 degrees of azimuth coverage," and will likely improve this capability shortly.[123] Bharath Gopalaswamy that China is still lagging behind the U.S. and Russia in the global SSA network, and he thinks that China still needs to develop more capabilities to make its global SSA network.[124]

Some assessments about the development of Chinese counterspace and ASAT capabilities suggest that China has rapidly expanded them in recent years. Observers believe in a possible Sino-U.S. armed conflict in future. According to Daniel Coats:

> We [U.S intelligence agencies] assess that, if a future conflict were to occur involving Russia or China, either country would justify attacks against US and allied satellites as necessary to offset any perceived US military advantage derived from military, civil, or commercial space systems.[125]

U.S. intelligence agencies believe that if Chinese space capabilities continue to grow at this pace, then Chinese counterspace capabilities "could endanger assets that are critical to Washington's launch-on-warning nuclear posture."[126] In 2015, China "has built a vast ground infrastructure supporting spacecraft and SLV manufacture, launch command and control (C^2), and data downlink."[127] China has developed counterspace capabilities that aim to "degrade and deny the use of space-based assets by adversaries during a crisis or conflict."[128]

Since the beginning of the twenty-first century, Chinese ASAT missile test 2007 has been the most widely discussed space incident. It was any state's first successful ASAT missile test after the Cold War. Before this test knocked out a defunct Chinese weather satellite, only the U.S. and the former Soviet Union could test such capabilities. The 2007 ASAT test allowed China to demonstrate its capability of hitting a satellite in space. In a discussion with Noah Shachtman, Geoffery Forden argues that Chinese test "threw the international community into a panic."[129] Forden argues that "U.S. forces have worried about an attack on U.S. satellites." These worries stem from the increasing pool of actors in space.[130] Likewise, Forden published his assessment of a possible Chinese space assault on American satellites in case of an armed conflict. He thinks that Chinese capabilities are insufficient to withstand U.S. space capabilities but are enough to damage U.S. intelligence-gathering satellites. Nevertheless, he concludes that if China can destroy half of U.S. navigation satellites and ISR capability in a worst-case scenario, the U.S. will continue to survive and provide data to its ground army to launch an attack on the Chinese military.[131]

China has developed high-tech microsatellites with proximity functions. China has made significant advancements in establishing a domestic industrial base to expand its satellite manufacturing industry. On January 9, 2018, a congressional hearing was held to assess China's pursuit of emerging and exponential technologies. During the hearing, Congressman Austin Scott asked a question about expanding China's satellite industry. The witnesses testified that China's satellite industry is rapidly expanding and is attracting worldwide customers.[132] Besides this observation, it is believed that China "envisions using microsatellites for numerous civil and military missions, using formations of smaller satellites to reduce vulnerability to attack."[133] Notably, China has launched numerous microsatellites over the years and plans to send them in GEO and Polar orbits. Likewise, China has built mobile SLVs to launch microsatellites and nanosatellites for military purposes.

China's manned space program is a significant source of its electronic intelligence as it is widely believed that the Shenzhou spacecraft provides substantial Electronic Intelligence (ELINT) and image-gathering capability.[134] Previously launched Shenzhou-6, 1, and 2 contained ELINT capability. The Shenzhou spacecraft has successfully docked in space. Shenzhou-8 docked with Tiangong-1, 340 km above sea level. Likewise, Shenzhou-9 also successfully docked with Tiangong-1 in 2012, and Shenzhou-10 docked with Tiangong-1 in 2013. The successful docking of the China Shenzhou spacecraft highlighted some key dual-use purposes. In 2008, China partially blinded one of the many U.S. reconnaissance satellites in LEO with its ground-based lasers. The targeting has shown that China has some advanced high-power laser systems. China has developed a laser with a capability ranging from 50 to 100 kW, which is believed to reach 1 MW in the future. A one MW laser can hit a target 5000 km away.[135]

U.S. space experts believe that Chinese counterspace capabilities severely threaten U.S. space activities. Ashely Tellis, a senior fellow at Carnegie Endowment for International Peace (CEIP), in a congressional hearing of the U.S. Senate Armed Committee's subcommittee, argued that current trajectory and evolving Chinese counterspace capabilities pose a serious threat to U.S. military operations in Asia–Pacific.[136] Tellis further stated that China's rapid development and diversity in its counterspace program, especially development of direct-ascent and co-orbital ASATs threaten U.S space operations. China is also increasing and fostering its EW capabilities and has shown a keen interest in developing its DEWs, radio-frequency weapons, and computer network attack capabilities. These capabilities are used for the soft killing of the satellites and are very difficult to respond to as there are attribution challenges.[137]

Ashley Tellis also thinks it is difficult for the U.S. to dissuade China from investing in counterspace capabilities. The only plausible reason is the Chinese thinking of having a geopolitical competition with the U.S. This thinking has driven its military planners to prepare an aggressive military space strategy and develop capabilities to neutralize U.S. space assets in any future armed conflict.[138] Chinese counterspace capabilities are diversified, remarkable, and comprehensive. China's major emphasis on developing counterspace capabilities is to build surveillance and identification systems, including DEWs for dazzling and blinding satellites, capabilities for EW to launch "attacks against space platforms and their associated links as well as against conventional forces and their warfighting operation," and "improving kinetic and non-kinetic forms of ground attack aimed at the control segments of an adversary's space infrastructure."[139]

China also has an incentive to target LEO satellites. These satellites are used for photographic reconnaissance and surveillance purposes, and Chinese counterspace capabilities can interfere with their function through laser dazzling. Likewise,

Chinese counterspace arsenal includes terrestrial and orbital communication satellites jamming. Michael Krepon argues that Chinese counterspace capabilities present during the Cold War are not new. At that time, the U.S. was focusing on the Soviet threat. Chinese counterspace capabilities are a new threat to U.S. space programs. The U.S. does not need further development of its counterspace capability "that messes space up for the other guy and us."[140]

China's space strategy primarily focuses on building A2/AD capabilities in the region. A reason behind building such capabilities is to deny the U.S. any strategic orientation to counter rising Chinese military and economic power in and around its mainland, especially in Southeast Asia. It is also building artificial islands in Southeast Asia, most of which were built to provide military support to PLA operations in the region.[141] China is building its space program to augment its A2/AD capabilities for this particular purpose. The post-Cold War, the geopolitical realities have changed and shifted eastward because of rising Chinese power.[142] Since 1950, the U.S. has protected and preserved its interests in the Eurasian region. To further consolidate its interests after the Cold War, the U.S. is making efforts under its rebalancing strategy to safeguard the Eurasian space and not let any local power emerge as a regional hegemon currently, AS rising Chinese power may pose a potential threat to the rebalancing efforts of the U.S. and the security of U.S. allies in Southeast Asia.

There are four underpinning elements to the rebalance strategy. First, China's rise is an enduring reality. Second, China must be managed in ways other than war. Although the U.S. has all the military means to coerce China, the luxury of war as an instrument to contain China would not be cost-effective. Such an assertion is that Chinese and U.S. economies are interdependent. This was not the case during the Cold War, as the U.S. and USSR did not share any interdependence, and it was easier to contain the Soviet Union. Third, China has risen so dramatically that an in-equilibrium has occurred in the East, increasing the U.S. allies' demands for an increased U.S. presence. The U.S. has to deal with China at the bilateral and multilateral levels to prevent its allies from bandwagoning with China, thereby enhancing Beijing's regional power. The rebalance is a way to sustain U.S. credibility as a regional security provider. The U.S. strategy is based on three core elements: military, economic, and diplomatic. Rebalance has involved an expansion of spatial components of U.S. strategy. This means the rebalance is not towards East Asia but the Indo-Pacific region.

The U.S. has significantly increased its military presence throughout the region. Guam, Australia, and the Philippines have seen U.S. military reinforcement. The U.S. is finding ways to defeat China's A2/AD strategy. If China can employ the A2/AD strategy and deny U.S. military reinforcement to reach the periphery of Asia, it will be the end of the U.S.-Asian alliance system. This is an essential and severe development as the U.S. sees Chinese counterspace capabilities with a pinch of salt. If the U.S. failed to counter Chinese A2/AD and its rising space power in the region, there would be serious setbacks to the U.S. rebalancing its core national interests in the Asian region.

Gopalaswamy regards China's military program as having significantly developed ASAT capabilities. China has developed kinetic-energy ASATs and has taken space "as a theatre to counter U.S. military space assets." China considers its kinetic-energy space weaponry essential to deter aggression on its space assets. Likewise, China is also developing non-kinetic ability since 2006. Chinese advancement in developing its kinetic and non-kinetic space weapons elements is troubling, creating vulnerabilities to U.S. space assets.[143]

India

On April 30, 1970, the U.S embassy in New Delhi sent a telegram titled *Indian Rocket and Satellite Launching Capabilities* to the State Department, Washington DC, highlighting a growing confusion in Indian space scientist community regarding "the size, range, payload, and status of development of launching vehicles and necessary propellants, guidance systems, etc."[144] The telegram also highlights that thirty American scientists were to help Indian scientists conduct scientific experiments at Thumba to get accurate information about the abovementioned issues.[145] The observations of India's space program activities in the past and their present status suggest that India has come a long way to achieving excellence in its space program. The long journey started in 1975 when India launched its first satellite in space, and in 1980, India became the sixth country to achieve its indigenous satellite launch capability.[146] A comparison between the last ten years for space launches by India and between 1975 and 2019 shows a drastic improvement in its space launches.

India's space program got help from the former Soviet Union and collaborated with Russia. Likewise, India got help from the U.S. at the beginning of its space program, and both countries are still collaborating in multiple areas.[147] The U.S. help to augment India's space program is evident from the history. However, it is also evident that on May 22, 1989, India became the first country in the world to test a strategic missile derived from a civilian space program, writes Gary Milhollin. On January 12, 2018, India launched its 100th satellite in space.[148] Likewise, Indian scientists claimed that the Indian Space Research Organization (ISRO) could manufacture a mini-PSLV in three days. The scientific achievement was revealed by the Former Director of Thiruvananthapuram-based Vikram Sarabhai Space Centre (VSSC), Dr K Sivan, while speaking to the journalists on the sidelines of a seminar titled *Indian Space Program* held in November 2017.[149] If India can manufacture and launch its mini-PSLV soon, it would be another feather in its space cap. India's civilian and controlled program progresses with a balanced and focused agenda. Likewise, according to the U.S. Defence Intelligence Agency's assessment, "India uses a building block approach to develop its space program."[150]

Moreover, India is just a small step away from making its first space shuttle. On May 23, 2016, Indian scientists announced that India would begin its mission to launch its first indigenous space shuttle.[151] The Reusable Launch Vehicle (RLV) is India's first reusable space vehicle to help ISRO reduce its satellite launch costs. It will be mounted on a rocket to form a two-stages-to-orbit (TSTO). The Indian government invested around $15 million in this project. ISRO says that if the project succeeds, it could revolutionize Indian space travel by reducing costs by ten times through reusable technology. This could mean that cost of transporting materials into space is cut to around $2,000 per kilogram. The main objective is to access space at the minimum cost possible.[152] Its space shuttle launch will put India in the pool of spacefaring nations that successfully tested the launch of space shuttles. It is not just a technology demonstration but proof that India has progressed in space exploration. The test aims at a larger plan to build fully functional two stages of an orbiting vehicle. It will make India more attractive to developing nations in the launcher market. ISRO showed the maturing of its expertise in different spheres of space technology, interplanetary journeys, flight testing of critical cryogenic engines, testing its heaviest rockets for stability during flight, and taking baby steps towards manned space missions.

Right from the beginning of its space program, India has been developing satellites for three major purposes: a) space-based communication, b) space-based remote sensing, and c) space-based meteorology.[153] Other areas of interest in space for India are navigation and geodesy. In addition, India has successfully built and launched its sounding rockets, space launch vehicle (SLV)-3, Augmented Satellite Launch Vehicle (ASLV), Polar Satellite Launch Vehicle (PSLV), and Geosynchronous Satellite Launch Vehicle (GSLV). Initially, PSLV production suffered major setbacks in India because of the non-availability of parts and materials to build PSLV and the procurement of vital parts for PSLV in the Missile Technology Control Regime (MTCR) in 1986. However, the MTCR restriction did not cause significant damage to India's PSLV fabrication, and India continued to invest in its domestic industrial base to indigenize PSLV manufacturing. As a result, more than three hundred private small and large companies can help the country manufacture its PSLV without any foreign help.[154]

India's space policy was initially pivoted around the country's socioeconomic development. However, with time, especially after the Kargil conflict in 1999, there were growing concerns about the lack of a military space program. Jacob Chriqui writes that during the Kargil conflict, when Pakistani troops entered the Indian-held Kashmir without the notice of Indian armed forces, pushed Indian policymakers to vigorously pursue its space program, especially for independent indigenous reconnaissance satellite capability.[155] As discussed earlier, India has 26 dedicated military satellites in space. The recent CartoSat series launch will further increase Indian imagery reconnaissance in space. ISRO scientists believe that the 2018 Cartosat launch is like placing an "eye in the skies," as the satellite will provide imagery data to Indian security agencies to track military activities in South Asia, covering Pakistan, Bangladesh, China, Nepal, and Sri Lanka.[156]

The *Joint Doctrine Indian Armed Forces-2017* suggests that India will ensure it has enough counterspace capability. India's Land Warfare Doctrine-2018 indicates that "continuous surveillance of our borders by developing and employment of satellites, to provide accurate inputs for planning of operations, mitigation of threats and integration of space based assets with ground based weapon platforms will be a priority area for development. Development of micro-satellites, lighter and greater capacity transponders, manoeuvrable and intelligent outer space satellites, with short life spans which can be launched on demand basis, will be the essential for future requirement for the Army". In this connection, Defence Space Agency (DSA) recently conducted maiden 'Exercise Antariksha Abyhas -2024' to enhance strategic readiness in space warfare. One of the objective of the maiden exercise was to validate doctrinal aspects and subsequently update doctrine, strategy and policy. India's policy change from purely a socioeconomic and non-military approach to an increased military space policy dates back to the Kargil conflict. The U.S. shut down GPS links to Indian Air Force (IAF) as a conflict management tool to stop the escalation of Indian and Pakistani armies fighting.[157] Benjamin Lambeth quoted Air Commodore Kaiser Tufail of PAF, saying that the IAF flew without GPS during the Kargil crisis and suffered initial losses. The IAF adopted makeshift solutions without GPS to fly their MiG-21, MiG-23BN, and MiG-27.

After Kargil, the Subrahmanyam Committee on Kargil report recommended that Indian government fasten its belt to develop India's navigation satellite system for military use.[158] That was when India decided to accelerate its space program for civil and military purposes.[159] Table 5.7 shows Indian space militarization capabilities. India has around 26 and Cartosat-2 satellites for the military space program.[160] Primarily, satellites are remote-sensing satellites, and their function is to keep an eye on India's borders on land and sea. Indian military uses Cartosat series and RiSAT satellites for surveillance purposes.[161] On the Cartosat-2 launch, then Pakistan's foreign office spokesperson, Dr Muhammad Faisal, responded to a query Essa Naqvi of Dunya News about the Cartosat-2 launch for surveillance purposes. Dr Faisal replied that.

> All space technologies, including earth observation satellites, are inherently dual-use and can be employed for civilian and military purposes. All states have a legitimate right to pursue peaceful uses of space technologies. However, given the dual-use nature of such technologies, such pursuits must not be directed towards a buildup of destabilizing military capabilities, which can negatively impact the regional strategic stability.[162]

India's space militarization capability is growing. India will likely expand its regional navigation satellite system into a global enterprise in the coming years. Likewise, it is also investing in its remote-sensing satellite network.

India has tested its ASAT capability in 2019. Statements in the past of India's Defence Research and Development Organization (DRDO), IAF, and ISRO chiefs have made it clear that India can test a ground-based kinetic-energy ASAT weapon to hit a target satellite in LEO.[164] Before 2019 test, Indian political leadership has not endorsed DRDO, IAF, and ISRO chiefs' statements.[165] However, India, believed that its capability to build an ASAT missile was real. India's main concern was the Chinese ASAT test. Like lessons learned from the Kargil War, Indian scientists and the military community began discussing building and neutralizing enemy satellites. Former DRDO chief and then scientific advisor to the defence minister, Dr V K Saraswat, stated, "India has all the technologies and building blocks that can be used for ASAT missions in LEO and polar orbits."[166] Saraswat's statement came after India's Agni-V ICBM test.

DRDO tested a short-range ballistic missile interceptor in 2011, a radio-frequency seeker and a fibre-optic gyroscope were key instruments in building a ground-based

Table 5.7 India's space militarization capabilities[163]

Space militarization capabilities	Current systems (satellites)
Communication	• GSAT-series 7 and 7A
Early warning	Rudimentary early warning capabilities
Geodesy	None
Positioning, Navigation, timing (PNT) (8)	IRNSS-IA, IB, IC, ID, IE, IF, IH and one more & satellite
Nuclear detection	None
Remote sensing (ISR) (15)	• CARTOSAT-series 9 satellites • RISAT 6 satellites
SIGINT/COMINT/ELINT (1)	EMISAT

Source: Indian Spacecraft," *ISRO*, accessed December 21, 2017, https://www.isro.gov.in/spacecraft; MV Dhekane, "Indian Space Programme: Ensuring Stable Use of Outer Space," (presentation, International Symposium on Ensuring Stable Use of Outer Space, Tokyo, March 3, 2016); "Satellites of India," *Gunter's Space Page*, accessed December 21, 2017, http://space.skyrocket.de/directories/sat_c_india.htm; Sobia Paracha, "Military Dimensions of the Indian Space Program," *Astropolitics* 11, no.3 (2013): 156–186; Rajeswari Pillai Rajagopalan, "India's Space Program: A Chronology," *India Review* 10, no.4 (2011): 345–350.

ASAT missile.[167] In another profound statement, Saraswat stated that the Agni-V successful missile launch test had allowed India to build its ASAT capability. He said, "An ASAT weapon would require reaching about 800 km altitude. Agni-V gives you the boosting capability, and the "kill vehicle," with advanced seekers, to home into the target satellite."[168] Before Saraswat's statement, IAF Chief PV Naik spoke in a lecture that "our satellites are vulnerable to ASAT weapon systems because our neighbourhood possesses one."[169] Indian military space program got the attention of Indian armed forces after the successful Chinese ASAT test in 2007. It was a wake-up call for India.

After the Chinese ASAT test, the scientific and technical communities and IAF started thinking about India's response and India's potential to build and test its ASAT. The statements from India's strategic organizations' chiefs showed a significant development towards building an ASAT capability. Rajagopalan believes that "India has a missile defence system under development, and the potential for India to acquire an ASAT capability is linked to missile defence capabilities."From IAF and DRDO chiefs' statements and the technological advancement in frequency seeker and fibre-optic gyroscope, India built an ASAT capability with slight modifications in its currently developed Prithvi Defence Vehicle (PDV-MKII). It is a fact that ASAT is a spin-off of ICBM/BMD capability.

On the other hand, many Indian space experts believe the scientific community was open to an ASAT test with extreme caution. However, India did an ASAT test in 2019. For building ASAT capability, advanced space-associated technologies like space-based sensors, synthetic aperture radars, electronics, and navigation/guidance systems in space were required. India made considerable capability development in the areas above. Experts believe developing an ASAT capability requires a real-time test or demonstration of capability. India demonstrated a capability in 2019.

Previously, Indian intelligence and strategic affairs pundits did not endorse a test of India's ASAT capability as it may propel China to declare India as an existential threat to its space assets. A consensus was emerged in India not to test its ASAT capability as long as China remains engaged with the U.S. and both major space powers continue to engage in a space competition. If India desires to test its ASAT capability, it has to assess its after-effects first and, if feasible, demonstrate its ASAT capability. However, Prime Minister Modi tested the ASAT missile Test to show India's technological prowess in space and gain political mileage in 2019 before the general election.

There are three thoughts; one believes 2019 test signified aggression and defiance of international norms. Moreover, India conducted an ASAT test that it thought put international sanctions and space technology transfer restrictions. But it did not happen. The second school believed that India should test its ability to see whether it can hit a target in LEO or India's ASAT is simply a white tiger. Another perspective was to check the efficacy of Indian GPS-aided GEO augmented navigation system (GAGAN) that how quickly it provides services at a regional level. GAGAN is phasing its signal in space with the help of the American navigation satellite system GPS.

The assessment of India's BMD and SLV capabilities suggests India has sufficient missile and SLV capability to develop more ASAT missile for LEO. A modified Prithvi Defence Vehicle with advanced frequency seekers and a gyroscope enable it to hit a target in LEO. DRDO claims that the Prithvi interceptor has a range of 1000 km and is a short-range ballistic missile (SRBM).

From this point of view, a modified PDV has been converted into an ASAT missile to hit its target in LEO. India has Geosynchronous Satellite Launch Vehicle (GSLV) rockets in its inventory to hit a target in other orbits. It is a three-stage rocket developed by ISRO to carry a payload of more than four tonnes.[170] On GSLV MK III's potential to hit a satellite in geostationary orbits, a difference of opinion has emerged in Indian strategic thinking. Indian space experts believe that GSLV Mk III can be modified with advanced seekers, navigational techniques, and equipment to target a satellite in the geostationary orbit. Other strategic thinkers on GSLV Mk III's argue that it may not hit a satellite in geostationary orbit as India may not have some advanced thermal imagery seekers that can locate and hit a target with pinpoint accuracy. In doing so, India augmented these techniques, developed and operationalized this capability, and tested it in LEO. Demonstrating India's ASAT capability has created hazardous space debris in LEO. In 2017, India recorded a world by sending 104 satellites in LEO. However, space experts believe that the powerful rocket created hazardous space debris in LEO, which ISRO experts denied, and it was stated by one ISRO scientist to Hindustan Times that:

> ISRO has developed the models and software for statistical analysis of risk due to space debris and close approach of debris to the functional satellites and to prevent in-orbit break-up by designing spacecraft to be not susceptible to on-orbit explosion.[171]

As spin-off affects of launching 104 satellites in 2017, India derived MIRVing capability. It tested MiRVed Agni-V in April 2024. India is cautious about the space debris, which annoys major spacefarers. India is a regional space power and will likely attain global status shortly. However, space is a unique environment; the crowded and congested domain will likely challenge U.S. superiority. Meanwhile, U.S. policy towards India's space program is not publicly stated. India and the U.S. signed the *Next Step in Strategic Partnership* (NSSP) in 2004, sparking nuclear and space cooperation. However, U.S. response to India's growing military space program is muted, and its response to Indian ASAT was not a considerable one.

Besides that, the Indian space program has tremendously contributed to developing its ballistic missile program. A Central Intelligence Agency (CIA) declassified the document, assessing India and Pakistan's ballistic missile capabilities, stated that India's Agni missile program was likely to be scrapped, and Indian scientists were unsure about its future. Indian officials claimed Agni was a "technology demonstrator not intended for production and deployment."[172] India's scientific community argued that the Agni missile program was tested and ceased after four test flights. India recently tested Agni-V with an officially declared range of 5,000 plus. India first tested Agni-V in 2012, rebuffing all past U.S. assessments about the Agni missile program. The reason behind India's extension of Agni series range is its space program.

ISRO and DRDO have separate mandates and expertise. However, the Agni-V missile is seemingly the joint product of India's SLV and ballistic missile programs. The possibility of interexchange components and technologies to build LRBMs and ICBMs cannot be ruled out. Ajay Lele argues that Medium Range Ballistic Missiles (MRBMs) and SLV capabilities are essentially used to develop ICBM capability. As discussed earlier, India is developing its GSLV MK III capability to carry a weight of 5500 lbs in space. If GSLV technologies are used to develop an ICBM, it is assessed that "it would be a major ICBM, capable of delivering a nuclear warhead up to 14,000 km."[173]

India and Israel are rigorously collaborating to develop India's military space program. Israel has helped India in developing Synthetic Aperture Radar (SAR), which serves India's tri-service Defence Intelligence Agency's (DIA) Defence Imagery Processing and Analysis Centre (DIPAC) at Gwalior.[174] The remote-sensing satellites DIPAC uses for reconnaissance can give an imagery resolution from 25 to 1 m. However, India's older reconnaissance satellites cannot see in cloudy or dark environments. Nevertheless, India has placed its RISAT series satellites with submetre resolution power and can see in cloudy or pitch-dark environments.[175] To improve its C^4I^2SR capability, India has made substantial advancements in building its navigational system.

The development of the Indian Regional Navigation Satellite System (IRNSS) is considered an alternative to or replaces U.S. GPS. ISRO considers establishing IRNSS a quantum leap in the Indian space program as India rigorously pursues its space navigation enterprise. "India's missiles are GPS-reliant for accurate targeting."[176] Learning from India's Kargil experience when the U.S. denied GPS as a conflict management tool, India will likely complete its regional navigation satellite constellation, GAGAN. The IRNSS is now operationally called Navigation with Indian Constellation (NavIC). The system gives two types of services. For multiple uses, Standard is available, and Restricted Service (RS) is "an encrypted service provided to specific (strategic) users."[177] The encrypted services are for tri-services. To make NavIC fully functional, fifteen ground stations across India are built to transmit the signals. "IRNSS is expected to provide a position accuracy of better than 20 m in the primary service area."[178] ISRO is developing satellites to complete the enterprise, but the network is still incomplete due to technical failures and glitches.

India has increased its military space capabilities to support its tri-services, especially IAF. In this regard, DSA was established with the inclusion of military personnel from tri-services. This also includes modernizing its C^4I^2SR capabilities. IAF is the fourth largest air force globally and largely depends on satellite navigation services. Besides this, India has build space capabilities for real-time SSA through space communication and space sensors, especially to monitor space weather.[179] India has to enhance its SAR capabilities with the assistance of Israel and other communications networks to cover the length and breadth of the country.[180] It is developing a two-layered BMD system to counter the rising missile capability of Pakistan and achieve targets in China. However, a comprehensive network of nuclear detection satellites and advanced space-based ISR capabilities is required to operationalize an effective BMD system with accurate and precise interception and targeting. India is also considering developing space assets to prevent hostile forces from jamming its satellites. Lele believes that to overcome this challenge of assisting the Indian BMD system, it will send one to two satellites annually with dual-use purposes to foster its military space program. However, it has not achieved such capability so far. These dual-use satellites will provide critical data and commands to its cruise missiles through these satellites.[181] India is also developing ELINT satellite clusters through its Defence Electronics Research Laboratory (DRDL), a dedicated DRDO facility. DRDL is primarily responsible for developing and providing electronic support to India's Integrated Guided Missile Development Program (IGMP). However, DRDL is also developing India's ELINT capability for its military space program.

India is also investing in building its "soft-kill" capability or non-destructive methods to neutralize enemy satellites and is developing laser technologies for this purpose. However, little has been reported on India's ambitions to explore laser technologies for blinding or jamming adversary satellite systems. Shoghi Communications Ltd. India has successfully developed an SCL-3411 system, a satellite jamming system to interfere with an enemy country's communication and television signals. The jamming system can jam the signals up to 12 C- and Ku-band frequencies. Likewise, the system is mobile and specially developed for covert operations.[182]

The private industry is making significant developments in Indian EW. Shoghi Communications Ltd. designed a GPS-based navigational jamming system, SCL-300, to block links between GPS receivers and satellite stations. The powerful system of 25 W strength is designed to cut off signals in "the GPS frequency bands and does not interfere with any communication other than GPS within the defined zone of operations." On activation, the system can turn off the GPS services in the tactical battlefield environment within 1.5 to 50 km or more. India has inducted and operationalized advanced jamming systems for its armed forces, which can be best used in a short battlefield or a surgical strike.[183] From India's perspective, an essential step towards solidifying its military space program was establishing an Aerospace Command or a possible establishment/creation of a Defence Space Agency (DSA). DSA has been established. Former IAF Chief Arup Raha in 2016 sent an email to an Indian journalist, N C Bipindra, in which he revealed that "the development of a space command stretching across the military needs to be expedited."[184] Rajeswari Rajagopalan believes that the establishment of the creation of DSA "was an interim arrangement until a full-fledged Aerospace Command will be in place."[185] India has an Integrated Space Cell (ISC) under the Integrated Defence Services (IDS) HQ, established in 2008.[186] However, she writes that establishing a full-fledged Aerospace Command is necessary as India needs to protect its regional and territorial interests and space assets.[187]

India's space capabilities are expanding, India's military space program is progressing, and its policy is now more tilted towards securing its space assets and developing counterspace capabilities. India has to achieved soft-killing capabilities of jamming, spoofing, hacking, and blinding its adversary's satellites, and testing of its ASAT weapon in future will be a test of its leadership's political will. Likewise, interim steps towards establishing an Aerospace Command and transforming a rudimentary ISR, ELINT, and Communication Intelligence (COMINT) capability into effective and operational capabilities are some of the challenges faced by India's military space program. However, the trajectory of India's space program suggests that it will likely overcome these odds shortly.

Pakistan

Pakistan has no SLV, but it is constructing a satellite launching pad for which SUPARCO requires enormous financial assistance. In Pakistan, an industrial base and scientific expertise can potentially start manufacturing the country's indigenous SLVs. Pakistan is a nuclear weapon state, and it has deterrence relations with its adversary, India. A credible nuclear deterrent capability requires delivery means for either counterforce or countervalue targeting. Pakistan has delivery means in a missile inventory range of 60 km to 2750 km. This includes SRBM: NASR to MRBM: Shaheen-III. The missile inventory also has Ababeel MRBM with multiple independent re-entry vehicles (MIRV).[188] It is widely believed that Pakistan's development of its missile capability has been in response to India's missile program. Pakistan's missile and nuclear weapons constitute a deterrent against "numerically superior Indian conventional forces."[189]

Donald Rumsfeld made a vital assessment of Pakistan's missiles in a U.S. commission. The commission's report was presented to the U.S. Congress in 1998, making profound statements on Pakistan's missile capabilities. The report suggests that "Pakistan's ballistic missile infrastructure is now more advanced than North Korea."[191] A particular section of the report predicted that Pakistan would develop a 2,500 km MRBM. Likewise, it was assessed that if Pakistan can develop an MRBM, it will give Pakistan a "technical base for developing a much longer-range missile system." However, it was argued that Pakistan "is not hostile to the U.S." Rumsfeld's commission report titled Commission to Access the Ballistic Missile Threats to the United States (1998) assessed that the growing hostilities between India and Pakistan may force both countries...

> ...additional technical assistance through cooperation with their current major suppliers-India from North Korea, Iran, and Russia; Pakistan from North Korea and China because of India's anxieties about China....

The Rumsfeld Commission report assessed the strategic rivalry between India and Pakistan. However, its prediction about Pakistan seeking technical assistance after 1998 from North Korea still lacks evidence. Whereas, U.S did not probe Indo-North Korea nexus in developing ballistic missiles for India. The commission's report did prove correct in assessing Pakistan's behaviour in developing MRBMs and Pakistan's testing of MRBM Shaheen-III with a 2700 + km range.[192] However, Pakistan has shown no interest in developing ICBMs or LRBMs. Pakistan's force posture and doctrinal statements pronounced its nuclear is doctrine India-centric with no objectives to move beyond South Asia.[193] It is important to discuss that Pakistan has made significant advancements in the recent past as it has launched Sea-Launched Cruise Missiles (SLCM), and Babur-3 with a range of 450 km.[194] Pakistan's missile capabilities are advancing gradually because of maintaining a strategic balance with India. Pakistan's missile experts also believe its missile technologies are superior to India's. Samar Mubarakmand, former Chairman of the National Engineering and Scientific Commission (NESCOM) and member of PAEC stated that "the calibre of Pakistan missile scientists, engineers and technicians is world-class and far more superior than their counterparts in India."[195] He also compared Pakistan's nuclear weapon capabilities with India and stated that "Pakistan's missile technology and nuclear weapons are far better than India."[196] The purpose of assessing Pakistan's missile capability is to assess whether there are possibilities that its SLV program germinates from its missile program or not. Will Pakistan develop its SLV in the future or continue seeking foreign help to launch its satellites? Does Pakistan have enough industrial and technical base to develop its SLV? Has Pakistan had enough strength to develop an ASAT missile? What are the possibilities for developing it? These are some of the important questions which need substantial investigation. In an important academic piece, Dinshaw Mistry and Bharath Gopalaswamy tested a hypothesis on ballistic missiles that can be reverse-engineered to make SLVs. They conclude that this possibility cannot be ignored.[197] Both scholars tested their hypothesis that "fourteen regional powers were involved in some thirty missiles and space launch program." The findings suggest that only a few regional powers could acquire missiles from SLVs. Likewise, in a reverse manner, some powers could also develop their SLVs from ballistic missiles. More elaborately, the findings suggest that

HATF-1 was a sounding rocket, and it was converted into a ballistic missile in the early 1980s with the collaboration and help of SUPARCO. Mistry and Gopalaswamy think Shaheen-2, an MRBM, can be converted into an SLV in the second scenario. However, Pakistan has more recently tested Shaheen-3 MRBM with a 2700-plus km range, and if Mistry and Gopalaswamy's hypothesis is applied to Shaheen-3, it can be converted into a future Pakistan's SLV. However, HATF-3, 4, 5, and 6 cannot be used as SLV. More recently, Pakistan demonstrated a test of a MIRV-capable Ababeel missile with a 2000 + km range. To further understand the possibilities of developing an SLV from a ballistic missile, experts have compared technologies used to develop ballistic missiles and SLVs. Some experts argue that there are significant physical differences between ballistic missiles and SLVs. As of this understanding, the possibility of building an SLV from a ballistic missile is bleak. On the contrary, some experts believe that technologies used in building SLV and ballistic missiles are "virtually interchangeable."[198] These interchangeable components, technology, and expertise include launching multiple satellites from SLV and ballistic missiles with MIRV capability. It is not difficult to understand that technologies used in building SLV and ballistic missiles are identical and interchangeable.[199] Likewise, stage control systems, satellite dispensers, coupling load analysis, upper-state solid-fuel engines, and kick motors are interchangeable components, technology, and expertise used in R&D and SLV manufacturing. From the scientific and engineering perspective, it is possible to "shift focus from space to missile to missile to space."[200] Applying this understanding on Pakistan's ballistic missile developments, a simple inference of the hypothesis will suggest that Pakistan will develop its SLV in the future. It is also necessary to mention that a multiple-launching satellite capability means the country has MIRV capability. However, having an MIRV capability refers to a state's capability to develop its SLV. A detailed comparison of the technologies suggests many similarities between SLV and ballistic missiles as both have similar re-entry vehicles, payload separation, inertial guidance and control systems, and strap-on boosters. However, this similarity is based on a case-by-case analysis comparison. In addition, staging mechanisms, propellants, airframes, motor cases, liners, and insulation are components, equipment, and technology that show many similarities.[201] SLVs are ballistic missiles used on the surface of space, and satellites are like payloads delivered by the SLV. Ballistic missiles and SLVs were covered with a path using navigation and similar propellants with little modifications. However, the difference is that one delivers satellites in the orbits, and the other is meant to deliver warheads.[202]From the above analysis of technologies used in ballistic missiles and SLVs, it is safe to say that Pakistan has enough technologies to build its SLVs. Over the past two decades, Pakistan has established an industrial base to develop its missiles. However, in a contradictory argument, A.H. Nayyar, a renowned Pakistani physicist, nuclear activist, and member of the International Panel on Fissile Materials (IPFM), believes Pakistan has a fragile industrial base and has not progressed far in building its rocketry. Pakistan lacks educational institutes and forums on modern technologies used in building space rocketry. He further states that Pakistan requires industrial base to build its rockets to explore the vast horizons of space. Nayyar thinks that space rocket development did not get the attention of Pakistan's policy-makers. Pakistan's discourse on its space program is unhealthy and suffers from total military and political leadership neglect. Few educational institutes and universities teach the basic knowledge of civilian space exploration.[203] Therefore, Pakistan has to seek Chinese help to develop its dying space program.[204] Can Pakistan build an ASAT missile? Rajeswari Rajagopalan opines that China is a principal source of Pakistan's emerging space program and has raised two major challenges to India's space program. Rajagopalan thinks that an independent Pakistani ASAT capability and expansion of its Pakistan missile program from MRBM to LRBM are two major threats to India. However, she also thinks it is not easy to develop an ASAT missile as it requires advanced navigation, frequency seekers, and a guidance system. But, she still argues that "it would not be hardest thing for Pakistan to achieve either."[205] Another renowned Indian space security expert, Ajay Lele, assessed that "Pakistan, being a missile capable state, is in a position to develop an ASAT system if need be."[206] On the other hand, Raja Mansoor believes that Pakistan's current space program will not allow it to build ASAT capability and will take decades.[207] Clay Moltz says that it will likely take decades of work in areas such as education, domestic economic reform, and favourable foreign investment policies to create the pre-conditions to enable Pakistan to generate its space technologies.[208] Despite Pakistan's missile capability to transfer into an SLV capability and an ASAT missile conversion, Pakistan's space ambitions are clear. Pakistan has not made any statement about Pakistan's space objective and activities, unlike India's DRDO chief's statement to develop an ASAT. It has not declared the development of its ASAT capability. Pakistan wants to develop its SLV capability but will test its nerves if it develops and tests any ASAT system.

Pakistan has not developed and does not possess any space weapon capability. However, Pakistan will likely progress its space program to launch and establish more satellites. Pakistan send remote-sensing PRSS-1 satellite to monitor the infrastructure development on the China-Pakistan Economic Corridor (CPEC) land routes.[209] Likewise, Air Chief Marshal Sohail Aman announced that Pakistan would send its first astronaut into space from China in 2020. The dream has yet to be realised.[210] Pakistan has also become the fifth user of China's BeiDou navigation satellite system (BDS) and actively uses BDS services.[211] This is a significant step towards exploring space technologies in Pakistan as the system's applications will provide Pakistani scientists with the opportunity to learn about techniques related to satellite navigation. In groundbreaking cooperation, Pakistan and China signed a Memorandum of Understanding (MoU) with Chinese Prime Minister Li Keqiang in May 2013.

Details of the MoU reported in the media tell that a Chinese company will build five ground stations and necessary infrastructure, including a processing centre in Pakistan, to put its navigation services on the system. Now, the system is fully operational, according to UniStrong Science and Technology Co. According to Chinese media reports, BeiDou will provide 2-cm accuracy to a foreign nation, and its services will be used for civilian and military purposes.

On March 25, 2016, former Director-General Strategic Plans Division (SPD) Lt General (R) Khalid Kidwai and now Advisor to National Command Authority

(NCA)was invited as a keynote speaker at the Institute of Strategic Studies Islamabad (ISSI) to speak on Pakistan's role in Nuclear Security Summit (NSS) process. During the interactive session, Raza Khan, a correspondent of Pakistan Television (PTV), asked General Kidwai about Pakistan's missiles using GPS. Khan argued that Pakistan's ballistic and cruise missiles are GPS-based. In case of a conflict with India, there is a possibility that the U.S. may deny GPS services to Pakistan, and its missiles may not be able to get proper guidance during their flight. Kidwai responded, saying that Pakistan's missile could hit its target without using GPS. He told the audience that Pakistan is not dependent on the U.S. GPS regarding its missiles.

Similarly, former DG Arms Control and Disarmament Affairs (ACDA) SPD, Air Commodore (retd) Khalid Banuri, was asked a question by the author on Pakistan's delivery means of achieving targets in a GPS-denied environment. The question was asked during a joint workshop titled *Defence, Deterrence, and Stability in South Asia* organized by the Centre for International Studies (CISS) Islamabad and the International Institute of Strategic Studies (IISS) London on December 13, 2016. Banuri replied that Pakistan would go for alternative methods and did not specifically mention whether Pakistan would adopt BeiDou as an alternative to GPS or whether the missile would use rudimentary navigation tools to achieve its target.[212] However, it is quite evident that the Pakistan Army is keen and interested in using BDS as an alternative to GPS. Sharing similar thoughts on Pakistan using BeiDou for military purposes, Air Commodore (retd) Kaiser Tufail told Agence France-Presse (AFP) that "Pakistan's armed forces cannot rely on US GPS because of its questionable availability during a conflict that has overtones of nuclear escalation."[213] IHS Jane's annual assessment of Pakistan's strategic weapons reported that the country's cruise missiles, Hatf-8 (Ra'ad) and Hatf-7 (Babur), require GPS services. Hatf-7 (Babur) is equipped with inertial Terrain Contour Matching (TERCOM) and Digital Scene Matching Area Correlation (DSMAC) guidance systems. IHS Jane assessed that "an alternative to U.S. GPS guidance has been sought, and access to the Chinese BeiDou regional system may have been agreed."

Mansoor Ahmed believes cruise missiles can achieve their target with higher precision and accuracy than ballistic missiles.[214] However, cruise missiles require advanced navigation and positioning services to hit counterforce targets. The primary reason behind Ahmed's understanding is the minimum Circular Error Probability (CEP). Hatf-8 (Ra'ad) has a minimum CEP of 20 m (66ft) and a maximum of 50 m (164ft).[215] Likewise, Hatf-7 has an expected CEP of 20–50 m and reported CEP of 3–10 m.[216] According to Ahmed, Pakistan does not have an indigenous GPS; therefore, it will likely use commercial services to navigate the cruise missiles. But in case of a crisis, those services can be turned off. Possibly, Pakistan will seek a Chinese BDS-II system for its cruise missile navigation. However, whether China continues to provide navigation services during a high-time crisis is still uncertain.[217]

Mansoor Ahmed and Feroz Hassan Khan write that BDS-II is expected to increase Pakistan's ballistic and cruise missile accuracy and precision. Pakistan does not have an indigenous navigation system. Since BDS-II covers all parts of India, its services are essential for minimizing the CEP of its cruise and ballistic missiles. They argue that Pakistan's inertial navigation system of Pakistan's cruise and ballistic missiles is likely to increase the CEP. Therefore, Pakistan will shift its cruise and ballistic missile from the inertial navigation system to the Chinese BDS-II navigation system. However, like IHS Jane's assessment, they also believe whether the services will be guaranteed in all situations is unclear.[218] Likewise, Moltz states that Pakistan can also purchase commercial imagery of its adversary, although perhaps not in as timely or focused manner as it might wish.[219]

Usman Ansari authored a report titled *China Provides Key to Pakistani Bandwidth Requirements.* He interviewed several experts on Pakistan-China cooperation in getting navigation services to Pakistan's military.[220] Ansari reported that Pakistani army officials favour acquiring navigation services for their missile program from their "strategic partner," China.[221] Ansari quoted Elizebeth Quintana saying, "Pakistan satellite capabilities are at the very early stage." Therefore, Pakistan could not develop its GPS or indigenous SATCOM capability for its military.

Pakistan may be likely to get BeiDou services for military purposes as well. Quintana also says that Pakistan may get Chinese support in providing navigation services in a conflict situation, and "Pakistani systems may utilize multiple PNT systems—BeiDou, GLONASS, GALILEO, GPS—which enhances resilience in the event of service failure or jamming."[222] According to IHS Jane's 2017 assessment of Pakistan's strategic weapons, Pakistan has no space weapons. The country is not unlikely to make any effort to initiate any project.[223] However, Pakistan may accelerate its efforts to utilize space for military purposes. It requires advanced ISR capability for its nuclear command and control infrastructure and maintains the credibility of its nuclear deterrent capability. In 2011, NCA approved the Pakistan Space Vision 2047. The vision discusses manufacturing, building, and launching SLVs and satellites for national security. Therefore, it is likely that Pakistan will accelerate its efforts to catch India in the ongoing space race in Asia and send satellites for military navigation and communication satellites in space. Pakistan wants to reduce the asymmetry in the region's ISR capability. During the 23rd meeting of the National Command Authority (NCA), under which all the strategic organizations are currently working, chaired by the then Prime Minister of Pakistan, laid a special focus on Pakistan's space program. The press release of the meetings stressed that the NCA members were briefed on the space program-2047, which was previously announced in another meeting held in 2011. NCA members endorsed the objectives of the Space Vision 2047 as it is "essential for future socioeconomic prosperity and growth." During the meeting, the participants discussed the current status of Pakistan's space program and agreed to provide resources.[224] However, recently released National Space Policy does not show any intention, and development of subsequent capabilities to compete at regional level except for socio-economic development by sending civil purpose satellites.

Conclusion

The study of space militarization and weaponization capabilities of the U.S., China, India, and Pakistan shows that space is militarized. Some of these states intensified efforts to follow the path towards weaponization. The U.S. is a leading actor in this path towards space weaponization. China has demonstrated that it can also possess enough capabilities to weaponize space. The former Soviet Union has been part of the Cold War space race and developed space weapons. Currently, Russia has those technologies to augment space weaponization capabilities. India has emerged as a regional space power with significant space militarization capabilities. It has developed space weapons, especially ASAT capability. Pakistan is the last of these states with no space militarization or weaponization capabilities. However, Pakistan is a nuclear weapon state with an intense rivalry with India. Independent security analysts and current nuclear weapons development in South Asia refer to an arms race between the two arch-rivals in South Asia, which could spill over to the space domain. However, the assumption has not proved.

At the global level, the U.S. considers growing Chinese and Russian counterspace capabilities a threat to its space assets. The U.S. has state-of-the-art space assets with all ingredients and components to weaponize space. This includes advanced ISR, communication, navigation, nuclear detection, and geodetic satellites, which have proven vital instruments for force enhancement. Likewise, the U.S. has developed, demonstrated, tested, and temporarily deployed space weapons. Its intra-state strategic engagement with the Soviet Union during the Cold War, now with China and Russia, has yielded to the augmentation of its space weapons. U.S. reliance on its space assets has resulted in insecurity of its space assets from the expansion of counterspace capability development in China and Russia.

In conclusion, the U.S. has followed the path from space militarization to weaponization. Its space doctrine, policy, and strategy highlight its objectives to lead and attain freedom of action in space. The U.S. has developed counterspace capabilities, which keeps the U.S. aware of space activities. A gradual expansion of U.S. defensive counterspace capability is hitting alarm bells in Russia and China. Fear of a similar response from China and Russia has germinated in response to U.S. continuous developments. Both countries have followed an action-reaction model to develop similar space weapons. China has been very active in this regard. The re-emergence of geopolitical and military rivalries between the U.S., China, and Russia has allowed them to follow the path towards space weaponization.

A major finding of the chapter is the discussion of the definition of space weapons. The experts' views, technical assessment reports, and existing literature depict a twisted and not universally accepted definition of space weapons. Most of the definitions are politically oriented; however, some are entirely technical. In addition, there is a complete lack of consensus among major, emerging, and aspiring space powers on definition of space weapons. Some states want to ban deployment of kinetic or destructive means of warfare. However, same group or alliance of states is not ready to accept non-destructive means or electronic warfare capabilities under the umbrella of space weapons. The lack of consensus on space weaponization at different arms control and disarmament forums has given more time and space for global space powers to develop offensive and defensive space capabilities. The states are becoming more aspirant of such technologies, giving them a non-destructive means to destroy their adversaries' space assets. A major takeaway from this chapter is the development of EW capabilities by the states. Considering this reality, the future of space weaponization will involve future development of EW capabilities as a tool to fight a war in space.

Another takeaway from the study on space capability is large-scale vertical proliferation of ground-based ASAT missiles. The U.S. has a large inventory of ground-based kinetic-energy ASATs. It tested these missiles during the Cold War in response to the former Soviet Union, and in 2008, another test was conducted to answer Chinese ASAT. On the other hand, China is vertically proliferating its ASAT capability, and it will likely conduct future tests of its kinetic-energy ASATs to bolster its space weapon arsenal. In 2022, Biden Administration announced a unilateral moratorium on testing of Direct Ascent ASAT missile. However, the ban does not include stockpiling, R&D, and future development of DA-ASAT missiles.

However, Russia has not declared anything such as restricting it from developing ASATs. India is fourth country in the world to test kinetic-energy ASAT. India's IAF, ISRO, and DRDO chiefs have stated that India can build and launch an ASAT missile if required. However, its political leadership has always been in the driving seat. Therefore, a political go-ahead was necessary for the country to test such capability. PM Modi availed the opportunity and tested its ASAT missile test in 2019. Pakistan is not on the path leading from militarization to weaponization. Pakistan has advanced missile technology, and it keeps on improving. Pakistan has missiles that can reach sub-orbits of space. It will be interesting to know when Pakistan can develop ASAT capability. Pakistan can transform its missile technology to build its SLV. The future development of ICBM in Pakistan will eventually help Pakistan develop its ASAT capability. However, there is no such indication that Pakistan can develop SLV and not near to develop ASAT missile.

An important aspect of space weaponization is the current development phase of the BMD system in different countries. The U.S. is actively pursuing BMD system capability and has conducted exoatmospheric, endoatmospheric and mid-course missile interception. Policymakers in the U.S. are now planning to give the go-ahead to the U.S. military to develop a space-based BMD system to intercept an incoming missile towards the mainland. Still, a novel idea in the U.S. China has recently conducted an anti-missile test showing that it is actively developing ASAT system to counter the U.S. or India BMD Shields. At the regional level, India is actively pursuing a two-layered BMD system to counter Pakistan and Chinese missiles simultaneously.

On the other hand, Pakistan has not shown any sign of the development of the BMD system. The mapping of BMD capabilities of the U.S., China, and India tells that space weaponization is not a distant reality for them. BMD capabilities, especially the mid-course interception of the missile, are visualized as the actual weaponization of space.

Notes

1. Cheng [1].
2. Michael Krepon (Co-Founder, Stimson Center) in discussion with the author, October 18, 2017.Krepon's argument is endorsed by Joanne Irene Gabrynowicz (Professor Emerita and Editor-in-Chief Journal of Space Law Editor-in-Chief) in discussion with the author, November 20, 2017; Malcolm Davis (Senior Fellow, Australian Strategic Policy Institute) in discussion with the author, November 20, 2017; and Damon Coletta (professor of political science at the US Air Force Academy) in discussion with the author, November 27, 2017.
3. Eligar Sadeh (Editor-in-Chief, Astropolitics) in discussion with the author, November 26, 2017.
4. Kaku [2].
5. Kaku, 9.
6. James Moltz (Professor at Naval Postgraduate School, U.S. and writer of Asia's Space Race (2012)) correspondence with author, November 28, 2017.
7. Kaku, foreword to *Weapon in Space,* 10.
8. To understand the social construct of space weaponization, there is a need admit the "bomb in the basement" approach where global space powers exhibit self-restraint and seem to adhere to a policy of "no first use." The global space powers possess space weapon capabilities, but this is not the same as deployed and active systems- implementation is restrained.
9. Lee Billing writes that "China, Russia and the U.S. are developing and testing controversial new capabilities to wage war in space despite their denial of such work." See, "War in Space May Be Closer Than Ever," *Scientific America*, August 10, 2015, https://www.scientificamerican.com/article/war-in-space-may-be-closer-than-ever/. Harsh Vasani argues that China is weaponizing outer space to counter U.S. military advantages. See, "How China is Weaponizing Space," *The Diplomat*, January 19, 2017, https://thediplomat.com/2017/01/how-china-is-weaponizing-outer-space/. Stratfor writes in its assessment that space militarization is in its advance stages and it will eventually lead towards space Weaponization. See, "The Battle to Militarize Space Has Begun," *Stratfor*, November 11, 2015, https://worldview.stratfor.com/article/battle-militarize-space-has-begun. Jim Sciutto, chief national security correspondent of CNN, writes that as the threat in space is increasing, U.S. prepares for possible space war. See, "US military prepares for the next frontier: Space war," *CNN*, November 29, 2016, http://www.cnn.com/2016/11/28/politics/space-war-us-military-preparations/index.html. Thomas Bell, USAF personnel, argued that space Weaponization is inevitable and "equally likely that Weaponization will occur with maturing of specific technologies over the next thirty years." The existing literature survey suggests that space technologies have been matured and U.S. and China has demonstrated these capabilities in last ten years. See, "Weaponization of Space: Understanding Strategic and Technological Inevitabilities," *Center for Strategy and Technology,* Air War College, Occasional Paper No.6, January 1999.
10. Kaku, foreword to *Weapon in Space,* 10.
11. Marboe [3].
12. UN General Assembly, Resolution 55/32, *Prevention of an arms race in outer space*, A/RES/55/32 (January 3, 2001), http://www.unoosa.org/pdf/gares/ARES_55_32E.pdf.
13. UN General Assembly, Resolution 18/1962, *Declaration of Legal Principles Governing the Activities of States in the Exploration and Use of Outer Space*, A/RES/18/1962 (December 3, 1963), http://www.un-documents.net/a18r1962.htm.
14. For details on legal perspectives especially from the international law's point of view on the word "peaceful purposes," see Rosas [4].
15. "Outer Space: Militarization, weaponization and the prevention of an arm race," *Reaching Critical Will*, accessed December 12, 2017, http://www.reachingcriticalwill.org/resources/fact-sheets/critical-issues/5448-outer-space.
16. Galloway [5].

17. For further details on the legality of space militarization, see, Hurwitz [6].
18. Galloway, review of *Legality of Space Militarization.*
19. Mueller [7].
20. See Marbo, "Militarization of Outer Space."
21. On space Weaponization, James Moltz firmly believes that space Weaponization has already happened and now states are taking next steps to build more space weapons and finally permanently place them in the orbits. The point is extracted from Moltz's correspondence with the author.
22. According to Jessie Canaday, "space capabilities can be used a force multiplier if these technologies are integrated into all military operations and exercises, develop space doctrine to drive requirements for technology, educate out people on space systems, develop a coherent space control strategy and win technology race and assess the future military requirements." See, for further details, "Space Technology: Force Multiplier or False Sense of Security," *Naval War College,* Department of the Navy, U.S, February 7, 1994, http://www.dtic.mil/dtic/tr/fulltext/u2/a279726.pdf, II.
23. "Space-An Enabler," *Army Space and Missile Defence Command,* Army Forces Strategic Command, U.S, 2003, http://www.dtic.mil/dtic/tr/fulltext/u2/a525767.pdf.(site discontinued)
24. According to Space Operation: Joint Publication (JP 3–14), space force enhancement is "to increase joint force effectiveness by increasing the combat potential of that force, enhancing operational awareness, and providing critical joint force support." See *Space Operations,* Joint Publication 3–14 (Washington DC: Joint Chief of Staff, May 29, 2013), XI & II-4, http://www.dtic.mil/doctrine/new_pubs/jp3_14.pdf.
25. Waldrop [8].
26. Director of the Center for Preventive Action at the Council on Foreign Relations (CFR) and writer of numerous articles and books on space security and militarization.
27. Stares [9].
28. Dahlitz [10].
29. Jasani [11].
30. Krepon and Katz-Hyman [12].
31. Lambakis [13].
32. Lambakis, 135.
33. Jasani, "Space Assets and Emerging Threats."
34. Lambakis, *On the Edge of Earth,* 135.
35. General (retired) James Cartwright (Commander (retired) U.S Marine Corps, Vice Chairman of the Joint Chiefs of Staff and Commander USSTRATCOM) in discussion with the author, December 14, 2017.
36. Weeden [14].
37. Weeden, 2010.
38. For to a comprehensive analysis of Ballistic Missile Defence and Space Weapons, see Garwin [15].
39. Cofield [16].
40. Lewis and Postol [17].
41. Krepon and Katz-Hyman, "Space Weapons and Proliferation," 325.
42. Krepon and Katz-Hyman, 325.
43. Davis, discussion.
44. Pasco [18].
45. Weeden, 2010.
46. Steinberg [19].
47. Pavelec [20].
48. See for details, Jasani and Lee, *Countdown to Space*; Sciutto [21]; Bowlby [22] Davenport [23]; Also read the analysis on the possibility of U.S.-China armed conflict in space, Broder [24],

49. Chun [25], "Viewpoint: Expanding the high frontier: Space Weapons in History," *Astropolitics* 2, no.1 (2004): 63–78; for U.S. space weapons, see Hitchens et al. [26].
50. For details, see MacDonald [27] and also see, Forden [28].
51. Zhang [29].
52. Oberg [30].
53. For details, see, Krepon and Katz-Hayman, "Space Weapons."
54. Jasani [31].
55. "Standard Missile-3: Beating ballistic missiles on land and at sea," *Raytheon*, accessed December 20, 2017, https://www.raytheon.com/capabilities/products/sm-3/?WT.mc_id=TWITTER_socialmedia_N/A&utm_source=TWITTER&utm_medium=paid&utm_campaign=N/A&linkId=45816805.
56. Krepon and Katz-Hyman [32].
57. Axe [33].
58. Axe, 2015.
59. Axe, 2015.
60. Tzu [34].
61. "Operationally Responsive Space," *Kirtland Air Force Base*, accessed December 20, 2017, http://www.kirtland.af.mil/Units/ORS/.
62. One particular incident of blinding of U.S.'s spy satellite in low-Earth orbit by Chinese ground-based LASER took place in 2006. U.S. National Reconnaissance Office (NRO) confirmed the illumination of U.S. satellite in 2006. However, there are several views on this kind of offence in space. Glenn Kessler believes that "in the context of satellites, "blinding" specifically refers to causing permanent damage to an imaging satellite's detector. Laura Grego of Union of Concerned Scientists was quoted by Kessler that blinding usually implied lasting damage to a remote-sensing satellite's sensor, which is offensive in nature. However, nuclear physicist Yousaf Butt of Federation of American Scientists argues that LASERS are "ineffective anti-satellite weapons," not producing desired results, but still can blind the satellite for short period of time. However, with the advancement in direct energy weapons (DEWs), a permanent damage can be caused to a satellite operating in different orbits depending on the range and power of the LASER light thrown on its sensors. For details, see, "Bachmann's claim that China Blinded U.S. satellites," *The Washington Post,* October 4, 2011. On this incident, Eligar Sadeh argues that U.S. deliberately remains silent and showed strategic restraint on this act of offence by China in space. For details on Butt's arguments, see "Effects of Chinese Laser Ranging on Imaging Satellites," *Science and Global Security* 17, no.1 (2009): 20–35.
63. "Fact Sheet: The Ballistic Missile Defence System," *Missile Defence Agency*, U.S, accessed December 21, 2017, https://www.mda.mil/global/documents/pdf/bmds.pdf.(site discontinued)
64. For details on Indian BMD and its implications for South Asia, see Jaspal [35]; Yusuf [36]; Mason [37].
65. For complete details on Chinese BMD, see MacDonald and Ferguson [38]; and for Chinese High-altitude missile test in 2010, see Lewis [39].
66. "China Says Carries Out another anti-missile test," *Reuters*, February 5, 2018, https://www.reuters.com/article/us-china-defence/china-says-carries-out-another-anti-missile-test-idUSKBN1FQ08X.
67. Stephen Walt criticized low development on the BMD system as he thinks missile defence systems have cost more than twice as much as the Manhattan Project. See, "Rush to Failure: The Flawed Politics and Policies of Missile Defence, *Harvard Magazine,* (May–June 2000).
68. Campbell [40].
69. For details on countermeasures, see Schwarz [41]; and also see, Lewis [42].
70. Grego [43].
71. Grego, 2011.
72. The technologies for ASAT and missile interceptors are closely interrelated. A missile interceptor designed to intercept a coming missile in its mid-course flight will almost "necessarily

have an ASAT capability at some altitudes and regions in space, since the task of locating, tracking and destroying a single satellite in orbit is much less demanding than defending against multiple missiles." For details and understanding the legality of the ABM and ASAT, see Chayes et al. [44].

73. A BMD system can also be modified into an ASAT capability. On Aegis, Laura Grego argues that "the current Aegis interceptors SM-3 Block IA/IB can reach only the relatively few satellites in orbits with perigees at or below 600 km altitude." For details, see Grego [45].
74. Wang [46].
75. On DEWs, see Carter [47].
76. For details on space-based BMD, see Frost [48]; Garwin [49]; Erlandson et al. [50].
77. Alwyn Young has discussed the countermeasures to different BMD (Land, Sea and Space) capabilities. For details on countermeasures and soft killing of the BMD capabilities by the adversary see, "Ballistic Missile Defence: Capabilities and Constraints," *The Fletcher Forum* 8, no.1 (1984): 153.
78. Paneerselvam and Soma [51].
79. For complete details, see *Space Operations*, Joint Publication 3–14 (Washington DC: Joint Chief of Staff, May 29, 2013), http://www.dtic.mil/doctrine/new_pubs/jp3_14.pdf.
80. See, *U.S. Military Uses of Space.*
81. For complete details, see Richelson [52].
82. *National Security Strategy of the United States of America* (Washington DC: The White House, December 2017), 31, https://www.whitehouse.gov/wp-content/uploads/2017/12/NSS-Final-12-18-2017-0905.pdf.
83. *National Security Strategy of the United States of America,* 31.
84. McCall and Darrah [53].
85. McCall and John Darrah, 7.
86. In presentation given by representatives of U.S. government accountability office to the Senate Armed Service Committee, there are four major functions of SSA network. First, SSA will detect, track and identify the different space objects, and distinguish between objects and their type and use. The second function is to characterize the temporary and permanent threats to U.S space assets from natural objects and from the space capabilities of hostile nations. The third important function is to create threat warning and assess the space weather and space system anomalies and their potential impact. The fourth function is integrating data and provides decision-level SSA information to the combatant commands. For details see U.S Government Accountability Office [54].
87. Hays [56]; For an overview on SSA function and capabilities see, Kennewell and Vo [55].
88. Hays [56].
89. *Space Operations*, Joint Publication 3–14, annex.
90. Gruss [57].
91. There are five Lagrange points in space. A Lagrange point is a location in space where the gravitational fields of the Earth and the Moon or the Earth and the Sun intersect each other. The intersection of the gravitational field will create a point of equilibrium where a spacecraft may be parked to perform a dual-use function. Elizabeth Howell highlights that three out of five points; L1, L2, L3; are unstable points with precarious equilibrium. On the contrary, the L4 and L5 are stable as compared to L1, L2 and L3. The L4 and L5 may be used to build space colonies; however, these are the points which can be best used to build a more advanced SSA network and well-placed communication satellites. If the U.S or China, which is currently developing capabilities to explore these points, are able to place their space assets then it will be making these assets physically untouchable for the adversary states in space. For stability of Lagrange points see, "Lagrange Points: Parking Places in Space," *Space.com*, August 21, 2017, https://www.space.com/30302-lagrange-points.html; and for military uses of these points see, John Thomas Didymus, "Is growing Chinese Space Power a threat to the U.S?" *Digital Journal*, October 25, 2011, http://www.digitaljournal.com/article/313327; and see commentary on Chinese efforts to explore Lagrange Points, Cheng [58].

92. Cartwright, discussion with the author.
93. Weeden [59].
94. Weeden, 2017.
95. For complete details on X-37B test and number of days spent in space. See, Weeden, 2017.
96. See, Davis [60].
97. For further details see, Ghoshroy [61].
98. Williams [62].
99. Rice [63].
100. Hyten [64].
101. Garamone [65].
102. Weisgerber [66].
103. Clark [67].
104. Quoted in Davis [68].
105. For details on space deterrence, Harrison et al. [69]; On multiple aspects of space deterrence and U.S. adversarial relations with China in Space, see an edited work of Krepon and Thompson [70]; Coletta [71]; Rendleman [72]; A detail work can be see, Bulkeley and Spinardi [73]; and also see the views on deterrence in twenty-first century, Gray [74]
106. The author attended the report launching ceremony at CSIS. For reference, Dickinson [75].
107. Satellite Industry Association [76].
108. Tellis [77].
109. Historically, China remained committed to exploring outer space for peaceful purposes, but in its first White Paper on space activities published in 2000, China considered its space program vital for its national security. See, Smith [78].
110. For more details and analysis on Chinese advancement in space see, Harvey [79],
111. Khan and Khan [80]; on its growing military space power, see Lele [81]; and also see Poduval [82].
112. Cordesman and Kendall [83].
113. Pham [84]; Philips [85].
114. For further understanding on China's military space strategy see, Tellis, "China's Military Space Strategy," 41–72.
115. Cordesman and Kendall [86].
116. *Military and Security Developments Involving the People's Republic of China 2017,* Annual Report to Congress (Washington DC: Office of the Secretary of Defence, May 5, 2017), 49.
117. Cordesman and Kendall, "Space for A2/AD."
118. *Worldwide Threat Assessment of the U.S. Intelligence Community, Before Select Comm. on Intelligence* (May 11, 2017) (statement of Daniel R. Coats, Director of National Intelligence), 8; and also see, *Worldwide Threat Assessment of the U.S. Intelligence Community, Before Select Comm. on Intelligence* (February 13, 2018) (statement of Daniel R. Coats, Director of National Intelligence), 13.
119. Tsujino [87]; and also read a detail assessment on the Chinese military space capabilities with a focus on its indigenous BeiDou system, Forden [88].
120. On China space weapons, see *IHS Jane's Sentinel Country Risk Assessments: China and Northeast Asia* (Coulsdon, Surrey, UK: IHS Jane's, IHS Global Limited, 2017), https://janes.ihs.com/ChinaNorthAsia/Display/1303170.
121. *IHS Jane's Sentinel Country Risk Assessments*, 2017.
122. See, *Assessment of the U.S. Intelligence Community,* (statement by Coast).
123. Tsujino, "Chinese Space Policy."
124. Bharath Gopalaswamy (Director, South Asia Center in Atlantic Council) in discussion with the author, January 5, 2018.
125. See, *Assessment of the U.S. Intelligence Community,* (statement by Coast), 13.
126. Gopalaswamy [89].
127. See, *Military and Security Developments*, 34.
128. *Military and Security Developments*, 34.
129. Shachtman [90].

130. *Ensuring America's Space Security* (Washington DC: Federation of American Scientists, 2004), https://fas.org/pubs/_docs/10072004163650.pdf; and for further details, see Moltz [91].
131. Forden, "China and Space War," 138–153.
132. *China's Pursuit of Emerging and Exponential Technologies,* 115th Cong. (2018), https://youtu.be/KnGTma-npvU.
133. See, *Country Risk Assessments: China.*
134. *Country Risk Assessments: China.*
135. *Country Risk Assessments: China.*
136. *People's Republic of China's Counterspace Program and the Implications for U.S. National Security,* Senate, 113th Cong., (January 28, 2014) (statement of Ashley Tellis, Senior fellow at the Carnegie Endowment for International Peace).
137. Gopalaswamy, discussion with author.
138. Tellis, testimony on *China's Counterspace Program.*
139. Tellis [92].
140. *People's Republic of China's Counterspace Program and the Implications for U.S. National Security*, Senate [93].
141. "A Constructive Year For Chinese Base Building," *Asia Maritime Transparency Initiative, Center for Strategic and International Studies,* accessed January 3, 2018, https://amti.csis.org/constructive-year-chinese-building/.
142. Tellis [94].
143. Gopalaswamy, discussion with author.
144. U.S Embassy India, *Indian Rocket and Satellite Launching Capabilities,* April 30, 1970, https://search.proquest.com/docview/1679140201?accountid=12084.
145. *Indian Rocket and Satellite Launching Capabilities.* 1970.
146. U.S Embassy India, Office of the Defence Attaché [95].
147. At the beginning of India's space program, US helped India in the SITE project to design and build a TV system for India. Likewise, former Soviet Union helped India in building Indian Scientific Satellite Project (ISSP), which was the first step towards Indian Satellites. For details see, U.S Embassy India [96].
148. "With 31 Satellites Abroad PSLV, ISRO launches its 100th Satellite," *DD News,* January 12, 2018, http://ddinews.gov.in/ISRO-satellites-single%20mission-31.
149. Singhi [97].
150. U.S Defence Intelligence Agency [98].
151. India's Reusable Launch Vehicle-Technology Demonstrator (RLV-TD), Successfully Flight Tested," *ISRO,* May 23, 2016, https://www.isro.gov.in/update/23-may-2016/india%E2%80%99s-reusable-launch-vehicle-technology-demonstrator-rlv-td-successfully.
152.
153. U.S Embassy India [99].
154. For details on development of SLV in India see, Nagappa [100]; On private sector involvement in India's space program, see Prasad [101].
155. Chriqui [102].
156. Jain [103].
157. Secretary SUPARCO/Executive Director ISNET Khan [104]; Srivastava [105]; and also see Lele [106].
158. *From Surprise to Reckoning:The Kargil Review Committee Report* (New Delhi: Sage Publications, 2000).
159. "How Kargil War with Pak propelled India to Elite Space Club," *Deccan Chronicle,* April 29, 2016, https://www.deccanchronicle.com/nation/current-affairs/290416/how-kargil-war-with-pak-propelled-india-to-elite-space-club.html.
160. On CartoSat-2 launch, see "PSLV-C40/Cartosat-2 Series Satellite Mission," *ISRO*, January 12, 2018, https://www.isro.gov.in/launcher/pslv-c40-cartosat-2-series-satellite-mission.
161. Singh [107].
162. Mehdi [108].

163. Quoted in Lambeth [109].
164. During the discussion with Dr. Ashley Tellis tells the author that India has achieved the capability to launch an ASAT missile to hit a target in LEO. He further argued that if India conducts its ASAT in future then it will be hit a target in LEO so that no space debris will be created. Ashley Tellis (Senior Fellow, Carnegie Endowment for International Peace) in discussion with the author, February 13, 2018.
165. Gopalaswamy and Kampani [110].
166. Subramanian and Mallikarjun [111].
167. Gopalaswamy and Kampani, "Anti-satellite technologies."
168. Pandit [112].
169. Quoted in Gopalaswamy and Pant [113].
170. For details see, "GLSV Mk III: About the Launch Vehicle," *ISRO*, accessed January 18, 2018, https://www.isro.gov.in/launchers/gslv-mk-iii.
171. Sharma [114].
172. "Ballistic Missiles in India and Pakistan," (official document, Washington DC: Directorate of Intelligence, copy date Jun 15, 1998), https://www.cia.gov/library/readingroom/docs/DOC_0000822286.pdf.
173. Hackett [115], quoted in Lele [116] and Feickert and Konstadt [117].
174. Sankaran [118].
175. Rai [119].
176. Rai, 2010.
177. "ISRO's inroads in Regional Navigation," *India Strategic Monthly*, May 2016, http://www.indiastrategic.in/ISROs_inroads_in_Regional_Navigation.htm; "Indian Regional Navigation Satellite System: All You Need to Know," *The Times of India*, August 31, 2017.
178. See, *IHS Jane's Sentinel Country Risk Assessments: South Asia* (Coulsdon, Surrey, UK: IHS Jane's, IHS Global Limited, 2017), https://janes.ihs.com/SouthAsia/Display/1304918.
179. Lele [120]
180. Lele, 379---393.
181. Lele, discussion with author.
182. "SCL-3411 C-/Ku-band DTH/VSAT jamming system," *IHS Jane's*, January 11, 2018, https://janes.ihs.com/C4iJoint/Display/1826566.
183. "SCL-300 GPS jammer," *IHS Jane's*, March 13, 2016, https://janes.ihs.com/C4iJoint/Display/1499039.
184. Bipindra [121].
185. Prasad and Rajagopalan [122].
186. Press Information Bureau, Government of India [123].
187. Press Information Bureau, 2008.
188. Ababeel [124].
189. Feicket [125].
190. "Missiles of Pakistan," *Missile Threat: CSIS Missile Defence Project*, accessed January 23, 2018, https://missilethreat.csis.org/country/pakistan/; Also see table 3 for list of Pakistani missiles' names, warhead weight, range, propellant and status, Khan and Ahsan [126].
191. Rumsfeld et al. [127].
192. Khan [128].
193. On Pakistan's strategic weapon systems, see *IHS Jane's Sentinel Country Risk Assessments: South Asia* (Coulsdon, Surrey, UK: IHS Jane's, IHS Global Limited, 2017), https://janes.ihs.com/SouthAsia/Display/1304920.
194. On Babur-3 (SLCM), Intern-Services Public Relations, news press release no. PR-10/2017-ISPR, January 9, 2017, https://www.ispr.gov.pk/front/t-press_release.asp?id=3671&print=1.
195. Khalid [129].
196. "Pak Missile Tech better than India's," *The Nation*, May 27, 2017.
197. Mistry and Gopalaswamy [130].
198. Kan [131].
199. Lele, *Asian Space Race*, 128.

200. Lele, 128.
201. Kan, *China,* CRS-14.
202. Lele, *Asian Space Race*, 128.
203. Mansoor [132].
204. Abdul Hameed Nayyar (Physicist, Nuclear Activist and member IPFM) in discussion with the author, January 24, 2018.
205. Rajagopalan, interview by Liang.
206. Lele, *Asian Space Race,* 57.
207. Mansoor, "Pakistan is Losing the Space Race."
208. Moltz, correspondence with author.
209. "Pakistan, China Sign Contract to Launch PRSS-1 System," *The News,* April 21, 2016.
210. "Pakistan to Send Astronauts into Space in Two Years," *Express Tribune,* December 7, 2017.
211. "Pakistan becomes first foreign nation to benefit from China's BeiDou System," *The News,* May 18, 2017.
212. Air Commodore (Retd.) Khalid Banuri was chairing a session of the workshop when the author asked him the question. See the press release of the event, "Big powers' Pressure May Win India NSG Entry, Fear Pakistani Officials," *DAWN*, December 14, 2016.
213. Kaiser's comments were reported by AFP Pakistan and the story was rehashed by several newspapers. See, "Pakistan Adopts Chinese GPS Satellite System," *Express Tribune,* May 18, 2013.
214. Mansoor Ahmed (Stanton Nuclear Security Junior Faculty Fellow, International Security Program and Project o Managing the Atom, Kennedy School's Belfer Center for Science and International Affairs) in discussion with the author, February 1, 2018.
215. "Ra'ad (Hatf-8)," *IHS Jane's,* updated March 2, 2017, https://janes.ihs.com/Janes/DisplayFile/JALWA049.
216. "Hatf-7 (Babur)," *IHS Jane's,* updated January 15, 2018, https://janes.ihs.com/Janes/Display/jswsa305-jsws.
217. Ahmed, discussion with author.
218. Khan [133]; Khan and Ahmed [134].
219. Motlz, correspondence with author.
220. Ansari [135].
221. "Space and Upper Atmosphere Research Commission (SUPARCO)," *IHS Jane's,* updated September 9, 2016, https://janes.ihs.com/Janes/Display/jsd_0712-jsd_.
222. "Space and Upper Atmosphere Research Commission (SUPARCO)."
223. See, *IHS Jane's Sentinel Country Risk Assessments: South Asia.*
224. Inter Service Public Relations [136].

References

1. Dean Cheng (Senior Fellow, The Heritage Foundation) in discussion with the author, November 6, 2017.
2. Michio Kaku, foreword to *Weapons in Space,* Karl Grossman (New York: Seven Stories Press, 2001), 9.
3. Irmgard Marboe, "Militarization of Outer Space: Present and Future Challenges from International Legal Perspective," *Academic Council on the United Nations System,* accessed November 22, 2017, http://acuns.org/wp-content/uploads/2012/06/Militarization-Outer-Space-Irmgard-Marboe-AM-2010.pdf, 1–10.
4. Allan Rosas, "The Militarization of Space and International Law," *Journal of Peace Research* 20, no. 4 (1983), 357–364.
5. Eilene Galloway, review of *The Legality of Space Militarization*, by Bruce Hurwitz, *The American Journal of International Law* 83, no.2 (April 1989):431–435.

6. Bruce Hurwitz, *The Legality of Space Militarization* (Amsterdam: Elsevier Science Publishers B.V., 1986).
7. Karl Mueller, "Totem and taboo: depolarizing the space weaponization debate," *Astropolitics* 1, no. 1(2003): 4–28.
8. Elizabeth Seebode Waldrop, "Integration of Military and Civilian Space Assets: Legal and National Security Implications," (MSc. Diss., Faculty of Law, Institute of Air and Space Law, McGill University, 2003), 5.
9. Paul Stares, *The Militarization of Space: U.S. Policy 1945–1984* (Ithaca, NY: Cornell University Press, 1985), 13; and also see "Space and U.S. National Security," in *National Interests and The Military Use of Space,* ed. William Durch (Cambridge, Massachusetts: 1984), 35.
10. Julie Dahlitz, "Preventing Space Weapons," *Journal of Peace Research* 25, no. 2 (1988): 109–114.
11. Bhupendra Jasani, "Space Assets and Emerging Threats," (presentation, Contribution of Space Law and Policy to Space Governance and Space Security in the 21st Century, Vienna, Austria, September 6, 2016).
12. Michael Krepon and Michael Katz-Hyman, "Space Weapons and Proliferation," *The Nonproliferation Review* 12, no.2 (2005): 323–341.
13. Steven Lambakis, *On the Edge of Earth: The Future of American Space Power* (Lexington, Kentucky: The University Press of Kentucky, 2001), 135.
14. Brian Weeden, "Space Weapons from a Technical Perspective," (presentation, Space Security Conference 2010, Geneva, Switzerland, March 29–30, 2010).
15. Richard Garwin, "Ballistic Missile Defence and Space Weapons," (presentation, The 11th PIIC Beijing Seminar on International Security: Building a Harmonious World of Stability and Win-Win, Qingdao, China, October 26–30, 2008); and also see, "Ground-based Midcourse Defence (GMD) System," Missile Threat Initiative: CSIS Missile Defence Project, accessed December 15, 2017, https://missilethreat.csis.org/system/gmd/.
16. Calla Cofield, "Missile-Intercept System Performed Flawlessly During Test, Boeing Says," *Space.com*, June 1, 2017, https://www.space.com/37048-missile-intercept-system-test-boeing-success.html.
17. George Lewis and Theodore Postol, "A Technically Detailed Description of Flaws in the SM-3 and GMD Missile Defense Systems Revealed by the Defence Department's Ballistic Missile Test Data," *MIT,* 2010, http://web.mit.edu/stgs/pdfs/White_Paper_Associated_With_May_2010_Arms_Control_Today_Article.pdf.
18. Xavier Pasco, "A Preliminary Assessment of the Space Weapon Issue," (presentation, UNIDIR, March 29, 2011), https://swfound.org/media/39984/xavierpasco-assessmentspaceweapon-unidir-2011.pdf.
19. Alan Steinberg, "Weapons in Space: The Need to Protect Space Assets," *Astropolitics* 10, no.3 (2012): 248–267.
20. Sterling Michael Pavelec, "The Inevitability of the Weaponization of Space: Technological Constructivism Versus Determinism," *Astropolitics* 10, no.1 (2012): 39–48.
21. Jim Sciutto, "US Military Prepares for the Next Frontier: Space War," *CNN,* November 29, 2016, http://www.cnn.com/2016/11/28/politics/space-war-us-military-preparations/index.html
22. Chris Bowlby, "Could a War in Space Really Happen?" *BBC,* November 19, 2015, http://www.bbc.com/news/magazine-35130478
23. Christian Davenport, "A Fight to Protect the Most Valuable Real Estate in Space," *The Washington Post,* May 9, 2016
24. Jonathan Broder "Why the Next Pearl Harbour Could Happen in Space," *Newsweek,* April 5, 2016.
25. Clayton Chun, "Viewpoint: Expanding the high frontier: Space Weapons in History," *Astropolitics* 2, no.1 (2004): 63–78
26. Theresa Hitchens, Michael Katz-Hyman and Jeffrey Lewis, "U.S. Space Weapons: Big Intentions, Little Focus," *The Non-proliferation Review* 13, no.1 (2006): 35–57; For details on China's space capabilities, see Department of Defence, *Military and Security Development*

Involving the People's Republic of China 2017 (Washington DC: Office of the Secretary of Defence, May 15, 2017).
27. Bruce MacDonald, *China, Space Weapons, and U.S. Security* (New York: Council on Foreign Relations, 2008)
28. Geoffrey Forden, "Viewpoint: China and Space War," *Astropolitics* 6, no.2 (2008): 138–153.
29. Hui Zhang, "Action/Reaction: U.S. Space Weaponization and China," *Arms Control Today* 35, no.10 (December 2005): 6–11
30. James Oberg, "Are We Setting Ourselves up for a Space Pearl Harbour?"*Jamesoberg.com*, June 12, 2001, http://www.jamesoberg.com/06122001pearlharbor_pol.html.
31. Bhupendra Jasani, "New Approaches to Achieving Space Security," in *Collective Security in Space: European Perspectives*, eds. Johan Logsdon, James Moltz and Emma Hinds (Washington DC: Space Policy Institute, Elliott School of International Affairs, The George Washington University, January 2007), 38.
32. Krepon and Katz-Hyman, "Space Weapons," 325; and also see Lambakis, *On the Edge of Earth*, 260.
33. David Axe, "When it Comes to War in Space, U.S. has the edge," *Reuters*, August 10, 2015.
34. Sun Tzu, *The Art of War*, tans., Samuel Griffith (New York & Oxford: Oxford University Press, 1982), 77, https://web.stanford.edu/class/polisci211z/1.1/Sun%20Tzu.pdf.
35. Jaspal, "The Introduction of Ballistic Missile Defence in South Asia: Implications for Strategic Stability," in *Nuclear Learning in South Asia: The Next Decade*, eds., Feroz Hassan Khan et al., (Monterey, CA: Naval Postgraduate School, 2014), https://www.nps.edu/documents/104111744/106151936/Nuclear+Learning+in+South+Asia_June2014.pdf/db169d3c-6
36. Moeed Yusuf, "Indian Missile Defence: A View from Islamabad," (presentation, Conference On Security And Cooperation In South Asia: A Global Perspective, Berlin, Germany, October 8–10, 2007)
37. Shane Mason, "India's Ballistic Missile Defence Program: Implications for Strategic Stability in South Asia," (presentation, Project on Nuclear Issues Fall 2013, Washington DC, December 17, 2013); and also see an Indian perspective on its BMD development, Summit Ganguly, "India's pursuit of Ballistic Missile Defence," *The Non-proliferation Review* 21, no. 3–4 (2014): 373–382.
38. Bruce MacDonald and Charles Ferguson, *Understanding the Dragon Shield: Likelihood and Implications of Chinese Strategic Ballistic Missile Defence* (Washington DC: Federation of American Scientists, 2015)
39. Jeffery Lewis, "Chinese Missile Defence Test," *Arms Control Wonk*, January 12, 2010, https://www.armscontrolwonk.com/archive/202588/chinese-missile-defense-test/.
40. Christopher Campbell, *Star Wars: Delusions and Danger* (Moscow: Military Publishing Press, 1985), 36.
41. Katie Schwarz, "Day-Long Symposium Examines SDI," *The Tech* 105, no.52 (November 26, 1985).
42. Kevin Lewis, *Possible Soviet Responses to the Strategic Defence Initiative: A Functionally Organized Taxonomy* (Santa Monica, CA: RAND Cooperation, 1986).
43. Laura Grego, "The Anti-satellite Capability of the Phased Adaptive Missile Defence System," *Union of Concerned Scientists*, 2011, https://www.ucsusa.org/sites/default/files/legacy/assets/documents/nwgs/2011-winter-anti-satellite.pdf.
44. Abram Chayes, Antonia Handler Chayes and Eliot Spitzer, "Space Weapons: The Legal Context," *Daedalus* 114, no. 3 (1985): 193–218.
45. Laura Grego, "Aegis as ASAT," *Union of Concerned Scientists*, April 26, 2012, http://allthingsnuclear.org/lgrego/aegis-as-asat.
46. Brian Wang, "USA SM-3 and Russia S500 Deployment of Continental Range Anti-ICBM Systems," *Next Big Future*, January 28, 2015, https://www.nextbigfuture.com/2015/01/usa-sm-3-and-russia-s500-deployment-of.html
47. Ashton Carter, *Directed Energy Missile Defense in Space–A Background Paper* (Washington, D. C.: U.S. Congress, Office of Technology Assessment, April 1984), https://www.princeton.edu/~ota/disk3/1984/8410/8410.PDF

48. Howard Frost, *Space-based BMD: A Multidimensional Analysis* (Cambridge: Massachusetts: Center for International Studies, MIT, 1985), https://dspace.mit.edu/bitstream/handle/1721.1/83072/15001760.pdf?sequence=1.
49. Richard Garwin, "Space-based Defences Against Ballistic Missiles," in *The Future of Smart Weapons*, eds., Eric Arnett et al (Washington DC: American Association for the Advancement of Science, 1992)
50. Robert Erlandson et al., "Development of Kill Assessment Technology for Space-Based Applications," *Johns Hopkins APL Technical Digest* 29, no.3 (2010): 289–29; "Fact Sheet: Space Based Missile Defence," *Union of Concerned Scientists,* May 2011, https://www.ucsusa.org/sites/default/files/legacy/assets/documents/nwgs/space-based-md-factsheet-5-6-11.pdf.
51. S Paneerselvam and P Soma, "Anti Satellite Weapons (ASAT): A Status Review and perception for an Indian ASAT," (presentation, Space, Science and Security: The Role of Regional Expert Discussions Conference, New Delhi, January 19–21, 2011).
52. Jeffery Richelson, *Space Sentinels: A History of the DSP and SBIRS Satellite Systems* (Lawrence, Kansas: University Press of Kansas, 2012).
53. Gene McCall and John Darrah, "Space Situational Awareness: Difficult, Expensive—and Necessary," *Air and Space Power Journal* 28, no.6 (2014): 7.
54. U.S Government Accountability Office, *Space Situational Awareness: Status of Efforts and Planned Budgets*, GAO-16–6R (Washington DC, 2015), https://www.gao.gov/assets/680/672987.pdf; and also see McCall and John Darrah, 8–14.
55. John Kennewell and Ba-Ngu Vo, "An overview of space situational awareness," (paper, 16th International Conference on Information Fusion 2013, Istanbul, Turkey), 1029–1036.
56. Peter Hays, "U.S Military Uses of Space: Issues and Challenges," (paper, International Symposium on Security Affairs 2015, Tokyo), 1–20.
57. Mike Gruss, "U.S Plans $ 6 Billion investment in Space Situational Awareness," *Space News*, October 19, 2015; and also see for complete breakdown of the funding, *Space Acquisitions: Some Programs Have Overcome Past Problems, but Challenges and Uncertainty Remain for the Future,* 114th Cong. (2015) (statement of Cristine Chaplain, Director Acquisition and Sourcing Management).
58. Dean Cheng, "China's Move to CIS-Lunar Space," *Space News Magazine*, November 21, 2016.
59. Brian Weeden, "Fact Sheet: X-37B Orbital Test Vehicle," *Secure World Foundation,* updated June 1, 2017, https://swfound.org/media/205879/swf_x-37b_otv_fact_sheet.pdf.
60. Malcolm Davis, "Why Russia and China Should Fear the X-37B Space Plane," *The National Interest,* October 19, 2016, http://nationalinterest.org/blog/the-buzz/why-russia-china-should-fear-the-x-37b-space-plane-18099.
61. Subrata Ghoshroy, "The X-37B: Backdoor Weaponization of Space," *Bulletin of Atomic Scientists* 71, no.3 (2015): 19–29.
62. Matt Williams, "Super-Secret X-37B Space Plane Nears One Year in Orbit," *Phys.org,* May 16, 2016, https://phys.org/news/2016-05-super-secret-x-37b-space-plane-nears.html.
63. Earle Rice, *Rockets and Satellites: Surveillance fromSpace* (New York: Enslow Publishing, 2017), 4–8.
64. John Hyten, interview by David Martin, *60 Minutes*, April 26, 2017, https://www.cbsnews.com/news/rare-look-at-space-command-satellite-defense-60-minutes/.
65. Jim Garamone, "U.S. Must Move Faster or Risk Losing Lead in Space," *U.S. Department of Defence*, December 2, 2017, https://www.defense.gov/News/Article/Article/1386361/us-must-move-faster-or-risk-losing-lead-in-space/.
66. Marcus Weisgerber, "As the U.S. Air Force Turns Its Focus to Space, This Small Team Could Lead the Way," *Defence One*, November 19, 2017, http://www.defenseone.com/business/2017/11/us-air-force-turns-its-focus-space-small-team-could-lead-way/142656/
67. Colin Clark, "SecAF Wilson Touts 'Offensive' Space Weapons; McMaster Details Framework," *Breaking Defence,* October 6, 2017.
68. Malcolm Davis, "The U.S. Thinks about Space Warfare," *Real Clear Defence*, October 18, 2017, https://www.realcleardefense.com/articles/2017/10/18/the_us_thinks_about_space_warfare_112491.html.

69. Todd Harrison et al., *Escalation and Deterrence in the Second Space Age* (Washington DC: Center for International Strategic Studies, 2017)
70. Michael Krepon and Julia Thompson (eds.), *Anti-Satellite Weapons, Deterrence and Sino-American Space Relations* (Washington DC: Stimson Center, 2013)
71. Demon Coletta, "Space and Deterrence," *Astropolitics* 7, no. 3 (2009): 171–192
72. James Rendleman, "A Strategy for Space Assurance," *Astropolitics* 8, no. 2–3 (2010): 220–255
73. Rip Bulkeley and Graham Spinardi, *Space Weapons: Deterrence or Delusion* (Totowa, N.J: Barnes and Noble Books, 1986)
74. Colin Gray, "Deterrence in the 21st Century," *Comparative Strategy* 19, no.3 (2000):255–261.
75. General James Dickinson, "Distributed Defence: New Operational Concepts for Integrated Air and Missile Defence," (speech, Report Launching Ceremony of Distributed Defence: New Operational Concepts for Integrated Air and Missile Defence, CSIS, Washington DC, January 25, 2018).
76. Satellite Industry Association, *2017 State of the Satellite Industry Report*, June 2017, http://www.sia.org/wp-content/uploads/2017/07/SIA-SSIR-2017.pdf
77. Ashley Tellis, "China's Military Space Strategy," *Survival* 49, no.3 (2007): 41–72.
78. Marcia Smith, *China's Space Program: An Overview*, CRS Report No. RS21641 (Washington, DC: Congressional Research Service, 2005), https://fas.org/sgp/crs/space/RS21641.pdf.
79. Brian Harvey, *China in Space: The Great Leap Forward* (New York: Springer, 2013).
80. Zulfqar Khan and Ahmad Khan, "Chinese Capabilities as a Global Space Power," *Astropolitics* 13, no. 2–3 (2015): 185–204
81. Ajay Lele, "China: A Growing Military Space Power," *Astropolitics* 3, no.1 (2005): 67–75
82. Sanjay Poduval, "China's Military Space Capabilities," *Maritime Affairs* 7, no. 1 (2011): 85–201
83. Anthony Cordesman and Joseph Kendall, *Chinese Space Strategy and Development* (Washington DC: Center for International Strategic Studies, 2016).
84. Sherisse Pham, "China Hits Milestone in Race to Create Hack-Proof Communications," *CNN*, June 16, 2017, http://money.cnn.com/2017/06/16/technology/china-quantum-satellite-success/index.html
85. Tom Philips, "China launches quantum satellite for hack-proof communications," *The Guardian*, August 16, 2016; and also see, "Chinese Satellite Sends Hack-Proof Message," *BBC*, August 10, 2017, http://www.bbc.com/news/technology-40885723.
86. Anthony Cordesman and Joseph Kendall, "How China Plans to Utilize Space for A2/AD in the Pacific," *The National Interest*, August 17, 2016, http://nationalinterest.org/blog/the-buzz/how-china-plans-utilize-space-a2-ad-the-pacific-17383.
87. TeruhisaTsujino, "Chinese Space Policy and Space-Related Activities (Especially SSA)," (presentation, International Symposium on Ensuring Stable Use of Outer Space, Tokyo, Japan, March 4, 2016)
88. Geoffrey Forden, "The Military Capabilities and Implications of China's Indigenous Satellite-Based Navigation System," *Science and Global Security* 12, no.3 (2004): 219–250.
89. Bharath Gopalaswamy, "Much ado about Nothing," *Bulletin of Atomic Scientists*, May 27, 2015, https://thebulletin.org/space-weapons-and-risk-nuclear-exchanges8346.
90. Noah Shachtman, "How China Loses the Coming Space War-Part 1," *The Wired*, October 1, 2008, https://www.wired.com/2008/01/inside-the-chin/.
91. James Moltz, *Crowded Orbits: Conflicts and Cooperation in Space* (Columbia University Press; New York, 2014).
92. Ashley Tellis, "China's Space Capabilities and U.S. Security Interests," *Carnegie Endowment for International Pace,* October 1, 2008, http://carnegieendowment.org/2008/10/01/china-s-space-capabilities-and-u.s.-security-interests-pub-22595.
93. Senate, 113th Cong., (January 28, 2014) (statement of Michael Krepon, Co-founded Stimson Center)
94. Ashley Tellis, "U.S' Asia Rebalance Strategy," (lecture, South Asia Strategic Stability Institute University, Islamabad, May 4, 2016).

95. U.S Embassy India, Office of the Defence Attaché, *Indian Space Program,* January 6, 1988, https://search.proquest.com/docview/1679139279?accountid=12084.
96. U.S Embassy India, *Status of Indian Space Program,* July 6, 1974, https://search.proquest.com/docview/1679140176?accountid=12084.
97. Surendra Singhi, "ISRO's Plan: A Rocket that Can be Made in 3 Days," *The Times of India,* updated November 22, 2017, https://timesofindia.indiatimes.com/india/isros-plan-a-rocket-that-can-be-made-in-3-days/articleshow/61746668.cms.
98. U.S Defence Intelligence Agency, *India's Civilian Space Program,* November 1986, https://search.proquest.com/docview/1679111547?accountid=12084.
99. U.S Embassy India, *Space Research and Development in India Government of India, Department of Space Report for 1972–1973 Included,* July 17, 1973, https://search.proquest.com/docview/1679111553?accountid=12084.
100. 101. Rajaram Nagappa, "Development of Space Launch Vehicles in India," *Astropolitics* 14, no. 2–3 (2016): 158–176.
101. Narayan Prasad, "Industry Participation in India's Space Program: Current Trends and Perspective for the Future," *Astropolitics* 14, no. 2–3 (2016): 237–255; "Traditional Space and New Space Industry in India: Current Outlook and Perspectives for the Future," in *Space India 2.0: Commerce, Policy, Security and Governance Perspectives,* eds. Rajeswari Rajagopalan and Narayan Prasad (New Delhi: Mohit Enterprises, 2017).
102. Jacob Chriqui, "Military Applications of India's Space Program: The Military Surveillance and Reconnaissance System," *Institute of Peace and Conflict Studies,* June 20, 2006, http://www.ipcs.org/article/india/military-applications-of-indias-space-program-the-military-surveillance-and-2043.html.
103. Rupam Jain, "India sends its 100th satellite into space to watch borders," *Reuters,* January 12, 2018, https://www.reuters.com/article/us-space-launch-india/india-sends-its-100th-satellite-into-space-to-watch-borders-idUSKBN1F10HR.
104. Secretary SUPARCO/Executive Director ISNET Haider Ali Khan, "Space Programs in South Asia," (lecture, 15th Senior Officers Management Course-2016, Pakistan Institute of Applied Engineering (PIEAS), Islamabad, April 22, 2016)
105. Ishan Srivastava, "How Kargil Spurred India to Design Own GPS," *The Times of India,* April 5, 2014
106. Lele answer to a question asked on IDSA website, see, "BhumishKhudkhudia asked: Is it true that the U.S had denied GPS to India during the Kargil War? Did the denial lead to the development of IRNSS by ISRO?" *IDSA,* accessed January 16, 2018, https://idsa.in/askanexpert/united-states-had-denied-gps-during-the-kargil-war
107. Surendra Singh, "Military using 13 satellites to keep eye on foes," *The Times of India,* June 26, 2017.
108. Zaman Mehdi, Political Counsellor in Pakistan's Embassy Washington DC, WhatsApp direct message to author, January 11, 2018.
109. 110. Benjamin Lambeth, "Airpower in India's 1999 Kargil War," *Journal of Strategic Studies* 35, no.3 (2012): 289–316.
110. Bharath Gopalaswamy and GauravKampani, "Piggybacking Anti-Satellite Technologies on Ballistic Missile Defence: India's Hedge and Demonstrate Approach," *Carnegie Endowment for International Peace,* April 19, 2011, www.carnegieendowment.org/publications/index.cfm?fa=view&id=43655.
111. T Subramanian and Y Mallikarjun, "Capability to neutralize enemy satellites proved," *The Hindu,* March 7, 2011
112. RajatPandit, "After Agni-V launch, DRDO's New Target is Anti-Satellite Weapons," *The Times of India,* April 21, 2012.
113. Bharath Gopalaswamy and Harsh Pant, "Does India Need Anti-Satellite Capability?" *Rediff.com,* February 9, 2010, http://news.rediff.com/column/2010/feb/09/does-india-need-anti-satellite-capability.htm.
114. Sanchita Sharma, "Space Junk is a Problem but Don't Blame it on ISRO," *Hindustan Times,* February 16, 2017.

115. Jim Hackett, "The Ballistic Missile Threat: India and Pakistan," *Center for Defence and International Security studies,* August 1996
116. Ajay Lele, *Asian Space Race: Rhetoric or Reality?* (London & New York: Springer, 2013), 134
117. Andrew Feickert and Alan Konstadt, *Missile Proliferation and the Strategic Balance in South Asia,* CRS report no. RL32115 (Washington DC: Congressional Research Service, October 17, 2003), CRS-25.
118. Jaganath Sankaran, "China-India Space Race: Rhetoric or Reality?" (presentation, Science, Technology and Energy Seminar, Belfer Center's South Asia Center, February 26, 2014).
119. Ranjit Rai, "Indian Navy: A C4ISR Nuclear Force," *India Strategic Monthly,* August 2010, http://www.indiastrategic.in/topstories717.htm.
120. Ajay Lele (Senior Fellow, IDSA) in discussion with the author, November 22, 2017. Also see, "Indian Armed Forces and Space Technology," *India Review* 10, no. 4 (2011): 379–393
121. N C Bipindra, "Space the Final Frontier for India Military Modernization Push," *Live Mint,* October 7, 2016, http://www.livemint.com/Politics/Mqe3HKnhRTUOGraAWzQKoN/Space-the-final-frontier-for-India-military-modernization-pu.html.
122. Narayan Prasad and RejeswariRajagopalan, "Creation of a Defence Space Agency: A New Chapter in Exploring India's Space Security," in *Defence Primer 2017: Today's Capabilities, Tomorrow's Conflict*, eds. Sushant Singh and Pushan Das (New Delhi: Observer Research Foundation, 2017), 97, http://cf.orfonline.org/wp-content/uploads/2017/01/Defence-Primer-2017.pdf.
123. Press Information Bureau, Government of India, "Special Cell Set up to Counter Growing Threat to Space Assets," press release no. 39503, June 10, 2008, http://www.pib.nic.in/newsite/erelcontent.aspx?relid=39503
124. On Ababeel, see Inter-Services Public Relations, news press release no. PR-34/2017-ISPR, January 2, 2017, https://www.ispr.gov.pk/front/main.asp?o=t-press_release&id=3705.
125. Andrew Feicket, *Missile Survey: Ballistic and Cruise Missiles of Foreign Countries,* CRS report no. RL30427 (Washington DC: Congressional Research Service, updated July 26, 2005), https://fas.org/sgp/crs/weapons/RL30427.pdf, 23.
126. 127. Ahmad Khan and Ali Ahsan, "Deterrence in Indo-Pak Context A Critical Appraisal," *Policy Perspective* 13, no.1 (2016): 53–76
127. Donald Rumsfeld et al., *Commission to Assess The Ballistic Missile Threat to the U.S* (Washington DC: 104th U.S Congress, July 15, 1998), https://fas.org/irp/threat/bm-threat.htm.
128. Ahmad Khan, "Pakistan's Missile Conscription and Essence of War," *Russian International Affairs Council,* March 12, 2015, http://russiancouncil.ru/en/analytics-and-comments/columns/digest/ahmad-khan-pakistan-s-missile-conscription-and-essence-of-wa/.
129. Hanif Khalid, "Pak Missile More Superior than India's: Dr Samar," *The News,* October 21, 2015.
130. 131. Dinshaw Mistry and Bharath Gopalaswamy, "Ballistic Missiles and Space Launch Vehicles in Regional Powers," *Astropolitics* 10, no.1 (2012): 126–151.
131. Shirley A. Kan, *China: Possible Missile Technology Transfers from U.S. Satellites Export Policy—Actions and Chronology,* CRS Report No. 98–485F (Washington, DC: Congressional Research Service, updated September 5, 2001),https://fas.org/sgp/crs/space/RS21641.pdf.
132. Raja Mansoor, "Pakistan is Losing the Space Race," *The Diplomat,* February 1, 2018, https://thediplomat.com/2018/02/pakistan-is-losing-the-space-race/.
133. Feroz Hassan Khan (Former DG ACDA SPD and writer of *Eating Grass: The Making of Pakistan's Nuclear* Bomb)
134. Feroz Hassan Khan and Mansoor Ahmed, "Pakistan, MIRVs, and Counterforce Targeting," in *The Lure and Pitfalls of MIRVs: From the First to the Second Nuclear Age,* eds. Michael Krepon, Travis Wheeler and Shane Mason (Washington DC: Stimson Center, May 2016), 160.
135. 136. Usman Ansari, "China Provides Key Pakistani Bandwidth Requirements," *Defence News* 28, no.10 (2013): 12.

136. Inter Service Public Relations, "23rd National Command Authority (NCA)," press release no. PR-615/2017-ISPR, December 21, 2017, https://www.ispr.gov.pk/front/main.asp?o=t-press_release&id=4459#pr_link4459
137. 138. Bruce Deblois, "The Advent of Space Weapons," *Astropolitics* 1, no.1 (2003): 30
138. 139. Barry Watts, *The Military Use of Space: A Diagnostic Assessment* (Washington DC: Centre of Strategic and Budgetary Assessment, 2001)
139. BhupendraJasani and Christopher Lee, *Countdown to Space War* (Stockholm International Peace Research Institute, 1984).
140. Petr Topychkanov, "Features of the Outer Space Environment," in *Outer Space: Weapons, Diplomacy and Security*, eds.Alexei Arbatov and Vladimir Dvorkin (Washington DC: United Book Press, 2010)
141. 142. Bob Preston et al., *Space Weapons Earth Wars* (Santa Monica, California: RAND Corporation, 2002).
142. NatáliaArchinard, "Space Security and Governance-The Role of Space Middle Powers," (presentation, Contribution of Space Law and Policy to Space Governance and Space Security in the 21st Century, September 5–8, 2016, Vienna, Austria)
143. U.S. Congress, Office of Technology Assessment, *Anti-Satellite Weapons: Countermeasures and Arms Control* (Washington DC: U.S. Government Printing Office, 1985), chap 4.
144. Laura Grego, "A history of Anti-Satellite Programs," *Union of Concerned Scientists,* January 2012, https://www.ucsusa.org/sites/default/files/legacy/assets/documents/nwgs/a-history-of-ASAT-programs_lo-res.pdf.
145. Union of Concerned Scientists, "UCS Satellite Database;" "Military Spacecraft-USA," *Gunter's Space Page,*http://space.skyrocket.de/directories/sat_mil_usa.htm.
146. Tyler Evans, "Space Coordinating Authority: Information Service from Space," in *Space Power Integration: Perspectives from Space Weapons Officers*, ed. Kendall Brown (Maxwell AFB, AL: Air University Press, 2006).
147. Eligar Sadeh, "Space Programs of the U.S of America," *Astroconsulting International LLC,* November 5, 2009."
148. Eric Heginbotham et al., *The U.S.-China Military Scorecard: Forces, Geography, and the Evolving Balance of Power 1996–2017* (Santa Monica, CA: RAND Corporation, 2015), chap 7 & 8; "Military Spacecraft-China," *Gunter's Space Page*, accessed January 1, 2018, http://space.skyrocket.de/directories/sat_mil_china.htm; and also see, *2017 Space Security Index,* 99–-100.

Chapter 6
Global and Regional Space Order

Introduction

This chapter answers following questions: what was the Cold War space order, what were the main actors that constituted it, and what are the present space order and its dynamics? Studying the past and present global space orders provides a closer look at the nature of relations between the U.S. and China globally and between China, India, and Pakistan at the regional level. This effort will highlight the nature of relations and their subsequent effects or implications for global and regional security. The chapter will answer the research questions highlighted at the beginning to prove that states follow the path from space militarization to weaponization. While following the path and studying the past and present space capabilities development trajectories in global and regional powers, an arms race between the powers discussed herein is evident.[1]

The Concept of International Order

Order is a contested term in political science, international relations, and strategic studies. Esteemed scholars in the fields above have been unable to provide a conclusive, comprehensive, universally agreeable, and well-structured definition of the word. Interestingly, the discourse analysis on "order" has generated a debate highlighting multiple factors contributing to formulating an international or world order. This debate's dominant schools of thought are realism, idealism, and liberalism.

This chapter draws from the Ph.D. research work of the author titled "Arms Race in Outer Space: A Paradigm Shift in International Security and Implications for South Asia," which was completed in 2019 and successfully defended in 2020 at Department of Strategic Studies, National Defence University, Islamabad.

A. Khan and E. Sadeh, *Sabre Rattling in Space*,
https://doi.org/10.1007/978-981-97-6050-3_6

Scholars from these schools of thought have given their perspectives on the nature, features, and characteristics of past, present, and future international/world order. However, the debate is not finished; it still defines and answer the questions: what is the exact nature of existing international/world order, and how will it transform? However, diverging thoughts on world order have only generated more confusion among scholars and policymakers.

What is an order? The Oxford English Dictionary defines order as "regular, methodical or harmonious arrangement in the position of things, contained in any space or area, or composing any group or body."[2] According to this definition, the order forms an arrangement of its entities through a methodological approach. The order is an arrangement of entities in their proper place and allows them to perform their proper functions in a particular manner. An order of entities also allows them to form relations with conformity with standards of method or conduct. The order has several interpretations across many fields. Political sciences and international relations scholars have tried defining order using their political understanding. The political or social order entities are states, groups, or people living close to a particular arrangement. In such subjects, states are usually referred to as entities of the order. It is generally believed that arrangement or the order's regularity is made according to relative power structure through military power. During the Cold War, the world was divided into two poles led by the U.S. and the former Soviet Union. The nations' politics focused on maintaining a balance of power through their relative military build-up. That formed an arrangement of bipolar world order. The world has been reshaped and transformed over time due to events in last four decades.

The changing nature of interstate relations is a prominent factor in shaping or transforming international order. Any study discussing past, present, or future world order would start with a question: "who are the entities that make up any given order?"[3] States are considered to be living organisms in international or world order. These organisms interact with each other and form relations in different mediums. Friedrich Ratzel, who gave the Organic Theory, explains that state is a "fragment of humanity on a piece of soil."[4] The fragment of humanity is organized and lives on it. Many fragments of humanity form a political community in which the fragments interact and continue to grow and expand. States' expansion depends on political and economic environment, or it may take place by war.[5] The expansion of state is also dependent on its military strength. And the states' military build-up or strength reshaped the post-Second World War order.

Examples of International "Orders"

The debate on world order has created more confusion among scholars and policymakers alike. One of many reasons behind such confusion seems to be volatile nature of state relations and different political understandings of major scholars in respective subjects. Kenneth Waltz, who belongs to the realist school of thought, discussed balance of power as fundamental characteristic of the world order.[6] Francis

Fukuyama argues that liberal democracy is a prominent feature of the world order.[7] On the other hand, Samuel Huntington, who wrote the famous book *The Clash of Civilizations*, took Fukuyama's argument at *the End of History* on liberal democracy a step ahead and talked about civilization's clash as a feature of future world order.[8] Robert Kaplan highlights the coming anarchy in the world due to overpopulation, ethnic and tribal rifts, crime, and disease. These factors will rapidly destroy societies' social fabric worldwide. These factors will reshape the future world order.[9] Jennifer Welsh, the author of *The Return of History*, argues for returning the world towards autocratic nationalism and illiberalism. She makes some fascinating arguments in the book. According to Welsh, the world order is reshaping, departing from Western-style liberal democracy towards illiberalism.[10] On the other hand, Anne-Marie Slaughter forces the reader of her book titled *The New World Order* to rethink the world's political structure and argues that the world is now witnessing an order with multiple ideas from the past and present.[11]

A fundamental characteristic of any given political order is relative military strength of the entities. The Cold War era suggests a rigorous competition between the two arch-rivals to foster their military capabilities, including nuclear, missile, and space capabilities, to shift the balance of power.[12] However, the end of the Cold War completely reshaped world order, its characteristics, and features. Military strength remains a fundamental characteristic, but the economy now plays a crucial role in reshaping world order.[13] Both factors are interlinked and intertwined to reshape. Military strength alone is not a measure or characteristic of world order during the Cold War. Its relative military and economic strength measure a state's role in world order.[14] Likewise, as discussed earlier, other factors can impact a given order. It can be viewed as a political and economic order, but military strength's importance remains.

The nuclear order may be exemplified to understand the importance of military power in the contemporary world and how it can still impact global politics. A so-called nuclear order is primarily based on distribution of relative nuclear forces. This nuclear order was primarily due to geopolitical changes in international system during the 1970s that had "important effects on the nuclear order, creating a North–South axis alongside the existing East–West axis." The nuclear order began to emerge after the Nuclear Non-proliferation Treaty (NPT) entered into force in 1970. The world was divided into nuclear "haves" and "have-nots." Disputes emerged on transferring nuclear technology to nuclear aspirant states. [15] Five declared nuclear weapon states are under the Non-proliferation Treaty (NPT). These states are also permanent members of the United Nations Security Council (UNSC) with veto powers.

However, the order has been gradually expanded. India detonated its first nuclear weapon in 1974 and then later in 1998, giving Pakistan a chance to respond with its nuclear detonations. Israel and North Korea are also nuclear weapons states. But NPT only recognizes the U.S., Russia, China, Britain, and France as legitimate nuclear weapons states. On the other hand, remaining states are de facto nuclear weapons states. All these states formed a nuclear order, which is, in fact, a disorder in itself. Ashok Kapur criticized the core understanding of Beltway scholars on nuclear order.[16] In Kapur's understanding, world order or nuclear order are political slogans and "more imagination and rhetoric than reality." The international order is a disorder, as is the nuclear order. It is not a regime as a set of rules does not govern it, somewhat manipulated by powerful states' core interests. It operates under the influence of rules set by major powers and their allies, which remain a stumbling block towards establishing a formal political world order. This order is neither regular nor a classification scheme, methodological, or systematic, and it is neither peaceable. It is full of anarchy, characterized by the changing nature of state interests, especially the interests of significant military and economic powers. Interestingly, the word anarchy means a world "without a ruler."[17] Likewise, the anarchists believe that "rule is unnecessary for preserving order." It is generally believed that "anarchy is order."[18]

The world order is primarily based on states' power distribution related to their military, economic, and political influence. Likewise, the power relationship, especially military and economic competition among states, is fundamental in shaping the world order. Kapur argues that "order is often shorthand for manageable instability."[19] William Walker authored comprehensive academic literature on nuclear order to understand normative basis and functionality. Walker divides nuclear order into two categories, one established during the Cold War and another after end of the Cold War.[20] Walker's division of nuclear order also lays a solid base to study the space order. The studies on nuclear order during and after the Cold War highlight factors implied or used to study the space order. Walker believes establishing a nuclear order during the Cold War was primarily the role nuclear weapons could play in achieving the state's political and military objectives. Walker summarizes the Cold War era's role as "instead of nuclear weapons losing value, they gained value, and dramatically so in some contexts." He refers to these contexts as two levels: international and regional. The major powers tried to maintain a monopoly on nuclear technology, know-how, and materials to build such weapons internationally. In that way, major powers tried to infuse their interests in the nuclear order. The continuous denial of technology and access to information forced some states to become aspirants of nuclear weapons at regional level. This suggests that "instead of strengthening order, there was an enveloping sense of disorder."[21]

The literature survey aims to understand the dynamics of space order during and after the Cold War. Space is a strategic domain and remained an area of contest and competition between the two superpowers during the Cold War. After the Soviet Union's demise, the U.S. gained the advantage of expanding its power without significant competition. It has reshaped global space order after the Cold War, but now U.S. interests are challenged by China's expanding space power. Likewise, the space order is now more complex than during the Cold War. The pool of space power aspirants is increasing, and it is now a crowded and contested domain with significant competition between major space powers.

Cold War Space Order

The story of the Cold War has many dimensions, and one key aspect was the space race.[22] History tells how the U.S. and the former Soviet Union competed to maintain their prestige in science and technology, defence, and soft power. This opening chapter of Space was primarily about these two major powers. However, other powers also started their space program during the Cold War.

The relations between the two strategic competitors were primarily based on the action-reaction syndrome that drove most technological developments. At the same time, both states developed space technologies for their needs. A key aspect of space rivalry was science and technology as a critical element of national diplomacy. The Cold War witnessed science and technology playing a catalytic role or as an "engine of progress," as well as the "direct index of national power." The contribution of science and technology in space during the Cold War helped both states "maintain a strong geopolitical position during the Cold War."[23] It is also a fact that space technologies apply to dual-use purposes. Space technologies were used for scientific developments in space exploration and defence.[24] Hence, both states saw any Cold War technological development in space through the lens of scepticism. It was development of technologies that further fuelled the Cold War.

Likewise, both countries had adversarial relations, so anything built for their domestic purposes was considered a response to technological development. From political and strategic views, any state's technological advancement to fulfil its needs was taken as a challenge to others' security, creating a security dilemma. The Cold War space order witnessed the "elements" of security dilemma between the two powers. Both countries were more technologically advanced space powers compared to other developing states. Robert Jervis analysed the U.S.-Soviet security dilemma during the Cold War with an exciting conclusion on the type of relations:

> Although the Cold War contained elements of the security dilemma and included episodes in which tensions and arms increased as each side defensively reacted to the other, the root of the conflict at best was a clash of the social system.[25]

Although both states defensively developed space technologies, these developments were considered a threat to other's national security. Both wanted to reflect advancement in space as the success story of their scientific and social culture. However, the nature of conflict portrayed advancement as a threat to each other's existence. Figure 6.1 highlights the dynamics of global space order during the Cold War. Consequently, aspiring national space programs were made to choose which bloc or camp they had to align with.

The Cold War space order highlights the U.S. and the former Soviet Union as the core states. These core states worked according to the baselines of structural realism as self-help.[26] In a self-help manner, they continued to balance each other through arms races and forming alliances. This alliance formation was a key factor in Cold War history. The Cold War space order also witnessed *realpolitik* in space order.[27]

The Cold War space order also suggests the emergence of new space technology aspirants: Brazil, South Korea, and Pakistan. China was third country globally to

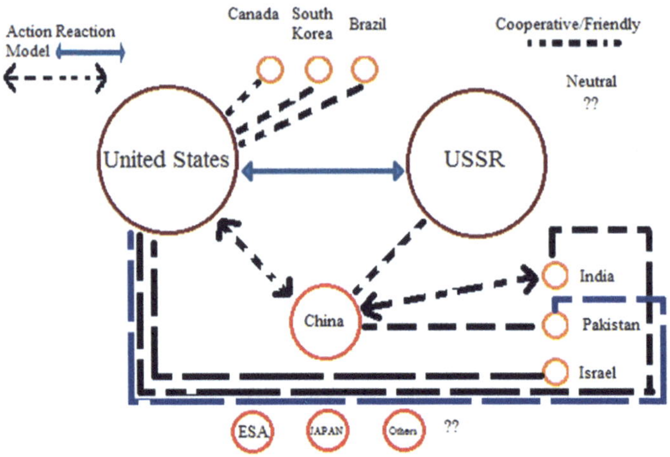

Fig. 6.1 Global space order during the Cold War

become part of the Cold War space order to explore for dual-use purposes.[28] The U.S. and the Soviets helped their allies build space power, transfer technological skills, and establish their space system. China was also the beneficiary of such technology transfers from the Soviet Union.[29] Pakistan's space program got critical space technology transfer from NASA; it helped Pakistan launch its first sounding rocket in the 1960s.[30] In India's case, NASA also facilitated technology transfer and helped Indian space scientific community solving some scientific glitches in their sounding rockets.[31] Likewise, India also remained aligned with the former Soviet Union during the Cold War. That led India to the so-called indigenization of space technology in the country. India got critical help from the U.S.in rocketry; French help in the field of liquid propulsion; and German help in guidance, rocket testing, and composite materials uses. No doubt, the Soviet Union help was paramount in structuring India's SLV and PSLV programs.

The beginning of modern history is demarcated with invention of aircraft as human quest to conquer different mediums: land, sea, and air; it reached its ultimate level when the first aircraft flew in air. The invention of aeroplanes was a living embodiment of revolution brought by science and technology in all fields of life, impacting world politics and states' economy and military.[32] The invention of aeroplanes revolutionized modern warfare, and human courtesy to fly in air to travel across all corners of the Earth became a reality.[33]

The doorway to scientific inventions and discoveries also opened at the beginning of the twentieth century. The dream of flying came true after the Wright Brothers made it possible.[34] Physicists discovered atom's structure and process to unleash atom's energy through nuclear fission. This also resulted in development of nuclear weapons, the most lethal and destructive weapon in history of humanity. Humans always wanted to travel beyond skies and saw space as the gateway to heaven. The quantum leap in history of humankind was successful sending of an artificial satellite into outer space.[35] That was made possible when first satellite was successfully launched by the former Soviet Union, heralding an unending space exploration story. States wanted the technology to explore space as it became a matter of national pride and prestige.[36] Space technology was the prime locus of any state's standing in science and technology. Space technology and subsequent development in space exploration, especially human-crewed missions to celestial bodies, were primary indicators of a state's international standing and progress. The U.S. and the former Soviet Union were the primary actors in all the progress in space technologies.[37] Besides that, many other states like China, India, the European Union, and Pakistan also became aspirants of space technologies to build their programs.

The Soviets gave a "physiological shock" to American public and policymakers with Sputnik-I's successful launch on October 4, 1957.[38] In November of the same year, the Soviets shocked Eisenhower's administration by launching Sputnik-II into space. The New York Tribune published a story on Sputnik-II telling American people that now the Soviet Union "will step out into space to reach the moon, the planets or even stars."[39]The exciting part of the story was about the Soviets' development of "rocket capability of dropping a hydrogen-bomb warhead on any spot on the earth and may even be in the process of stockpiling several such rockets."[40] Sputnik-I and II's launch changed American public opinion and created public doubts about American scientific knowledge of its space program. It was a major setback to Eisenhower's administration and American prestige.[41] The pressure was mounting to place an American satellite into space. Several programs were initiated before the launch of Sputnik to send satellites into space, but they failed to escape Earth's gravity. Finally, on January 31, 1958, U.S. Army successfully launched its space rocket Explorer I in space to send its satellites.[42] From onward, an intense race was started between two strategic competitors, and "Sputnik would seem to qualify as a historical catalyst" of the space race of the First Space Age.[43]

Walter McDougall writes about the post-Sputnik world witnessing "scientific and technological revolution" as "capitalism itself altered its law, and Leninist doctrine was modified to include science as a direct productive force."[44] McDougall opines that

> The four realms most often cited as the loci of revolutionary change in the Space Age are 1) international politics, 2) the political role of science and scientists, 3) the relationship of the state to technological change, and 4) political culture and values in nations of technology.[45]

McDougall aptly points out main drivers behind the first Space Age. In addition, prestige and national security were the intervening drivers who set the pace of the U.S.-Soviet space rivalry. As space rivalry intensified, both states shifted gears to achieve nuclear superiority. Missiles are vital delivery means of nuclear weapons, and mutual fears of a widening missile gap were also germinated in both states. As a result, the space race and development of Intercontinental Ballistic Missiles (ICBMs) to reach each other's heartland intensified in the 1960s.

The post-Sputnik era's chronicles suggest a growing American perception of the Soviet Union's keen interest in developing ICBMs. Declassified top-secret CIA documents highlight U.S. anxiety over the Soviet Union's desire to achieve an ICBM capability.[46] However, the advancement in U.S. satellite reconnaissance and aerial photographic capability and subsequent assessment of once-denied territories and Soviet missile capabilities disapproved the missile gap perception in the U.S. The shooting down of an American U-2 spy plane and pilot Gary Powers' capture gave much attention to U.S. aerial reconnaissance of Soviet territories. For this, the U.S. built Badaber Peshawar Air Station, 10 miles from the Pakistani city. President Eisenhower had authorized the flight of Gray Power, an experienced pilot, to carry out Operation GRAND SLAM. However, it was later caught by the Soviets after its air defences shot down U-2.[47] Cold War estimates of U.S. intelligence agencies revealed that the Soviet space program played a significant role in developing and fostering its ICBMs due to Sputnik I & II's success.[48] The U.S. assessed that the Soviet space program was actually "an off-shoot of its efforts to develop a nuclear-tipped ICBM."[49] That forced the U.S. to shift gears to increase its space and aerial reconnaissance of Soviet missile facilities.

Another aspect of the Soviet-U.S. space race was achieving nuclear superiority and sending rockets with military payloads. Bradley Shreve argued that:

> Historiographically, the role of the greater good in space exploration has not been recognized. Instead, nearly all of the literature on the U.S. and USSR's endeavours into outer space has focused on the space race as an extension of the Cold War, virtually ignoring all the cooperative efforts and conciliatory words.[50]

Shreve's argument about the first space age suggests that both powers' primary focus was to achieve their military objectives by amalgamating all their powers, including nuclear and space. Both were trying to maximize nuclear numbers to shift balance of power in their favour, thinking about victory in an armed conflict. U.S. intelligence agencies assessed Soviet intentions and capabilities as they would seek victory in a nuclear crisis.[51] Likewise, the Soviets accused the U.S. of massively developing nuclear weapons to seek superiority.[52] Mathew Kroening investigated past-armed events between Cold War competitors and argued that "states that enjoy nuclear superiority over their opponents are more likely to win nuclear crises."[53] However, none of the past-armed conflicts escalated to where both countries tried to nuke each other. Likewise, the two strategic powers continued to augment their space for military purposes and militarize outer space.

Sputnik-I and II's successful launch temporarily shifted balance of power in Soviet Union's favour and had profound implications for geopolitical order. As highlighted earlier, the U.S.'s primary fear was ICBM's development as an associated product of space technology development in the Soviet Union. The perceived threats from Soviet's continuous development of its space program caused a political and technological stir in the U.S. As a result. The U.S. also accelerated its efforts to compete with the Soviets to reach space. In doing so, the U.S. space program became the top political priority and a must-win battleground to maintain U.S. prestige in world politics.

The exciting part of the space race was from 1957 to 1983. Between these years, the two states focused on launching satellites for military purposes, exploring the Moon with human-crewed missions, and developing missile programs as an associated product of their space programs.

The militarization of space is not a new concept; it dates back to the Second World War.[54] General Henry Arnold and his counterpart Theodore von Karman sensed the importance of a U.S. military space program. The concept of space as a strategic domain was presented at that time, and efforts were initiated to acquire and develop U.S. missile and space programs.[55] USAAF's efforts to augment space and missile technologies were to develop long-range ballistic missiles and heavy-lifting rockets to send artificial satellites into space.

Initial efforts to materialize the reality of space militarization were begun in the Eisenhower era. However, it was the Soviets who brought the novelty into reality by sending Sputnik I and II. In that period, American policymakers felt danger of a surprise attack from the Soviets. To securitize, policymakers in Eisenhower Administration proposed the construction of an enterprise of reconnaissance satellites to take imagery of the Soviet Union's denied territories, where they feared presence of missile launching pads and military airports, troop movements, their extent and direction with a 10–15 per cent error.[56] Likewise, both powers developed satellites for passive military purposes, including intelligence gathering, surveillance, reconnaissance (ISR), communication, navigation, geodesy, ocean surveillance, meteorology, etc.[57]

Less than five years after the launch of Sputnik I, President Kennedy announced the U.S. plans to land Americans on the Moon in his speech at the height of the Cold War. The U.S. was making rigorous efforts to surpass tactical advantage gained by the Soviets from the Sputnik launch. The most pressing issue was to get the images of denied Soviet territories, and in doing so, the U.S. had created an "extraordinary series of reconnaissance satellites." The CORONA series played an important role in it.[58] Likewise, on the other side, the Soviets' Zenit series of reconnaissance satellites was countermeasure to CORONA. The most significant part of the space race history came after Kennedy. The space race was so intense that it established several key research and development (R&D) agencies in the U.S. The National Reconnaissance Office (NRO) was established at that particular time. New agencies were established within the U.S. Department of Defence (DoD), e.g. Advanced Research Projects Agency (ARPA), now Defence Advanced Research Projects Agency (DARPA). The space race started to take over the government machinery of both powers. The Soviets also started similar efforts to develop spy satellites. Loring Wirbel notes the dual-use space technology development as:

> The civilian space satellite program served as cover for a wide-ranging spy satellite program. That came as little surprise to an academic community already accustomed to the idea that the civilian race to the Moon has been little more than a Cold War stunt.[59]

Wirbel and Väyrynen's observations about development of space technologies during the Cold War primarily addressed getting real-time information about enemy military developments. The space technologies used for civilian purposes were by-product of the space race. Jeffery Richelson noted the U.S. desire during the Cold War was to outnumber the Soviet Union in reconnaissance satellites. The U.S.

was looking towards detecting other hotspots beyond Soviet territory, and for that purpose, it continued to send more reconnaissance satellites.[60] In addition, the U.S. and Soviets also developed military communication satellite systems, as well as position-navigation-timing (PNT) systems (the U.S. developed its Global Positioning System (GPS), and the Soviets developed GLONASS). The primary reason behind developing reconnaissance and communication satellite systems was to expand the space spy network, "gauging threat accurately and possibly circumvents potential hostilities."[61]

Paul Stares gave a significant analytical assessment of Soviet-U.S. space competition to expand their space militarization capabilities. Stares assessed the development of spy satellites for various purposes by both sides during the Cold War peak. He argued that academics and experts usually saw space as the "new high ground or a new dimension of the arms race." The primary reason for this assertion was the intense development and subsequent launching of satellites in space, which indicated a new trend in space militarization. Stares analysed the post-Sputnik era as a period of uncertainty for a short duration. In that era, both sides realized the profound implications of any conflict in space. Stares argues that both sides developed military satellites to fulfil their domestic requirement "rather than in response to the activities of the other."[62] Likewise, other key variants of any military competition between two adversaries were absent from the Soviet-U.S. space race. However, as their reliance on satellites for military purposes or ancillary activities to the military increased over the decades, "space has remained, in effect, an adjunct to the overall arms race" between the two Cold War competitors.[63]

In the mid-1950s, the U.S. started the development of ICBMs. The Soviets were aware of the threats across the Atlantic Ocean with an incoming ICBM from the U.S. mainland and advanced their ICBM capability. To counter a nuclear-tipped incoming Soviet missile, the U.S. Army proposed building an anti-ballistic missile (ABM) shield. Bell Telephone Laboratories was tasked to prepare a feasibility report about the possibility of hitting a missile with another missile. This report assessed the American capability to build an ABM shield and the Soviet's capabilities to do the same. Notably, the report suggested that the U.S. had achieved significant "technological advancement in radar, electronic computing, nuclear explosives, and rocketry" and that "it was indeed feasible to build an ABM with a simple objective."[64] To build an ABM shield, policymakers in the U.S. agreed to the Nike Zeus Project in 1956.

The ABM Treaty defines ABM system as "a system to counter strategic ballistic missiles or their elements in flight trajectory." The elements include ABM interceptors, ABM launchers, and ABM radars. The ABM shield includes sea-based, air-based, space-based, or mobile land-based assets. Notably, the space-based ABM components were the most alarming development. However, a prominent part of ABM history during the Cold War was the U.S.-Soviet action-reaction syndrome.[65] Hence, both states agreed to limit ABM development altogether. Both agreed to end that action-reaction syndrome to expand a thin layer of ABM to an Iron shield because an ABM shield was extremely destabilizing and less of a confidence-building measure. The primary reasons behind this agreement on signing the ABM Treaty were its "advantages outweighed by the disadvantages. Under the best circumstances, the ABM seemed prone to obsolescence (as new offensive missiles appeared), uncertainty effective, enormously expensive, and politically inexpedient."[66]

The technological revolution and the Revolution in Military Affairs (RMA) were key aspects of the Cold War space order.[67] This factor fuelled the political feud between two powers as it became a matter of prestige. A detailed history of that period will highlight the role of technological advancement in setting up the pace of U.S.-Soviet strategic competition. Both sides continued to build expensive defence systems for military purposes. This technological advancement overlapped during the Cold War. Consequently, development of one defence system made another system a significant development in BMD system, and ABM shield resulted in making of anti-satellite system, and all these were related technologies.

The first technological breakthrough in space exploration was launch of Sputnik-1. The Sputnik-I launch was just tip of the iceberg as it was the beginning of the space race, an expensive race to send satellites into space. As highlighted earlier, the competition between two strategic rivals was so intense that the peaceful exploration of space was never the top priority in the U.S. or the Soviet Union. A primary example could be establishment of NASA to avoid the complexity created due to lack of information about the peaceful exploration of space. Both countries wanted to know each other's military developments. Thus, half of the Cold War space race was about sending spy satellites into space to help them see "enemy's backyard." Spy satellites changed the course of Cold War history by introducing intelligence collection, surveillance, and imaging gathering methods, making nations less "fearful and, thus, less prone to pre-emptive aggression."[68]

The intense space race also lured both countries into thinking about methods to hamper, disrupt, or destroy enemy eyes in the sky. To do so, ASAT missiles were developed. The designed mission of ASAT missiles was to destroy the enemy's network of eyes and ears in sky, including its forces' command and control. The objective of developing kinetic-energy ASATs was to blind enemy satellites in space in a crisis. Most spy satellites are in low Earth orbit (LEO) and give images of territory through photo-reconnaissance. Likewise, LEO satellites can also be used for Electronic Intelligence (ELINT), meteorology, and geodesy. The ASAT developments in the U.S. and the Soviet Union were to target these LEO satellites. Both states also placed satellites for strategic early warning and military and civil communication in Highly Elliptical Orbits (HEO). Both countries developed ASAT missiles to target each other's LEO/HEO satellites. The Soviets again shocked U.S. policymakers and the public by hitting a satellite with an ASAT in 1968. Consequently, Carter Administration authorized development of an advanced U.S. ASAT missile program under command of the USAF in 1977. The primary objectives of U.S. ASAT were to deter the Soviets from committing any action in space, "to protect U.S. military united from observation by Soviet satellites, and to induce the Soviet Union to reach an ASAT arms control agreement."[69]

ASAT development resulted from "dedicated systems and residual systems development capabilities for other purposes, notably defence against ballistic missiles."[70] The U.S. and the Soviet Union developed their ASAT capability due to significant overlapping technologies for developing BMD and ABM systems. Technologically, an ASAT is a residual or the by-product of missile interception technology. An ASAT missile can be developed by looking at the BMD system hitting an incoming ballistic missile at three different stages in its time of flight: boost-phase, mid-course, and terminal or re-entry phase. Any boost-phase BMD system has great ASAT potential. Likewise, mid-course BMD systems have a great tendency towards ASAT. However, a terminal BMD system may not be an ASAT.[71] The Cold War space race's noticeable point was development of ASAT missile as a designated or residual product of many other associated defence systems with specific political, military, and economic implications.[72] Both powers continued to develop their BMD system. As a result, more lethal by-products or designated missiles were also developed. During the Cold War, spy satellites launched by both sides rekindled Soviet-U.S. interest in developing ASAT missiles. The more they continued to rely on satellite systems for military purposes, more they became prone to develop ASAT weapons to threaten each other.

Another aspect of the weaponization of space during the Cold War was the inception of the Strategic Defence Initiative (SDI) concept during President Ronal Reagan's era. The Reagan era's pursuit of technologies to build an iron shield around the homeland departed previous administrations' narrative of space sanctuary. The announcement of SDI in 1983 marked the death of space sanctuary narrative. Space sanctuary doctrine promotes space exploration for peaceful purposes and maintains space for military uses, except not weaponizing space.

Before Reagan, Carter and Ford administrations had points of view of preserving space as a sanctuary. However, announcement of SDI and subsequent establishment of Strategic Defence Initiative Organization (SDIO) to oversee development of technologies marked the beginning of path followed by states towards the weaponization of space. On March 23, 1983, President Reagan asked the people to save lives rather than avenge them.[73] His message was to develop a shield to protect the homeland from Soviet ballistic missiles. The speech also marked a change in U.S. strategy from Mutually Assured Destruction (MAD) to Mutually Assured Survival (MAS).[74] The American perspective on taking such a revolutionary step was that it was because of Soviet violations of the ABM Treaty. The Reagan administration assessed that the Soviets invested far greater resources in building their strategic defence by expanding their ASAT missile, BMD, and conventional capabilities.[75]

The primary objectives of the SDI were to deter any Soviet aggression and increase strategic stability and the security of the U.S. homeland and its allies. For that purpose, a concept of a three-layered missile defence shield orchestrating multiple technologies, including space-based director energy weapons, kinetic kill vehicles, and ground-based missile interception.[76] The whole SDI architecture was based on various technologies, as mentioned earlier. Besides direct and kinetic energy technologies, there were technologies for "detecting a ballistic missile launch, surveillance, acquisition, and tracking of attacking missiles and with battle assessment."[77] In addition, SDI also conceived of increasing lethality of weapons and making that era's weapons more survivable. Likewise, attention was paid to assessing battle management and control techniques and developing countermeasures to defeat future defences.[78] The SDI program marked the doorway towards space weaponization. Although the system was never installed to counter an incoming missile, residual technologies or by-product of R&D in the SDI were politically helpful in deterring the Soviets and pushing their defence spending to breaking point.

During the Cold War, another key aspect of space exploration was formulation of bilateral and multilateral arms control treaties to prevent the deployment, detonation, and placement of Weapons of Mass Destruction (WMD) in outer space on celestial bodies. The treaties to prevent such deployment resulted from the enormous strategic capabilities produced by the two powers. To avoid any catastrophe in space, a common human heritage, the Soviets and the U.S. were the principal parties in arms control and disarmament treaties in nuclear, conventional, or space fields. The treaties and bilateral agreements negotiated and later formulated are the Limited Test Ban Treaty (LTBT), the Outer Space Treaty (OST), The Moon Agreement, the ABM Treaty, and inclusion of the Prevention of Arms Race in Outer Space (PAROS) issue in the Conference on Disarmament (CD) core agenda list. These bilateral and multilateral treaties were meant to prevent the weaponization of space, but none of these treaties, except the PAROS issue, discusses the fine aspects of the weaponization of space and has many loopholes.[79] Unfortunately, PAROS, the fourth core agenda item in the CD was initially discussed at the forum in 1985 but remained not negotiated because it would take rest of measures under its prohibition umbrella. This stalemate in CD shows the major powers' political will towards any negotiations prohibiting true weaponization of space.[80]

Humans have always remained curious to explore and travel in outer space. The curiosity to climb as the first step of the ladder was when human flight in the air became possible with aircraft. The next step towards achieving excellence became possible when German military scientists explored a new technology to send objects from one place to another with much more speed, the V series rocketry. After World War II, human curiosity became essential to state's ambitions and national security objectives. That was not peaceful as it was all about developing delivery means of nuclear weapons. However, most technologies are dual-use, and it is always a matter of time, choice, and setting up priorities when peaceful side of technology is explored for much more significant benefits for humanity. Sputnik-I's launch made the world realize that another side of space technology needs attention: exploring deep space and other planets and stars. Sputnik was the pre-eminent milestone in history of the space race,[81] and it provided an opportunity to test human scientific understanding of stars, planets, and the Universe. Sputnik was not the only step in that direction, as it also motivated the U.S. to go beyond the Earth's atmosphere after multiple initial failures to send an artificial satellite.[82]

Onward the Sputnik and Explorer mission, a race was in full swing between the Soviet Union and the U.S. to reach the Moon and other planets. Some authors noted earlier that the dual-use technology for space exploration was primarily meant for defence, and peaceful exploration was residual product of overall efforts. However, Peter Hays disagrees with this notion, believing that both states made significant steps towards space cooperation during the Cold War.[83] Establishing the International Space Station (ISS) is an example of space cooperation between two powers, even during the Cold War.[84] Space has proved to be an exclusive medium where competition and cooperation between two superpowers have occurred.[85] The voices raised in U.S. policymaking corners by public, space experts, media, and NASA personnel "reveal how early space exploration is a prime example of the blurring lines between military and civilian activities in the Cold War."[86] Both states have realized importance of space exploration for collective good of humanity. The race to conquer space "lifted the Soviet-American conflict out of the military sphere into a peaceful competition, with astronauts fighting a symbolic battle, an alternative to nuclear war," writes Werth.[87] Space exploration has helped both states' apparent misperceptions and misunderstandings about each other. The U.S. still depends on Russia's rockets to launch its big satellites into high orbits.[88]

Second Space Age and Present Space Order

The fall of Berlin Wall and Soviet withdrawal from Afghanistan in the late 1980s were the most debated modern history. These events were among many other factors that proved to cause the demise of the Soviet Union.[89] Some said it was the end of history and beginning of a unipolar world with a single dominant force with all military and economic might and a strong and undoubted political will to enforce its "New World Order."[90] The Soviet collapse cleared all the stumbling blocks from American way to achieving its global military, economic, and political pre-eminence. This marked the end of a great competition in which two powers never directly engaged in a war but continued to build all means of military power to shift what was believed to be a balance of power in their favour.[91] The chronicles of the Cold War tell a rigorous and intense arms race at nuclear and conventional levels.[92] Concerning overall competition, a new dimension had emerged, and it was the medium of space, in which they competed with all available national resources to maintain their prestige and create hegemony. The space race had many ups and downs, as for a short time, a party was leading in scientific and technological advancement, creating a national embarrassment for other parties failing to respond similarly. A time came when one actor left no stone unearthed to show its scientific and technological advancement by sending its human-crewed mission to the Moon, which was indeed a setback for another party.

Similarly, both actors had parity in nuclear weapons and other dimensions of military competition, known as a détente.[93] Both realized that it was time to negotiate bilaterally and participate in multilateral arms control negotiations. Time passed, and the space age witnessed both sides' efforts to build space weapons and BMD systems. The space race witnessed intense scientific and technological advancement for military purposes and international prestige. But, at the end of the Cold War, only a single power remained ready to shape the entire space order.

Both states tried to achieve nuclear superiority during the Cold War, but real game-changer was space power. Like Britain became a mighty empire because of its super navy, space power made the U.S. a superpower after the Cold War. The U.S.

demonstrated military space power during Operation Desert Storm in 1991 Gulf War. The analysis of operation suggests that the U.S. armed forces "came to the desert battlefield with a near-total dominance of Earth orbits and marshaled unprecedented space-dependent military capabilities to help it achieve a decisive victory."[94] The unprecedented space power used by the U.S. during Operation Desert Storm and its open declaration and employment of space control has made it the "undisputed leader in space-assisted warfare."[95]

Russia's space program came under severe budget cuts and suffered a lack of attention from the leadership because of its deteriorating economic, military, and political infrastructure. That gave a comfort zone for the U.S. to maintain its dominance in the space arena. New actors in space include China, India, Japan, and the European Space Agency (ESA). The end of the Cold War also ended the space race between two powers. It marked the beginning of the second space age and reshaped the space order (see Fig. 6.2).

During the 1991 and 2003 Gulf Wars, China observed U.S. space power, which helped reinvigorate its space program.[96] According to Ashley Tellis, China's space program has been a key characteristic of its overall national power, and China is continuing to expand this as it has become a symbol of its soft power.[97] China tagged its space program as an element of its soft power in setting up its relations with the world. China launched "cooperative measures," declaring its aims and objectives to explore space for scientific and peaceful purposes "as part of a larger strategy to increase its soft power and enhance its international reputation and influence within Asia and across the globe."[98] China took a quantum leap in its space program in 2003 when its first taikonaut, a Chinese astronaut, reached orbit and returned safely to Earth.[99] The next step that shocked the entire world was successful Chinese ASAT missile test in 2007. It reignited chances of ASAT proliferation.[100] Chinese

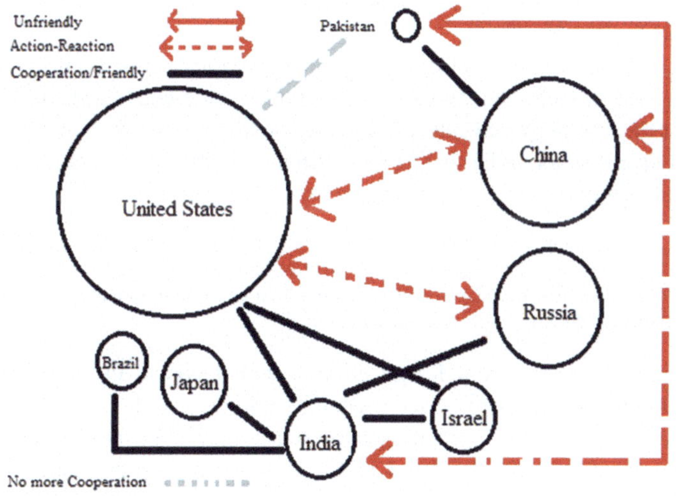

Fig. 6.2 Post-Cold War space order

space power continues to grow, surpassing Russia's several active satellites in outer space.[101] China is presently disinclined to accept U.S. space supremacy or dominance and poses asymmetric military challenges to the U.S.[102]

After ASAT missile test, China's other ASAT weapon test was the blinding of a U.S. reconnaissance satellite in LEO. There are different opinions on technological capabilities of laser used in that incident. However, there is a consensus that China partially blinded the satellite, implying that China has paced up its effort to achieve destructive and non-destructive means to hit satellites in space. The U.S. response to partial blinding was non-reactive, and observed a strategic silence. One reason behind U.S. strategic salience over the partial blinding was that the U.S. wishes to maintain freedom of action in space. U.S. protest with China could potentially mitigate U.S. counterspace programs. Onward, a new chapter in space security began, and space rivalry between the U.S. and China began. The dynamics of this adversarial relation have reshaped the global order.[103]

China has a footprint of Soviet space technologies and launched its missile program by testing its first Dongfeng (DF)-1 missile in 1960. The cooperation between two Communist states in space is historical, and it remained complex regarding technology transfer. However, neither country reacted to development of each other's space capabilities. In the Cold War, the Sino-Soviet space cooperation remained focused on achieving economic, scientific, and social objectives.[104] However, in past three decades after the Soviet demise, Sino-Russian space relations have developed a platform to counter U.S. space capabilities, especially in diplomatic forums, such as by presenting proposals to prohibit the placement of weapons in outer space and other initiatives. A research article by De Leon Petta Gomes da Costa on Sino-Russian space cooperation suggests that both countries must cooperate in space; otherwise, they will be restricted if they create a rivalry. He thinks Sino-Russia cooperation can play a "decisive role in this planet's future" if they wish to collaborate.[105] Recently, both sides signed 20 deals in energy and space technology transfer and exploration.[106]

India's space program's history tells us that India cooperated with both superpowers to get space technology for socioeconomic development during the Cold War. India's first successful space venture tested the sounding rocket Rohini-560 in 1972–73. In subsequent years, India sent its first artificial satellite, codenamed Aryabhatta, to a Soviet Cosmodrome for scientific purposes. However, OnkarMarwah wrote:

> Like the nuclear program, Indian policymakers will inherit military-launch capabilities, where at least intermediate-range missiles should become available to the country by the early 1980s. If the circumstances required, it would not be difficult to match the weight of nuclear warheads with those of scientific satellites.[107]

India learned lessons from Kargil conflict with Pakistan in 1999 and understood the importance of space power, especially military capabilities in space. After Kargil, India began to invest in its space program, gaining momentum. Bharath Gopalaswamy writes that the initial phase of Indian space program was developing technologies for scientific, agricultural, and information technology purposes between the 1960s and 2000s. But in 2001, India began exploring space for military purposes and sent its first military satellites in 2001.[108] According to the Annual Publication of the Institute of International Strategic Studies (IISS), Military Balance 2024, India has 26 military satellites in space.[109] In addition, India is developing counterspace (kinetic and non-kinetic) capabilities to enhance the scope of its military space program.

India is a regional space power with global space ambitions. Its space cooperation is increasing with regional partners globally, like Japan and Brazil. India is an essential member of the Asia–Pacific Regional Space Agency Forum (APRSAF) alongside Japan. It is believed that to counter rising Chinese commercial space ventures in Asia, India, and Japan will likely cooperate at APRSAF. Still, China is on top of the Asian Space Race. Recently, both countries signed various agreements to boost cooperation in space technology and exploration.[110] In a comparative study with Brazil, Renata Ribeiro's analysis of India's space program notes that from the beginning, India's strategy to establish international cooperation in acquiring space technology and expertise from other countries has been successful. He writes that "India realized that international embargoes impeded its satisfactory progress within the sector, which continued to buy foreign technology."[111] Launching 104 satellites from different countries and making a world record in space launches reflects India's successful space cooperation and diplomacy.[112] India's position in the Cold War and post-Cold War space order has remained non-reactive, and its space objectives are primarily motivated to achieve technological achievement in planetary exploration and other associated fields. However, after 2007, the Indian political, military, and scientific community started considering building ASAT missiles and other counterspace capabilities to counter China's emerging space threat to India's space program. In 2019, the testing of ASAT was aimed to signal China. In 'Antariksha Abhyas' Space War Game, it was identified that the primary threat to India is Chinese space assets. Likewise, Pakistan was also considered an Indian adversary in space.

The current space order has multiple layers. At global level, the space order is witnessing the "rise of China," "resurgence of Russia," and "to a lesser extent, India." The expanding capabilities of these three countries and significant devotion of national resources to foster their respective space programs for various reasons, including prestige and national security, have made the current space order multipolar. Furthermore, ESA, Japan, and Israel's development of critical space technologies and enhancement of their cooperation with other developing countries have made orbits more congested and crowded, leading to military and economic competition. Moltz, on the characteristics of the present order, said that:

> The U.S. has certain military, commercial, and civil space advantages over other players that make it the most powerful actor among other countries in space today. The U.S. will likely narrow over time, but it will remain the leading space power for the foreseeable future, particularly due to the likely expansion of its commercial sector.[113]

Moltz aptly characterizes features of current space order. In addition, there is a misunderstanding-misperception dynamic between three major space powers regarding development of their space weapons and increase in military space capabilities. States have covered significant distances while following a path towards the weaponization of space. This is also a strong argument that the weaponization of space has already been done, and states are just waiting to wave each other off in a weaponized space environment.[114]

Furthermore, complexity, uncertainty, and dynamic international security environment have shaped the space environment. The states are lost in space towards a "misguided drive toward building anti-satellite weapons," exploring kinetic and non-kinetic means to disrepair, permanently or temporarily damage the functioning of the adversary's satellite.[115] "Conflict remains a prominent feature of international relations," becoming more complicated because of many ungoverned areas of technology transfer and regional powers gaining modern nuclear, conventional, and space technologies.[116] The more states develop military capabilities by self-help for their survival, the more likely they are to establish a deterrent relationship with their adversaries. Likewise, in the rise of illiberal world order,[117] more states economically become interdependent, more they solidify their deterrent relations. Nicolas Peter categorized history of space exploration into three different orders: "proto-space age" (pre-World War II), "Space 1.0" (Cold War), and "Space 2.0 (post-Cold War)."[118] Space 2.0 has witnessed multipolar characteristics and increasing commercialization of space for various national reasons, including national economy, public services, and national security. However, more the misunderstanding-misperception dynamic grows in any bilateral or trilateral relation, more chances of escalation and conflict, making complex space deterrent relations.[119]

A dominant narrative in current literature, policy statements, and experts' views on space security concerns increasing activities in space. The debate is mainly U.S.-based. Space is now more congested and crowded than it was in the Cold War. The Cold War was about two powers' relations, but space technologies increased the pool of states aspiring to become space powers. As a result, several states other than three major space powers, the U.S., China, and Russia, and international companies now own many satellites orbiting the Earth. These international companies are also actively collaborating, and major spacefarers are stakeholders in their investment as part of their commercialization of space. Roger Harrison believes that

> Some "golden" orbits are more desirable than others, which are becoming crowded, with some jostling apparent. "Cheap launch," if it becomes a reality, will worsen the problem: the business plan for the new commercial launch companies depends on slim margins and high volumes, and this portends a large increase in the number of satellites encumbering a fixed number of useful orbits and crowding available spectrum.[120]

This has made the space crowded and congested.[121] But from a space security view, more the reliance on satellites grows, more they are vulnerable to attacks, especially hacking and physical destruction, because of increasing fear of states moving towards a tipping point where they regard weaponization as inevitable.[122] Those at helm of affairs in U.S. military space organizations believe that with increasing number of nation-states in space owning a significant number of satellites with space launch capabilities, they are likely to increase hostile ISR and intelligence capabilities to

U.S. national security. U.S. military space commanders believe a need to re-evaluate their space strategy to counter emerging challenges to U.S. space supremacy and freedom of action in space.[123]

Space is a strategic domain, and major and emerging space powers want to have their place in it. States are shifting their gear to maintain their position in space in the twenty-first century primarily because of military and economic benefits. India, China, and Japan have declared planetary exploration missions, which were only part of the Soviet Union and U.S. policies in the Cold War. After its end, the world witnessed a gradual increase in military and peaceful space assets and technologies of states other than the U.S. and Russia. States like India, China, Japan, South Korea, etc., are expanding their international partnership to send other states' satellites into outer space. This has broken monopoly of the U.S. and Russia over only the two powers to send satellites to other states; in fact, China and India have sent alternative platforms for developing countries to send their satellites more cheaply than from U.S. and Russian launching pads. In addition, North Korea, South Korea, and soon Pakistan, Turkey, Brazil, and Argentina will join the club to advance their space launch proficiency. The expansion of space-faring nations' pools has made the skies and space more competitive.

However, there is a need to understand that today is not like a Cold War competition. Although there is an element of prestige in present space order as it was in the Cold War order, it does not mean that it will shape present-day order similarly. The Cold War was about bipolar world, and the space order was also bipolar, but today's space order is very much multipolar. China has emerged as a global space power, India is also following suit, and Japan is not lagging. European states have also jointly developed indigenous technologies to explore space. The Russian space program is coming out of a two-decade-long hibernation. Likewise, there are increasing numbers of space users. In sum, the contemporary space order is more complex, may be reactive, and may see more efforts from states to weaponize outer space and competition to shift space economic balance in their favour by giving cheap space launches. The end of the Cold War marked beginning of an era of space commercialization. Advanced space powers are deregulating their space launch industry to allow them to send private satellites owned by non-state actors. "The space industry is thriving and highly competitive, attracting both emerging established technological and industrial powers," according to Stratfor's space assessments.[124]

Likewise, other than states' vital interest in space, common human life in an interconnected world depends on space-based infrastructure, e.g. internet, communication, navigation, etc. Living without these facilities, largely dependent on satellites, would be complicated. The World Wide Web (WWW) is a by-product of space race during the Cold War. After Soviet demise, the "Internet profoundly subverted the ability of powerful institutions (governments, newspapers) and economic/geographic factors (distance, costs of publishing and mailing) to control and shape the flow of information."[125] Internet services after the Cold War were like "the invention of the printing press." It was like "Martin Luther used to erode the clergy's power by printing the Bible in German so that ordinary folk could read the word of God."[126] So, it is evident that living without internet in this modern-day world, which is very much interconnected and was never before in history of humankind, would be extremely difficult. In this regard, satellites undoubtedly are basic building blocks of this interconnected world, and from a commercializing point of view, more satellites are in space, more the world will be interconnected, and people will have more freedom of action on social media. However, satellites providing these services are also under, if not at all, a constant threat of being knocked out through electronic and destructive means.

The tensions between the U.S. and North Korea have renewed the catastrophic consequences of an Electromagnetic Pulse (EMP) attack on U.S. satellites by the latter.[127] Peter Vincent Pry appeared as a witness in joint hearing before the subcommittee on national security, explaining the disastrous effects of a North Korean EMP attack on U.S. satellites. He testified that a North Korean EMP attack would knock out U.S. navigation and communication satellite systems and ground and air traffic control systems, blinding surviving aircraft. Furthermore, "cars, trucks, trains, and traffic control systems would be damaged." Consequently, life in the U.S. will be dead as cities suffer from gigantic traffic jams, vehicles will be rendered inoperable, and massive blackouts in major cities will halt all fields of life. In 2024, U.S intelligence agencies warned Biden administration that Russia is building a nuclear capable ASAT weapon in space. U.S. first tried to bring a UNSC resolution on Article IV of the OST. But Russia vetoed it. The U.S. again tabled the resolution in the UNGA First Committee, where it was passed. Pakistan also voted in favour of the resolution.

Interestingly, the renewed threat from North Korea, and Russia has meant recommendations from experts to strengthen the U.S. BMD system, land and space-based systems, and reconsidering old SDI to avert the chances of an EMP attack by North Korea and Russia.[128] Besides these imminent threats due to multilateral adversarial relations in international system, there is also an environment of competition in subject of space science and technologies as states are rigorously competing to project their scientific achievements, which has given space-related institutions "an interest in space science studies as well as general earth studies."[129] However, despite some negativity, the one good side of this competition is progress of science and technology for society's good. Technology is always dual-use but always pays back for good despite being negatively used for destruction. In case of space, technology has paid back in the past and will continue to pay back in the future.

The space order is multipolar with multidimensional characteristics primarily focused on economic and military avenues for states to explore in parallel. The security challenges are tremendous, and states compete globally. Space power's importance for military purposes as a force-enabling capability has increased twice in the Cold War. Likewise, commercialization of space has grown exponentially over past two decades, creating new horizons of space tourism, deep space exploration, and set space stations with many states participating in building them. Besides that, there are many similarities between post and pre-Cold War space order. Both orders lack international governance or a code of conduct to explore space.[130] There is no universally accepted treaty to prohibit all kinds of space weaponization. States still feel vulnerable in space. Space military capabilities are increasing to counter each other. However, unlike the Cold War space order, present-day space order may involve an assured deterrent relation between states, or states may complete the path towards space weaponization and bring doomsday clock more seconds closer to space Armageddon.

In present space order, states are rapidly increasing their space weaponization capabilities, and there is an increasing sense of space as a warfighting domain.[131] Likewise, there is also a sense in major space powers that space weaponization is inevitable, and there is a need to take steps ahead of space militarization. There are growing concerns in the U.S. that Russia and China can attack U.S satellites, and if it happens, the U.S. should prepare for war in space.[132] U.S. policymakers believe that U.S. dependence on their space assets is critical for their national security, and if attacked, the U.S. will have no option but to respond similarly. The U.S. military has prepared strategies like the National Security Strategy and National Defence Strategy, explicitly discussing counterspace capabilities and space as a warfighting domain.

On the other hand, China and Russia are also aware that the U.S. intends to add more lethality to its space weapons and will likely follow suit. The current space order is becoming complex because of geostrategic and geopolitical competition between these three powers, thus reshaping the current global space order. There is a chance that the U.S. will increase its space fleet, as there is a chance of a Sino-Russia bilateral response to U.S. space capabilities. China's PLA has increased its ASAT defence capabilities,[133] and the Kremlin has announced building "an invincible intercontinental cruise missile and a nuclear torpedo that could outsmart all American defenses."[134] Chinese and Russian investments in their missile defence systems will have a spin-off effect on their counterspace capabilities. They will likely affect their lethality, precision, accuracy, and targeting in space and push them to rigorously follow a path towards space weaponization, increasing chances of a space arms race.

Asian Space Race

Within the layers of global space order, a layer tells the space race between Asian space powers. China, India, and Japan are three major Asian space powers. Space power is vital for these states' national, international prestige and soft power. All these states have announced plans to explore deep space and other solar system planets. Likewise, all provide opportunities for other states to jointly manufacture/build and launch satellites to increase commercial activities in space.

China took the lead from other Asian space powers at regional level cooperation and established the Asia–Pacific Multilateral Cooperation in Space Technology and Applications (AP-MCSTA) in November 1992. Establishing AP-MCSTA was presented by China, Pakistan, and Thailand and later became the Asia–Pacific Space Cooperation Organization (APSCO). Pakistan, Bangladesh, China, Iran, Mongolia, Peru, Thailand, and Turkiye are Member States of APSCO, dominated by China as a core state.[135] Interestingly, China asked South Korea to become a Member State, but it did not sign the document, nor did Japan and India.[136] APSCO was modelled on ESA format, and its goal was to achieve space technologies for peaceful purposes.

James Moltz sees China's help in establishing APSCO space platform to crowd in aspiring space powers in region but with " perspective of regional leadership and has apparent aims of integrating space economics of members, although most of membership has only rudimentary space technology."[137] In addition, APSCO Member States see China as principal innovator of space technology, and they see APSCO as a platform to seek Chinese space technology know-how and transfer it to build their space program infrastructure. Under APSCO, China is "providing data, ground stations, scientific training, and practical experience in helping to construct spacecraft, which they would not otherwise be able to gain." One prime example of Chinese efforts is BeiDou navigation satellite system. Pakistan has ended its reliance on U.S. GPS as Chinese BeiDou system started providing services in Pakistan.[138] China also cooperates with other countries to help them build their space program. However, China has not successfully convinced other space powers like India, Japan, and South Korea to join the organization because of cold Chinese relations with said states. Likewise, these states are unlikely to accept Chinese monopoly in Asian region, "making it difficult for China to see the organization emerging as a basis for region-wise institutionalized cooperation anytime soon."[139]

Asia–Pacific Regional Space Agency Forum (APRSAF) is another regional space cooperation forum led by Japan and India to counter Chinese-led APSCO in Asia. China is also a member of APRSAF, but its main regional cooperation is through APSCO. APRSAF is mainly funded by the Japan Aerospace Exploration Agency (JAXA). APRSAF has a different mandate and objectives than APSCO as it is more related to scientific knowledge sharing and space relation information sharing. Japan is primarily leading the organization in active collaboration with India. During Prime Minister Shinzo Abe's visit to New Delhi in 2017, both countries signed MoUs to increase cooperation in sharing space technologies and expertise in launching lunar and planetary exploration missions in future at APRSAF platform.[140]

The existence of parallel space forums reflects existence of a space race in Asia. The two Asian poles attract periphery states to become part of APSCO or APRSAF. Rong Du argues that space cooperation in Asia is suffering from a status quo, and space order in Asia presents a bifurcation structure driven mainly by three distinctive space powers: China, India, and Japan.[141] Likewise, two organizations' structural differences have reduced institutional interactions between the space platforms. Instead, core states in these two organizations use platforms to project their soft power in and outside Asia, inviting competition.

Furthermore, difference between two organizations has made it "unfeasible for initiatives to carry out substantial cooperation with each other. The subregionalization and fragmentation of space cooperation in Asia will likely be magnified if no cooperation agreement is reached among China, India, and Japan."[142] However, Asif Siddiqi believes that APSCO provides a bigger platform for Asia states to cooperate and globalize space technology. China is well-prepared to counter Indo-Japan-led APRSAF as APSCO gives strategic consideration to China with "larger issues of political and economic influence in Asia."[143]

China, India, and Japan rapidly increased their space capabilities and sub-regional, regional, and international cooperation.[144] However, this rapid expansion has been "accompanied by rapid growth in leadership competition among these states."[145] Likewise, most space capabilities development in China, India, and Japan are due to regional strategic environment for military purposes. There were proposals to integrate these two organizations into a single forum where all Member States of both organizations discuss issues related to space cooperation in Asia, but all ended in vain because neither of states wanted to share a single stage.[146] Neither state wants to be subordinate to others even though all three have primarily developed technologies indigenously, and by sharing their experience about space, technology could help establish Pan-Asian cohesion in space technology experience.[147]

Thus, the core states in this regional and sub-regional space order are China, Japan, and India. China is leading APSCO, whereas India and Japan are core states in APRSAF. See Fig. 6.3. These two organizations are shaping the regional and sub-regional space order.[148] As a space technology principal and increasing regional diplomacy in South Asia, India has tried to create a rule-based sub-regional space order under South Asian Association for Regional Cooperation (SAARC) Satellite initiative.[149] During 2014 SAARC Summit in Nepal, Prime Minister Modi announced the launch of SAARC satellite for mutual benefit of SAARC countries, which will provide a full range of space applications and services to India's neighbouring states, including Pakistan. But, Pakistan refused to become part of India's rule-based sub-regional space order created. India launched the satellite without Pakistan's participation, whereas remaining SAARC countries are part of SAARC satellite program.[150] India considers it a gesture of goodwill to its neighbouring countries and sees it as a sign of cooperation between regional countries and India. However, Sri Lanka and Pakistan continue to cooperate with China to manufacture and launch their satellites in space, likely to blow India's initiative to increase rule-based sub-regional space cooperation and influence.[151]

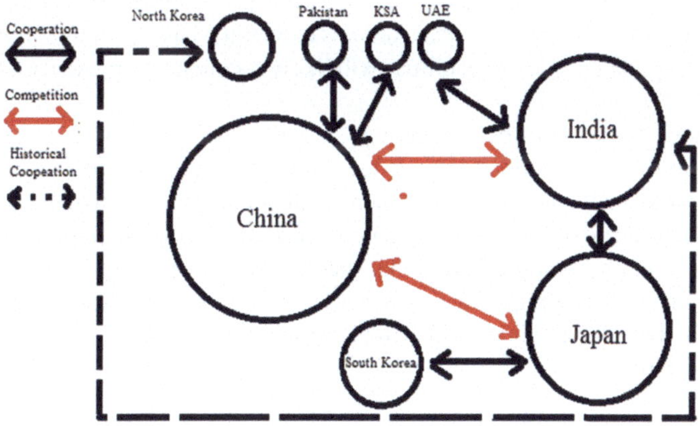

Fig. 6.3 Asian space order

Interestingly, Asia's desire to achieve space supremacy and space race between core and periphery states are gaining pace. However, Asian space order is also influenced by the U.S. as an external force. The U.S. has significant space cooperation with India, Japan, Indonesia, and South Korea. On the other hand, the U.S. perceives China as its adversary in space and feels vulnerable to its counterspace capabilities. Hence, it is a fact that rule-based global, regional, and sub-regional space orders have complex interactions and are likely to be more security-driven than focusing on increasing cooperation to explore space.[152]

Conclusion

This chapter aims to understand combined effect of space capabilities and intentions of major and emerging space powers. This combined effect of global and regional space capabilities and intentions forms rule-based global, regional, and sub-regional space order. States' space capabilities are growing in line with their political, military, and economic intentions, which help them secure a prominent global space order. States in prominent places tend to influence other states' behaviour and project and maintain their soft power and prestige. States with significant space militarization and weaponization capabilities possess power to reshape rule-based global, regional, and sub-regional space order. It is also evident that capabilities are instrumental in shaping the strategic environment in space. Likewise, intention-driven policies are also important, but a real game-changer is industrial base and subsequent development of national infrastructure to help a state develop its capability to influence other states.

The U.S. is dominant space power in global space order, with a historical tendency to influence other states' behaviour. It is also evident that any capability developed in U.S. threatens or challenges other states' national security. Russia is also resurging in space with a history of engaging the U.S. in a race, and China has also emerged as a global space power. The present space order is capability-based, not intention-driven. States with expanding space capabilities will likely dominate the present global space power.

At regional level, states depend on region's principal innovator to provide them with the know-how, expertise, knowledge, and information related to space technology to build their own. However, there is also complexity involved in it, as in Asia. Two parallel space forums compete for different strategic purposes, and this competition has given birth to a regional space race known as the Asian space race.

In conclusion, the current global space order is complex, crowded, congested, and competitive. The global space order will likely see more congestion and competition in coming years.

Notes

1. The author has evaluated the spending on the space technologies development for defence purposes in major, emerging and aspiring states using scientific methods involving statistical modelling and analysis, and concluded that "To the best of my knowledge, such strong general evidence of arms racing and security dilemma dynamics for military spending has not been presented before. Arms racing among proximate states are not just an intuitive theory; it also seems to be an underlying fact of international relations." See Goldsmith [1].
2. Quoted in Vincent [2].
3. Sorensen [3].
4. Quoted in Hagan [4].
5. Hagan, 478–490.
6. Kenneth Waltz has authored pioneer work on structural realism and balance of power as one the characteristics of world order. See Waltz [5]; "The Emerging Structure of International Politics," *International Security* 18, no.2 (1993): 44–79; "Structural Realism after Cold War," in *America Unrivalled: The Future of the Balance of Power,* ed. John Ikenberry (Ithaca, NY: Cornell University Press, 2002).
7. Fukuyama [6]; *The End of History and the Last Man* (New York: Avon Books, 1992).
8. Huntington [7]; *The Clash of Civilization and the Remaking of World Order* (New York: Simon and Schuster, 1996).
9. Kaplan [8]; *The Coming Anarchy: Shattering the Dreams of the Post Cold War* (New York: Random House, 2000).
10. Welsh [9].
11. Slaughter [10]; *New World Order* (Princeton: Princeton University Press, 2004).
12. See Nuechterlein [11].
13. See Mearsheimer [12].
14. See Treverton and Jones [13].
15. Holloway [14].
16. Kapur [15].
17. Shantz [16].
18. Proudhon [17], quoted in Shantz, "Anarchy Is Order."
19. Kapur, "International Nuclear Order," 421.
20. Walker [18]; Also see other publications of Walker on nuclear order, "International Nuclear Order: A Rejoinder," *International Affairs* 83, no.4 (2007): 747–756; "Nuclear Enlightenment and Counter-Enlightenment," *International Affairs* 83, no.3 (2007): 431–54; "The Quest for International Nuclear Order," *Die Friedens-Warte*83, no. 2–3 (2008): 35–55.
21. Walker, "Nuclear Order and Disorder," 712.
22. The authors have highlighted the emerging technologies used in space exploration and the narrative built during the space race to use those technologies to reach the Moon and conquer outer space. See AsifSiddiqui [19].
23. Muir-Harmony [20].
24. The dual-use item is defined as "an item (knowledge, technology, artefact) is dual-use if there is a (sufficiently high) risk that it can be used to design or produce a weapon, or if there is a (sufficiently great) threat that it can be used in an improvised weapon, where is neither case is weapons development the intended or primary purposes." The definition can also be applied to space technology and the history of the Cold War space race suggests that space technologies for peaceful exploration were also used for defence purposes. See Forge [21].
25. Jervis [22].
26. Goldgeier and McFaul [23].
27. On realpolitik in space, see, Dolman, *Astropolitik,* 1, 2, 60, and 78.
28. "China Joins the Space Age," *Science* 97, no. 18 (May 2, 1970): 427–428.
29. Moltz [24].

30. The technical report highlighting technical cooperation between NASA and SUPARCO was written by director science and research, SUPARCO in March 1972. Rehmatullah [25]; Also see the history of NASA-SUPARCO cooperation in space exploration, "Pakistan Derives its First "Hatf" Missiles from Foreign Space Rockets," *Wisconsin Project on Nuclear Arms Control,* October 1, 1995, https://www.wisconsinproject.org/pakistan-derives-its-first-hatf-missiles-from-foreign-space-rockets/; Khan [26].
31. Merbaum [27].
32. On the role of science and technology in the early twentieth century, see Wise [28].
33. On aeroplane invention and its demand in different fields, see, Simonson [29].
34. Read details, Roach [30].
35. See, Siegel [31].
36. On space as a matter of world's prestige, see, Mieczkowski [32].
37. Dolman [33]; "Geostrategy in the Space Age: An Astropolitical Analysis," *Journal of Strategic Studies* 22, no.2–3 (1999): 83–106.
38. Ryan and Keeley [34]; "Sputnik and the Dawn of the Space Age," *NASA*, accessed February 23, 2018, https://history.nasa.gov/sputnik/.
39. Ubell [35].
40. Ubell [35].
41. Michael [36].
42. "Explorer I Overview," *NASA*, February 23, 2018, https://www.nasa.gov/mission_pages/explorer/explorer-overview.html.
43. McDougall [37].
44. McDougall, 1011.
45. McDougall, 1011.
46. See CIA's declassified documents with assessments on Soviet's missile developments pre-and post-Sputnik edra, "What was the Missile Gap?" *Central Intelligence Agency*, February 23, 2018, https://www.cia.gov/library/readingroom/collection/what-was-missile-gap?page=2; On Soviet's ambition to develop its Long-range Ballistic Missile, see "Creation of a Long-Range Missile with a Nuclear Warhead," (official memorandum, Presidium of the CPSU Central Committee, November 25, 1953), http://digitalarchive.wilsoncenter.org/document/165389.
47. For history of U-2 flights, see section "over flights" in Richelson [38].
48. "Decree of the USSR Council of Ministers, 'On a New Test Range for the USSR Ministry of Defense'," *History and Public Policy Program Digital Archive,* February 12, 1955, Published in Baturin (2008), 46–47, selected, edited, and annotated by AsifSiddiqi, and trans., Gary Goldberg, http://digitalarchive.wilsoncenter.org/document/165390.
49. "The Dawn of the Space Age," *Central Intelligence Agency,* updated February 5, 2013, https://www.cia.gov/news-information/featured-story-archive/2007-featured-story-archive/the-dawn-of-the-space-age.html.
50. Shreve [39].
51. Gwertzman [40].
52. Erlanger [41].
53. Kroening [42].
54. Johnson-Freese [43].
55. Spires [44], Stares [45].
56. Väyrynen [46].
57. Väyrynen, 44–49.
58. Cloud [47].
59. Wirbel [48].
60. Richelson [49].
61. Richelson, 38–45.
62. Stares [50].
63. Stares, 128.
64. York [51].

65. *Arms Control in Space: Workshop Proceedings* (Washington, D. C.: U.S. Congress, Office of Technology Assessment, May 1984), 33.
66. Rothstein [52].
67. See, Cooper [53], Owens and Deitchman [54]
68. Motschiedler [55].
69. Gottfried and Lebow [56].
70. Grego [57].
71. See, *Arms Control in Space,* 35.
72. *Anti-Satellite Weapons, Countermeasures, and Arms* (Washington DC: Office of Technology Assessment, Government Pressing Office, September 1, 1985), 49–50.
73. See, Lord [58].
74. "MAD, the theatre threat and ABM," *The Adelphi Papers* 27, no. 225 (1987): 15–18.
75. Yonas [59].
76. See, *Strategic Defense Initiative: Survivability and Software* (Princeton, NJ: Office of Technology Assessment, 1988), Chap 2; Jasani and Lee [60].
77. Yonas [61].
78. Yonas, 185–189.
79. See, Van Ness [62].
80. Zhang [63], Moltz [64]; and also see, Rademaker [65], Hitchens [66].
81. Mcdonald [67].
82. See MacDonald [68].
83. Peter Hays (writer and visiting professor, George Washington University) in discussion with the author, February 26, 2018.
84. See Neal [69].
85. A detailed assessment suggests the history of U.S.-Soviet space cooperation during the Cold War, see *U.S.-Soviet Cooperation in Space* (Washington, DC: U.S. Congress, Office of Technology Assessment, July 1985).
86. Werth [70].
87. Yonas, 563–587.
88. "Why Washington Cannot Ban Russia's RD-180 Rocket Engines," *Space Daily* May 3, 2016, http://www.spacedaily.com/reports/Why_Washington_cannot_why_Russias_RD_180_rocket_engines_999.html.
89. "Soviet Union Timeline," *BBC,* October 31, 2013, http://www.bbc.com/news/world-europe-17858981.
90. See, Nye [71]; Oakley [72].
91. The research article gives a sceptical view of events that happened just before and after the end of the Cold War. See Artaud [73].
92. An interesting piece telling the morality of nuclear arms race in the Cold War, see, Wood [74].
93. On détente, see the views of Robert [75].
94. Lambakis [76].
95. Lambakis, 418.
96. Moltz, *Asia's Space Race,* 91–92.
97. Ashley Tellis (Senior Fellow, Carnegie Endowment for International Peace) in discussion with the author, February 13, 2018; Also see his article, "China's Space Capabilities and their Impact on U.S. National Security," *Carnegie Endowment for International Peace,* May 20, 2008, http://carnegieendowment.org/files/AshleyJTellisUSCCTestimonyMay2020082.pdf.
98. Chambers [77].
99. Solomone [78].
100. An edited book published by Stimson Center gives a detailed study on the proliferation of ASAT and its likely impacts, see Krepon [79].
101. See details, Khan and Khan [80].
102. Lewis [81].

103. A detailed study draws a holistic picture of U.S.-China space rivalry including doctrines, policies, capabilities and future programs. See, Erik Seed house, *Space Race: China Vs. the U.S* (Chichester, UK: Praxis Publishing, 2010).
104. Mathieu [82].
105. da Costa [83].
106. "China, Russia agree to Further Cooperation," *China Daily,* updated November 2, 2017, http://www.chinadaily.com.cn/world/2017-11/02/content_34000566.htm.
107. Marwah [84]; also see Thomas [85].
108. Gopalaswamy [86].
109. See, *The Military Balance 2018: The Annual Assessment of Global Military Capabilities and Defence Economies* (London: IISS, 2018), chapter 6: Asia, 261.
110. "India, Japan Set to Boost Space Cooperation," *Sputnik News,* September 9, 2017, https://sputniknews.com/asia/201709121057319030-india-japan-cooperation-/.
111. Ribeiro [87]; also see Kasturirangan [88].
112. Safi [89].
113. James Moltz (Professor at Naval Postgraduate School, U.S. and writer of *Asia's Space Race*) email correspondence to the author, November 28, 2017.
114. Hallman [90].
115. Krepon [91].
116. Berkowitz [92].
117. See detail analysis on rise of illiberal world, Boyle [93].
118. Peter [94].
119. See a detail study on space deterrence published by U.S Air Force Academy's (USAFA) Eisenhower Center for Space and Defence Studies, Harrison et al. [95].
120. Harrison [96].
121. Representatives of U.S, Bahrain, Indonesia, EU, Egypt, France, Kazakhstan, Cuba, Kuwait, Canada, and Brazil in the UN First Committee expressed their nations' concerns about the increasing activities in outer space and space race in their statements. See, United Nations, "Outer Space Increasingly 'Congested, Contested and Competitive', First Committee Told, As Speakers Urge Legally Binding Document to Prevent its Militarization," press release no. GA/DIS/3464, October 23, 2012, https://www.un.org/press/en/2013/gadis3487.doc.htm.
122. Hitchens [97].
123. Kitfield [98].
124. "Space: The Increasingly Crowded Frontier," *Stratfor*, March 25, 2016, https://worldview.stratfor.com/article/space-increasingly-crowded-frontier.
125. Ruffin et al. [99].
126. Ruffin et al., 319.
127. Dorminey [100].
128. Dorminey, 2017.
129. See, "Increasingly Crowded Frontier."
130. On challenges facing in establishing international space governance and Code of Conduct see "U.S Space Policy and the Challenges of Integrating Emerging Powers," (proceedings, Conference on U.S. Space Policy under International Institutions and Global Governance Program, Council on Foreign Relations, New York, U.S, June 30, 2011).
131. See the statement of USSTRATCOM Commander General Hyten, United Senate, "Opening Remarks of Chairman Rogers," press release, March 7, 2018, https://armedservices.house.gov/news/press-releases/opening-remarks-chairman-rogers-22.
132. *HASC-SF Hearing on the President's Fiscal Year 2019 Budget Request for Strategic Forces: Nuclear, Space, and Missile Defence,* 117th Cong., (March 7, 2018) (statement of John Rood, Under Secretary of Defence for Policy)
133. Dominguez [101].
134. MacFarquhar and Sanger [102].
135. "Welcome to APSCO: APSCO Member States," Asia–Pacific Space Cooperation Organization, accessed March 9, 2018, http://www.apsco.int/AboutApsco.asp?LinkNameW1=APSCO_Member_States&LinkCodeN=11.

136. Moltz [103].
137. Moltz, 128.
138. "Pakistan's Reliance on US GPS Ends as China's Beidou Navigation Satellite Systems has started to Cover Entire Pakistan," *Times of Islamabad,* February 13, 2018, https://timesofislamabad.com/13-Feb-2018/pakistan-s-reliance-on-us-gps-ends-as-china-s-beidou-navigation-satellite-system-has-started-to-cover-entire-pakistan.
139. Moltz, "Asian Space Rivalry," 130.
140. Ministry of External Affairs, "India-Japan Joint Statement during Visit of Prime Minister to India," press release, September 14, 2017, http://www.mea.gov.in/bilateral-documents.htm?dtl/28946/IndiaJapan+Joint+Statement+during+visit+of+Prime+Minister+of+Japan+to+India+September+14+2017.
141. Rong Du, "Space Cooperation in Asia: A Mystery," (paper, 65th International Astronautical Congress, Paris, France, October 3, 2014).
142. Du, 2014.
143. Siddiqi [104].
144. Sheehan [105].
145. Aliberti [106].
146. Moltz [107].
147. Quintana [108].
148. Pekkanen [109].
149. Shounak Set [110].
150. Arora [111].
151. *The Hindu,* "Editorial—Space For All: South Asia Satellite Launch A Positive Signal to the Neighbourhood," May 8, 2017.
152. Boyd [112].

References

1. Benjamin Goldsmith, "Arms Racing in Space: Spatial Modeling of Military Spending around the World," *Australian Journal of Political Science* 42, no.3 (2007): 419-440.
2. R.J. Vincent, *Nonintervention and International Order* (Princeton: Princeton University Press, 1974), 328.
3. Georg Sorensen, *A Liberal World Order in Crisis: Choosing Between Imposition and Restraint* (Ithaca, NY: Cornell University Press, 2011), 11.
4. Charles Hagan, "Geopolitics," *The Journal of Politics* 4, no.4 (1942): 478-490.
5. Kenneth Waltz, *Theory of International Politics* (Reading: Addison-Wesley, 1979).
6. Francis Fukuyama, "The End of History," *The National Interest,* no.16 (Summer 1989): 3–18.
7. Samuel Huntington, "The Clash of Civilization," *Foreign Affairs* 72, no.3 (1993): 22-49.
8. Robert Kaplan, "The Coming Anarchy," *Atlantic Monthly* 273, no.2 (1994): 44-76.
9. Jennifer Welsh, *The Return of History: Conflict, Migration, and Geopolitics in the Twenty-First Century* (Toronto: House of Anansi Press, 2016)
10. Anne-Marie Slaughter, "The Real New World Order," *Foreign Affairs* 76, no.5 (1997): 183-98.
11. Donald Nuechterlein, *U.S National Interests in a Changing World* (Lexington, KY: University Press of Kentucky, 1973), 171–194.
12. John J. Mearsheimer, "Structural Realism," in *International Relations Theories: Discipline and Diversity,* eds. Tim Dunne, MiljaKurki, and Steve Smith, 3rd Edition (Oxford: Oxford University Press, 2013), 77–93.
13. Gregory Treverton and Seth Jones, *Measuring National Power* (Santa Monica, CA: RAND Cooperation, 2005).
14. David Holloway, "Conclusion: Reflections on the Nuclear Order," *The International History Review* 40, no.2 (Special Issue 2018): 1–9.

15. Ashok Kapur, "Rogue States and the International Nuclear Order," *International Journal* 51, no.3 (1996): 420-439.
16. J. Shantz, "Anarchy Is Order: Creating the New World in the Shell of the Old," *The Journal of Media and Culture* 7, no.6 (2005).
17. Pierre-Joseph Proudhon, *Selected Writings of Pierre-Joseph Proudhon* (Garden City: Anchor Books, 1969)
18. William Walker, "Nuclear Order and Disorder," *International Affairs* 76, no.4 (2000): 703-724.
19. AsifSiddiqui, "Competing Technologies, National (ist) Narratives, and Universal Claims: Toward a Global History of Space Exploration," *Technology and Culture* 51, no. 2 (2010): 425–443.
20. Teasel Muir-Harmony, "The Role of Space Exploration in Cold War Diplomacy," *Physics Today,* May 6, 2015, http://physicstoday.scitation.org/do/https://doi.org/10.1063/PT.5.2027/full/.
21. John Forge, "Responsible Dual-Use," in *On the Dual Uses of Sciences and Ethics: Principles, Practices, and Prospects,* eds. Brian Rappert and Michael Selgelid (Canberra, Australia: ANU Press, 2013), 121.
22. Robert Jervis, "Was the Cold War a Security Dilemma?" *Journal of Cold War Studies* 3, no.1 (2001): 58.
23. James Goldgeier and Michael McFaul, "A Tale of Two Worlds: Core and Periphery in the Post-Cold War Era," *International Organization* 46, no.2 (1992): 467-491.
24. James Moltz, *Asia's Space Race: National Motivations, Regional Rivalries, and International Risks* (New York: Columbia University Press, 2012), chap 3.
25. Rehmatullah, *Upper Atmosphere Wind and Temperature Structure at Sonmiani Derived from the Rocket-Grenade Experiments Conducted During 1965–67* (Karachi: SUPARCO, 1972)
26. Feroz Hassan Khan, *Eating Grass: The Making of Pakistani Bomb* (New Delhi & Stanford: Stanford University Press, 2012), 236.
27. Alan Merbaum, "The U.S. Industry Perspective," in *Space Security and Global Cooperation,* eds. AjeyLele and Gunjan Singh (New Delhi: Academic Foundation, 2009), 234.
28. George Wise, "Science and Technology," *Osiris* 1, no.1 (1985): 229-246.
29. G.R. Simonson, "The Demand for Aircraft and the Aircraft Industry, 1907-1958," *The Journal of Economic History* 20, no.3 (1960): 361-382.
30. Edward Roach, *The Wright Company: From Invention to Industry* (Athens: Ohio University Press, 2014).
31. Irving Siegel, "Scientific Discovery and the Rate of Invention," in *The Rate and Direction of Inventive Activity: Economic and Social Factors* (Princeton: Princeton University Press, 1962), 441–458, http://papers.nber.org/books/univ62-1.
32. YanekMieczkowski, *Eisenhower's Sputnik Moment: The Race for Space and World Prestige* (Cornell University Press, 2013), chap 12.
33. Everett Dolman, *Astropolitik: Classical Geopolitics in the Space Age* (London: Frank Cass Publishers, 2002), 85-86.
34. Amy Ryan and Gary Keeley, "Sputnik and U.S. Intelligence: The Warning Record," *Studies in Intelligence* 61, no. 3 (2017): 1-17
35. Earl Ubell, "Sputnik II Opens Era of Travel into Space," *New York Tribune,* November 4, 1957, ProQuest Historical Newspapers.
36. Donald Michael, "The Beginning of the Space Age and American Public Opinion," *The Public Opinion Quarterly* 24, no.4 (1960): 573-582.
37. Walter McDougall, "Technocracy and Statecraft in the Space Age—Toward the History of a Saltation," *The American Historical Review* 87, no.4 (1982): 1010-1040.
38. Jeffrey Richelson, *The Wizards of Langley: Inside CIA's Directorate of Science and Technology* (Boulder, CO: Westview Press, 2001).
39. Bradley Shreve, "The U.S., the USSR, and Space Exploration, 1957–1963," *International Journal on World Peace* 20, no.3 (2003): 68.
40. Bernard Gwertzman, "Russians Debate Nuclear Victory," *The Washington Star,* February 21, 1967, CIA's Electronic Reading Room.

41. Steven Erlanger, "U.S. Seeks Nuclear Superiority, Soviet Officer Says," *Boston Globe,* October 23, 1985, CIA's Electronic Reading Room.
42. Mathew Kroening, "Nuclear Superiority and the Balance of Resolve," *International Organization* 67, no.1 (2013): 141-171.
43. Joan Johnson-Freese, *Space as a Strategic Asset* (New York: Columbia University Press, 2007), 83.
44. David Spires, *Beyond Horizon: A Half Century of Air Force Leadership* (Washington DC: Air University Press, 2002), 15
45. Paul Stares, *Space Weapons and U.S. Strategy: Origin and Development* (London: Croom Helm, 1985), 24–25.
46. Raimo Väyrynen, "Military Uses of Satellite Communication," *Instant Research on Peace and Violence* 3, no.1 (1973): 44-49.
47. John Cloud, "Imaging the World in a Barrel: CORONA and the Clandestine Convergence of the Earth Sciences," *Social Studies of Science* 31, no.2 (2001): 231-251.
48. Loring Wirbel, *Star Wars: U.S. Tools of Space Supremacy* (London: Pluto Press, 2004), 19.
49. Jeffery Richelson, "The Future of Space Reconnaissance," *Scientific American* 264, no.1 (19991): 38–45.
50. Paul Stares, "U.S. and Soviet Military Space Programs: A Comparative Assessment," *Deadalus*114, no.2 (1985): 127.
51. Herbert York, "ABM, MIRV, and the Arms Race," *Science* 169, no.3942 (July 17, 1970): 257–260.
52. Robert Rothstein, "The ABM, Proliferation and International Stability," *Foreign Affairs* 46, no.3 (1968): 487-502.
53. Jeffery Cooper, "Another View of the Revolution in Military Affairs," in *In Athena's Camp: Preparing for Conflict in the Information Age,* eds. John Arquilla and David Ronfeldt (Santa Monica, CA: RAND Cooperation, 1997)
54. W.A. Owens and S.J. Deitchman, "The Revolution in Military Technology," *Issues in Science and Technology* 11, no. 1(1994): 5–6
55. Motschiedler, Review of *Spy Satellites and other Intelligence Technologies that Changes History,* by Thomas Graham and Keith Hansen, *International Affairs* 84, no.1 (2008):171.
56. Kurt Gottfried and Richard Ned Lebow, "Anti-Satellite Weapons: Weighing the Risks," *Daedalus* 114, no.2 (1985): 147-170.
57. Laura Grego, "The History of Anti-Satellite Programs," *Union of Concerned Scientists,* January 2012, https://www.ucsusa.org/sites/default/files/legacy/assets/documents/nwgs/a-history-of-ASAT-programs_lo-res.pdf, 2.
58. Carnes Lord, "A Strategic Defence Initiative: Building A Better Shield," *The National Interest* 76, no. 7 (Summer 2004): 84–92.
59. GeroldYonas, "The Strategic Defense Initiative," *Daedalus* 114, no.2 (1985): 73–90.
60. BhupendraJasani and Christopher Lee, *Countdown to Space War* (London: Routledge, 1984).
61. Gerold Yonas, "Research and the Strategic Defense Initiative," *International Security* 11, no.2 (1986): 185-189.
62. Peter Van Ness, "The Time Has Come For A Treaty to Ban Weapons in Space," *Asian Perspective* 34, no.3 (2010): 215-225.
63. Hui Zhang, "Action/Reaction: U.S. Space Weaponization and China," *Arms Control Today* 35, no.10 (2005): 6-11
64. James Moltz, *Crowded Orbits: Conflict and Cooperation in Space* (New York: Columbia University Press, 2014), chap 7
65. Stephen Rademaker, "The Conference on Disarmament: Time is Running Out," *Arms Control Today* 36, no.10 (2006): 13–15
66. Theresa Hitchens, "Rushing to Weaponize the Final Frontier," *Arms Control Today* 31, no.7 (2001): 16-21.
67. Fraser Mcdonald, "Space and the Atom: On the Popular Geopolitics of Cold War Rocketry," *Geopolitics* 12, no.4 (2008): 611-634.

68. Alexander MacDonald, *The Long Space Age: The Economic Origins of Space Exploration from Colonial America to the Cold War* (New Haven, CT: Yale University Press, 2017), chap 4.
69. Valerie Neal, *Spaceflight in the Shuttle Era and Beyond: Redefining Humanity's Purpose in Space* (New Haven, CT: Yale University Press, 2017), chap 5.
70. Karsten Werth, "A Surrogate for War—The U.S. Space Program in the 1960s," *Amerikastudien/American Studies* 49, no. 4 (2004): 563-587.
71. Joseph Nye, "What New World Order?" *Foreign Affairs* 71, no. 2 (1992): 83-86
72. Robert Oakley, "The New World Order: Myth and Reality?" *Pakistan Horizon* 44, no.3 (1991): 9-18.
73. Denise Artaud, "The End of the Cold War: A Skeptical View," *Diplomatic History* 16, no. 2 (1992): 256-261.
74. James Wood, "The Nuclear Arms Race and the Churches," *Journal of Church and State* 25, no. 2 (1983): 219-229.
75. Robert Schulzinger, "The End of the Cold War, 1961-1991," *OAH Magazine of History* 8, no.2 (1994): 13-18.
76. Steven Lambakis, "Space Control in Desert Storm and Beyond," *Orbis*39, no.3 (1995): 418.
77. Rob Chambers, "China's Space Program: A New Tool for PRC "Soft Power" in International Relations?" (M.Sc. diss., Naval Postgraduate School, Monterey: CA, March 2009), 1.
78. Stacey Solomone, "China's Space Program: The Great Leap Upward," *Journal of Contemporary China* 15, no.47 (2006): 311-327.
79. Michael Krepon, "Space and Nuclear Deterrence," in *Anti-Satellite Weapons, Deterrence and Sino-American Space Relations,* eds. Michael Krepon and Julia Thompson (Washington DC: Stimson Center, 2013), chap 1.
80. Zulfqar Khan and Ahmad Khan, "Chinese Capabilities as a Global Space Power," *Astropolitics* 13, no, 2-3 (2015): 185-204
81. James Lewis, "Reconsidering Deterrence or Space and Cyberspace," in *Anti-Satellite Weapons, Deterrence and Sino-American Space Relations,* eds. Michael Krepon and Julia Thompson (Washington DC: Stimson Center, 2013), 77.
82. Charlotte Mathieu, "Assessing Russia's Space Cooperation with China and India," *European Space Policy Institute,* report 12, June 2008.
83. De Leon Petta Gomes da Costa, "Chinese Geopolitics: Space Program Cooperation among China, Brazil, and Russia," *Astropolitics* 14, no.1 (2016): 96.
84. Onkar Marwah, "India's Nuclear and Space Programs: Intent and Policy," *International Security* 2, no. 2 (1977): 104
85. Raju Thomas, "India's Nuclear and Space Programs: Defence or Development?" *World Politics* 38, no.2 (1986): 315-342.
86. Bharath Gopalaswamy, "Space Security: India's Perspective," in *Crux of Asia: China, India, and the Emerging Global Order*, eds. Ashley Tellis and Sean Mirski (Washington DC: Carnegie Endowment for International Peace, 2013), 173-185.
87. Renata Ribeiro, "Comparative Perspective of the Brazilian and Indian Space Programs," *Astropolitics* 15, no.3 (2017): 231
88. K. Kasturirangan, "India's Space Enterprise—A Case Study in Strategic Thinking and Planning," in *The First Ten K R Narayanan Orations: Essays by Eminent Persons on the Rapidly Transforming Indian Economy*, eds. Raghbendra Jha (Canberra, Australia: ANU Press, 2006).
89. Mihchael Safi, "India launches record-breaking 104 satellites from single rocket," *The Guardian,* February 15, 2017.
90. Wesley Hallman, "A Fast-following Space Control Strategy," *Astropolitics* 3, no.1 (2005): 35-42.
91. Michael Krepon, "Lost in Space: The Misguided Drive toward Anti-Satellite Weapons," *Foreign Affairs* 80, no.3 (2001): 2-8.
92. Marc Berkowitz, "Shaping the Outer Space and Cyberspace Environments," in *Conflict and Cooperation in Global Commons: A Comprehensive Approach for International Security*, ed. Scott Jasper (Washington, DC: Georgetown University Press, 2012),

93. Michael Boyle, "The Coming Illiberal Order," *Survival* 58, no.2 (2016): 335-66.
94. Nicolas Peter, "The New Space Order: Why Space Power Matters for Europe," *Space and Defence* 4, no.1 (2010): 56.
95. Roger Harrison, Deron Jackson, and Collins Shackelford, "Space Deterrence: The Delicate Balance of Risk," *Space and Defence* 3, no.1 (2009): 1-22
96. Roger Harrison, "Unpacking the Three C's: Congested, Competitive, and Contested Space," *Astropolitics* 11, no.3 (2013): 123-131.
97. Theresa Hitchens, "War in Space in Increasingly Possible. That Would be Terrible for Everyone," *National Post,* November 17, 2017, http://nationalpost.com/opinion/war-in-space-is-increasingly-possible-that-would-be-terrible-for-everyone.
98. James Kitfield, "Crowded, Congested Space," *Air Force Magazine* 93, no.8 (2010): 24-29.
99. Holt Ruffin et al., *The Post-Soviet Handbook: A Guide to Grassroots Organizations and Internet Resources,* revised edition (London: University of Washington Press, 1999), 319.
100. Bruce Dorminey, "North Korean EMP Attack Would Cause Mass U.S. Starvation, Says Congressional Report," *Forbes,* October 23, 2017, https://www.forbes.com/sites/brucedorminey/2017/10/23/north-korea-emp-attack-would-cause-mass-u-s-starvation-says-congressional-report/#19ad76dd740a.
101. Gabriel Dominguez, "China Conducts mid-course anti-missile test," *IHS Jane's*, February 8, 2018, http://www.janes.com/article/77752/china-conducts-mid-course-anti-missile-test.
102. Neil MacFarquhar and David Sanger, "Putin's Invincible Missile is Aimed at U.S. Vulnerabilities," *New York Times,* March 1, 2018.
103. James Moltz, "Asian Space Rivalry and Cooperative Institutions: Mind the Gap," in *Asian Designs: Governance in the Contemporary World Order*, ed, Saadia Pekkanen (Ithaca: Cornell University Press, 2016), 128.
104. Asif Siddiqi, "Asia in Orbit: Asian Cooperation in Space," *Georgetown Journal* 11, no.1 (2010): 138.
105. Michael Sheehan, "Rising Powers: Competition and Cooperation in the New Asia Space Race," *The RUSI Journal* 155, no.6 (2010): 55-50.
106. Marco Aliberti, "Regionalization of Space Activities in Asia?" *European Space Policy Institute,* ESPI Perspective no.66, February 2013, https://www.files.ethz.ch/isn/163952/ESPI_Perspective_66.pdf, 6.
107. James Moltz, "Asia's Space Race," *Nature* 480, no.7378 (2011): 171-173.
108. Elizabeth Quintana, "The Asian Space Race," in *Raisina Files: Debating the World in the Asian Century*, eds. Harsh Pant and RitikaPassi (New Delhi: Observer Research Foundation, 2017).
109. SaadiaPekkanen, "China and Japan Vie to Shape Asia's Approach to Outer Space," *Forbes,* October 31, 2016, https://www.forbes.com/sites/saadiampekkanen/2016/10/31/china-and-japan-vie-to-shape-asias-approach-to-outer-space/#1f3249a52606.
110. Shounak Set, "India's Regional Diplomacy Reaches Outer Space," *Carnegie Endowment for International Peace,* March 7, 2017, http://carnegieendowment.org/files/7-3-2017_Set_IndiaRegionalDiplomacy_Web.pdf.
111. MedhaviArora, "India Launches Satellite for South Asia Countries, Pakistan Says No Thanks," *CNN,* May 5, 2017, https://www.cnn.com/2017/05/04/asia/india-pakistan-satellite/index.html.
112. Alan Boyd, "Asia's Space Race Gathers Pace," *Asia Times,* January 6, 2018.

Chapter 7
U.S.—China Bilateral Relations in Space

Introduction

The study's research problem is to analyse the implications of an arms race in outer space for South Asia. The study's title is *Sabre-rattling in Space: A South Asian Perspective,* and it seems that a significant chunk of book will focus on studying China, India, and Pakistan. However, it would be impossible to understand the dynamics of global and regional space orders and Astropolitics without examining the U.S. space program. Likewise, study also focuses on a key important feature of South Asia's geopolitical and geostrategic environment: the security trilemma.

Moreover, the study will be incomplete if the implications of space power and the security trilemma for South Asia are not adequately studied. A more comprehensive review will investigate role of the United States as a core state, which has political, economic, and military power, resources, and influence to shape rule-based global, regional, and sub-regional space order. The United States possesses enough power in space to influence other states to change their behaviour. However, the U.S. faces challenges from additional global space power, China and Russia. China has ascertained second position in international space order, built sufficient space capabilities, and showed its Astro-intentions to Asia to be recognized as an Asian Space power. However, China has become a global space power, creating challenges and vulnerabilities for U.S. space supremacy.

The U.S.-China power dynamics in missile and space dimensions have spillover effects on South Asian security calculus. The Sino-U.S. competition in missiles and space has positive and negative implications for South Asia. Several questions germinate here: How can Sino-U.S. competition affect South Asia? What is the

---

This chapter draws from the Ph.D. research work of the author titled "Arms Race in Outer Space: A Paradigm Shift in International Security and Implications for South Asia," which was completed in 2019 and successfully defended in 2020 at Department of Strategic Studies, National Defence University, Islamabad.

A. Khan and E. Sadeh, *Sabre Rattling in Space*,
https://doi.org/10.1007/978-981-97-6050-3_7

nature of Sino-U.S. relations in space? What is space security trilemma? What are possible political and military implications of Sino-U.S. competition in space for South Asia? In general, will global, regional, and sub-regional competition in space bring a paradigm shift in international security? Likewise, the questions answered in previous chapters are backbone of this research. Analysing answers to questions asked during last chapters and explanations of this chapter will provide a base to prove study's hypothesis.

First, the chapter will explain nature of Sino-U.S. political, military, and economic relations. It will further explain nature of Sino-U.S. relations in space. Is there a kind of action-reaction model between the two space powers, or do they have complex interdependence that will engage them in assured space deterrence relations? A prominent part of their competitive relations is implications for South Asia. It is a fact that space power cannot be seen in total isolation as space capabilities work as a force enabler, and space power military, political, and economic benefits and create security challenges for adversaries.

U.S.—China Dynamics

> The United States and China are indispensable pillars of world order.[1]
>
> —Henry Kissinger, a Famous U.S strategist and diplomat.

"Yangtze Civilization" originated five thousand years ago when people living near the Yangtze River started knitting a "complex of great cultures."[2] Chinese civilization represents the existence of other civilizations, e.g. the Yellow River Valley, but the Yangtze River has deep footprints on China's five-thousand-old civilizations.[3] A brief study of Chinese civilization suggests that gaining political power to rule China was winning wars to obtain legitimacy. The history of tradition goes back to four thousand years ago. Dean Cheng believes that the five-thousand-year-old Chinese Civilization suggests that War begun by China or inflicted upon it was by choice.[4] The five-thousand-year-old Chinese history highlights fighting War as a prominent feature. As a result, Chinese thinkers and military generals authored some of most acceptable military thinking and strategy, e.g. Sun Tzu.[5]

The most acceptable perspectives of Chinese civilization are intellectualism and meritocracy, self-governance in civil society, and unified language and cohesive culture. These factors have helped China for over five thousand years.[6] Likewise, among many profound characteristics of ancient Chinese civilization are its relations with neighbouring and far-reaching states. During different Chinese dynasties, its civilization had "played as the foundation head of the oriental cultural rim and became increasingly prominent."[7] It is evident from history books that ancient China had a profound impact on world culture. In reciprocity, Chinese people also learned from civilization of their neighbours and other countries. The Western writings on Chinese civilization suggest that it has an "order, stability, symmetry, rationality," unlike the "divided, uneasy, strike-ridden world."[8] China's civilization was complex, but it was ordered. This orderliness in Chinese civilization shows how to interact with other civilizations in ancient times.

The purpose of highlighting some core features of Chinese civilization is to understand its impact on China's foreign relations with major powers. China has a five-thousand-year history, and it deeply reflects on modern China and its relations with thc world. It is important to understand the core values of Chinese civilization before understanding its relations with the United States. Fighting a war, winning it, and establishing cordial relations with its neighbours are paramount in Chinese foreign relations. China is a rising global power and has been a responsible power since the End of the Cold War.[9]

The post-Cold War order witnessed the rise of China at the regional and global levels. China emerged as a global economy in last three decades of the twentieth century, and next three decades of the twenty-first century will "bring them the completion of that rise."[10] From data gathered on world economies by the Economist's Intelligence Unit, China will likely retain the second position in the global economic order in 2024. At the end of the Cold War, dominant paradigm was the emergence of interplay of geopolitics and economy.[11] The interplay of these dominant themes in world politics gave birth to a new era of geoeconomics, and China realized the importance of being an economic power after the Cold War ended.[12] Another aspect of Chinese rise is its active role in geopolitics at regional and global levels. Chinese leaders have "refashioned their country's foreign policy" to meet China's foreign policy and economic and national security challenges in changing regional and global geopolitical landscape.[13] In past years, China has adopted a proactive approach to meet challenges in regional and global changing economic affairs and an active strategy to engage with cultural, technological, and educational affairs at regional and international levels.[14]

Rising China in changing world order riddled with realities of geopolitics and geoeconomics has many obstacles and daunting challenges. Among these knee-jerk challenges is sustaining economic growth in a competitive regional and global environment. Likewise, another obstacle to Chinese defence and foreign policies is peaceful engagement with major powers, especially the United States, without involvement in political, military, and economic competition, highlighting its ambitions and power to change the existing political and economic power.[15] China's foreign, economic, and defence policies engage with the U.S. and other major powers.[16] China-U.S. bilateral relations are undoubtedly the jewel of the crown of twenty-first-century political and economic order. As highlighted at beginning of this section, both countries are two prominent pillars of present international order. Both countries have massive economic, military, and political capacities.[17] It is important to understand how China sees the world.

The answer to this question is deeply interlinked with its bilateral relations with the United States. China sees a multipolar world without U.S. primacy.[18] The world has been turning upside down since 9/11 in the United States. After the terrorist events, the United States launched a war against the Global War on Terror (GWOT), and in subsequent years, it also waged War on Iraq. Onward, discussion about a "unipolar versus multipolar" world became prominent in global political discourse.

Likewise, China's discussion started as an emerging political, economic, and military player on the world stage. The gradual rise of China in the post-9/11 world has germinated fears that it will eventually surpass the U.S. military and economic power.[19] But that is only one side of picture. Many Chinese political and strategic analysts disagree with this revisionist thought. They argue that China does not harbour any grand revisionist ambition and will be happy to "play a larger role in the existing system and is prepared to attempt to achieve this goal" by bringing more political independence, economic reforms, and smoothing foreign relations with its neighbouring countries and with major powers including the United States.[20]

Likewise, China-U.S. political, economic, and military relations will also be highlighted to understand how the two powers interact in outer space.

Political Relation

A general political thought about U.S.-China relations in the early years of the post-Cold War was that they were neither friends nor foes.[21] Both countries were not engaged in a rivalry fashioned in a Cold War manner. A central or core feature of U.S.-China relations is "mutual distrust of long-term intentions, termed strategic distrust."[22] The perception and image of any state in international political system matters, and when it comes as a central theme of two pillars of global order, it becomes lethal for normal relations. However, China and the United States have different histories, languages, cultures, civilizations, social norms, institutions, and political thoughts about present world order but are still engaged in a vicious cycle of misperception and misunderstanding.[23] The issue of misperception and misunderstanding in the international system is arguably best studied by Robert Jervis. He summarized the dynamic between the two actors:

> In determining how he will behave, an actor must try to predict how others will act and how their actions will affect his values. Therefore, the actor must develop an image of others and their intentions. However, the image may be inaccurate; the actor may, for several reasons, misperceive both others' actions and their intentions.[24]

The misperception-misunderstanding dynamic is prevalent in U.S.-China bilateral relations. The current relations can be framed as what Jervis has hypothesized. Jervis argued about misperception in the two states' policy and decision-making spheres. Still, in U.S.-China relations, this element of misperception is now trickling down to the general public, making the relationship more complex in the last decade. The dynamic of strategic mistrust between the two countries is now the combination of misperception at the decision-making and public levels.

Due to different cultures, civilizations, governance, economy, etc., the impact of public opinion on overall policymaking process in both countries is unlike. American public opinion profoundly affects its policymaking, whereas, in China, public opinion seems to have less impact on policymaking. However, it cannot be discounted in current urban China.[25] Mathew Hirshberg has analysed history of American public opinion on China during and after the Cold War. Hirshberg developed an American Patriotic Schema framework in his research to describe the American public opinion on the Soviet Union and the People's Republic of China (PRC).[26] He analysed that most American public opinion during the Cold War was negative towards China, tagged as "Red China." PRC, a Soviet puppet, communist, evil, and oppressive to its people, was perceived in the U.S.[27] During many ups and downs in Sino-U.S. relations, a time came when "Sino-Soviet confrontation led to Sino-American accommodation," resulting in a wave of positivity in American public opinion towards China. But this positivity did not remain consistent, "China remained as communist and undemocratic."[28] During the Cold War, China was a communist and oppressor because of American public. Change in public opinion is a gradual and slow process, but near the end of the Cold War, American public opinion surveys gave China "favourable ratings."[29]

The post-Cold War era had some major trends, including collapse of communism, trade replacing territorial expansion, and economic and political reforms in many countries.[30] In the post-Cold War, China's image drastically changed American public opinion. Although reforms began in China in 1979 when the government decided to bring Market Reforms, real reforms were political reforms after Tiananmen Square.[31] During the Cold War, China struggled to liberalize economy and bring political reforms. That seems to change Chinese image in American public of being an oppressor and a communist country. After all these efforts, China has become the second-largest economy globally, surpassing Japan in 2010. However, American public opinion about China is more or less similar to the Cold War image of China. Many Americans believe that Chinese government does not respect political rights of its citizens, and around 55% of Americans still have negative views about China. However, Americans seem little impressed with a factor that is mostly driving U.S.-China relations in the twenty-first century: the economy. Around 49% of Americans view China's economy from a positive angle.[32] China's economy is rising at a consistent growth rate, and there are many predictions about it taking over the American economy in the coming decades.[33] This fear or anxiety, if not wrong, has become a challenge for the U.S. to deal with to maintain its global supremacy.

Economic Relations

It is written on the wall that the United States is undoubtedly a military and economic might. However, it is also hard that "America's economic and military edge relative to the world's other great powers will inevitably diminish over several decades."[34] The United States has fought two major wars at the beginning of the twenty-first century, one in Afghanistan and one in Iraq. These two wars' economic and political cast has created a dent in American economic, political, and military power. It has paid the huge financial cost of these two wars in Afghanistan and Iraq. One estimate suggests that the United States federal government has spent the U.S. $ 4.8 trillion in two wars.[35] In a political context, America's ability to attract others is declining because of rising anti-Americanism in recent years.[36] More recently, its soft power has further declined.[37] The United States' soft power declined primarily because of two wars it fought and a subsequent economic spillover effect on its economy. However, rising economic competition with China is a prominent aspect of its soft power and financial crunch decline.

In the contemporary world, China is "a dynamic factor in the world economy."[38] China's trade partnership with its neighbours, Central Asian Republics (CARs), Western Industrial powers, especially the United States.

Zi Zhongyun defines the political nature of Sino-U.S. relations well. He concludes political context of Sino-U.S. economic relations as present economic relations will "probably be governed more by economic laws than by political development."[39] Here are some facts about bilateral trade between the United States and China.[40]

a. The total volume of trade and services between the United States and China was U.S. $ 610.3 billion in 2023.
b. China received United States' goods and services in 2023 worth U.S. $ 147.7 billion.
c. China was the number one country to export its goods to the United States in 2023, worth U.S. $ 462.6 billion.

The numbers represent that the U.S. economy depends primarily on Chinese exports. The United States' dependence has grown as Chinese exports of goods and services have significantly increased.[41] Likewise, China's dependency on the United States as a major importer of its goods has tremendously increased in several years, making China a global economic engine.[42] As a result, Americans and the rest of the world's appetite to import low-priced Chinese products have increased.

Deterrent Relations

A core aspect of U.S.-China relations is strategic relations in terms of nuclear deterrence. The central figure or referent state in Chinese deterrent calculus is the U.S.[43] Chinese development of Intercontinental Ballistic Missiles (ICBMs), scope and capabilities of its nuclear forces, nuclear strategy, and force posturing are by and large influenced and shaped by changing global environment, and the U.S. has played a significant role in shaping nuclear force and missile capability development during and after the end of the Cold War.[44] The changing geopolitical and geostrategic environment has played a significant role in shaping a nuclear weapon state's nuclear strategy, force posturing, and missile development. China's deterrent relations are directed to assess and counter U.S. military build-up around Chinese territories.

George Friedman argues that the United States Navy in the South and East China seas is China's most significant military threat.[45] China sees U.S. forces around Chinese seas as an existential threat. China's five-thousand-year-old history suggests that it has considered any military force on its borders an existential threat to national security. It is a fact that the overall Chinese military, economic, and political approach, doctrine, policy, and strategy are deeply intertwined, linked, and connected with essential geographical parts connected with its borders. Likewise, China has also felt threatened when there is a military presence on its seas and, incredibly, when its export routes come under military surveillance.[46]

China has developed advanced missiles and launch platforms to counter the United States military in the East and South China seas. The missile development in China is akin to the U.S. military presence on Chinese seas, and it is also shaping Chinese nuclear posturing and strategy.[47]

China has felt vulnerable and fearful of growing United States' nuclear primacy, and its reaction is "conditioned by broader strategic context." The primary aim of Chinese nuclear capability acquisition was to establish a useful military capability to deter the United States. Likewise, another significant objective of acquiring nuclear weapons was to achieve a "status of world power and increase its influence internationally and throughout the world." Besides, China aims to develop nuclear weapons is to seek "additional means for establishing Chinese hegemony in Asia."[48]

Jeffery Lewis has summarized that U.S. policymakers are debating whether or not it should recognize its so-called mutual vulnerability with China.[49] China has a relatively small nuclear weapon arsenal. According to the SIPRI Yearbook 2024, China has 500 nuclear weapons in its arsenal.[50] However, the U.S. is still not recognizing that it is vulnerable to Chinese nuclear strikes and continues to rely on its Cold War era strategy to accept mutual vulnerability in response to Chinese nuclear force development.[51] U.S. policymakers are unwilling to accept mutual vulnerability as they think it will establish U.S.-China relations in a peer competition and incentivize China to proliferate vertically. However, this mutual vulnerability has become a reality for the U.S.[52] It seems that the U.S. is inching towards accepting the reality. Global strategic stability depends upon U.S.-China competition, and U.S.-China strategic stability is pivotal to it based on mutual vulnerability.[53]

In 2022, the National Security Strategy of the United States of America clearly defined its policy towards countering rising Chinese military might and, from their perspective, a revisionist state. The document suggests that China wants to shape the world order and displace the United States in the Indo-Pacific region. China pursues a policy to expand its state-driven economic model and realign the region according to its choice.[54] A prominent aspect of U.S.-China deterrence relations is a complex security dilemma.[55] One example is U.S. Nuclear Posture Review (NPR) under President Trump's administration and the Chinese response.

Under the 2018 NPR, the Trump administration seeks to develop low-yield nuclear weapons "to preserve" U.S. credible deterrence against regional aggression.[56] Analysts fear that the U.S. added more weapons to its nuclear arsenal after the 2018 NPR. China condemned US NPR and called it representing the U.S. Cold War mentality.[57] In response, China has increased its nuclear arsenal. But it is unlikely to fill the present number gap.[58] China pursues limited or minimum nuclear deterrence force structure, institutional capacity, expertise, or lack of resources to fill the gap. However, this is likely to limit the nuclear modernization program.[59] Perhaps that is why the U.S. does not explicitly recognize China as its peer competitor, but China still has enough nuclear weapons with its advancement in ICBM, cyber, and space technologies to deter the U.S. However, China is interested in mutual strategic reassurance and restraint between both countries, without confrontation, with mutual respect, cooperation, and benefits.[60] On the other hand, the recently launched National Security Strategy (2022) indicates that the U.S. sees China as a competitor with a reluctance to accept U.S. nuclear primacy.

Complex Interdependence

The post-Cold War world witnessed competition and cooperation between states and non-state actors. International organizations (I.O.) and multinational companies (M.C.s) tremendously influence states' foreign policies. States have moved beyond the traditional concept of preserving their security and meeting challenges to their national security. The world has become more globalized in that a state's survival is not only measured by its military power; instead, it has become a combination of realist and liberal perspectives of having military might and a strong economy. In the Cold War era, a state's survival was linked with its relative military power.

States' foreign and defence policies were predominantly labelled and studied from a neorealist paradigm, especially maintaining or shifting balance of power linked with power distribution. However, the end of the Cold War ended a bipolar world. In bipolar world, military dependence of states was on other state. A core state built a bloc, and a periphery state depended on core states for arms build-up. However, the end of bloc politics marked the beginning of more complex relations as state's economy became a parallel factor to military might and instrumental to the state's sovereignty and integrity. According to liberal perspective, state's economy is core of state's survival in this anarchic world. From this perspective and living in a globalized world, mutual dependence between states, even if adversaries are required, must cooperate instead of competing to solidify each other's economies.[61]

Robert Keohane and Joseph Nye were not satisfied with core assumptions of neorealist international relations perspective.[62] Keohane and Nye laid the foundation stone of theory of Complex Interdependence. They co-authored a research work titled *Power and Interdependence: World Politics in Transition,* in which they discussed the increasing economic interdependence between states, non-governmental organizations, and their networks.[63] The phenomenon of complex interdependence is now frequently observed in the age of information revolution and globalization.[64]

Studying details of concept is beyond the scope of study. The question arises here: is it observable between China and the U.S. in the age of information and globalization? Are these two having a complex interdependence with each other?

A baseline of liberal perspective is that all roads to peace lead from economic interdependence. Scholars believe that global commerce germinates peace, and economic relations between states solidify peace.[65] Katherine Barbieri talked about no links between economic interdependence and occurrence of armed conflict. On the contrary, there are strong arguments and hard-core economic and political assessments of facts prevalent in intra-state relations, given historical analysis combined in a study widely cited. The study concludes that economic cooperation or interdependence between two states dramatically influences the occurrence of wars. This is due to confounding influence of contiguity, military capabilities, alliance commitments, and regimes. The study also concludes that extensive economic interdependence increases the likelihood of that dyad, which will engage states in militarized interstate disputes. Besides, the study also highlights that chances of peace are possible through bilateral trade between two adversaries, but extreme economic interdependence could cause armed conflict.[66]

From above perspective, it is evident that "capitalist peace" between two states depends on regime type, military capabilities, and regional and global relations with other states of respected states. Likewise, notion of "power money is probably the most reliable"[67] as primary source of complex interdependence is a mere existence between states with different regional and global ambitions. Likewise, there is strong evidence that public opinion is an important variable that likely influences states' foreign and defence policies. If public remains ignorant about state's trade and service relations with its adversary, it can provide greater representation to protectionist interests.[68]

As far as U.S.-China relations are concerned, policymakers of both countries have realized the growing interdependence between both countries. Both countries' political leadership has realized the importance of developing a new framework for mutual economic cooperation to decrease chance of belligerence.[69] The capitalist peace between two countries is growing. The facts and figures between two states' annual trade suggest that both countries move fast to solidify their capitalist peace. Likewise, this indicates that despite asymmetrical trade and service relations, both countries are heavily interdependent, bolstering capitalist peace between them. However, capitalist peace is mere evidence without any theoretical framework, as it can still not guarantee the non-occurrence of conflict.[70]

The changing global economy is a primary factor in complex interdependence between the U.S. and China. China has conceived a plan to implement its idea of restructuring old Silk Road. It has come with the One-Belt-One-Road (OBOR) project. It is now actively participating in BRICS, ASEAN, SCO, AIIB, CPEC, and other regional forums to capitalize on the growing global economy. Likewise, the U.S. is signing economic and trade agreements with India and other Asian powers to contain the rise of China's regional economics. But, their mutual trade is a prominent part of the U.S-China complex interdependence. Much of their economic growth depends on mutual trade and services and Foreign Direct Investment (FDI).[71]

On Barbieri's lines, the conflict between two countries cannot be entirely ruled out. The bilateral relations are framed in a model of complex interdependence due to bilateral economic interdependence. However, there are unlikely thoughts on inevitability of conflict between both states. Zhiqun Zhu assesses U.S.-China relations since 1990 and tentatively concludes that "a potential power transition from the U.S. to China is most likely to be peaceful."[72] On the implications of the U.S.-China conflict for regional and international peace and stability, Aaron Friedberg argues that if U.S.-China engaged in a turf war, it could divide whole of European Eurasia into a new Cold

War and fuel the fire between the two countries. Likewise, if economic interdependence prevails between both countries, it may increase chances of resolving many regional and international disputes and strengthen sustained worldwide economic growth.[73]

From a war and political studies point of view, confrontation is inevitable between a rising power and an old hegemon, who are not accommodating[74]unless they make some "concessions" to each other. Some strong assessments favour present Sino-US complex interdependence phenomenon due to economic dependence as a token to avoid War. However, a strong and rising feeling in Washington is that China wants to supersede the United States in economic field. The current asymmetry or imbalance in bilateral trade and services catalyses American policymakers' thinking and intentions. Likewise, American policymakers see China as a regional hegemon with an "aggressive and expansionist" attitude in South China Sea. China is militarily and economically bullying its neighbours, "including U.S. allies."[75] On the contrary, China always feels vulnerable to U.S. military presence on its borders, threatening its territorial integrity and sovereignty. China is particularly fearful of President Obama's Asia Rebalance Strategy to contain China's economic and military rise.[76]

Academics and experts have tried to understand U.S.-China relations through different theories of international relations, like theory of complex interdependence, capitalist peace, power-transition theory, structural realism, etc. Hardcore facts and figures encompassing military, economic, and political realities help prove theories. Facts and figures are backbones of theory because they provide a path for a theory to prove itself. A brief literature survey on Sino-US relations, culture, history, civilization, economic, military and political power distribution, regional influence, geography, doctrines, policies, strategies, and alliance commitments provides multiple perspectives. The analysis of survey suggests that War is inevitable. A dominant theme has emerged within the layers of varying thoughts, perspectives, and analyses: peace between two powers is a choice, not a necessity. It is also evident that their bilateral military, economic, and political relations have profound implications for their political, economic, and military allies and partners. A war between the U.S. and China is more likely. As a rising power, China is challenging a hegemonic power, and bloodshed between both is imminent.[77]

U.S and China in Space

An essential understanding of space is its uniqueness. Space is a strategic domain but also one of important global commons. Space is akin to land, sea, and air. It is a fact that states have accepted that War in space is now a reality. The evolutionary process of warfare suggests that humans have prepared first-generation warfighting tools to fight with each other. The thousands of years old history of warfare has entered into a fourth generation of warfare and space in a relatively new medium of warfare. Strategically, space has now become fourth medium of warfare. Space's strategic importance for major powers has increased since the first satellite in outer space.

The reliance on space capabilities and applications for communications, navigation, intelligence gathering, photographic reconnaissance, surveillance, and early warning purposes has increased for major powers. Likewise, space for peaceful purposes, especially economic benefits of manufacturing and launching satellites for states and non-state actors, has increased the significance of commercialization of space. Space has become a new venture for states and international companies to earn revenues. Space's military and economic aspects have made it an area of intra-state competition. But it is also important to understand that space is a unique medium, and intra-state competition has profound implications for international and regional peace and stability.

Space had been militarized when the first satellite was launched into outer space, and in subsequent years, states have conceived ideas to weaponize space and have successfully built space weapons. This has started the countdown to space warfare. Three major space powers, the United States, China, and Russia, are standing at the doorstep of space weaponization. They have the capability and have shown their intentions by launching and testing various space weapons. Now, they are following a path from militarization to weaponization of space and looking at each other who will blink their eye first. They look at each other and who will first put space weapons. In this regard, U.S.-China relations have profound implications for global and regional stability, especially for South Asia. In general, both considered strategic competitors in space and saw each others' capabilities with a pinch of salt and high scepticism. The scepticism is primarily due to a lack of dialogue and disagreement on the code of conduct in space, which has given birth to strategic distrust between the two space powers. This is akin to their overall misunderstanding-misperception dynamic.

China is ranked third as the most powerful military in the world.[78] It is the world's second-largest economy, surpassing Japan's in 2010.[79] China has surpassed Russia in space and has become the second nation in terms of the active number of satellites orbiting the Earth.[80] China has tremendous political, economic, and military influence over its neighbouring and far-reaching nations.[81] All these economic, military, and political accumulations of power show China as a rising global power, akin to its rising power in space. Chinese space thinking is akin to its land, air, and sea power thinking, and it has become part of its overall national power.[82] Chinese space thinking is comprehensive, and its program is based on full-spectrum concept. This includes launching microsatellites, the manned space program, building high-powered lasers to blind satellites in LEO ASAT weapons, and meeting its civilian and military space requirements.[83] Chinese military space strategy is coloured with space nationalism, primarily driven by political realism, strategic competition, and hostility and belligerence from the first-ever space hegemon, the United States. The strategy augments Chinese space power to secure a geostrategic advantage over the U.S. The current rate of space capabilities development reflects that China is also looking to dominate this medium.

John Logsdon described growing Chinese space ambitions as an indication of attaining global leadership status. He also argued that Chinese space leadership aims to achieve legitimacy in space akin to land, sea, and air powers associated with great power status.[84] However, it is also a fact that Chinese civilian space policy is based on technological determinism. China is actively engaged with its neighbouring countries and outside Asia to share its space technology with them and build, manufacture, and launch its space satellites. China sees its space program as instrumental in projecting its soft power.[85] Overall, space power for China is now necessary to solidify its political, economic, and military influence and power. China has consistently progressed in its space program in the past two decades.[86] It adopted a building block approach to orchestrating its space power. The Chinese space program in public diplomacy is playing an instrumental role. Over the years, China has successfully projected its image of a technologically advanced country, and wildly, it has convinced many of its neighbouring countries, as well as from Africa and Latin America, that China has achieved significant achievements in space technology and it has the potential to help them in their space programs. Likewise, Chinese space program has also played a role in the world order as a responsible nuclear and space power. China and Russia have proposed arms control proposals and initiatives in space at the Conference on Disarmament (CD). China projected itself as a reliable space power respecting global norms, initiatives, and rights for the safe conduct of activities in space. The Chinese space program has projected its image that it is "a partner instead of an enemy."[87]

Gregory Kulacki and Jeffrey Lewis analyse the Chinese space program's aims, objectives, and history and write that China's space ambitions revolve around finding an equitable position in the global space order. China's actions are to find "a place for one's mat,"[88] which means China is looking towards developing its program as a necessary tool to achieve a prominent position in space and among other space actors. Chinese leadership sees space as a domain to achieve scientific and technological advancement, to project its soft power, and to increase its industrial and economic cooperation with other states. Chinese technological determinism means "having a space program proves to others and, more importantly, to themselves that the Chinese deserve a seat at the table."[89] It is evident that over the years, China has made many efforts to achieve a seat at the global space table, aiming to become a world-leading space power by 2045.[90] However, it is also important to understand costs and benefits. The incentives and benefits of pacing up its space program for achieving commercial and military objectives are tremendous. Still, these incentives will come at the cost of creating an environment for competition in space with the U.S. It has exacerbated U.S. vulnerabilities in space, as fears of a Space Pearl Harbour are still looming over U.S. space primacy.

As far as the United States space program is concerned, it is a jewel of this scientific, technological, informational, military, economic, and political success and power in the hierarchy of nations. The U.S. is indisputably the first space hegemon, and space program is crucial for its soft power projection and international prestige. The U.S. dominates with the world's largest civil, government, non-governmental, and military satellite fleet. The U.S. competed with the USSR for domination and shifting balance of power in space. Convincingly, the U.S. became first hegemon in space with unmatchable space resources and capabilities and growing intentions of full-spectrum dominance in air, land, sea, and space. The assessment of U.S. national space policies and strategies suggests that the U.S. wants to preserve its hegemonic power in space, deny space to others, and maintain its dominance. However, China has emerged as a challenger to negate U.S. space dominance. The U.S. considered Chinese military space capabilities offensive towards the U.S. space program. The U.S. consistently observes the Chinese space program, its civilian and military capabilities, and growing international and regional cooperation in space. So, the question arises: is there a competition between the two states in space, and what is level of political, economic, and military cooperation between them?

There is competition between the U.S. and China in space, and several factors are behind it.[91] China's space capabilities are real and a growing threat to U.S. hegemony in space. This perspective has limited scope of political, military, and economic cooperation between the two states. In fact, after the Chinese ASAT missile test in 2007, the mutual distrust over each other's space capabilities and intentions widened.[92]

At the political level, there is little cooperation. In the Conference on Disarmament, China and Russia have placed two draft proposals for the Prevention of Placement of Weapons in outer space (PPWT). But, neither of the proposals can get the United States' endorsement or support to prohibit the weaponization of outer space. Likewise, China and Russia worked together on an initiative, "No First Placement of Weapons in Space," but once again, it received little attention in the U.S., and it has not agreed to negotiate the proposals and initiatives drafted by China and Russia. U.S. behaviour towards Chinese and Russian arms control proposals and initiatives means neither country can compete in space technology and capabilities. Therefore, they want to fight diplomatically with the U.S. to restrict its military space program. The Chinese White papers on its space program have repeatedly favoured a treaty prohibiting the weaponization of space. However, the U.S. considers the Chinese position on space weaponization dubious. The U.S. believes that China is involved in making space weapons but simultaneously prohibits the weaponization of space. Politically, the U.S. takes Chinese steps in the U.N. arms control and disarmament forum as a threat to its freedom of action in space. Likewise, the U.S. thinks China wants to achieve high moral grounds by advocating the prohibition of arms placement in space, projecting its soft power, and maintaining its prestige in the diplomatic community.

On the other hand, China considers blocking the negotiation on the Prevention of Arms Race in Outer Space (PAROS), PPWT I and II draft proposal to be a U.S. effort to maintain its space primacy. China thinks the U.S. does not want a conclusive negotiation on the PAROS as it will bring its mid-course and terminal phase BMD systems and ABM shield under space weapons. China fears that the U.S. wants vague and politically driven definitions of space weapons recognized by U.N. forums so that its BMD system may not fall under banned space weapons. Strategically, U.S. BMD systems are very offensive to China's military as China's vulnerabilities to U.S. BMD have increased. China has shown concerns about the U.S. deployment of the THAAD system in South Korea. China thinks that the regional THAAD will be connected with the U.S. missile command in Alaska, and it will be connected with the U.S. global missile and space command to intercept Chinese ICBMs and cruise missiles in and outside Asia.[93] So, both share divergent political views, resulting in less political cooperation on space security, including arms control and disarmament affairs concerning space weaponization. The divergent priorities have caused stained cooperation in space issues at the political and diplomatic level, resulting in a mere possibility of future cooperation.[94]

The space cooperation between two states is an interesting story at economic level. Multilateral Missile Technology Control Regime (MTCR) and U.S.-led International Traffic in Arms Regulations (ITAR) are two major forums where states can cooperate on space technology transfer. However, China is not a Member State of either of the forums. China has applied for membership in MTCR, but its application is still pending. Likewise, China is not a Member State of ITAR, mainly dealing with dual-use sensitive space technology transfer. There are difference of opinions on chinese application for MTCR. China believes that it did not apply for MTCR membership formally. Western countries believe that there was no consensus on the membership application.

Technology transfer is necessary to establish sustainable and long-term economic cooperation in contemporary world. Interestingly, it is important to mention that it did not significantly impact China's space program. However, it reflects the divergence of interests between the U.S. The U.S. steers MTCR and ITAR regimes, and both forums' rules and regulations are cognizant of U.S. export control laws and Entity List.

Space commercialization is crucial for the U.S. economy and national security. Space activities worldwide are rapidly commercialized with a sharp decrease in government footprints. The U.S. is a key actor in global space commercialization. But to maintain its primacy in this field, it has played an important role in establishing above export control regimes to regularize export and import of space technology for launching vehicles and manufacturing satellites. The space industry is an emerging market, and the U.S. wants to be centre of gravity of space commerce.[95] So far, both countries have taken baby steps in civil space cooperation because of stringent U.S. export control laws.[96] The U.S. knows "China's burgeoning space program" and its commercialization with new space powers. This has created significant challenges for the U.S. in maintaining its dominance over other space actors.[97] The U.S. has put the Chinese government and private companies on its export control "Entity List." The U.S. Congress passed a bill, P.L. 105–261, Section 1512, in 1999. The bill gave the President the authority to "certify to U.S. Congress before any export to China of missile equipment or technology that specifically proposed export is not detrimental to U.S. space launch industry and the equipment or technology to be exported, including any indirect technical benefits, will not measurably improve China's missile or space launch capabilities."[98] Now, the authority is delegated to the Secretary of Commerce. There is little cooperation between China and the U.S. in space commercialization due to competing attitudes. The Wolf Amendment was passed by the United States that prohibits NASA from using government funds to engage in direct cooperation with Chinese space entities. The U.S. and Soviet Union competed during the Cold War for various reasons. This includes prestige, hegemony, and soft power. But economic benefits of space were last priority. The end of the Cold War rationalized the economic outcome of space power as a top priority.[99] Currently, China is barging with ambitions to be a space superpower. In 2016, China, for the first time, launched more rockets than Russia and just as many as the U.S. It placed robotic landers on the Moon and Mars and is looking to send astronauts there. The Chinese government and private companies are launching rockets into space with backing from universities and hedge funds. As a result, several space start-ups have emerged from China, increasing pressure on U.S. space agency NASA and private U.S. space companies such as SpaceX and Blue Origin. OneSpace and SpaceX in space commercial market to give U.S. private space companies an ease in lifting small satellites into orbit. Likewise, LandSpace has also entered the club. China's overall space budget is around the U.S. $ 11.94 billion, comparable to NASA's U.S. $ 61.97 billion. China's push for space supremacy is an effort to bring national pride, but its economic implications are tremendous. China's economy has been making little progress for the last two to three years as its global domestic product (GDP) has not been growing as fast as other emerging economies like India. China considers that its space ambitions may boost its state and private enterprises. Any breakthrough in space commerce could free China from growth fuelled by cheap labour and low-end manufacturing. It is believed that China's role in new space race has forced NASA to pull back. At present, governments and private companies are shaping future of space economy altogether.[100]

From a military point of view, there is little cooperation and staunch competition. The United States monitors China's ICBM and space launch capabilities. Likewise, the U.S. is also critical of China's space militarization capabilities. Moreover, the ASAT tests by China have raised the bar of concerns and vulnerabilities to U.S. space assets from a Chinese ASAT attack in future. In conclusion, China is an opponent of U.S. space militarization and weaponization efforts and receives the same kind of critical bashing from the U.S. As a result, there is a complete lack of cooperation between two states in military space programs.

So, what is the perfect recipe for War in space between two states? From an economic perspective, no interdependency can prevent bloodshed between two states in space. There is no capitalist peace in space between the United States and China, leading to peace. From a political point of view, China is a rising global space power, and the U.S. is first-ever space hegemon, so a hegemonic power like the U.S. will not accommodate a rising space power like China. Likewise, the U.S. space program is declining, and there is a lack of coherence in space policymaking in the U.S. to utilize the growing space industry in the world market.

On the other hand, China is increasing its regional space cooperation for economic benefits and reaching other regions. This has undermined U.S. space dominance. China will likely take the lion's share in space-based commerce in next three decades. From a power-transition theoretical perspective, China may become a space superpower in next decade. Its growing space power may give it enough power to shape the world order. But, all this growth is slow and gradual. China is inching towards achieving such status with a slow, steady win-the-race approach. There is now economic dependency between two states in space, which can avoid a bilateral collision.

The possibility of conventional or nuclear War between two countries is very bleak. However, chances of conflict cannot be ruled out. However, if China and the U.S. fight a war, it will be in cyberspace through non-destructive and electronic means. United States authorities believe that many persistent and unexplained cyber-attacks on U.S. critical and national security architecture have been undeniably launched from China. For both countries, it is a new domain of warfare, and both countries see it differently.[101] "A growing number of states are developing means not merely to access and exploit space, but to conduct space warfare."[102] China has also developed warfighting capabilities in space. But, interesting and most important aspect of the War in space will be using electronic means to destroy, disrepair, and permanently or temporarily damage electronic parts of adversary's satellites.

In contemporary world, public, government, and military satellite reliance has increased tenfold in past decade. If Chinese hackers hack U.S. satellites and jam only navigation and communication services in the U.S., the impacts will be devastating for the U.S. economy and national security. Likewise, if U.S. hackers hack Chinese satellites, it will be a setback for the rising Chinese power. The National Security Strategy (2022) highlights the importance of cyber and space attacks. In the strategy, the Biden administration pledges to respond.

Brett Biddington authored a report, in which he argued that Chinese endeavour is to achieve space parity with the U.S.[103] China's satellite-based global timing and navigation systems are now moving to global coverage. The BaiDou Satellite System (BDS) will improve Chinese intelligence capabilities in South China Sea. In space, and with particular reference to BDS, China is actively cooperating with other nations that operate global navigation satellite systems, including the U.S. (GPS), Russia (GLONASS), Europe (Galileo), Japan (Quasi-Zenith Satellite System—QZSS), and India. According to the Union of Concerned Scientists database on active space assets of all space-faring nations, China has surpassed Russia regarding several space assets. The BDS covering all the global provides sufficient accuracy to Chinese MIRVed ICBMs, a concern for U.S. policymakers. The Sino-U.S. space race for hegemony in space is focused on seeking military dominance. The new space race can destabilize the relationship between Washington and Beijing. The U.S. plans to spend U.S. $ 2.3 billion on space-control space superiority and space domain awareness measures in 2024–25 to augment its space defence systems to protect its satellites dealing with sensitive national security issues. Increasing China's civilian space activities now further threatens U.S. space dominance. The fear is that at some point in the foreseeable future. In conclusion, a "Thucydides Trap" exists for the United States and China in space. The U.S. is first space hegemon with enormous military and civil space capabilities to maintain its space primacy and dominance, and China has emerged as a challenger to this primacy.

Conclusion

China has many incentives to be the next space superpower as it may shape global space order for a power transition in the next few decades. It depends on whether these two space powers do not get into a Thucydides Trap in space. Both countries know the uniqueness and importance of space power and subsequent economic benefits, but if the old and first space hegemon does not accommodate the rising space power, a collision may likely increase. There are no sufficient and necessary conditions for space activities that can prevent a conflict in space largely because of the absence of a universally accepted treaty to prohibit the weaponization of space, especially the non-destructive means. There is no global space governance system in which states follow a code of conduct and adopt confidence-building measures to prevent the weaponization of space. Hence, present conditions may likely incentivize major space powers to use their lethal force in space against each other in case a conflict emerges on land.

Notes

1. Kissinger [1].
2. Xu [2].
3. Rousseau [3].
4. Xia [4].
5. Rong [5].
6. Wright [6].
7. Zhang and Austin [7].
8. Golley and Song [8].
9. Baru [9].
10. Ross and Øystein [10].
11. Ferchen [12].
12. Dahlman [13].
13. Shenkar [14].
14. Medeiros and Fravel [15].
15. Ikenberry [16]
16. Pei [17].
17. Rapoza [18]
18. Li [19].
19. Decker [20].
20. Lieberthal and Jisi [21].
21. Ma [22]
22. Jervis [23]
23. Shapiro [24]
24. Hirshberg [25].
25. Zagoria [26].
26. Brick [27].
27. Hu and Khan [28]
28. Art [29].
29. Nye [30].
30. Nye [31]
31. Kissinger [32].
32. Zhongyun [33].
33. Garnaut [34].
34. Heginbotham et al. [35].
35. Friedman [36]
36. Beckley [37].

37. Lieber and Press [38].
38. Lewis [39].
39. Rimland [40]
40. Kulacki [41].
41. Twomey [42]
42. Jianqun [43]
43. Kulacki [44]
44. Fravel and Medeiros [45].
45. Xia [46]
46. Rana [47].
47. Keohane [48]
48. Keohane and Nye [49]
49. Rogerson [50]
50. Milner [51].
51. Gartzke et al. [52], Braddon [53]
52. Barbieri [54].
53. Kant [55].
54. Tanaka et al. [56].
55. Wang [57].
56. Weede [58].
57. Echeverri-Gent et al. [59]
58. Zhu [60].
59. Friedberg [61].
60. Ikenberry [62]
61. Schake and Manuel [63]
62. Allison [64].
63. Etzioni [65].
64. Khan and Amin [66]
65. Saunders [67].
66. Khan and Khan [68]
67. Fernandez and Hogenboom [69].
68. Chapman [70].
69. Weeden [71]
70. Dellios [72].
71. Dillow et al. [73]
72. Williams [74]
73. Kuipers [75]
74. Chambers [76]
75. Kulacki and Lewis [77].
76. Chi [78]
77. MacDonald [79]
78. Steinberg [80]
79. Ohlandt [81]
80. Ali [82]
81. Seedhouse [83]
82. Meyers and Landsberg [84]
83. Hitchens and Chen [85].
84. Quingley [86].
85. Tronchetti [87].
86. Hampson [88].
87. Foust [89].
88. Hilborne [90].
89. MacDonald [91].
90. Dillow [92].

91. Hagestad [93]
92. Harold et al. [94]
93. Kelly et al. [95]
94. Lieberthal and Singer [96]
95. Potter [97].
96. Kleinberg [98].
97. Biggington [99].

References

1. Henry Kissinger, *World Order* (London: Penguin Press, 2014).
2. ChaolongXu, "Viewing the Reconstruction of the framework of the Chinese Civilization," *Japan Review,* no.9 (1997): 205–222.
3. Richard Rousseau, "Strategic Perspectives: Clausewitz, Sun-Tzu and Thucydides," *Khazar Journal of Humanities and Social Sciences* 15, no.2 (2012): 74-83.
4. Guang Xia, "China as a Civilization-State: A Historical and Comparative Interpretation," *Procedia—Social and Behavioral Sciences* 140, no.1 (2014): 43–47.
5. ZangRong, "The Treatment of Foreign Relations in Ancient China in the New History Textbook," *Chinese Education and Society* 36, no.6 (1999): 83.
6. Arthur Wright, "The Study of Chinese Civilization," *Journal of the History of Ideas* 21, no.2 (1960): 233.
7. Yongjin Zhang and Greg Austin, "China and Responsibility of Power," in *Power and Responsibility in Chinese Foreign Policy*, eds. Yongjin and Greg Austin (Canberra, Australia: ANU Press, 2013), chap 1.
8. Jane Golley and Ligang Song, "China's Rise in the Changing World," in *Rising China: Global Challenges and Opportunities*, eds. Jane Golley and Ligang Song (Canberra, Australia: ANU Press, 2011), chap 1.
9. SanjayaBaru, "Geo-economics and Strategy," *Survival* 54, no.3 (2012): 47–58.
10. Robert Ross and TunsjøØystein "Introduction," In *Strategic Adjustment and the Rise of China: Power and Politics in East Asia*, eds. Robert Ross and TunsjøØystein (Ithaca: Cornell University Press, 2017), chap 1.
11. Avery Goldstein, "A Rising China's Growing Presence: The Challenges of Global Engagement," in *China's Global Engagement: Cooperation, Competition, and Influence in the 21st Century*, eds. Jacques Delisle and Avery Goldstein (Washington, DC: Brookings Institution Press, 2017), 1.
12. Matt Ferchen, *China, Economic Development, and Global Security* (Washington, DC: Carnegie-Tsinghua, Center for Global Policy, December 2016)
13. Carl Dahlman, "Technology, Globalization, and International Competitiveness: Challenges for Developing Countries," in *Industrial Development for the 21st Century: Sustainable Development Perspectives* (New York: UN Sustainable Development Knowledge Platform, 2006), 29-75.
14. OdedShenkar, "China's Economic Rise and the New Geopolitics," *International Journal* 61, no.2 2006): 313–319.
15. Evan Medeiros and Taylor Fravel, "China's New Diplomacy," *The New York Times,* October 22, 2003.
16. John Ikenberry, "Introduction," in *America, China, and the Struggle for World Order: Ideas, Traditions, Historical Legacies, and Global Visions*, eds. John Ikenberry, Zhu Feng, and Wang Jisi (New York: Palgrave, 2015), chap 1.
17. Minxin Pei, review of *Debating China: The U.S.-China Relationship in Ten Conversations*, by Nine Hachingian, *Foreign Affairs* 93, no.2 (2014):143–147.

18. Kenneth Rapoza, "The Future: China's Rise, America's Decline," *Forbes,* March 26, 2017, https://www.forbes.com/sites/kenrapoza/2017/03/26/the-future-chinas-rise-americas-decline/#6d1b0eab3b2f.
19. Mingjiang Li, "Rising from Within: China's Search for a Multilateral World and Its Implications for Sino-U.S. Relations," *Global Governance* 17, no.3 (2011): 346.
20. David Decker, "The People's Republic of China and the Clinton Administration," in *China in Transition*, eds. PhylisLan Lin and David Decker (Indianapolis, Indiana: University of Indianapolis Press, 1997), 11.
21. Kenneth Lieberthal and Wang Jisi, *Addressing U.S.-China Strategic Distrust* (Washington, DC: The Brookings Institute, March 2012), 1–49.
22. Damien Ma, "Friend/Foe: The Contradictions in How Americans and Chinese See Each Other," *The Atlantic,* July 13, 2012.
23. Robert Jervis, "Hypotheses on Misperception," *World Politics* 20, no.3 (1968): 454
24. Robert Shapiro, "Public Opinion and American Democracy," *The Public Opinion Quarterly* 75, no. 5 (2011): 982-1017
25. Matthew Hirshberg, "Consistency and Change in American Perceptions of China," *Political Behaviour* 15, no.3 (1993): 247-263.
26. Donald Zagoria, "The End of the Cold War in Asia: Its Impact on China," *Proceedings of the Academy of Political Science* 38, no. 2 (1991): 1-11.
27. Andrew Brick, *Reform in China After Tiananmen Square* (Washington, DC: The Heritage Foundation, August 5, 1989), 1–6.
28. Zuliu Hu and Mohsin Khan, *Why Is China Growing So Fast?* (Washington, DC: International Monetary Fund, April 1997), 1–9.
29. Robert Art, "The United States and the Rise of China: Implications for the Long Haul," *Political Science Quarterly* 125, no.3 (2010): 359.
30. Joseph Nye, "The Decline of America's Soft Power," *Foreign Affairs* 83, no.3 (2004): 16-20.
31. Joseph Nye, "Donald Trump and the Decline of U.S. Soft Power," *Project Syndicate: The World's Opinion Page*, February 6, 2018, https://www.project-syndicate.org/commentary/trump-american-soft-power-decline-by-joseph-s--nye-2018-02.
32. Henry Kissinger, "The Future of U.S-Chinese Relations: Conflict Is a Choice, Not a Necessity," *Foreign Affairs* 91, no.2 (2012): 47.
33. Zi Zhongyun, "A Multidimensional Approach to Sino-U.S. Relations," in *U.S.-China Economic Relations: Present and Future*, eds. Richard Holton and Wang Xi (Berkeley, CA: Institute of East Asian Studies, 1989), 19.
34. Ross Garnaut, "China: New Engine of World Growth," in *China: New Engine of World Growth*, eds. Ross Garnaut and Ligang Song (Canberra, Australia: ANU Press, 2012), chap 1.
35. Eric Heginbotham et al., *China's Evolving Nuclear Deterrent: Major Drivers and Issues for the United States* (Santa Monica, CA: RAND Cooperation, 2017), 17.
36. George Friedman, "In China, a Strategy Born of Weakness," *Stratfor,* October 18, 2017, https://geopoliticalfutures.com/in-china-a-strategy-born-of-weakness/.
37. Michael Beckley, "Balancing China: How the United States and Its Partners Can Check Chinese Naval Expansion," *War on the Rocks,* November 15, 2017, https://warontherocks.com/2017/11/balancing-china-united-states-partners-can-check-chinese-naval-expansion/.
38. KeirLieber and Daryl Press, "U.S. Nuclear Primacy and the Future of the Chinese Deterrent," *China Security,* no. 5 (2007): 71.
39. Jeffery Lewis, *Paper Tigers: China's Nuclear Posturing* (London: Institute of International Strategic Studies (IISS), 2014), chap 1, 33.
40. Ben Rimland, "The U.S. Should Admit its Vulnerability to Chinese Nuclear Attacks," *The Diplomat*, May 3, 2016, https://thediplomat.com/2016/05/the-us-should-admit-its-vulnerability-to-chinese-nuclear-attacks/.
41. Gregory Kulacki, "Mutual Vulnerability with China a Reality, Not a Choice," *Union of Concerned Scientists,* October 11, 2013, https://allthingsnuclear.org/gkulacki/mutual-vulnerability-with-china-a-reality-not-a-choice.

42. Christopher Twomey, "The U.S-China Strategic Dialogue: Phase IX Report," *PASCC,* Naval Postgraduate School, report no. 2017–001, December 2016.
43. TengJianqun, "The Sino-U.S. Security Dilemma: The Root Cause and Way Out," *Observer Research Foundation* (ORF), February 8, 2017, http://www.orfonline.org/research/the-sino-us-security-dilemma-the-root-cause-and-way-out/.
44. Gregory Kulacki, "China's Nuclear Force: Modernizing from Behind," *Union of Concerned Scientists,* January 2018, https://www.ucsusa.org/sites/default/files/attach/2018/01/modernizing-from-behind.pdf?_ga=2.82376593.645215538.1521151248-2061194595.1521151248.
45. Taylor Fravel and Evan Medeiros, "China's Search for Assured Retaliation: The Evolution of Chinese Nuclear Strategy and Force Structure," *International Security* 35, no.2 (2010): 48-87.
46. Liping Xia, "China's Nuclear Doctrine: Debates and Evolution," *Carnegie Endowment for International Peace,* June 30, 2016, http://carnegieendowment.org/2016/06/30/china-s-nuclear-doctrine-debates-and-evolution-pub-63967.
47. WaheedaRana, "Theory of Complex Interdependence: A Comparative Analysis of Realist and Neoliberal Thoughts," *International Journal of Business and Social Science* 6, no.2 (2015): 290–297.
48. Robert Keohane, "Institutional Theory in International Relations," in *Realism and Institutionalism in International Studies*, eds. Michael Brecher and Frank Harvey (Ann Arbor, MI: University of Michigan Press, 2002),
49. Robert Keohane and Joseph Nye, *Power* and *Interdependence*: *World Politics in Transition* (Boston: Little, Brown, 1977)
50. Kenneth Rogerson, "Information Interdependence: Keohane and Nye's Complex Interdependence in the Information Age," *Information, Communication and Society* 3, no.3 (2000): 415-436
51. Helen Milner, "Power, Interdependence, and Nonstate Actors in World Politics: Research Frontiers," in *Power, Interdependence, and Nonstate Actors in World Politics*, eds. Helen Milner and Andrew Moravcsik (Princeton: Princeton University Press, 2009), chap 1.
52. Erik Gartzke, Quan Li, and Charles Boehmer, "Investing in the Peace: Economic Interdependence and International Conflict," International Organization 55, no.2 (2001): 391-438
53. Derek Braddon, "The Role of Economic Interdependence in the Origins and Resolution of Conflict," Revue D'économiePolitique122, no.2 (2012): 299–319
54. Katherine Barbieri, "Economic Interdependence: A Path to Peace or a Source of Interstate Conflict?" *Journal of Peace Research* 33, no.1 (1996): 29.
55. Immanuel Kant, *Perpetual Peace: A Philosophical Essay,* trans, Campbell Smith (London: Swan Sonnenschein Co., 1903).
56. Seiki Tanaka, Atsushi Tago and KristianSkredeGleditsch, "Seeing the Lexus for the Olive Trees? Public Opinion, Economic Interdependence, and Interstate Conflict," *International Interactions* 43, no.3 (2017): 337-396.
57. Jianwei Wang, "Building Conceptual Framework for U.S.-China Relations," in *Challenges to Chinese Foreign Policy: Diplomacy, Globalization, and the Next World Power,* eds. YufanHao, George Wei, and Lowell Dittmer (Lexington, KY: University of Kentucky Press, 2009), chap 2.
58. Erich Weede, "The Capitalist Peace and the Rise of China: Establishing Global Harmony by Economic Interdependence," *International Interactions* 36, no.2 (2010): 206-213.
59. John Echeverri-Gent, April Herlevi, and Kim Ganczak, "Economic Interdependence and Strategic Interest: China, India, and the United States in the New Global Order," (paper, ISA Asia-Pacific Conference, Hong Kong, June 25, 2016).
60. Zhinqun Zhu, "Power Transition and U.S.-China Relations: Is War Inevitable?" *Journal of International and Area Studies* 12, no.1 (2005): 1.
61. Aaron Friedberg, "The Future of U.S-China Relations: Is Conflict Inevitable?" *International Security* 30, no. 2 (2005): 7-45.
62. John Ikenberry, "From Hegemony to the Balance of Power: The Rise of China and American Grand Strategy in East Asia," *International Journal of Korean Unification Studies* 23, no.2 (2014): 41-63

63. KoriSchake and Anja Manuel, "How to Manage a Rising Power—or Two," *The Atlantic*, May 24, 2016, https://www.theatlantic.com/international/archive/2016/05/china-india-rising-powers/484106/
64. Graham Allison, "The Thucydides Trap: Are the U.S. and China Headed for War?" *The Atlantic*, September 24, 2015, https://www.theatlantic.com/international/archive/2015/09/united-states-china-war-thucydides-trap/406756/.
65. AmitaiEtzioni, *Avoiding War with China: Two Nations, One World* (Charlottesville, VA: University of Virginia Press, 2017), 151.
66. Zulfqar Khan and Fouzia Amin, "Pivot and Rebalancing: Implications for Asia-Pacific," *Policy Perspectives* 12, no.2 (2015): 3-28
67. Philip Saunders, "China's Rising Power, the U.S. Rebalance to Asia, and Implications for U.S.-China Relations," *Issues and Studies* 50, no.3 (2014): 19-55.
68. Zulfqar Khan and Ahmad Khan, "Chinese Capabilities as a Global Space Power," *Astropolitics*13, no. 2–3 (2015): 185–204
69. Alex Fernandez and Barbara Hogenboom, "China's Growing Economic and Political Power: Effects on the Global South," *The Asia-Pacific Journal* 5, no.12 (2007): 1-15.
70. Bert Chapman, "Chinese Military Space Power: U.S. Department of Defence Annual Reports," *Astropolitics* 14, no.1 (2016): 71-89.
71. Brian Weeden, "China's Plans for Space," (presentation, Goddard Memorial Symposium, Greenbelt, Maryland, March 7, 2017)
72. Rosita Dellios, "China's Space Program: A Strategic and Political Analysis," *Cultural Mandala* 7, no.1 (2005): 1-15.
73. Clary Dillow, Jeffery Lin, and P.W. Singer, "China's Race to Space Domination," *Popular Science*, September 20, 2016, https://www.popsci.com/chinas-race-to-space-domination.
74. Matt Williams, "The Surprising Scale of China's Space Program," *Phys.org*, January 11, 2018, https://phys.org/news/2018-01-scale-china-space.html.
75. LysanKuipers, "A Space Oddity? The Use of the Chinese Space Program in Public Diplomacy Strategies," (M.Sc. Diss., Leiden University, 2017)
76. Rob Chambers, "China's Space Program: A New Tool for PRC Soft Power in International Relations?" (MSc. Diss., Naval Postgraduate School, 2009)
77. Gregory Kulacki and Jeffery Lewis, *A Place for One's Mat: China's Space Program, 1956—2003* (Cambridge: American Academy of Arts and Science, 2009), 3, 30 and 31.
78. Ma Chi, "China Aims to be World-Leading Space Power by 2045," *China Daily*, updated November 17, 2017, http://www.chinadaily.com.cn/china/2017-11/17/content_34653486.htm.
79. Bruce MacDonald, *China, Space Weapons, and U.S. Security* (Washington, DC: The Heritage Foundation, September 2008)
80. James Steinberg, *Strategic Reassurance and Resolve: U.S.-China Relations in the Twenty-First Century* (Princeton: Princeton University Press, 2014), chap 7
81. Chad Ohlandt, "Competition and Collaboration in Space between the U.S., China, and Australia," *Asian Survey*, 54, no. 2 (2014): 395-417
82. Muhmud Ali, *U.S-China Strategic Competition: Towards A New Power Equilibrium* (New York, Springer, 2015)
83. Erik Seedhouse, *The New Space Race: China Vs. the United States* (New York: Springer, 2010)
84. Jessica Meyers and Mitchell Landsberg, "A Growing Competition: China and the U.S. Space Program, Year by Year," *Los Angeles Times*, May 11, 2017
85. Theresa Hitchens and David Chen, "Forging a Sino-U.S. Grand Bargain in Space," *Space Policy* 24, no.3 (2008): 128-131.
86. Erik Quingley, *Geo-political Considerations to China's Rise in Space Power* (Maxwell, AL: Air Command and Staff College, Air University, 2009).
87. Fabio Tronchetti, "Preventing the Weaponization of Outer Space: Is a Chinese-Russian-European Common Approach Possible?" *Space Policy* 27, no.2 (2011): 81-88.
88. Joshua Hampson, *The Future of Space Commercialization* (Washington, DC: The Niskanen-Center, January 25, 2017).
89. Jeff Foust, "One Small Step for U.S.-China Space Cooperation," *Space News*, July 10, 2017.

90. Mark Hilborne, "China's Rise in Space and U.S. Policy Responses: A Collision Course?" *Space Policy* 29, no. 2 (2013): 121.
91. Alexander MacDonald, *The Long Space Age: The Economic Origins of Space Exploration from Colonial America to the Cold War* (New Haven, CT: Yale University Press, 2017).
92. Clay Dillow, "China's Secret Plan to Crush SpaceX and the U.S. Space Program," *CNBC*, updated March 28, 2017, https://www.cnbc.com/2017/03/28/chinas-secret-plan-to-crush-spacex-and-the-us-space-program.html.
93. William Hagestad, *21st Century Chinese Cyberwarfare*(Cambridgeshire Business Park, Cambridge: IT Governance Publishing, 2012), chap 1
94. Scott Warren Harold, Martin Libicki, and Astrid StuthCevallos, *Getting to Yes With China in Cyberspace* (Santa Monica, CA: RAND Cooperation, 2016), chap 1
95. Terrence Kelly et al., *The U.S. Army in Asia, 2030–2040* (Santa Monica, CA: RAND Cooperation, 2014)
96. Kenneth Lieberthal and Peter Singer, *Cybersecurity and U.S-China Relations* (Washington, DC: The Brookings Institute, 2012)
97. Robert Potter, "The U.S-China Cybersecurity Disconnect," *Modern War Institute*, November 16, 2016, https://mwi.usma.edu/us-china-cybersecurity-disconnect/.
98. Howard Kleinberg, "On War in Space," *Astropolitics* 5, no.1 (2007): 1.
99. Brett Biggington, "Parity in Beginning to Emerge between America and China in Space," *The National Interest,* July 5, 2016, https://nationalinterest.org/blog/the-buzz/parity-beginning-emerge-between-america-china-space-16844.

Chapter 8
Space Security Trilemma and Strategic Implications for South Asia

Introduction

The relationship between three major South Asian powers may be termed a security trilemma since India, Pakistan, and China have enmity and amity, respectively. The security trilemma was observed between these three nations as it came into view in the early 1960s, and it was remerged during the bilateral conflicts, Indo-Pak during the three major wars in 1948, 1965, and 1971, whereas during the Sino-India War in 1962. Consequently, the associations among the nations have advanced from "diplomatic rivalry" to war. In succeeding years, the relationship has been further transformed from war to a security trilemma as Sino-U.S. relations have spilled over effect on South Asia's security calculus.

The importance of this relationship between three geographically and "strategically" associated countries, China, India, and Pakistan, is well observed in space as a space security trilemma. The overall security trilemma, which is quite observable in space as well in other mediums of warfare between these three countries, has twisted their division of military powers along with the criterion of their relationship—of war, rivalry, enmity, weapons proliferation, diplomatic alignments and the design of economic relationship after the end of the Second World War. The study of space security trilemma between these three countries has its significance and manifestation because of the "intensity" and "durability" of their diplomatic and military connections among them.

This chapter draws from the Ph.D. research work of the author titled "Arms Race in Outer Space: A Paradigm Shift in International Security and Implications for South Asia," which was completed in 2019 and successfully defended in 2020 at Department of Strategic Studies, National Defence University, Islamabad.

A. Khan and E. Sadeh, *Sabre Rattling in Space*,
https://doi.org/10.1007/978-981-97-6050-3_8

China-India

The 1962 India-China War started over persisting territorial disputes between the two, which resulted in India's military defeat. In the aftermath, their relations became more estranged. Meanwhile, their adversarial relationship continued on the same trajectory in the post-Cold War period. However, economic ties between two gradually progressed, creating a complex state of interdependence. Moreover, a diversified Sino-India relationship improved their economic, diplomatic, and political relations. Though military ambitions of two remained on adversarial path, competition in outer space, parallel with military tension over disputed territories, continued to intensify.[1]

Dinshaw Mistry observes that India's space motives and objectives were "influenced by prevailing political circumstances and economic philosophies, socioeconomic development, political objectives, military spin-offs, and commercial applications."[2] Also, "India's space program is backed by strong political support from country's policymakers, and it remained its top strategic and political priority." "The objective is to project India's soft power and to show India's high-technology achievements to enhance its prestige further internationally."[3]

Another significant dimension to India's space program continued to be associated with its future military and plans to elevate its relative power and geostrategic role in international politics. This is ostensibly a clear shift from India's traditional space policy, envisioned by its first premier, Nehru—to focus on the imperatives of socioeconomic development through space technology, which has been tilting towards utilizing space assets for military objectives for the past two decades. The Indian space program has significantly grown and has become a vital element of its national security strategy policy. The *Joint Doctrine Indian Armed Forces-2017* document emphasized the importance of space for military purposes[4] and highlighted growing relevance of space power for national security policy:

> India's space capabilities are driven mainly by civil and commercial requirements, and steps are being undertaken to exploit space for military applications. Leveraging space power would include protecting our National space assets and exploiting space to enable defence capabilities across the conflict spectrum.[5]

Indian Army released Land Warfare Doctrine in 2018 and it stated that:

> Continuous survilliance of our borders by developing and employment of satellites, to provide accurate inputs for planning of operations, mitigation of threats and integration of space based assets with grand based weapon platforms will a priority area for development. Development of microsatellites, light and greater capacity transponders, with short life span which can be launched 'on demand basis,' will be the essential future requirement for the Army.

The Indian policymakers are paying significant attention to developing space-based command and control and communication assets with advanced C^4ISR capabilities. India has been developing a two-layered Ballistic Missile Defence (BMD) system which, created an ASAT capability.[6] One Indian analyst—Ajay Lele observes that India's space security policy seeks to establish a tri-service space command for obvious strategic military purposes. India's space program may build capabilities to enhance space situational awareness capabilities and develop strategic technologies to increase its reliance on space assets for intelligence gathering, communications, navigation, and operating various weapon systems,[7] writes Ajay Lele. The author also suggested "establishing the National Authority for Space Security under the Ministry of Defence to supervise its space security-related issues and develop ISR capacity." The Indian Space Research Organization (ISRO) has released Space Activities bill in 2017 to lay down a solid basis for development of legal frameworks, structures, and strategy as to how to respond to any hostile outer space activity that may be imping upon its vital security interests.[8]

Currently, India possesses 26 active military satellites. India's military space capabilities are developing quickly, including reconnaissance, intelligence gathering, and communication satellite capabilities. This will help India counter the conventional Chinese military threat. Likewise, India's growing space capabilities will effectively counter China-Pakistan strategic balance versus India in South Asia. Moreover, India's testing of an ASAT capability has pressured China to preserve its space assets from rivals' ASAT capability. India managed to build a strong military space program based on satellite reconnaissance and communication-backed conventional capabilities to change the strategic equation of South Asia. India seems to be fast emerging as a strong challenger to China's dominance in Asia in exploration, commercial space sector, and use of space for military purposes.

Cameron Hickert argues that regional rivalry between India and China has long simmered, and next frontier increasingly appears to be space. Both countries increasingly invest in space programs to develop their national powers. The appeal of building their hard power through space programs is clear. Likewise, both consider space a domain to project their hard and soft powers. Both offer cost-effective satellite manufacturing, launching, and scientific cooperation with neighbouring countries to bolster their commercial space program.[9] Currently, Indian space program has the world's largest commercial space customers. This domain of space exploration offers tremendous incentives for India and creates an environment of competition between India and China. However, there is negligible bilateral cooperation between India and China in diplomatic, and political, domains. India and China compete for (regional and global) markets, resources, and influences on land, sea, and the Indian Ocean.[10] He argues that this competition is spilling over into outer space.

Both countries compete to take their share in the commercial satellite building and launching business. Regarding the competition for military space, India's military space program largely depends on its collaboration with the U.S and Russia. The Indo-U.S. nuclear deal of 2005 and the formalization of strategic partnership as a countervailing power to China's economic and military rise resulted in India's siding with U.S. by vetoing the Prevention of Arms Race in Outer Space (PAROS) in 2005 in Conference on Disarmament (CD).[11] India does not endorse China's initiatives of PPWT and No First Placement of Weapons in Outer Space in CD. Likewise, both share opposing views regarding the peaceful uses of outer space in the First Committee of the UN. However, both agreed and part of the consensus report of the Group of Govermental Experts on PAROS-2023/24 to recommend possible elements of legally binding instrument on PAROS.

China-Pakistan

The history of Pakistan-China friendly diplomatic and bilateral relations and strategic cooperation is over six decades old. China is investing in China-Pakistan Economic Corridor (CPEC), a flagship project of China's Belt and Road Initiative (BRI). CPEC reflects Pakistan-China's budding strategic cooperation in region's economic, military, industrial, diplomatic, and geopolitical affairs. Both countries enjoy friendly relations under the ambit of their long-term strategic relationship. Furthermore, the development of CPEC in Pakistan is likely to build a Space Silk Road by sending many remote sensing satellites into outer space. Pakistan and China have agreed to enhance their cooperation in space exploration, technologies, and communication. For instance, China Pakistani remote sensing satellites into orbit—Pakistan Remote Sensing Satellite (PRSS-1) and Pakistan Technology Evaluation Satellite (PakTES-1A).[12] China also send PakSAT-MMI and iCube-Qamar in 2024. Likewise, China will reportedly take a Pakistani astronaut into space. Pakistan also joined its collaboration on a groundbreaking lunar exploration mission in partnership with China's Chang'e 8 mission, set to launch in 2028. SUPARCO's lunar rover, weighing approximately 35 kgs, will join the Chang'e 8 mission, which is part of the larger International Lunar Research Station (ILRS) initiative. The expanding orbit of Pakistan-China space cooperation demonstrates their flourishing space technological cooperation as a benchmark of their friendship in all spheres of technology. To further strengthen their twenty-year-old space cooperation agreement, Pakistan's first communication satellite geostationary, PakSAT-1R, was launched into space from the Xichang Satellites Centre in Sichuan province, which shows much-developed space cooperation between the two countries.[13] Launch of PakSat-MMI and establishment of Pakistan Space Center with the help of China reflects Pak-China Iron bond in space cooperation.

The Indo-U.S. space cooperation, from Pakistani perspective, is further fracturing and creating trouble spots in South Asia, undermining region's strategic stability, peace, and security. The challenges to the region's security are primarily due to India's arms build-up. Pakistan and China know the Indo-U.S. partnership's challenging impact on region's security architecture. China has been a "time-tested" and "all-weathered" friend of Pakistan that has always stood by Pakistan in every conflict and crisis. Similarly, China's assistance to enhance Pakistan's defence, security, and space potentials has become a hallmark of their longstanding strategic and technological cooperation" and friendship framework in fast-transforming world that is laying down new foundations of regional realignments/alliances, which are presently shaping the geostrategic trajectory, not only of South Asia but also of entire Asia.[14]

India-Pakistan

The bilateral relations between India and Pakistan are action-reaction type syndrome. Since 1947, Pakistan and India have fought three major wars—1948, 1965, and 1971. There also was a localized war of Kargil in 1999 and a 2001–2002 military standoff/twin peak crisis paralleled with a frequent eruption of skirmishes along the Line of Control.[15] The most significant tension between India and Pakistan is the acquisition of destabilizing military technologies by India and expanding orbit of India-US technological and strategic partnership. Indian acquisition/development of Ballistic Missile Defence (BMD) system is challenging Pakistan's credible minimum deterrence strategy. Pakistan's development of nuclear weapons is aimed to deter India from committing any aggression against it. However, Pakistan has developed adequate delivery systems, for instance, from the Short-Range Low-Yield Ballistic Missile (SRLYBM), NASR, to Medium-Range Ballistic Missile, Shaheen III, to counter India's apparent aggressive military doctrinal restructuring and tilting towards pre-emptive policy. In the 1980s, India started a program to develop the Integrated Guided Missile Development Program (IGMDP), under which India developed different missile systems with a minimum range of 150 km up to 12000 km.[16] According to Zahid Hussain and Raja Qaiser, India claims to have a strategic need to develop a missile weapon with more than 4000 km range. However, China and Pakistan can be deterred by Agni-IV being inducted into the military after successful tests.[17] However, India has not stopped here and extended Agni-V's from 5000km to 8000km. Likewise, it is developing Agni-VI and Surya ICBM that will bring major Western countries' capitals in its targeting list. A worrisome development for Washington, Paris and London. The primary objective of India's missile development is to counter any incoming missile from Pakistan and also from the Chinese. However, there is a major stumbling block to achieving this strategic objective. This stumbling block is the lack of adequate remote sensing satellites in India's Low Earth Orbit (LEO). It is generally believed that India's BMD system cannot work effectively without having a constellation of remote sensing satellites in LEO. The primary reason is geographical proximity between India and Pakistan. The travel distance or time of flight of a Pakistani Intermediate Range Ballistic Missile (IRBM) is considered to be less than 10 min. Therefore, to effectively intercept any incoming Pakistani IRBM by the Indian BMD system, the latter would require adequate early warning, detection, photographic reconnaissance, and surveillance systems based on remote sensing satellites operating in LEO.[18] Hussain and Qaiser stress that:

> India's TES, RISAT-1, and RISAT-2 can provide proper surveillance with a camera with less than 1-m resolution, but these satellites, being in LEO, cannot offer a reliable remote sensing system. LEO satellites cannot map wide areas due to small swaths. For continuous and complete coverage of sectors between Karachi and Islamabad, more than 100 satellites would be required to monitor 1100 km. TES and RISAT series have only five to seven-year in-orbit lifespans, so India would have to send satellites continuously to replace the retired satellites. Even the in-orbit positioned satellites deceive camouflage and use window opportunities and other means.[19]

India is consistently developing its ballistic missiles with extending ranges and BMD programs to enhance its nuclear capability and strategic outreach. India recently acquired S-400 Triumf air defence system from Russia to counter Pakistan's aircrafts, UAVs and cruise missiles. The growing conventional forces' asymmetry between India and Pakistan is to India's advantage. It has further stalemated their relations and intensified tension along the LoC that seems to have motivated New Delhi to strategize the imposition of a swift limited war under its Cold Start Doctrine (rebranded as Dynamic Response after Palwama Fiasco in 2019) creating a security dilemma for both nuclear powers. In parallel, India is also massively investing in space programs for strategic military and civilian objectives, including economic, communication, and meteorological. In this context, the Indo-US space cooperation architecture is raising eyebrows in China and Pakistan. India-US cooperation is further negatively undermining the security environment of South Asia.[20] India signed agreements with the U.S., on space cooperation including SSA Data Sharing Agreement, COMCASA, BECA, the Joint Working Group on civil space cooperation, the earth observation data sharing agreement, CSLA, the framework for civil space cooperation and TSA agreements, to bolster its space program.

The Indo-US space cooperation dates back to 1963 when India launched a U.S.-manufactured sounding rocket from its Thumba Equatorial Rocket Launching State (TERLS) for first time. In addition to the U.S. space collaboration, India had also received assistance from the Soviet Union, France, the UK, and West Germany. U. R. Rao, the Indian Space Research Organization writes in his book—*India's Rise as a Space Power* that the sounding rocket program at TERLS was initiated through a unique international cooperative arrangement with NASA of US, CNES of France, and the Hydro-Meteorological Service of the Soviet Union.[21] In the subsequent decades, the U.S. and other countries assisted India in producing and launching over 350 sounding rockets. This Indian launch site emerged as a meteorology and atmospheric research centre. Incidentally, in 2013, India launched the Mars Orbiter Mission (MOM) program with the assistance of the US National Aeronautics and Space Administration (NASA). Incidentally, the Indian launch of MOM elevated it to the space club. NASA and the Indian Space Research Organization (ISRO) have also established a close space cooperative initiative by signing different agreements, including setting up Joint Working Groups to enhance India's space program." In 2012, both countries signed more agreements for the US-led Global Precipitation Measurement project, the Megha-Tropiques, and the OceanSat-2 satellites. Moreover, both countries expressed resolve to channel data-sharing mechanisms. To further expand the orbit of their space cooperation, in September 2018 during '2 + 2' Dialogue in New Delhi, both India and US reached a consensus to earmark long-term space goals in consonance with their ongoing strategic partnership framework."

The states always desire to gain more and more power, particularly military power. As we have entered the fourth generation of warfare with so much technological advancement and space whose strategic importance cannot be denied, it has become a medium of conflict in the region. Global changes have deeply influenced space politics in the region, and the ongoing space competition between the U.S. and China has also created a space security trilemma in South Asia. The growing Indian missile defence program and its military space program are gaining too much attention due to its utilization of outer space for national development. India also developed the anti-satellites (ASAT) capability. Previously, China's ASAT test in 2007 had incited Indian space policymakers to take countermeasures, which amplified both Indian and U.S efforts to enhance their space cooperation. The recent expansion into outer space has changed the discourse of regional and international cooperation in outer space.

Strategic Implications

The strategic implications for space militarization and weaponization are profound for South Asia. India has emerged as a regional space power with global ambitions. Its military doctrines have envisioned space as a vital instrument to bolster its national power in the region and beyond. Pakistan, another aspiring space power, considers India's conventional, nuclear, and space developments as attempts to establish regional hegemony and subdue Pakistan and other South Asian countries. While China, an increasingly established global space power, competes with the US, India sees it as its main Asian rival in space. China's position on Indian space ambitions may not be public, but it is very cognisant. All these developments in space are interlinked with India, China, and Pakistan's nuclear deterrence and conventional forces, as space capabilities are force multipliers and enhancers. Satellites offer cutting-edge command and control mechanisms for nuclear forces, and delivery means. Likewise, space assets offer crucial infrastructure and BMD capabilities. However, there are chances of proliferation of ASAT capabilities in South Asia. Both India and Pakistan are adding nuclear weapons to their arsenal, and the military and political leadership of both nuclear-armed forces continue to flaunt their nukes for deterrence purposes. All these issues combined to make South Asia a complex region with numerous security challenges, mostly emanating from immediate neighbours.

Given the above discussion, the strategic implications of space militarization and weaponization are proffered as:

Ballistic Missile Defence System: India has invested heavily in building its BMD capabilities. Experts on South Asian security believe that the primary rationale behind India's development of a BMD system is to counter any incoming missiles from Pakistan. However, India has increased its BMD capabilities' scope, range, and firepower. Now, China has come under its radar. It is still unknown whether India will be able to intercept any Chinese missile or not.

On top of that, India continues to test-fire its other missiles, including interceptors, SLBMs, and ICBMs. In response, Pakistan also tests its missiles' range, accuracy, and precision. Thus, the BMD is inheritably destabilizing. Table 8.1 shows the ratio of missile testing by India and Pakistan from 1998 to date. The ratio suggests that India is moving faster than any other country in Asia to test, develop, and induct nuclear-capable missiles in its arsenal. This table was last updated in 2022.

Table 8.1 Ratio of missile testing between India and Pakistan (1998-to-date)

	India	No. of tests	Pakistan	No. of tests
Ballistic missiles				
1.	Prithvi-I (150 km)	23	Abdali (180 km)	12
2.	Prithvi-II (250 km)	32	Ghaznavi (290 km)	10
3.	Prithvi-III (350 km)	4	Shaheen-I (700–750 km)	11
4.	Dhanush (350 km)	11	Shaheen-II (2000–2500 km)	7
5.	Prahaar (70–150 km)	1	Shaheen-III (2750 km)	2
6.	Agni-I (700 km)	18	Ghauri (1300–1800 km)	12
7.	Agni-II (2000 km)	12	Nasr (60–70 km)	6
8.	Agni-III (3500 km)	8	Ababeel (2200 km)	1
9.	Agni-IV (3500–4000 km)	7		
10.	Agni-V (8000 km)	6		
11.	K-15 (750 km—submarine launched)	6		
12.	K-4 (3500 km—submarine launched)	3		
Cruise missiles				
13.	Nirbhay (1000 km—land, air, sea)	5	Ra'ad (350 km)	6
14.	Brahmos (290 km—land, air and sea)	40	Babur (700 km) Babur—II (700 km) Babur—III (450 km)	9 1 3
Total number of missile tests				
	India	***176***	**Pakistan**	**80**

Ratio of missile testing between India and Pakistan is **2.3:1**

With several reasons behind this assertion, it is also argued that India may not achieve what it desires from its BMD capabilities. First, India requires advanced ISR capabilities to monitor entire Pakistan extensively, requiring more than a hundred satellites to do so continuously. This will be a mammoth step in developing such a remote sensing constellation in space. India still lacks considerable resources and will be unlikely to launch such a huge number of satellites shortly. As a result, its BMD capabilities will continue to be under pressure from Pakistan's missiles mainly because of geographical proximity. Likewise, continued missile testing by both sides further destabilizes regional strategic stability and peace. India has developed maneuverable hypersonic missile with a range of 1500 km. This will further destablize strategic stability in South Asia. The test will enhance India's temptations to counterforce targeting in South Asia. India will also try to dominant during escalation with its neighbouring countries.

Another exciting aspect of India's BMD development is the exaggerated statements made by its scientific community in the past. Indian scientists claimed to have achieved an over 90% target acquisition/interception rate. On the other hand, the US BMD and Ground-based Midcourse Defence (GMD) target acquisition/interception rates are less than 70%. All this scientific flaunting is primarily to project India's BMD system and gain public support. Nevertheless, it is a fact that India's BMD cannot be so accurate and precise without a large constellation of remote sensing satellites in LEO. The claiming of 90 % interception may give India a false sense of security.

Anti-satellite Weapon Proliferation: China tested its ASAT capability in 2007, and India tested its ASAT in 2019. India has the scientific, industrial, and military base to develop ASAT weapons. It has developed technologies that have spin-off effects to develop ASAT capabilities. India's political and military leadership was reluctant to do so in the past, mainly for several reasons. One is space debris. In the past, space experts in India have realized that any Indian ASAT test may likely disturb its relations with China and the US, given that the US would not like to see other states have such a capability. However, the 2019 ASAT test has killed the assumptions. India's space weaponization ambitions are unclear and remain ambiguous, though India may prefer ambiguity. Nevertheless, it is a fact that India does have all the industrial and technological requirements to build a weapon/missile to target and hit a satellite, other than LEO.

Pakistan also has an advanced missile inventory. Its Shaheen-III long-range ballistic missile (LRBM) has 2750 km range. Pakistan may likely convert its LRBMs into an ASAT missile with few modifications needed in the future. However, it is indeed a tall ask for Pakistan's scientific community to do so, given that the Pakistani political leadership has repeatedly opposed space weaponization. From political and military point of view, Pakistan would not like to develop ASAT weapons in near future. Pakistan's Full Spectrum Deterence has been able to pursuade India not to commit any couse of aggression. However, FSD does not reflect any space-based response to India.

Nuclear Deterrence in South Asia: From one perspective, credible minimum deterrence is primarily based on maintaining credible minimum nuclear forces with an adequate early warning and command and control system. The credibility of deterrence comes from nuclear capability and communication. Both India and Pakistan follow credible minimum deterrence principles. However, both continue to develop conventional and non-conventional military capabilities to undermine each other's deterrence credibility.

India has a large conventional army, and its space program is advanced, with a growing number of military space assets. On the other hand, Pakistan is conventionally weak state with no military satellites in space. However, it is a nuclear-weapon state. According to independent think tanks that evaluate nuclear arsenals worldwide, India is estimated to have more nuclear weapons than Pakistan in 2024. Hence, the two states have asymmetry in conventional and space assets. Conventional asymmetry is believed to be inversely proportional to nuclear thresholds, leading to lowering of nuclear thresholds in South Asia.

On top of that, space asymmetry will further exacerbate this ongoing regional security environment. India has realized that it cannot have credible deterrence without military space capabilities. On the other hand, Pakistan has tried to compensate for this conventional asymmetry by inducting Short-Range Low-Yield Ballistic Missile (SRLYBM) to put hot water on its Cold Start Doctrine. India has now rebranded Cold Start Doctrine to Dynamic Response. India has also tested maneuverable hypersonic missile. Naval version of this weapons is more lethal. However, Pakistan has also tested maneuverable Fetah-II and SMASH P282. Pakistan also tested MIRVed Ababeel. Pakistan's list of military response is exhaustive but adopted a subtle strategic approach to counter Indian aggression. Pakistan's SRLYBM, MIRVing and maneuverability tactics developments are to pour hot waters on Indian conventional forces and prepare response to India's Dynamic Response strategy to balance regional power. However, Pakistan still requires military space assets to maintain a strategic balance with India and maintain deterrence credibility.

The Possibility of Inadvertent War: Jay Wise argues that nuclear-armed India and Pakistan are involved in a competition that can lead both states towards a nuclear exchange in an armed conflict. The perfect recipe for such a catastrophic exchange is the development of SRLYBM by both sides, eventually lowering the nuclear thresholds in South Asia. While the actual chances of nuclear warfighting in South Asia are rare, they cannot be ruled out. Both countries have little trust, only prescribing limited conventional and nuclear confidence-building measures (CBMs). These limited CBMs cannot promise to prevent future-armed conflict, mainly a nuclear exchange. The security situation is getting more complicated because of technological advancements in defence sectors and military build-ups. In this case, the role of the US as a third-party mediator may become conflictual as India and the US have established strategic partnership, and US-Pakistan relations became more unstable after the U.S forces withdrawal from Afghanistan.

However, specific proposals are to chalk out CBMs beyond traditional wisdom to meet the challenge of nuclear eventuality in South Asia. That possibility requires unprecedented political will from India and Pakistan's political and military leadership. Wise proposes that specific measures should be taken to reduce the chances of unauthorized and accidental use of nuclear weapons in South Asia. He thinks that it is possible through the imagery collection of Indo-Pak borders. Remote sensing imagery could be a viable option to analyse the situation of borders and reduce the incentive for a nuclear option in a conflict situation. He argues for a limited transparency regime during bilateral talks between India and Pakistan, enabled by remotely sensed commercial imagery employed by a third party, potentially reducing nuclear risks in the subcontinent.

Conclusion

This chapter concludes that Sino-U.S. relations in outer space "is the triggering point of space security trilemma in South Asia." For the U.S., space is a domain that has to maintain its presence and primacy with complete freedom of action. For China, space power is an important component of its overall national power, and it wants to play safely in a tricky space environment. Overall, both countries have adversarial relations while having a complex interdependence. China considers the U.S. a key market for its manufactured goods, with almost half of Chinese exports going there. The U.S. also has deep trade ties with China but sees Beijing as an adversary. China has made considerable nuclear and missile build-up, irking the U.S. Both have uneasy, complex, and complicated relations not only on land, sea, and air but also in space. Their military space developments have germinated a space arms race, bringing a paradigm shift in outer space. However, it is a fact that both countries have adopted a cautious approach towards each other's military and space development and build-ups while embracing a strategic salience over any economic, political, and military provocations. However, the U.S. is an old hegemon with immense military power and is unlikely to accept the Chinese rise in space. China continues to provoke the U.S. by challenging its interests in different regions and realms. China has proved itself highly cautious in projecting its military power across its immediate area of influence, which is not the case in the U.S. However, it is still valid reasoning that both countries are trapped in a dilemma where an old hegemon is ensuring that the new power may be unable to replace it.

Sino-U.S. relations also have ramifications for South Asia. India is not a friendly state in Chinese eyes, while Pakistan enjoys deep ties with China. Pakistan and India have a history of armed conflict. India is a close ally of the United States, and the U.S. wants to contain China, with India playing an instrumental role in U.S. Asia Rebalance Policy. All these bilateral relations are the source of insecurity and instability in South Asia. Three major nuclear powers reside here. All three have different types of relations with the U.S. The U.S.-China relations plague all three bilateral relations between India-Pakistan, Pakistan-U.S., and China-India to a level where misunderstanding, misperception, and mutual distrust continue to halt regional economic and political progress. As a result, a strategic chain reaction based on military action-reaction dynamics gets accelerated. Eventually, it poses a grave threat to the peace and security of the region and may also create strategic instability in South Asia. This strategic chain reaction involving the United States, India, China, and Pakistan has profound implications for their bilateral relations and for their behaviour as states.

Notes

1. Khan and Khan [1].
2. Mistry, [2].
3. Mistry, "India's Emerging Space Program."
4. *Joint Indian Armed Force 2017* (New Delhi: Ministry of Defence, India, April 2017), 25–26, http://ids.nic.in/dot/JointDoctrineIndianArmedForces2017.pdf.
5. *Joint Indian Armed Force 2017*.
6. Khan and Khan, "Space Security Trilemma," 4–22.
7. Lele [3].
8. Lele, India's Space Security Policy.
9. Hickert [4].

10. Ramachandran [5].
11. Khan and Khan, "Space Security Trilemma," 4–22.
12. "Space Silk Road: Pakistan and China Enhance Space, Science and Technology Cooperation," *Space Watch*, https://spacewatch.global/2018/11/pakistan-and-chinaenhance-space-science-and-technology-cooperation/
13. "Space Silk Road."
14. Khan and Khan, "Space Security Trilemma," 4–22.
15. Khan and Khan, "Space Security Trilemma," 4–22.
16. Khan and Khan, "Space Security Trilemma," 4–22.
17. Hussain and Ahmed [6].
18. Hussain and Ahmed, "Space Programs of India and Pakistan."
19. Hussain and Ahmed, "Space Programs of India and Pakistan."
20. Khan and Khan, "Space Security Trilemma," 4–22.
21. Jha [7].

References

1. Zulfqar Khan and Ahmad Khan, "Space Security Trilemma in South Asia," *Astropolitics* 17, no. 1 (2019: Special Issue on Space Power and Security Trilemma in South Asia edited by Ahmad Khan): 4–22.
2. Dinshaw Mistry, "India's Emerging Space Program," *Pacific Affairs* 71, no. 2 (1998): 161.
3. Ajay Lele, "India's Space Security Policy: A Proposal," *IDSA, policy brief*, https://idsa.in/policybrief/indias-space-security-policy_alele_280416
4. Cameron Hickert, "Space Rivals: Power and Strategy in the China-India Space Race," Schwarzman Scholars, https://www.schwarzmanscholars.org/news-article/space-rivalspower-strategy-china-india-space-race/
5. Sudha Ramachandran, "Chinese and Indian Competition in Space Heats Up," *The Jamestown Foundation*, https://jamestown.org/program/chinese-indian-competitionspace-heats/
6. Mian Zahid Hussain and Raja Qaiser Ahmed, "Space Programs of India and Pakistan: Military and Strategic Installations in Outer Space and Precarious South Asian Regional Strategic Stability," Space Policy (2018).
7. Martand Jha, "Fifty Years of TERLS," *The Hindu*, March 1, 2018.

Chapter 9
Contemporary Challenges to International Space Governance

Introduction

The Cold War space order was shaped by the US and the Soviet Union's bilateral relationships and competition to dominate space environment. However, rapid development in space technologies and growing reliance on space-based assets for civilian and military uses have encouraged state and non-state actors to enhance their prowess in this domain. Contemporary space governance is shaped by states' simultaneous pursuit of space weaponization and competition and shifting of economic balance of space in their favour. This chapter highlights challenges posed to international space governance, primarily due to a lack of consensus among competing powers over a desirable code of conduct to regulate space-based activities for civil and military utilization. The strategic distrust continues to grow among major spacefarers, creating uncertainty in current space environment. The chapter concludes that there is an ongoing race to explore lunar resources and risks of space anarchy that would continue to grow without a binding international agreement to prohibit space weaponization. It merits sustainable efforts to deal with challenges of space weaponization and fragile international space governance. This looming threat highlights the need for a binding international agreement or a treaty to prevent an arms' race in outer space. Major spacefaring nations, e.g. the UK and the US, promote non-binding instruments in space due to a lack of consensus over binding agreements in the Conference on Disarmament, the UN First Committee, and the UN General Assembly. On the other hand, Russia, China and Pakistan support legally binding instrument on PAROS. UK and US support UNGA resolution on responsible behaviour in space based on norms and behaviours. Whereas, Russia, China

This chapter draws from the Ph.D. research work of the author titled "Arms Race in Outer Space: A Paradigm Shift in International Security and Implications for South Asia," which was completed in 2019 and successfully defended in 2020 at Department of Strategic Studies, National Defence University, Islamabad.

A. Khan and E. Sadeh, *Sabre Rattling in Space*,
https://doi.org/10.1007/978-981-97-6050-3_9

and Pakistan support PAROS, Further Practical Measures on PAROS, No First Placement of Weapons in Outer Space, and Transparency Confidence Building Measures resolutions on legally binding instruments on the prevention of an arms race in outer space.

On the other hand, states like Pakistan and G-77 advocate binding instruments at multilateral forums to deal with the contemporary challenges to international space governance. They argue to negotiate a binding treaty to regulate the states' behaviour in space and prevent the vertical and horizontal proliferation of space weapons, thus creating a favourable environment for cooperation rather than competition. However, due to a lack of consensus, the UK, the US, and their Western allies promote non-binding instruments. They understand that there is a need first to bring transparency confidence-building measures through norms by behaviour approach and then negotiate a treaty to prohibit the arms race in outer space. On the contrary, other states think that non-binding instruments are not preferential; binding instruments should be negotiated first.

Contemporary Challenges to Space Governance

The ongoing race to explore and use lunar resources is a significant challenge for international space governance. The race for Moon resources has led to the emergence of the Artemis Accords and the International Lunar Research Station (ILRS). To date, 44 countries have joined the Artemis Accords upon receiving bilateral invitations from the US. The China-Russia-led ILRS is also inviting like-minded states to join the project. Both projects highlight the exploration, exploitation, and use of lunar resources for scientific value, socioeconomic development, and financial burden sharing. However, these projects face legal and political challenges because of international space law.

Regarding legal obligations (militarization, and weaponization), major space powers exploit grey areas in the existing international space laws, describing these endeavours as soft legalization of deviation from the 1967 Outer Space Treaty. Artemis Accords and ILRS could violate the spirit of the corpus of international law sponsoring space law. The emergence of such initiatives reflects the improbability of universal agreement on legal norms concerning governance of space resources as reflected in the Moon Agreement, which has extremely low adherence since its entry into force. Instead, the two competing sides would like to invite a maximum number of countries, including those that have ratified the Moon Agreement, in their respective initiatives to enhance their legitimacy and inclusive character and to the evolution of a desirable international regulatory regime. The Moon Agreement championed the governance of lunar resources, providing an intelligent approach to governing future feasibility of extraction of resources through equitable sharing, as promised in Article XI. However, none of the Artemis Accords and ILRS founding states adheres to the Moon Agreement, taking it as a moratorium on extracting lunar resources. In this case, instead of adhering to existing space laws concerning exploration, exploitation, and the use of space resources, the founding states of two initiatives legitimize extraction of resources through norm-building and state practices, keeping existing space law at bay. This provides further rationalization and the need to fulfil the Moon Agreement's promise to establish an international regime to govern the lunar resources and placement of WMDs on lunar surface.

Spacefaring nations seek to establish decisive dominance, at least in the military domain. This approach consequently heightens competition by stimulating tensions and encouraging military countermeasures. Given the ongoing geopolitical competition in space, whereby this domain has emerged as the fourth medium of warfare, any model for space governance must not overlook the inherent competitive tendencies among states and promise more incentives through cooperation.[1] The rationale behind global space governance revolves around the notion that the irrational behaviour of spacefaring nations would be equally disadvantageous for their pursuits in this domain despite having competing interests. Recognizing these states' inherent instinct to compete, the authors suggest that cooperation towards space governance should aim to reduce threats cooperatively and not overlook their grounded self-interests. Therefore, the idea of global space governance seeks to maximize the prospects of peaceful exploitation of this global common by encouraging responsible behaviour.

The current space order has multiple layers. The space order is witnessing the rise of China, a resurgence by Russia, and, to a lesser extent, the emergence of India.[2] The expanding capabilities of these three countries and the significant devotion of national resources to foster their respective space programs for various reasons, including prestige and national security, created a multipolar contemporary space order.[3] European Space Agency (ESA), Japan, and Israel are also developing critical space technologies and enhancing cooperation with other developing countries. As a result, orbits have become more congested and crowded, and competition in military and economic dimensions has increased. The US is a pre-eminent space power enjoying dominance in military, commercial, and civilian space activities compared to other players. For these reasons, the U.S. is the most powerful actor among other countries in space today.[4]

A prominent feature of contemporary space order is the misunderstanding and misperception of dynamics between the three major space powers mentioned above. The development of space weapons has contributed to a cycle of misunderstanding and misperception. These issues can significantly impact international space governance system. This suggests that states are following a path of space militarisation and weaponization. Likewise, major spacefaring nations are not interested in solidifying contemporary space governance, leaving behind several legal and political loopholes.[5]

Renewed Interest in Lunar Resource Exploration

Major spacefaring nations have expressed renewed interest in lunar resource exploration primarily due to strategic reasons and pursue their plans to extract rare materials. The rivalry between major spacefaring nations is to re-establish their reach to lunar surface. The US is undoubtedly the only space power in the past, and right now, it can reach and establish its bases on the Moon's surface. During the Cold War, former Soviet Union and US were engaged in an aggressive race to reach the Moon. They spent their precious national resources to build lunar missions. However, the US won the race by reaching the Moon's surface and landing the first human on the Moon's surface.[6] However, it must be noted that the Soviet Union faced multiple failures in landing human missions on the lunar surface.[7] These failures and US landing on the Moon's surface resulted in the loss of appetite for the two strategic competitors to continue the race to explore the vast horizons of space.

After 50 years of Apollo XI, what triggered the major spacefaring nations to reach the Moon's surface again? Why the states are pursuing lunar resource exploration so vigorously? However, the conclusions pivot around whether the Cold War space law still applies to cater to major spacefaring nations' renewed interest in lunar exploration and arms race in outer space. It is indeed a fact that present space law governing outer space activities was negotiated during the height of the Cold War. Both strategic competitors were enthusiastic about bringing future activities to lunar surface under an agreed framework that conceived five outer space treaties. However, both space powers lost interest in lunar exploration programs, ending the first race for Moon exploration. The US also spent nearly USD 25.4 billion to make the Apollo XI mission successful.[8] That amount is almost USD 152 billion at the moment.[9] But the result is zero material return. However, it cannot be discounted that it was a quantum leap towards future space activities and use of space by humanity since it came into being.

The US claimed its technological prowess in space and attained prestige, but it did not financially pay back the desired dividends. The economic viability of lunar exploration missions impacted the US appetite to do the same in coming years. The US administrations after President Kennedy paid little attention to land on the lunar surface again. The crash of X-15 no 3 in November 1967, the near loss of Apollo XIII in 1970, the crash of Challenger in 1986, and the annihilation of Columbia in 2003 almost ended US plans to go into lunar exploration programs and missions.[10] Likewise, the Soviet Union suffered major setbacks because of manned space flight disasters, including Soyuz I in 1967 and Soyuz II in 1971.[11]

The main reasons behind the two superpowers not going to the Moon were unstable financial funding, lack of technology to sustain living on the lunar surface, and, importantly, diversion to other strategic developments. The great powers also looked towards technological accomplishments and motivation through prestige. The past seven decades have witnessed dwindling focus and attention towards space exploration and can be divided into three ages.[12] The Soviet took the initial setup towards the above factors by launching Sputnik-I in 1957, which marked the beginning of first space age. This development raised concerns in the US that Soviet Union had taken the lead in this unparalleled scientific advancement and also sparked fears that the latter was going far in developing missile technology.[13] The US won the second part of this first space age by sending the Apollo XI manned mission.

Interestingly, after accomplishing these factors, the interests faded on each side. Nevertheless, this interest in reaching the lunar surface renewed five decades later. Several key factors reinvigorated the great powers' lost appetite to relaunch their Moon missions. The first space age witnessed humans landing on the Moon surface and continued throughout the Cold War until the Soviet Union was dismantled in 1990.

The militarization of space and genesis of norms for space governance were the two hallmarks of this first space age. Given the ongoing strategic rivalry between the two states, militarization of space continued, albeit retaining relative stability, as the two competing space programs intended to complement their respective nuclear postures. It is estimated that around 70% of satellites launched between 1950 and 1990 were primarily military satellites for operations like missile warning, communication, and intelligence collection.[14] Nevertheless, despite these developments, the first age witnessed an era of stability as the relative balance in space capabilities refrained both sides from interfering with each other's military satellites due to the shared belief that any conflict in space would trigger nuclear conflict between them.[15] Simultaneously, this era also witnessed efforts to create norms and enact a structure for space governance through institutional frameworks like legally binding treaties and the United Nations General Assembly's (UNGA) adoption of resolutions and other measures.[16] The establishment of the United Nations Committee on the Peaceful Uses of Outer Space (UN-COPUOS) in 1958 and the Outer Space Treaty in 1967 are the most noteworthy steps.

The second space age began in 1991 when the world saw the emergence of a New World Order. The space commercialization and diversification of relations between states were witnessed as the main features of the second space age. As technological know-how also spread around the globe, commercial firms and new aspirant states started to jump into this domain after the end of the Cold War. However, it must be noted that there were no renewed interests in reliving manned missions to the Moon or landing on the surface for mining or extracting resources at that time. Nevertheless, commercializing space sectors in different countries and diversifying international relations opened the gate for new interest in space.

The newcomers sought to acquire space technologies to launch their space programs with significant interest in sending unmanned and manned lunar missions in the future.

The third space age marks an era in the twenty-first century when the world is witnessing the revival of great power rivalry and eventually transitioning from a unipolar world to a multipolar one. Space exploration and uses of space for military and economic interests are the hallmark of the third space age. These also provide an impetus to explore the lunar resources and gain prestige. The prominent actors in the third space age are China, India, Russia, and the US.

In October 2020, NASA's Sofia mission found evidence of water on the Moon.[17] The idea and possibility of establishing bases and colonizing the lunar surface got another life after this earth breaking development. Likewise, mapping mineral resources and helium to be used for nuclear energy production prompted the rethinking of going to the Moon.[18] The commercialization initiated after the Cold War ended further grew in the third space age. States are now looking forward to bringing down rare lunar surface materials. The US has been considering establishing military bases on the Moon surface, and cislunar space is also a prime factor in going beyond Earth orbits.[19] Likewise, the third space age has also witnessed the emergence of non-governmental entities as new actors in space. Although these entities are rigorously pursuing their commercial and economic interests, they may be able to overshadow the government entities' interests. Their emergence provides renewed interest in lunar exploration and extraction of rate materials.

At present, economic and military interests are the key motivational sources behind the renewed interests of major spacefaring nations. Pursuing these two interests also indicates a more intense resource-consuming space race than the Cold War model of space exploration by great powers. The spacefaring nations are concerned about who will claim more lunar territory and its resources. Meanwhile, the old space law provides major guiding principles, but the loopholes and legal lacunas remain unresolved, and the renewed interests of the major spacefaring nations in exploring lunar resources remain unresolved.

Legality of Space Exploration

In 1966, US presented a draft treaty in the UNCOPUOS on the issue of governing the exploration of the Moon and the other celestial bodies. The primary focus of the draft treaty was on the issue of governance of space's natural resources. The draft contained many provisions of the OST and primarily called for the freedom of exploration and scientific investigation of space resources. The draft also discussed banning the stationing of weapons of mass destruction and other military installations on the Moon and other celestial bodies. In continuous efforts by states to establish a legal treaty to govern the Moon and other celestial bodies, Argentina 1970 submitted a draft of a treaty on the activities of states on the Moon. The text represented the view of the developing states. The draft remained focused on the legal status and the exploration of the natural resources of the Moon and other celestial bodies, and it called the Moon the "common heritage of all mankind." The draft also indicated that benefits should be available to everyone without discrimination. The draft was supported by many developing countries; former Soviet Union also submitted a draft treaty concerning the activities of states on the Moon. The draft excluded "common lunar heritage of mankind and other celestial bodies. The draft also challenged the non-appropriation principle concerning states' activities on the Moon. In the end, the major challenges faced during the negotiation process on the Moon treaty were the scope of the agreement, whether to include other celestial bodies in the treaty or not, the principle of common heritage of mankind, benefit sharing derived from lunar resources extraction, and perceived moratorium on space mining. After tough negotiations, the agreement governing the activities of states on the Moon and other celestial bodies (Moon Agreement) was adopted by the UN General Assembly. After 47 members of the UNCOPUOS approved the process, the UNGA in 1979 adopted the Moon Agreement by consensus. The Agreement was opened for signature in December 1979 and entered into force in 1984 after the date of redeposit of the fifth instrument of ratification. Although it was adopted by consensus, it has garnered only 18 ratifications with the US, Russia, China, United Kingdom, Japan, etc. All these states actively participated in the negotiation process of the Moon Agreement, but none have signed and ratified it. India and France have signed the Agreement but did not ratify it. Pakistan, on the other hand, acceded to the agreement. Recently, KSA withdrew from the agreement. The low adherence to the Moon Agreement has raised questions about whether it is even part of international law.

The Moon Agreement has been described as a treaty ahead of its time. It foresaw the possibility of exploitation of natural resources of space and the Moon. While the exploitation of lunar resources was still considered a fictitious thought when the agreement was agreed upon, it is argued that it is increasingly becoming possible for the major spacefaring nations to exploit lunar resources due to overwhelming technological advancements in space science and applications. Programs like ILRS and Artemis Accords are pressing hard to make this exploitation a reality. Private space sector and rising interests of global technological industries in space sector are making efforts to make the exploitation of lunar resources a reality with a growing sense that technically and economically feasibility of the exploration and exploitation of extra-terrestrial resources, referred to as space mining, is imminent, the Moon Agreement has gained great topicality.

Developed and technologically high-end countries argue that utilizing space resources is essential and critical to long-term viability of space operations and activities. However, Article II of the OST is an important aspect of the existing space law. Many developing and developed countries support this particular Article. The Article reiterates basic legal principles of the non-appropriation and equitable access to outer space, which is the common province of humankind. Developing countries argue and debate that any approach for exploration, exploitation, and use of space resources, including lunar resources, should be equitable, constructive, collaborative, consensus-based, and, above all, not leave behind or unfairly create disadvantages for the developing countries. Activities on lunar surface require increased international efforts to safeguard free exploration and use by all states without discrimination, based on equality and following international law.

In this context, the most relevant provision of the Moon Agreement is its Article XI, which declares Moon and its natural resources' the common heritage of mankind', as against the vaguer notion of "the province of all mankind" used in the 1967 OST. This Article, like Article II of the OST, stipulates that Moon is not subject to national appropriation, and the extracted resources will be distributed equally between states under the supervision of an international regime. The Article II of the OST and Article XI of the Moon Agreement clearly state that no state can claim sovereignty on the surface and subsurface of the Moon by any claim and that all state parties have "the right to exploration and use of Moon without discrimination of any kind, based on equality and under international law and terms of Moon Agreement." It is argued that the most articulate mandate for this regulation is not found in Article I of the OST, but in the Moon Agreement. However, major states, e.g. Russia, China, the US, and the UK are not parties to this agreement, which leaves little reinforcement mechanism to be implemented to make the exploration, exploitation, and use of space resources equitable, including lunar resources.

The Moon Agreement envisages the establishment of an international regime, including appropriate procedures, to govern the exploitation of the natural resources of the lunar surface. Such an international regime would enable orderly and safe development of the natural resources of the Moon and equitable sharing by all states' parties in the benefits desired from these resources, whereby interests and needs of developing countries, as well as the efforts of those countries which have contributed either directly or indirectly to the exploration of the Moon, shall be given special consideration.

As a major spacefaring nation, the US believes that OST does not provide a comprehensive international regime for space resource utilization activities. It sees neither a need nor a practical basis to create such a regime. In defence of Artemis Accords, the belief that Accords underscore critical principles and norms as a starting point for future work on space resources exploitation, exploration, and uses. Understandably, the Moon Agreement is vague, and Article XI does not provide a comprehensive framework for governing activities concerning space exploration, exploitation, and use. The US advocates that Artemis Accords signatories intend to use their experience under the Accords to contribute practices and rules applicable to extraction and utilization of space resources, including through ongoing efforts at UNCOPUOS.

States are emphasizing the development of a specific international regime for exploring, exploiting, and utilizing space resources based on internationally agreed rules and standards. In this regard, many developing countries argue that the exploration, exploitation, and use of space resources, including lunar resources must be ensured irrespective of their degree of economic or scientific development benefit from lunar-based activities, without taking away the investment incentives for public and private space flight. In this regard, the state parties to the Moon Agreement advocate that it provides ample leads to other countries to build a regime governing space resources. On the other hand, those who have joined U.S.-led Artemis Accords advocate that OST provides principles, but these are insufficient to manage ongoing lunar exploration activities in the long term. Artemis Accords signatories also believe that the existing values do not make explicit requirements related to the conservation and long-term management of space resources. In this connection, multilateral rules and norms for space uses are needed to reinforce the peaceful, safe, and sustainable use of lunar resources. The economic potential related to utilization of space resources has been increasingly recognized as of universal relevance by multiple stakeholders: Artemis Accords and ILRS partners.

Even as the number of states parties to the Moon Agreement has remained par less, the Cold War legislation on the extraction of lunar resources is considered a moratorium on lunar mining. States in this regard are moving towards unilateral and domestic legislation to allow private space entities to launch Moon mission under state ownership. For instance, the Commercial Space Launch Competitiveness Act (CSLCA) enacted by the US in 2015 grants private companies the right to own, sell, and profit from sources extracted from the Moon and other celestial bodies. While it may still take time until such activities are carried out commercially and profitably, national or domestic legislation has been enacted more recently, making space mining all the more pertinent to address the international law framework in which such activities may be undertaken. Luxembourg, which has an advanced space industry, followed suit in 2017 by permitting private commercial actors based on its territory to appropriate space resources. These developments are fraught with consequences. For one, their legality under existing space law is questionable. These unilateral legislations lower the Moon Agreement's relevance, and the results appear. Although it would be the right kind of example, but the recent withdrawal of KSA from the Moon Agreement after joining Artemis Accord is a worrisome development for the significance and relevance of an already under-stressed Moon Agreement.

On the other hand, the US promotes Artemis Accords as an alternative approach to legalize the exploitation, exploration, and use of space resources, including extracting lunar materials. The US advocates that Artemis Accords, in which commercial utilization is also included, is consistent with four UN treaties. There is an urgent need to ensure that all nations engaged in space resource activities share a common set of fundamental beliefs: in the rule of law, transparency, and peaceful purposes. Artemis Accords underscores these critical principles and forms the starting point for future work on space resources. Artemis Accords signatories intend to use their experience under the Accords to contribute to multilateral rules applicable for the extraction and utilization of space resources, including through ongoing efforts at the COPUOS. The signatories of the Accords also advocate that these provide non-legally binding guidance for outer space exploration and sustainable use and will enable the next generation of international partnerships to explore the Moon and beyond. However, it may be noted that such developments are legally questionable. Secondly, these could not only lead to conflict over space resources (linked by some to colonial wars) and widen the gap between spacefaring and non-space faring nations but also lead to contamination of space through the generation of artificial debris. These unilateral developments have led to calls for a universal legal framework to regulate space mining, for which the Law of Sea Conventional could serve as potential model.

Efforts are underway at UNCOPUOS and its two subcommittees, the scientific and technical subcommittee and legal subcommittee, to address gaps concerning the exploration and use of space resources in the existing space treaties. The states parties to the UNCOPUOS emphasize that adherence to the UN treaties would create a safe, secure, and sustainable atmosphere for developing space operations. There is a need to plug the gaps in the UN treaties to make them acceptable to the states that have not yet become parties to the Moon Agreement. State parties may stick to main principles of the OST, including freedom of access to space for peaceful uses, preservation of security and integrity of space objects, consideration of a rule-based international order for space, etc., and universal adherence to UN treaties may guarantee the peaceful exploration and use of outer space for all mankind.

At the 47th session of the LSC of the COPUOS, the states' parties made a unique declaration of the Moon Agreement to make it more acceptable and called for its adherence. There are only 17 states parties to the Moon Agreement, even though major spacefaring nations negotiated it during the Cold War. However, interestingly, none of the present spacefaring nations is state party to the Moon Agreement. Pakistan was the leading country in the declaration of 2008 that called the major spacefaring nations that the Moon Agreement is very much part of international space law.

The declaration encouraged the major spacefaring nations to become part of it and pointed out that the Agreement had unique provisions that clarified and complemented the OST. It showed the way forward in building an international legal regulatory framework for space mining while balancing the interests of developed and developing countries. The declaration clearly stated that Article XI refers to natural resources of the Moon as Common Heritage of Mankind (CHM). Article XI foresees the future possibility of exploiting natural resources in space. This Article is not a moratorium on exploitation of natural resources rather, and it allows the space mining subject respect for CHM principle applicable to outer space. Article XI provides legal solution to the exploitation, exploration, and use of space resources. Although an international legal regime has not formed so far as promised in Article XI of the Moon Agreement, it adopts an intelligent approach to the states parties to define, set up, and implement such regimes per CHM and other principles of OST along with considering relevant political, legal, and technical facts into account. However, the matter has been on the agenda of UNCOPUOS, where views continue to be divergent. It has been pointed out that Agreement has not hindered current or future activities aimed at the study, exploration, and use of the Moon and that activities undertaken by states to the Moon Agreement are consistent with the provisions of the other four UN treaties on outer space. Still others continue to think that discussions about space mining are premature. However, it is believed that negotiations at UNCOPUOS and LSC on establishing an international legally binding instrument defining, setting up, and guiding international commercial activities in outer space could play an important role in expanding the use of outer space.

Presently, efforts are underway to set principles for exploration, exploitation, and uses of lunar resources at the Legal Subcommittee of the UNCOPUOS. A Working Group was established in 2022 in the LSC to formulate principles governing lunar resources. Recently, the 63rd Session of the LSC was conducted. However, LSC failed to adopt its final report for the first time in history due to geopolitical rifts between the US and Russia. Meanwhile, the chair and co-chair of the Working Group on exploration, exploitation, and uses of space resources informed that draft five principles on this subject will be finalized and presented in the 2025 Scientific and Technical Subcommittee of the UNCOPUOS. Likewise, Romania has presented an idea in the STSC session of 2024 to establish "an Action Team on Lunar Activities Consultation (ATLAC) within the framework of COPUOS to establish an international consultative mechanism on sustainable lunar activities to facilitate addressing numerous operational issues facing future missions. To share best practices and lessons learned, as well as building capabilities, and identify common needs and concerns of lunar operators. Such a mechanism may approach topics connected to sustainable lunar exploration and settlement in and around the Moon, including for lunar operators to share information on their ongoing and planned operations and to engage in consultations to coordinate operations, facilitate interoperability, improve safety, avoid interference, protecting the lunar environment, mitigating the creation of debris in lunar orbit, coordination of landing sites, ensuring the protection of sites of significant scientific and cultural importance etc." Efforts are underway to established norms and principles to govern international activities on lunar surfaces that are transparent, sustainable, and financially viable. More recently, pursuant to UNGA Resolution 78/238, a Group of Governmental Experts was established in 2022. It first session was held in 2023 and final session in 2024. The GGE was mandated to recommend possible elements of a future legally binding instrument on PAROS, inter alia, prevention of placement of weapons in outer space. The Group adopted a censensus report supporting efforts and measures on legally binding instruments on PAROS. The report will be transmitted to the Conference on Discrarment in 2025 to start discussions on PAROS (legally binding instrument). However, the geopolitical rift may likely create more polarization at UN forums dealing with regulatory, scientific, and technical matters.

Conclusion

The rapid growth in activities for lunar exploration comes amidst the visible weaknesses in the prevailing lunar governance structure. This has raised several critical questions regarding the relevance of Cold War-era space laws in modern times, characterized by ongoing geostrategic competition and renewed interest among multiple powers in lunar exploration. The absence of a universally agreed framework for lunar governance raises concerns about potential conflicts in space, especially as major spacefaring nations vigorously pursue lunar resource exploration. Unilateral legislations, such as the withdrawal of KSA from the Moon Agreement in favour of the Artemis Accords, underscore the legal uncertainties surrounding lunar activities. While the Artemis Accords are positioned as a contemporary alternative, their legality is questioned, potentially leading to conflicts over space resources and environmental hazards. Efforts at UNCOPUOS to address gaps in existing space treaties and the push for universal adherence to UN treaties offer hope for a more comprehensive and equitable regulatory framework for lunar exploration, emphasizing the need for a rule-based international order in space. The unique declaration by states parties to the Moon Agreement, despite its limited adoption, emphasizes the importance of the Agreement in providing legal solutions for space resource exploitation. The ongoing discussions at UNCOPUOS and LSC play a crucial role in shaping the future of international commercial activities in outer space, emphasizing the need for a collaborative and legally binding instrument to guide such endeavours.

Notes

1. Khan and Khan [1].
2. Peter [2].
3. Moltz [3].
4. See Moltz [4], Johnson-Freese [5]; see also Weichert [6].
5. Hallman [7].
6. Launius [12].
7. Launius, *Reaching for the Moon.*
8. Korb [13].
9. Brnadau [14].
10. Shayler and Burgess [15].
11. Volf [16].
12. Harrison et al. [17].
13. "Milestones: 1953–1960," *Office of the Historian, U.S. Department of State*, https://history.state.gov/milestones/1953-1960/sputnik, accessed 19 December 2023.
14. Harrison et al., "Space as a Contested Domain".
15. Harrison et al., "Space as a Contested Domain".
16. Tepper, "Big Bang of Space Governance," 488.
17. Bandari [18].
18. "Helium-3 mining on the lunar surface," *The European Space Agency*, https://www.esa.int/Enabling_Support/Preparing_for_the_Future/Space_for_Earth/Energy/Helium-3_mining_on_the_lunar_surface#:~:text=Unlike%20Earth%2C%20which%20is%20protected,not%20produce%20dangerous%20waste%20products., accessed 22 December 2023.
19. Willis [19].

References

1. Zulfqar Khan and Ahmad Khan, "Space Security Trilemma in South Asia,"*Astropolitics* 17, no.1 (2019): 4.
2. Nicolas Peter, "The New Space Order: Why Space Power Matters for Europe" *Space and Defence* 4, no.1 (2010): 56.
3. James Clay Moltz, *Crowded Orbits: Conflict and Cooperation in Space* (New York: Columbia University Press, 2014).
4. James Clay Moltz, "The Changing Dynamics of Twenty-First-Century Space Power," Jounral of Strategic Security 12, no.1 (2019): 15–43
5. Joan Johnson-Freese, *Space as a Strategic Asset* (New York: Columbia University Press, 2007)
6. Brandon J Weichert, "The High Ground: The Case for U.S. Space Dominance," *Orbis* 61, no.2 (2017): 227–237.
7. Wesley Hallman, "A Fast-following Space Control Strategy," Astropolitics 3, no.1 (2005): 35–42.
8. Michael Krepon, "Lost in Space: The Misguided Drive toward Anti-Satellite Weapons" *Foreign Affairs* 80, no.3 (2001): 2–8.
9. Marc Berkowitz, "Shaping the Outer Space and Cyberspace Environments" in *Conflict and Cooperation in Global Commons: A Comprehensive Approach for International Security*, Scott Jasper, ed, (Washington, DC: Georgetown University Press, 2012).
10. Michael Boyle, "The Coming Illiberal Order," *Survival* 58, no.2 (2016): 35–66.
11. Roger Harrison, Deron Jackson, and Collins Shackelford, "Space Deterrence: The Delicate Balance of Risk," *Space and Defence* 3, no.1 (2009): 1–22.
12. Roger D. Launius, *Reaching for the Moon: A Short History of the Space Race* (Michigan: Yale University Press, 2019).

13. Lawrence Korb, *Memories of the Apollo and Space Shuttle Programs* (New York: Page Publishing Inc, 2017).
14. Daniel Brnadau, "One Nation, Two Astrocultures? Rocketry, Security and Dual Use in Divided Germany, 1949–61," in *Militarizing Outer Space*: Astroculture, *Dystopia, and the Cold War*, eds., Alexander C. T. Geppert, Daniel Brnadau and Tilmann Siebeneichner (New York: Palgrave Macmillan, 2021), 196.
15. David J. Shayler and Colin Burgess, *NASA's First Space Shuttle Astronaut Selection: Redefining the Right Stuff* (Cham: Springer International Publishing, 2020), 366.
16. Darina Volf, "Evolution of the Apollo-Soyuz Test Project: The Effects of the "Third" on the Interplay Between Cooperation and Competition," *Minerva: A Review of Science, Learning and* Policy 59, no.1 (2021): 411.
17. Todd Harrison, Zack Cooper, et al., "The Evolution of Space as a Contested Domain," *Center for Strategic and International Studies*, 2017, https://www.jstor.org/stable/pdf/resrep23194.3.pdf?refreqid=fastly-default%3A4f4e726032e72e298ffcf6c71dca3eee&ab_segments=&origin=&initiator=&acceptTC=1.
18. Anashe Bandari, "Study Reveals Map of Moon's Water near its South Pole," *NASA*, 15 March 2023, https://www.nasa.gov/solar-system/study-reveals-map-of-moons-water-near-its-south-pole/.
19. Shawn Willis, "To the Moon: Strategic Competition in the Cislunar Region" *A Journal of Strategic Airpower and Space Power* 2, no.1 (2023): 17–30.

Conclusions[1]

The research problem highlights that states are following a path from space militarization to weaponization. This indicates that states can weaponize outer space depending on the political, economic, and strategic circumstances. China and the U.S are two major space powers. Both have adversarial relations in outer space; however, they have complex interdependence, likely preventing a conflict between them. But it is not likely to restrict or prohibit the misunderstanding overcoming the little they have to prevent conflict in outer space. All this explanation and analytical description of China's bilateral relations and the U.S in outer space are based on a framework built on a realist perspective. U.S and China compete with each others to take the lion's share in the global commons' vast resources. Both recognize strategic importance of space and try to get whatever augments their military and national power.

Major space power, including the U.S and China, has followed a path from space militarization to space weaponization. The analysis of primary sources suggests that there is an arms race in outer space. However, quantifying analytical part of discourse is quite tricky. The limitation in research continues to persist because of concealed nature of space programs of countries. It is entirely plausible that a civil launch may contain a military-grade payload. Independent analysis of China and the U.S' space launches often fails to identify launch's actual payload. Likewise, it is widely observed that the U.S continues to deny military nature of X-37B STB and never released specifications and nature of the STB operation. This creates confusion in the minds of experts and analysts about whether space has been weaponized or not. The existing literature fails to clear the dust gathered on space weaponization programs of the U.S and China. However, some glimpses about their space weaponization capabilities enable independent space experts and analysts to connect the dots. The

[1] This chapter draws from the Ph.D. research work of the author titled "Arms Race in Outer Space: A Paradigm Shift in International Security and Implications for South Asia," which was completed in 2019 and successfully defended in 2020 at Department of Strategic Studies, National Defence University, Islamabad.

A. Khan and E. Sadeh, *Sabre Rattling in Space*,
https://doi.org/10.1007/978-981-97-6050-3

study has briefly analysed all available resources to investigate a research problem, and it concludes that space weaponization capabilities are possessed by the U.S, China, India and Russia, but they are waiting for each other that who will start placing space weapons first. The research concludes that once any major spacefarers initiate the weaponization of space, the others will follow suit.

Since Sputnik-I's successful launch into space, the U.S fear of a surprise nuclear attack had reached beyond their strategic calculations. In addition, the U.S was trying hard to make such a defensive shield against the Soviet Union's ICBMs, which could make its defence unconquerable against any missile attack from it. Simultaneously, many defence analysts firmly believe that militarization of space has occurred since the first space launch. During the Cold War, the U.S and the Soviet Union invested heavily to build up their space assets, including communication, photographic reconnaissance, meteorological, and arms control verification satellites. Both have tried their level best to make a comprehensive reconnaissance capability. SDI was the first step towards weaponizing space, including GPALS, NMD, GMD, TMD, and BMD. The world's major powers wanted to have their space to protect their self-interests and create their dominance. During the Cold War, satellites were extensively used for military purposes, and states still use them for military advantages.

The announced GPALS program gave birth to several other programs like NMD and THAAD, in which the space-based interceptors became an integral part of the defence against the ICBMs. After 9/11, in 2001, President Bush unilaterally withdrew from the ABM Treaty and announced the BMD program- refurnishing all previous missile defence programs. These programs mentioned outer space as a vital ground for their implementation. These programs increased militarization of outer space, thus initiating a new debate on weaponization of outer space.

The space race between the U.S and the Soviet Union has also made China, India, and Pakistan one space exploration aspirant. China, in this regard, has augmented its space exploration power for a couple of decades. The U.S and Soviet Union ambitions to create their hegemony, especially the U.S policy of full-spectrum dominance, have prompted other nations to exploit outer space for their military purposes. In this regard, China is also building its space power by constructing its satellite systems in outer space. Similarly, it has also demonstrated its anti-satellite capability in 2007 by destroying one of its defunct satellites- creating a considerable amount of hazardous space debris in outer space. This has revived the whole discourse of weaponization of space.

India, in this whole story, has also contributed a lot. Its space activities since the 1990s have created a security dilemma for Pakistan. India is aiming to build its BMD and ABM system to contain Pakistan and China in South Asia. Although it has not achieved a significant dedicated military satellite constellation in outer space, its growing BMD capabilities- incorporation with U.S, Israel, and Russia, can bolster its strategic aspirations in region.

The growing number of states in outer space, which has increased space trafficking, has added more vulnerability for survivability of defenceless space assets of the U.S and has forced it to take offensive countermeasures in outer space. The U.S. reliance on its space assets has increased, and so have its future requirements for conducting its combat mission. Therefore, outer space has become a strategic field for major powers. It is argued that space weapons can be deployed which could create a conflict of interest among the nations. Therefore, space as we know it is a strategic domain that could play a determining factor in future engagements.

The U.S unilateral withdrawal from the ABM Treaty in 2001 and its initiation of BMD and NMD has prompted Russia and China to revisit their strategic force posture. Both countries are continuously increasing their military capabilities at a moderate level because of the U.S offensive missile defence system in Europe and the Far-East. Because of this, there is a chance of horizontal proliferation of space weapons worldwide. Similarly, North Korea and Iran, on the other hand, are in pursuit of building their nuclear capabilities. North Korea has developed its nuclear device, whereas Iran is searching to accomplish its strategic goal to become a nuclear power. Both countries have the necessary infrastructure for space technologies; therefore, any move from these countries will not be welcomed. Now, there is a possibility that they will move towards building ASATs in upcoming years, which will raise chances of vertical proliferation of space weapons.

In the absence of an international agreement to prohibit weaponization of outer space, there is an urgent need of an international agreement or treaty, which could bar proliferation of space weapons—both horizontally and vertically.

Space exploration's role for nations' economic development is well established. Similarly, it has also played a significant part in intensifying the nations' military capabilities. In this regard, Pakistan must also boost space exploration efforts to foster its economy. On the other hand, efficient and reliable surveillance and early warning systems in outer space need to maintain its credible minimum deterrence in region. Therefore, it has to build satellites for early warning and surveillance.

From the analysis of existing literature, mostly from primary sources, it is safe to say that the possibility of battle in space is growing. In addition, militarization of space started long ago, and now states are rigorously following the path from space militarization to weaponization of outer space. Another vital factor that is a source of concern for major spacefaring nations is that pool of spacefaring nations increases. The U.S. is an indisputable space power, and its reliance on space is enormous. Likewise, the U.S. fears that its space assets face the potential threat of attack in orbit because of increasing number of states in space. Therefore, the U.S. is creating new capabilities and systems to establish assured space deterrence against its adversaries. U.S. orbital assets are meant mainly to provide global navigation, reconnaissance, surveillance, early warning, intelligence gathering, acquiring targets, and other crucial activities to bolster integrated deterrence.

An essential feature of space security is kinetic and non-kinetic threat to major space-faring nations' satellite constellations. The non-kinetic threats, including jamming signals, operational hacking software, and dazzling, are dangerous for creating a conflict in space.

The U.S. invests in a second-generation surveillance system known as Space Fence to establish its assured space deterrence. In addition, the U.S. has an extensive self-Awareness Space Situational Awareness (SSA) system aimed at collecting data on space debris and activities of its adversaries.

Moreover, the Operationally Responsive Space Office (ORS) is funding the development of the Spaceborne Payload Assist Rocket-Kauai (SPARK) launch system, which will send the miniaturized satellite into LEO and sun-synchronous orbit. Considering all these space developments, it can be deduced that the U.S., China, Russia, and other major spacefaring nations are getting far more serious about threat of space warfare ever, any war in space would be as devastating as a nuclear war on Earth. The consequences of space war would be severe for entire humankind. The world is facing a looming threat of space warfare. This threat has emerged as a reality due to non-agreement of significant powers on framing any legal instrument/ treaty that prohibits weaponization of outer space. Russia and China have proposed several drafts to prevent space weaponization, like PPWT and No First Placement of Weapons in Space, but the U.S. and its allies are not agreeing on such draft proposals. These efforts suggest that Russia and China are unwilling to fight the war in space and more inclined towards framing legal instruments to avoid space war. On the other hand, the U.S. is not interested in any treaty restricting its freedom of action in space.

The U.S considers its space program as the jewel of the crown. No nation in the world allocates such an enormous budget in its fiscal year as the U.S to its civil and military program. Likewise, strategic importance of this domain has increased manifold for the U.S. Space has been an uncontested domain for decades. Hundreds of miles from above the Earth's surface, the ultimate high-ground U.S Air Force (USAF) has owned this high-ground space for decades, and the other nations and other air forces only dream of making such a claim. What if their dreams come into reality? U.S' military and political leaders believe that major revisionist powers want to achieve their dreams and have a renewed focus on their aggression.

Regarding China's space program, it is concluded that China's space ambitions are to harness vast resources available in space to sustain its economic rise. There are three areas where China's space activities are focused: building Space-Based Solar Power (SBSP), lunar and asteroid mining, and establishing its space station. SBSP can harness solar power in space, where the sun's rays are constant, and beam that energy from satellites using microwave technology to receiving stations on China's next big ambition is to exploit rare materials in space like titanium, helium-3, and water from the Moon's far side. The lunar exploration program, launched on Long March rockets, is an ongoing robotic mission to the China National Space Administration's Moon. China, prevented from participating in the International Space Station (ISS) by an Act of the U.S. Congress in 2011, has invested heavily in developing its space station in 2020, named Tiangong (Heavenly Palace). China is focused on long-term activities to generate resources and establish a permanent space presence.

The ambiguity of international space law concerning property ownership in space will work to China's advantage as it will be based on "first-come, first-serve." China plans to stay in space and expand its presence there. China has the most active and ambitious space program in the world. China is increasing its navigation satellite system to make the U.S. like the global enterprise of space navigation, reconnaissance, and surveillance system. It entered space race late but is now a force to be reckoned with. The Chinese space program development suggests it will achieve parity in space with its strategic competitor, the U.S., in upcoming years. Likewise,

China provides cheap launching pads for developing countries to send satellites into space. The Chinese space program is a vital element of its national power. Currently, China's space program begets economic growth and development, supports China's focus on education, science, and technology, and is a source of considerable national pride and unity. The financial and development benefit China's space program fit squarely into government's campaigns for economic growth and prosperity. The global impact of China's space program is perhaps evident in its military applications. The development of China's fleet of dual-use satellites has benefitted China in its quest to establish security, assert regional hegemony, and reach military parity with the India's space.

India's space program is a top political priority, with a renewed interest in its civil and military leadership to reach next level of prestige in international political and strategic system. India considers its space program a tool for projecting its soft power in the region. It is a reality that India has excelled in achieving space technologies to indigenize its space program with the foremost ambition to achieve socioeconomic benefits for well-being of a common Indian. It is also a fact that India's scientific community and political leadership have collectively recognized importance of its space program; that is why planetary exploration is a crucial part of ISRO mission. Otherwise, it becomes a headache for political leadership if they opt for an expensive venture without earning any political mileage. However, civil and political leadership in India is on one page to lift the country's image, prestige, and power by developing space power.

Pakistan's space program has gained momentum after a stalemate for decades. The program has never remained a priority of civil and military leadership, and all the focus has remained on developing Pakistan's nuclear capability. But space is a domain that every country wants to reach and mark its footprints. Pakistan has also realized its dream of marking its presence in the world's prime location.

The research concludes that a real threat in space could germinate seed of armed conflict. The U.S and China do not trust each other, and there is strategic distrust between two adversaries, which could be triggering point of an armed conflict in outer space. U.S' concerns are emanating from China's military and economic rise, and the U.S. wants to contain China in its region of influence. China considers space as a building block of its national power. This germinates a strategic distrust between two space powers, diminishing chances of cooperation between two states. This also incentivizes both states to build their military space programs to counter each other's space power. Both countries have developed kinetic and non-kinetic means to disrupt, disrepair, and damage each other's space assets. All these efforts are a perfect recipe for competition in outer space. Space is one of the global commons providing crucial resources for humanity. But the environment of competition is what the world desires to progress on Earth. Likewise, competition is relatively new to what the world has observed in nuclear and conventional military build-up. The military build-up in outer space has brought a paradigm shift in international security as fear of war in space would cause catastrophe on Earth. The problem of space debris in the aftermath of a future space war may last centuries, to clear debris in space. Therefore, the development of space weapons on the Earth by major spacefarers and these doctrines and strategies to fight a war in space have brought a paradigm shift in international security.

The research has comprehensively covered theoretical understanding of security complex in South Asia. Chapter three comprises the theoretical knowledge of the security environment at international, regional, and individual levels of security. The literature on selected nations' space militarization and weaponization capabilities was analysed in subsequent chapters to understand security complex's implications in South Asia. The study concludes that space for competition between the U.S and China is in outer space with its ramifications for South Asia. In addition, these bilateral relations are triggering point of space security trilemma in South Asia. This may likely intensify because of destabilizing technology development in South Asia. Specifically, Indian development of its BMD capabilities is extremely offensive towards Pakistan's national security. India's BMD capabilities are incomplete without effective development and deployment of space-based assets by India. Hence, space for competition in South Asia between China and India and India and Pakistan is looming, leaving little space for cooperation. However, space is a domain where interstate cooperation is entirely plausible, creating space for cooperation. Therefore, there is also a space for cooperation depending upon South Asian leadership's political will.

Like nuclear deterrence, there is also a healthy debate on deterrence in space. A conflict in space is as deadly as a nuclear war on Earth. A nuclear war may obstruct functions of life in a particular area on the Earth in case of a nuclear exchange. But, a war in space could jeopardize proper functioning of life on the globe. People living on the planet Earth may come to a near halt if the space assets providing communication, navigation, and other essential functions of life are hit and damaged in an armed conflict. The destructive nature of fighting a war in space has created assured space deterrence between adversaries. It becomes assured by development of space weaponization capabilities by major spacefarers. The major space powers are cognizant that if they hit a target in space, their assets will also come under attack, and their survival chances are incredibly bleak. One particular example of space deterrence is strategic patience shown by the U.S. when one of its Iridium satellites was blinded by China's laser attack. The U.S. did not respond similarly or strike back to maintain its freedom of action in space. Hence, the study concludes that space weaponization is inevitable, but assured space deterrence is likely to prevail.

The study also concludes the revival of space sanctuary school of thought in major spacefarers' doctrine, policies, and strategies. It is quite observable that their actions entail high-ground perspectives, but due to rising competition in space, the sanctuary school of thought is reviving its roots. The study briefly analyses space policies of selected states, and it is found that states have never-ending desires to exploit outer space for civil and military purposes. The states will never end their efforts to augment their military power and see space power as a force multiplier. But the rising pool of states also restricts them from demarking their space territories.

The research concludes that conflict in space is entirely plausible as states build military space capabilities to fulfil their national security goals. The conflict on the ground has also been inevitable, and its nature and characteristics are transforming and changing. However, debate is about how to resolve dispute and mitigate its effects if transformed. Likewise, states are also in rigorous debate to formulate a global framework to prevent arms race in outer space. In this regard, several multilateral forums under the United Nations discuss and establish treaties for arms control and disarmament affairs. The PAROS issue has been under discussion in CD for the last four decades, but a consensus has not emerged between states at the forum. The negotiation process has been suffering from a perfect stalemate. As a result, much progress has not been made to prevent space weaponization in all these three decades.

The study also finds a complete lack of consensus among the Member States, even on the definition of peaceful uses of outer space and space weapons. All these litigations regarding the demarcation of definition require undying commitment from the Member States to come across all the odds and discuss a verifiable arms control and disarmament mechanism not to make space accessible of weapons. Many efforts were made in past, but other space powers' high scepticism has not allowed negotiation process to come from embryonic state. Therefore, study concludes a desire to negotiate a universally accepted arms control and disarmament treaty in space. In this regard, the recommendations of Transparency Confidence Building Measures (TCBMs) and report of the Group of Governmental Experts (GGE) may allow a way forward to break the stalemate on establishing legally binding instrument on PAROS.

Index

A
Anti-Satellite (ASAT), 1, 2
APSCO
Asia-Pacific Space Cooperation Organization, 7

B
Ballistic Missile Defence (BMD), 2, 12, 13

C
Chandrayaan-1, 5
Command, control, communication, computers, intelligence, information, surveillance, and reconnaissance (C^4I^2SR), 5
Conference on Disarmament (CD), 3
Countermeasures, 6
Credible Minimum Deterrence (CMD), 6, 12, 13

D
Defence Research and Development Organisation (DRDO), 5

E
ESA
European Space Agency, 7

G
GPS
Global Positioning System, 19

I
Inadvertent, 2
India, 2, 4–6, 11, 12
Indian Space Research Organization (ISRO), 5
International Relations (IR), 15, 28
ISR
Intelligence, Surveillance, Reconnaissance, 19

K
Kinetic Kill Vehicles (KKVs), 2

L
Low Earth Orbit (LEO), 2

M
Military power, 1
Miscalculated, 2

N
NASA
National Aeronautics and Space Administration, 7
NC^2
Nuclear Command and Control, 6
Next Steps in Strategic Partnership (NSSP), 5
NSA
Non-State Actors, 18
NSSP
Next Steps in Strategic Partnership, 5

A. Khan and E. Sadeh, *Sabre Rattling in Space*,
https://doi.org/10.1007/978-981-97-6050-3

P
PAROS
Prevention of Arms Race in Outer Space, 3
PNT
Positioning, Navigating, and Timing, 7
Prevention of Placement of Weapon Treaty (PPWT), 3

R
Research and Development (R&D), 1
Revolution in Military Affairs (RMA), 3, 19, 28
RSC
Regional Security Complex, 9

S
SLF
Space Launch Facility, 7
SLV
Space Launch Vehicle, 7
Soviet Union
Country, 1–4
Space Test Bed (STB), 2
Sputnik-I
Satellite, 1, 3
SUPARCO
Space Upper Atmosphere Research Commission, 7

U
Unauthorised war, 2
United Nations, 11–13
United Nations General Assembly (UNGA), 3
United States, 2, 4, 11, 12

X
X-37B, 2, 11, 12

The manufacturer's authorised representative in the EU is Springer Nature Customer Service Centre GmbH, Europaplatz 3, 69115 Heidelberg, Germany. If you have any concerns regarding our products, please contact ProductSafety@springernature.com

Printed and bound by CPI Group (UK) Ltd, Croydon, CR0 4YY
01/10/2026
02225910-0006

SPRINGER NATURE

GPSR Compliance

The European Union's (EU) General Product Safety Regulation (GPSR) is a set of rules that requires consumer products to be safe and our obligations to ensure this.

If you have any concerns about our products, you can contact us on ProductSafety@springernature.com

In case Publisher is established outside the EU, the EU authorized representative is:

Springer Nature Customer Service Center GmbH
Europaplatz 3
69115 Heidelberg, Germany